Joseph Solodow

CAMBRIDGE CLASSICAL TEXTS AND COMMENTARIES

19

VELLEIUS PATERCULUS: THE TIBERIAN NARRATIVE

(2.94–131)

VELLEIUS PATERCULUS

THE TIBERIAN NARRATIVE
(2.94–131)

EDITED WITH AN INTRODUCTION AND COMMENTARY

BY

A. J. WOODMAN
University of Newcastle upon Tyne

CAMBRIDGE UNIVERSITY PRESS

CAMBRIDGE

LONDON · NEW YORK · MELBOURNE

PUBLISHED BY THE PRESS SYNDICATE OF THE UNIVERSITY OF CAMBRIDGE
The Pitt Building, Trumpington Street, Cambridge, United Kingdom

CAMBRIDGE UNIVERSITY PRESS
The Edinburgh Building, Cambridge CB2 2RU, UK
40 West 20th Street, New York NY 10011–4211, USA
477 Williamstown Road, Port Melbourne, VIC 3207, Australia
Ruiz de Alarcón 13, 28014 Madrid, Spain
Dock House, The Waterfront, Cape Town 8001, South Africa

http://www.cambridge.org

First published 1977
First paperback edition 2004

A catalogue record for this book is available from the British Library

Library of Congress catalogue card number: 76–22985

ISBN 0 521 21397 5 hardback
ISBN 0 521 60935 6 paperback

CONTENTS

TO MY MOTHER AND FATHER

PREFACE

This preposterous volume is the first instalment of a commentary on Velleius Paterculus which I hope in due course to complete. Although Velleius is the only historian of Roman affairs to have survived from the period which separates Livy and Tacitus, no commentary of comparable scale or scope has been published since the beginning of the nineteenth century.

The neglect of Velleius by commentators has extended to scholars in most other branches of classical learning and is due almost entirely to his treatment of the man who occupies what is marginally the largest single portion of his work – Tiberius. A historian who describes Tiberius in such enthusiastic terms, it is argued, cannot be trusted on any other matter and his work may be safely dismissed. The Tiberian narrative, which forms the last thirty-eight chapters of Velleius' work and covers the years 23 B.C.–A.D. 29, is thus of primary importance for any consideration of his history as a whole. It is for this reason that I am publishing the present volume here and now.

Although it is principally Velleius' value as a historian that has been called into question, the emphasis of this book is upon textual and literary, rather than historical, matters. Since we cannot assess an author's historical value unless we first know as accurately as possible what he wrote, and since Velleius' text is not only notoriously corrupt but has also suffered at the hands of most nineteenth- and twentieth-century editors through their misplaced confidence in MS A, the need for a detailed reappraisal of the text will, I hope, be understood. There has after all been no such thorough treatment since Kritz's outstanding commentary of 1840, which, apart from certain introductory sections, is concerned with textual criticism to the exclusion of all else. Whether the literary emphasis of this book will be equally welcome, I am not sure. But if one believes that in the ancient world the writing of history was primarily a literary activity and that historians were concerned rather with the structured and dramatic presentation of their narrative than with the more 'scientific' aspects of their craft, there is every reason why works of ancient history should require a literary treatment. Indeed it is the persistent refusal of scholars to see Velleius' Tiberian narrative in terms of the literary tradition that has largely contributed to the general disparagement of his history. Naturally my discussions of textual and literary matters have regularly led me into areas which more properly belong to experts in early imperial history; but I have often been able to limit my historical incursions by referring to such works as the latest comprehensive treatment of Tiberius available to me, the exemplary biography by Robin Seager, where a fuller account and bibliography may invariably be found. I nevertheless hope that by providing an improved text and by explaining the nature and meaning of the narrative I shall have done some service to those who wish to use Velleius as a historical source.

I have not thought it useful to provide either an account of Velleius' family background and career or an outline of modern Velleian scholarship, tasks which have recently and admirably been taken up by G. V. Sumner and J. Hellegouarc'h respectively. Nor have I said anything in this volume about the dates of Velleius' composition or the genre of historiography to which he belongs, since these are subjects which I have already discussed elsewhere.

I have several acknowledgements to make. Mr and Mrs E. H. Prater, through the kind offices of Dr B. R. Rees, passed to me the notes on Velleius which had been collected by their late son, John Prater, formerly Temporary Lecturer in Classics at Cardiff and Sheffield, and Assistant Classics Master at Bristol Grammar School at the time of his death. His bibliographical material was particularly helpful, on one notable occasion disclosing a brilliant emendation of 99.2 by Withof which had escaped successive editors of Velleius and which otherwise would certainly have escaped me. I am extremely grateful to Mr and Mrs Prater for their thoughtfulness and generosity.

PREFACE

Dr A. H. McDonald started me off on my research in Cambridge more than ten years ago: although he has not seen this book, I would like to believe that it contains evidence of his wise teaching. Miss Dorothy Monk kindly read the whole of the book in typescript and made a number of corrections and observations for which I am most grateful. In grappling with many of the historical, literary and textual problems which arose during the book's preparation I was greatly helped by Mr J. J. Paterson and Professor D. A. West, whose kindness, patience and scholarship I have shamelessly exploited.

Professor G. B. A. Fletcher, who first suggested Velleius to me as a topic for research, has read the whole of this book in typescript and generously furnished me with numerous valuable lexical notes which I have acknowledged throughout by the letter 'F.'. In addition he placed at my disposal his personal copies of the *editio princeps* and Kritz's now unobtainable commentary, the latter of which I have had on loan for five years. Professor F. R. D. Goodyear, who supervised my work for a year in Cambridge, has also read this book in typescript and given me the benefit of his penetrating criticism and expert knowledge of early imperial historiography. In addition he was of particular assistance when the book was approaching readiness for publication. To these two friends above all I am indebted for their many suggestions and corrections: without the aid of their scholarship and erudition the book would have been greatly impoverished.

The book would not have been published at all if my University had not provided financial assistance of an order which would have been most generous under ordinary economic circumstances but which in the present crisis places me all the more in its debt. Finally I owe my thanks to Mr I. M. Le M. DuQuesnay for nobly agreeing to read the proofs, and to the staff of the Cambridge University Press for their kind and expert attention.

University of Newcastle upon Tyne A.J.W.
June 1976

REFERENCES AND ABBREVIATIONS

References to Book 1 and to chapters 1–18 of Book 2 of Velleius are always given in full; other references to Book 2 omit the book number. In the commentary I often omit also the chapter number when reference is being made to a different section of the same chapter.

A. ABBREVIATIONS

Note. This list includes neither current periodical abbreviations, for which I generally follow the system used in *L'Année philologique*, nor the familiar abbreviations of certain standard works.

ALL	*Archiv für lateinische Lexikographie und Grammatik*
BMC Emp.	Mattingly, H.–Carson, R. A. G. (1923–62). *Coins of the Roman Empire in the British Museum.* Vols. 1–6. London
CAH	Cook, S. A.–Adcock, F. E.–Charlesworth, M. P. (1923–39). *Cambridge Ancient History.* 1st edn. Cambridge [references are invariably to Vol. 10]
EJ	Ehrenberg, V.–Jones, A. H. M. (1955). *Documents illustrating the reigns of Augustus and Tiberius.* 2nd edn. Oxford [references are to entries unless otherwise stated]
F.	Fletcher, G. B. A. [notes privately communicated: see p. xi]
H–W	Hainsselin, P.–Watelet, H. (1932). *Velleius Paterculus et Florus. Texte revu et traduit.* Paris
K–S	Kühner, R.–Stegmann, C. (1971). *Ausführliche Grammatik der lateinischen Sprache.* Vol. 2 *Satzlehre.* Parts 1 and 2. 4th edn. Repr. Hanover
L–H–S	Leumann, M.–Hofmann, J. B.–Szantyr, A. (1972). *Lateinische Grammatik.* Vol. 2 *Syntax und Stilistik.* Revised edn. Munich
L&S	Lewis, C. T. & Short, C. (1879). *A Latin Dictionary.* Oxford
OLD	*Oxford Latin Dictionary* (1968–). Oxford
PIR[2]	Groag, E.–Stein, A.–Petersen, L. (1933–). *Prosopographia Imperii Romani.* Vols. 1– . 2nd edn. Berlin
RG	*Res Gestae Diui Augusti*
RIC	Mattingly, H.–Sydenham, E. A. et al. (1923–67). *Roman Imperial Coinage.* Vols. 1–9. London
S–H	Schanz, M.–Hosius, C. (1959). *Geschichte der römischen Literatur.* Vol. 2[4]. Repr. Munich

B. CRITICAL EDITIONS AND COMMENTARIES

Note. I always refer to critical editions etc. of Velleius by the name of the editor or commentator. This list includes only those works to which I refer in this volume: more complete inventories will be found in Krause 61–104, Kritz cxxviii–cxxxvi, Stegmann viii–xii.

Acidalius, V. (1590). Padua
Aldus [see Manutius, A.]
editio Bipontina (1780). Zweibrücken
Boeclerus, J. H. (1642). Strasbourg
Bolaffi, E. (1930). Turin
Bothe, F. H. (1837). Zürich
Burman, P. (1719). Leyden [the elder Burman]
Cellarius, C. (1707). Leipzig
Cludius, A. H. (1815). Hanover
Ellis, R. (1898). Oxford
Gelenius, S. (1546). Basel
Gruner, J. F. (1762). Coburg
Gruter, J. (1607). Frankfurt
Haase, F. (1884). Leipzig [the first edn appeared in 1851]
Halm, C. (1909). Leipzig [a reprint of the first edn of 1876]
Heinsius, N. (1678). Amsterdam
Krause, J. C. H. (1800). Leipzig
Kreyssig, J. T. (1836). Meissen
Kritz, F. (1840). Leipzig
Lipsius, J. (1591). Leyden
Manutius, A. (1571). Venice [grandson of the 'great' Aldus Manutius, hence often called Aldus Nepos]
Miller, J. P. (1756). Berlin
Orelli, J. C. (1835). Leipzig
Popma, A. (1620). Franeker
Puteanus, C. (1608). Paris
Rhenanus, B. (1520). Basel [the *editio princeps*]
Ruhnken, D. (1779). Leyden
Schegk, J. (1589). Frankfurt
Stegmann de Pritzwald, C. (1965). Stuttgart [a reprint of the first edn (1933), with some recent bibliographical material added by H.-D. Blume]
Vascosanus, M. (1538). Paris
Vossius, G. (1703). Frankfurt [this edn, by the third son of G. F. Vossius, first appeared in 1639]

REFERENCES AND ABBREVIATIONS

C. OTHER WORKS

Note. This list includes only those works of which I do not give full details elsewhere or to which I refer by author's name: where an author is responsible for several works, these are distinguished either by a date or by an abbreviation, as indicated below. This list is not a bibliography of all the works cited in this volume; nor is it a bibliography of modern work on Velleius, for which see Hellegouarc'h, *ANRW*.

Abraham, F. (1885). *V. und die Parteien in Rom unter Tiberius.* Berlin

Avenarius, G. (1956). *Lukians Schrift zur Geschichtsschreibung.* Meisenheim am Glan

Bacherler, M. (1915). 'Die Namengebung bei den lateinischen Prosaikern von V. bis Sueton', *WKlPh* 32.1049–56, 1075–8

Badian, E. (1966). 'The early historians' in *Latin historians* (ed. T. A. Dorey), 1–38. London

Baehrens, W. A. (1912). 'Beiträge zur lateinischen Syntax', *Philologus* Supplementband 12.233–556

Bardon, H. (1952–6). *La littérature latine inconnue.* Vols. 1 and 2. Paris

Barnes, T. D. (1974). 'The victories of Augustus', *JRS* 64.21–6

Béranger, J. (1953). *Recherches sur l'aspect idéologique du principat.* Basel

Bolaffi, *Sallustio* = Bolaffi, E. (1949). *Sallustio e la sua fortuna nei secoli.* Rome

Boot, J. C. G. (1877). 'Adversaria critica in V.P. . . . libros', *Mnem.* 5.165–74

Brunt, P. A. (1963). Review of H. D. Meyer, *Die Aussenpolitik des Augustus und die augusteische Dichtung* (Cologne, 1961), in *JRS* 53.170–6

Burdeau, F. (1964). 'L'empereur d'après les panégyriques latins' in *Aspects de l'empire romain* (ed. F. Burdeau–N. Charbonnel–M. Humbert). Travaux et recherches de la Faculté de Droit et des Sciences Économiques de Paris. Série 'Sciences Historiques' 1.1–60. Paris

Cairns, F. (1972). *Generic composition in Greek and Roman poetry.* Edinburgh

Canfora, L. (1972). *Totalità e selezione nella storiografia classica.* Bari

Castiglioni, L. (1931). 'Alcune osservazioni a V.P.', *RAL* 7.268–84

Cornelissen, J. J. (1877). 'Coniecturae Velleianae', *Mnem.* 5.47–55

(1883). 'Ad Vell. Pat.', *Mnem.* 11.411–20

(1887). 'Kritische Aanteekeningen op V.P.', Verslagen en Mededeelingen der Kon. Akad. van Wetenschappen. Afdeeling Letterkunde 3.4.102–50

Curtius, E. R. (1953). *European literature and the Latin Middle Ages.* Eng. trans. by W. R. Trask. London

Damsté, P. H. (1905). 'Ad Vell. Pat.', *Mnem.* 33.398–420

Dihle, A. (1955). 'C. Vell. Pat.', *RE* 8A.1.637–59

Dobiáš, J. (1960). 'King Maroboduus as a politician', *Klio* 38.155–66

Doblhofer, E. (1966). *Die Augustuspanegyrik des Horaz in formalhistorischer Sicht.* Heidelberg

Draeger, *Hist. Synt.* = Draeger, A. (1878–81). *Historische Syntax der lateinischen Sprache.* Vols. 1 and 2. 2nd edn. Leipzig

Dupraz, L. (1963). 'Autour de l'association de Tibère au principat', *MH* 20. 172–85

Durry, M. (1938). *Pline le Jeune: Panégyrique de Trajan.* Paris

Earl, D. C. (1961). *The political thought of Sallust.* Cambridge

Esteve-Forriol, J. (1962). *Die Trauer- und Trostgedichte in der röm. Literatur.* Diss. Munich

Fechter, D. A. (1844). *Die Amerbachische Abschrift des V.P. und ihr Verhältniss zum Murbacher codex und zur Editio princeps.* Basel

Fletcher = Fletcher, G. B. A. *either* (1964). *Annotations on Tacitus.* Brussels; *or* (1971). 'On the *Annals* of Tacitus', *Latomus* 30.146–50

Fraenkel, E. (1957). *Horace.* Oxford

Frei-Stolba = Frei-Stolba, R. (1967). *Untersuchungen zu den Wahlen in der röm. Kaiserzeit.* Zürich

Frei-Stolba, R. (1969). 'Inoffizielle Kaisertitulaturen im 1. und 2. Jahrhundert', *MH* 26.18–39

Freitag, P. (1942). *Stilistische Beiträge zu V.P.: Pleonasmus und Parenthese.* Unpubl. diss. Vienna

Friebel, C. (1837). 'Emendationes in V.P. Hist. Rom.' in *Graecorum Satyrographorum Fragmenta* (ed. F. Larsow), 146–53. Berlin

Gelzer, M. (1969). *The Roman nobility.* Eng. trans. by R. J. Seager. Oxford

Georges, H. (1877). *De Elocutione V.P.* Diss. Leipzig

Goodyear, *Comm. Tac.* = Goodyear, F. R. D. (1972–). *The Annals of Tacitus: Books 1–6.* Vols. 1– . Cambridge

Grant, *Aspects* = Grant, M. (1950). *Aspects of the Principate of Tiberius.* NY
FITA = Grant, M. (1946). *From Imperium to Auctoritas.* Cambridge
RAI = Grant, M. (1950). *Roman Anniversary Issues.* Cambridge

Grenade, P. (1961). *Essai sur les origines du principat.* Paris

Gutzwiller, H. (1942). *Die Neujahrsrede des Konsuls Claudius Mamertinus vor dem Kaiser Julian* [= *Pan. Lat.* 3]. Basel

Häussler, *Nachträge* = Häussler, R. (1968). *Nachträge zu A. Otto: Die Sprichwörter und sprichwörtlichen Redensarten der Römer.* Hildesheim
Tac. = Häussler, R. (1965). *Tacitus und das historische Bewusstsein.* Heidelberg

Halm (1875) = Halm, K. (1875). 'Ueber die handschriftliche Ueberlieferung des V.P.', *RhM* 30.534–54

Hand, *Turs.* = Hand, F. (1969). *Tursellinus seu de particulis latinis commentarii.* Repr. Amsterdam

Haupt, M. (1875). 'Kritische Bemerkungen über V.P.' in *Opuscula* 1.265–76. Leipzig

Havet, L. (1911). *Manuel de critique verbale appliquée aux textes latins.* Paris

Hellegouarc'h, *ANRW* = Hellegouarc'h, J. 'État présent des travaux sur l'histoire romaine de V.P.' in *Aufstieg und Niedergang der röm. Welt* (ed. H. Temporini). Vol. forthcoming. Berlin–New York

VL = Hellegouarc'h, J. (1963). *Le vocabulaire latin des relations et des partis politiques sous la république*. Paris

Hellegouarc'h, J. (1964). 'Les buts de l'œuvre historique de V.P.', *Latomus* 23.669–84

(1974). 'L'impérialisme romain d'après l'œuvre de V.P.' in *L'idéologique de l'impérialisme romain* 69–90. Colloque de Dijon. Publications de l'Université de Dijon 46. Paris

Henzen, W. (1874). *Acta Fratrum Arvalium*. Berlin

Herel, J. F. (1800). 'Adnotationes criticae ad V.' in Krause 559–78

Janson, T. (1964). *Latin prose prefaces*. Stockholm

John, W. (1963). 'P. Quinctilius Varus', *RE* 24.907–84

Kaiser, P. (1884). *De Fontibus V.P.* Diss. Berlin

Kenney, E. J. (1974). *The classical text*. Berkeley–Los Angeles–London

Klebs, E. (1890). 'Entlehnungen aus V.', *Philologus* 49.285–312

Klingner, F. (1958). 'Tacitus und die Geschichtsschreiber des 1. Jahrhunderts n.Chr.', *MH* 15.194–206

Kloft, H. (1970). *Liberalitas Principis*. Kölner Historische Abhandlungen 18. Vienna

Koestermann, E. (1953). 'Der pannonisch-dalmatinische Krieg 6–9 n.Chr.', *Hermes* 81.345–78

Kornemann, E. (1930). *Doppelprinzipat und Reichsteilung im Imperium Romanum*. Leipzig–Berlin

Krebs, J. P.–Schmalz, J. H. (1905–7). *Antibarbarus der lateinischen Sprache*. Vols. 1 and 2. Basel

Kühnast, *Liv. Synt.* = Kühnast, L. (1872). *Die Hauptpunkte der livianischen Syntax*. 2nd edn. Berlin

Lana, I. (1952). *V.P. o della propaganda*. Turin

Latte, K. (1960). *Römische Religionsgeschichte*. Munich

Laurent, J. C. M. (1836). *Loci Velleiani*. Altona

Leo, F. (1901). *Die griechisch-römische Biographie*. Leipzig

Levick, B. (1966). 'Drusus Caesar and the adoptions of A.D. 4', *Latomus* 25.227–44

(1972). 'Tiberius' retirement to Rhodes in 6 B.C.', *Latomus* 31.779–813

(1975). 'Mercy and moderation on the coinage of Tiberius' in *The ancient historian and his materials: Essays in honour of C. E. Stevens* (ed. Barbara Levick), 123–37. Westmead, Farnborough

Lindgren, H. (1935). *Studia Curtiana*. Uppsala

Litchfield, H. W. (1914). 'National *Exempla Virtutis* in Roman literature', *HSCP* 25.1–71

Löfstedt, *Synt.* = Löfstedt, E. (1942, 1933). *Syntactica*. Vols. 1² and 2. Lund

Lundberg, E. (1906). *De Elocutione Val. Max.* Vol. 1. Diss. Falun

Madvig, J. N. (1871–3). *Adversaria Critica.* Vols. 1–3. Copenhagen

Magie, D. (1950). *Roman rule in Asia Minor.* Vols. 1 and 2. Princeton, N.J.

Maguinness, W. S. (1932). 'Some methods of the Latin Panegyrists', *Hermathena* 47.42–61

Manitius, M. (1892). 'Zu Curtius und V.', *RhM* 47.465–8

Marsh, F. B. (1931). *The Reign of Tiberius.* Oxford

Massauer, B. (1968). *Historisch-antiquarischer Kommentar zur Augustus-Partie des V.P. (II. 90–123).* Unpubl. diss. Vienna

Michels, M. (1949). *De V.P. arte biographica quaest. selectae.* Unpubl. diss. Bonn

Milkau, F. (1888). *De V.P. genere dicendi quaest. selectae.* Diss. Königsberg

Momigliano, A. (1971). *The development of Greek biography.* Cambridge, Mass.

Mommsen = T. Mommsen's Velleian emendations in Haase vii–xii

Mommsen, *Staatsr.* = Mommsen, T. (1887). *Römisches Staatsrecht.* Vols. 1^3, 2^3, 3. Leipzig

Nägelsbach, K. F. von (1905). *Lateinische Stilistik.* 9th edn. Nürnberg

Neue, F.–Wagener, C. (1892–1905). *Formenlehre der lateinischen Sprache.* Vols. 1–4. 3rd edn. Leipzig

Norden, *AK* = Norden, E. (1958). *Die antike Kunstprosa.* Vol. 1^5. Stuttgart
AP = Norden, E. (1939). *Aus altrömischen Priesterbüchern.* Lund
Tac. Germ. = Norden, E. (1923). *Die germanische Urgeschichte in Tacitus' Germania.* 3rd edn. Leipzig–Berlin

Novák, R. (1884). 'Příspěvky ke kritice textu V.P.', *Listy filol. a paedagogické* 11.212–17
(1906). 'Zur Kritik des V.P. I', *WS* 28.283–305
(1907). 'Zur Kritik des V.P. II', *WS* 29.130–49

Ogilvie, R. M. (1965). *A commentary on Livy Books 1–5.* Oxford

Ogilvie (1967) = Ogilvie, R. M.–Richmond, I. (1967). *Cornelii Taciti de Vita Agricolae.* Oxford

Orth, W. (1970). *Die Provinzialpolitik des Tiberius.* Diss. Munich

Otto, A. (1890). *Die Sprichwörter und sprichwörtlichen Redensarten der Römer.* Leipzig

Paessens, H. (1938). 'Zum Partikelgebrauch bei V.P.', *RhM* 87.286–8

Paladini, M. L. (1953). 'Studi su V.P.', *Acme* 6.447–78

Peter, *GL* = Peter, H. (1897). *Die geschichtliche Litteratur über die röm. Kaiserzeit.* Vols. 1 and 2. Leipzig
HRR = Peter, H. (1914, 1967). *Historicorum Romanorum Reliquiae.* Vol. 1^2, Leipzig; Vol. 2^2, Stuttgart
WK = Peter, H. (1911). *Wahrheit und Kunst.* Leipzig–Berlin

Pluygers, W. G. (1881). 'ἀπομνημονεύματα Gul. Geo. Pluygers' (ed. C. G. Cobet), *Mnem.* 9.21–32

Prater, J. H. [see p. x]

Premerstein, A. von (1937). *Vom Werden und Wesen des Prinzipats.* Munich

Purser, L. C. (1897–9). 'Professor Ellis's edition of V.', *Hermathena* 10.369–96
Rambaud, M. (1970). 'Recherches sur le portrait dans l'historiographie romaine', *LEC* 38.417–47
Rau = Rau, R. (1925). 'Zur Geschichte des pannonisch-dalmatinischen Krieges der Jahre 6–9 n.Chr.', *Klio* 19.313–46
Rau, *Chronologie* = Rau, R. (1922). *Chronologie und Quellenfrage bei V.P.* Unpubl. diss. Tübingen
Rawson, E. (1972). 'Cicero the historian and Cicero the antiquarian', *JRS* 62.33–45
Rockwood, F. E. (1893). *Velleius Paterculus. Book II, chapters xli–cxxxi. Edited with introduction and notes.* Boston–New York–Chicago
Rogers, R. S. (1943). *Studies in the reign of Tiberius.* Baltimore
Rosenheyn, J. S. (1810). *Lectionum Velleianarum Specimen.* Berlin
Sauppe, H. (1896). 'M. Vell. Pat.' in *Ausgewählte Schriften* 39–72. Berlin
Schäfer, W. (1912). *Tiberius und seine Zeit im Lichte der Tradition des V.P.* Leipzig–Halle
Schoepfer, C. (1837). *Adnotationes Criticae.* Quedlinburg
Seager, R. (1972). *Tiberius.* London
Shipley, F. W. (1924). *Velleius Paterculus: Res Gestae Divi Augusti, with an English translation.* (Loeb edn.) London–Cambridge, Mass.
Stadter, P. A. (1972). 'The structure of Livy's History', *Historia* 21.287–307
Steffen, H. J. (1954). *Die Regierung des Tiberius in der Darstellung des V.P.* Unpubl. diss. Kiel
Sumner, G. V. (1970). 'The truth about V.P.: prolegomena', *HSCP* 74.257–97
Sutherland, C. H. V. (1951). *Coinage in Roman imperial policy 31 B.C.–A.D. 68.* Oxford
Syme, *Amm.* = Syme, R. (1968). *Ammianus and the Historia Augusta.* Oxford
DP = Syme, R. (1971). *Danubian Papers.* Bucharest
RR = Syme, R. (1939). *The Roman Revolution.* Oxford
Sall. = Syme, R. (1964). *Sallust.* Berkeley–Los Angeles
TST = Syme, R. (1970). *Ten Studies in Tacitus.* Oxford
Tac. = Syme, R. (1958). *Tacitus.* Oxford
Syme, R. (1933). 'Some notes on the legions under Augustus', *JRS* 23.14–33
(1934). 'Galatia and Pamphylia under Augustus: the Governorships of Piso, Quirinius and Silvanus', *Klio* 27.122–48
(1956). 'Seianus on the Aventine', *Hermes* 84.257–66
(1959). 'Livy and Augustus', *HSCP* 64.27–87
Thomas, E. (1893). *De Vell. voluminis condicione aliquot capita.* Berlin
Thomas, P. (1919). 'Notes critiques sur V.P. et sur Tacite', *Bulletin de l'Acad. Roy. de Belgique* (5th series), 5.305–20
(1921). 'Observationes ad scriptores latinos', *Mnem.* 49.17–21

Timpe, *Arminius* = Timpe, D. (1970). *Arminius-Studien*. Heidelberg
Germanicus = Timpe, D. (1968). *Der Triumph des Germanicus*. Bonn
Ungewitter, J. (n.d. [1904]). *De V.P. et Val. Max. genere dicendi quaest selectae*. Diss. Donauwörth
Ursinus, F. (1595). *Fragmenta Historicorum Romanorum*. Antwerp
Verhaak, H. J. W. (1954). *V.P. en de rhetoriek van zijn tijd*. Grave
Walsh, *Livy* = Walsh, P. G. (1961). *Livy: his historical aims and methods*. Cambridge
Walsh, P. G. (1961). 'Livy and Augustus', *PACA* 4.26–37
(1974). *Livy. Greece & Rome* New Surveys in the Classics 8. Oxford
Warde Fowler, W. (1911). *The religious experience of the Roman people*. London
Weber, W. (1936). *Princeps*. Vol. 1. Stuttgart–Berlin
Weinstock, S. (1971). *Divus Julius*. Oxford
Wells, C. M. (1972). *The German policy of Augustus*. Oxford
West, M. L. (1973). *Textual criticism and editorial technique*. Stuttgart
Wilhelm, F. (1928). *Curtius und der jüngere Seneca*. Paderborn
Wilkes = Wilkes, J. J. (1969). *Dalmatia*. London
Wilkes, J. J. (1965). 'ΣΠΛΑΥΝΟΝ-SPLONVM again', *AAntHung* 13.111–25
Williams, G. (1968). *Tradition and originality in Roman poetry*. Oxford
Wimmel, W. (1960). *Kallimachos in Rom. Hermes* Einzelschriften 16. Wiesbaden
Winterbottom, M. (1970). *Problems in Quintilian. BICS* Suppl. 25. London
Wirszubski, C. (1950). *Libertas as a political idea at Rome*. Cambridge
Wiseman, T. P. (1971). *New Men in the Roman senate 139 B.C.–A.D. 14*. Oxford
Wölfflin, E. (1933). *Ausgewählte Schriften* (ed. G. Meyer). Leipzig
Woodman, *EA* = Woodman, A. J. (1975). 'Vell. Pat.' in *Empire and aftermath: Silver Latin II* (ed. T. A. Dorey), 1–25. London
Woodman, A. J. (1968). 'Sallustian influence on V.P.' in *Hommages à M. Renard* 1.785–99. Brussels
(1975). 'Questions of date, genre and style in V.: Some literary answers', *CQ* 25.272–306
Yavetz, Z. (1969). *'Plebs' and 'Princeps'*. Oxford

Note on emendations. Almost every emendation recorded in this volume may be traced to its original source by using the works listed under B and C above. However, some early emendations were originally proposed in works which are now almost inaccessible and for which reference should be made to the editions of Krause and Kritz: in the main such emendations have long since been assimilated into the common stock of Velleian scholarship.

INTRODUCTION

1 THE TEXT

Modern textual criticism of V.'s work may be said to have begun with Orelli's edition of 1835.[1] If since that date V. has been deserted by commentators and historians, he has certainly not been deserted by editors and textual critics.[2] Besides the work of Kritz, which I have already mentioned in the Preface, there were editions from Kreyssig, Bothe, Haase, Halm, Ellis, Bolaffi and Stegmann. This last scholar stated that between 1873 and 1933 more than 1,500 emendations were proposed for V.'s text, a figure which lends considerable support to the view that 'pendant longtemps le texte de Velléius Paterculus n'ait présenté d'autre intérêt, pour beaucoup de savants, que celui de leur offrir un terrain où ils puissent exercer leur ingéniosité'.[3] It is the purpose of this Section to sketch the background to this textual activity and also to explain the position of the present editor.

THE MURBACH CODEX: (M)

A solitary codex of V., probably written in a minuscule script in the eighth century,[4] was discovered early in 1515 by Erasmus' friend Beatus Rhenanus in the Benedictine monastery at Murbach, Alsace.[5] As we learn from his writings of

[1] See below, pp. 11ff.

[2] Nor was he deserted by textual scholars before that date: see the list of editions etc. in Krause 64–104, Kritz cxxviii–cxliv, Dihle 655–7.

[3] Hellegouarc'h, *ANRW*; cf. Stegmann v.

[4] Estimates of the age of the (now lost) codex have varied. Burer (on whom see below, pp. 6–11) informs us on 29.5 that the codex had there written *a* in the form of *cc*, a characteristic of Caroline minuscule script which had apparently died out by the ninth century (Havet 164 § 646; also W. Clausen, *CP* 71 (1976), 42 n. 26). This date would be confirmed by the information given below, p. 12 n. 1, provided that it derives from other evidence than that just mentioned. It is also likely that (M) wrote *s* and *l* similarly (see below, p. 22 n. 2), a further characteristic of Caroline minuscule (Havet 162 § 621).

[5] The exact date of the discovery is unknown, but must have preceded 30 March 1515, the date of the dedication of the edition of Sen. *Apoc.* in

1520,[1] Rhenanus was at once struck by the corruptness of the codex: 'cum primum hunc ... reperissem, et uiderem tam prodigiose corruptum ut omnia restituere non foret humani ingenii'.[2] And he had some sharp words for its unfortunate copyist. 'Ausim iurare eum qui illum descripserat, ne uerbum quidem intellexisse: adeo omnia erant confusa absque ullis punctis aut distinctionibus... imo nihil erat non deprauatum: in singulis pene uerbis haerebatur.'[3] Rhenanus was also struck by the incompleteness of the MS, from which V.'s preface and the greater part of Book I were missing. For this loss he blamed not so much the ravages of time as 'hominum incuriam'. 'Poterant exemplaria aetatis uitio obsolescentia describi, poterant...restitui, si fuissent quos huius rei cura tetigisset. Et certe fuerunt, qui tametsi parum docti, praestiterunt tamen quod potuerunt: quibus habendam gratiam censeo, quod horum saltem opera qualicunque miseras bonorum autorum reliquias licet mendosissime exceptas, conseruatas uideamus, si modo conseruari est, tam deprauate esse descriptum.'[4] In view of these deficiencies Rhenanus decided to postpone publication of the text until he could have access to a better MS which G. Merula was supposed to have discovered in Milan.[5] But he first arranged for the codex to be copied, which was done 'properanter...ab amico quodam'.[6]

THE 'EDITIO PRINCEPS': P

The Milan codex failed to materialise, and Rhenanus, presumably either in 1518 or 1519, began to arrange for the publication of the *editio princeps*.[7] In producing the edition he saw his

which Rhenanus cites V. 'quem nos nuperrime in Murbacensi bibliotheca reperimus'. Cf. R. Sabbadini, 'La scoperta di V.P.', *RFIC* 47 (1919), 346f.

[1] These writings, upon which our knowledge of such matters depends, are: the dedication of the *ed. pr.* to the Duke of Saxony; the addresses to the reader on the first and final pages of the *ed. pr.*; Rhenanus' letter of 16 Dec. 1520 to the Duke's employee, G. Spalatinus. For the text of this last, cf. Fechter 42.

[2] *ed. pr. dedic.*

[3] *ed. pr.* pp. 69–70.

[4] *ed. pr.* p. 1.

[5] *ed. pr. dedic.*

[6] *ed. pr. dedic.*

[7] Again the exact date is uncertain. In *ed. pr. dedic.* Rhenanus says that he waited 'iam treis annos' for the codex, but on p. 69 he says 'iam in quartum annum emendatius exemplar expectando'.

role as that of scholar-editor. 'Vtinam uero quidam autores extarent, quamlibet mendose scripti. Possent in illis multa restitui per uiros eruditos, ac iudicio praeditos.'[1] He claimed to have eliminated many corruptions from the text, with varying degrees of success ('Curauimus autem nos multa uulnera perfecte: nonnulla sic, ut cicatrix etiamnum appareat: quaedam splenio tantum obduximus'), all of which took him some considerable time. 'Proinde cogita quantis mihi uigiliis constiterit haec qualis qualis castigatio...Quod si tu scires quam ego laborarim in hiis fragmentis utcunque restituendis, credo fateberis te mihi non nihil debere. Neque enim quia tu multa absque offensione legis, idcirco codex planus erat.'[2] And he quickly dismissed those who might have objected to his conjectural method: 'Quasi uero qui iam olim poetas enarrarunt, aut nostro saeculo sunt interpretati, non coniecturas plerunque sequantur!'[2]

In many respects Rhenanus' confidence, not unmixed with an agreeable diffidence, was justified, as will be seen below (pp. 20–5); but in one respect at least Rhenanus' method seems to have been seriously defective. His restoration of the text was apparently based not on the original codex but on the copy made by his anonymous friend.[3] The matter seems incapable of definite proof, but there are several indications that this was so. First, when Rhenanus sent the text to J. Froben to be printed, he sent both the Murbach MS and its copy, often warning Froben's men 'ut uetus exemplar non minus quam exemplum inspicerent'.[4] Second, Rhenanus on occasion proposes as an emendation of his own a reading which was in the original codex.[5] Third, writing a few days after the *editio*

---

[1] *ed. pr.* p. 1.
[2] *ed. pr.* pp. 69–70.

[3] So Fechter 52ff.; also Ellis ix; G. Pasquali, *Storia della tradizione e critica del testo*[2] (1952), 100. There is no authority in any of the three sources mentioned above (p. 4 n. 1) for Kritz's statement that Rhenanus 'ipse codicem Murbacensem descripsit' (lxxvi). See too below, n. 5.

[4] *ep. Spalat.*

[5] Thus *aciem* and *at ea* at 112.3–4, assuming (with Krause 62) that Rhenanus' marginal formula 'alias' is not a method of referring to the text of the codex. There are in fact only two places in the whole *ed. pr.* where Rhena-

princeps had been published, Rhenanus claimed that he had been deceived as to the accuracy of the copy of the codex: 'in quo multum falsus sum, quod exemplar fidelissime descriptum arbitrabar'.[1] Fourth, the inaccuracy of this copy was revealed by a late *collatio* which Rhenanus refrains from specifying as his own: 'cum postrema sed nimium sera collatio librarii oscitantiam arguat'.[2] None of these four circumstances is likely to have taken place if Rhenanus had had the original Murbach codex in front of him while preparing his text for Froben. However much we may regret Rhenanus' omission, it was characteristic of his age: Lipsius was to act similarly when he produced his edition of Tacitus in 1574.[3]

BURER'S APPENDIX: B

The bulk of the *editio princeps* – that is, the text and Rhenanus' marginal notes – seems to have been completed in November 1520, the date printed on its (unnumbered) seventy-first page. It was then that one of Rhenanus' scribes, J. A. Burer, happened to notice an error which led him to retrieve the Murbach MS from Froben and collate it with the *editio princeps*. 'Cum Velleium typis excusum uidissem, casu inspecto recenti libro erratululum[4] quoddam deprehendi, leuiusculum quidem illud, sed adeo non leue, quin dignum uideretur obseruatu: atque ex hoc uno (quod aiunt) caetera omnia spectare coepi, uetustum Vellei codicem a Io. Frobenio repetens animo conferendi eius ...Contuli itaque Velleium a capite (quod aiunt) usque ad

nus seems to mention the codex: his note on 109.1 ('nam hic in exemplari lacunulam omissae dictionis offendimus') and his final remarks on p. 70 ('nam in exemplari versus aliquot erant erasi'). The former could be either an assumption on Rhenanus' part, or information derived from the copy of the codex; the latter is similarly explicable, but might equally be due to Rhenanus' recollection of the codex when he discovered it five years before.

1 *ep. Spalat.*, completely misinterpreted by Kritz lxxxii.

2 *ep. Spalat.*

3 Cf. C. O. Brink, 'Justus Lipsius and the text of Tacitus', *JRS* 41 (1951), 33 n. 9; Kenney 53.

4 Other copies of the *ed. pr.* have 'erratulum': cf. Kritz cxxix; also below, p. 7 n. 7.

calcem.'[1] It is this *collatio* to which Rhenanus referred in the passage quoted near the end of the preceding paragraph;[2] and it revealed many discrepancies between the book and the codex for which Rhenanus blamed both Froben's printers, who contrary to his warnings had failed to consult the MS as well as its copy,[3] and also his anonymous friend, who had made that copy 'infeliciter'.[4] If the above reconstruction is true, however, the blame should rest with Rhenanus himself.

Burer's collation takes up ten unnumbered pages at the end of the *editio princeps*. The book then seems to have gone back to Froben, for he added not only Rhenanus' dedication and *Vita Vellei*, dated 8 and 13 December 1520 respectively, but also, on p. 70, an emendation by Rhenanus of 112.4 which is so self-evidently correct that even Burer, had he been able to see it, would scarcely have bothered to advance his own wrong emendation of the same passage.[5] The book was finally published at some point between 13 and 16 December,[6] but even that seems not to have stopped Rhenanus' tinkering: there are several places where different copies of the *editio princeps* have different readings.[7]

---

1 Burer's address 'historiarum amatoribus' on the (unnumbered) p. 73 of *ed. pr.*

2 This seems clear because Rhenanus' statement 'meus amanuensis uolumen typis excusum denuo cum uetusto contulit' follows directly upon his reference to 'postrema sed nimium sera collatio' (*ep. Spalat.*). It must be admitted that the words *denuo* and *postrema* imply that the codex had been collated previously; but I think Rhenanus here means the *collatio* which he had expected Froben's men to perform.

3 'Illi non obtemperarunt, magis curantes, ut quam primum labore defungerentur, quam ut liber bene haberet' (*ep. Spalat.*). Such discrepancies as 1.4.3 *Graeciae* for *Graecae* or 1.16.2 *clausa capsa* for *clausa capso* might reasonably fall into this category: see also below, p. 17 n. 3, p. 21.

4 *ed. pr. dedic.*

5 For the unreliability of Burer's emendations see below, p. 9 n. 4.

6 The respective dates of the *Vita* and the letter to Spalatinus, in which latter the book is referred to as published.

7 See e.g. Haase iv–v, who says that at 35.2 (on p. 27, not 37, of *ed. pr.*) some copies have *homo*, others *non* (the former is correct, the latter the reading of the codex); and that at 83.2 some copies have *hunc mox auunculum*, others *mox autem hunc auunculum* (the latter is the reading of the codex and probably nearer the truth than the former). See too Orelli xii–xiii; Stegmann on 73.1, 76.3; also above, p. 6 n. 4.

Rhenanus does not emerge from this story with much credit, and to that extent his edition may be said to have been 'badly executed';[1] but his acceptance of Burer's collation as an appendix, while admittedly 'nimium sera', does at least give some grounds for the view that 'maximae Rhenano curae fuisse, ut editio princeps quam accuratissime ad codicis fidem excuderetur'.[2]

That Burer took his job seriously seems not to be in doubt. He regularly expresses an interest in and knowledge of old MSS and their characteristics, observing their orthographical habits (on which he quotes Politian), their abbreviations, the habits of scribes, and the way in which corruptions might have arisen. He remarks upon such items as erased words in (M), its marginal notes, and the different hands which it exhibited; and he confirms Rhenanus' impression of the codex by such statements as 'uestigia literarum uix poterant uideri prae uetustate' (103.3).[3] It is not surprising that such a man should introduce his collation with the following claim. 'Cum hunc recentem uetusto Vellei codici conferrem, non modo uersum uersui, sed etiam syllabam syllabae, & (quod alicui plus quam curiosum ac pene stultum uideri queat) etiam literam literae contuli.'[4]

Burer's normal practice was to print a lemma from P and follow it by the formula *exemplar uetustum habet*, which he would in turn follow by his reading of (M). Although he occasionally made mistakes, we shall see that he generally maintained a very high level of accuracy in his transcriptions.[5] Thus he notices

---

[1] Goodyear, *Comm. Tac.* 1.6 n. 5. [2] Kritz lxxxiii.

[3] Burer makes similar statements on several other occasions, esp. towards the end of his collation (cf. Krause 51).

[4] *ed. pr.* [= p. 73]. Rhenanus testifies that Burer acquitted himself 'plus quam diligenter' (*ep. Spalat.*).

[5] See below, p. 16. Although some scholars like Burman and Gruter questioned Burer's fidelity, he was defended, in my opinion rightly, by Ruhnken (*praef.* 2), Krause 52–3, and Kritz lxxxi–lxxxiv. Some exs. of Burer's errors are as follows. He apparently omits *gladiorum* from his reading of the codex at 22.2 (for the controversial case at 120.1 see my n. ad loc.) and occasionally seems to attribute to (M) two different readings of the same word: 1.2.1 *incies* and *ncies*, 115.2 *in integras* and *in integritas*; the same may have happened at 107.1 *metumque* and *motumque*, but the case is more uncertain. Even though in almost every instance Burer's reading of (M) will

Scpiones at 127.1; and he is excellent at noting such normally elusive items as omissions, transpositions, and alterations of numerals. On roughly half the occasions on which Burer notes the divergence of P from (M), the reading of P is in fact correct,[1] often quite blatantly so. From this we are compelled to conclude that Burer saw himself strictly as a collator and that to him a *uera lectio* was the reading of (M), which he proposed to record, regardless of its merits, on as many occasions as he noticed that P diverged from it. If true, this conclusion is of great importance (see below, pp. 16–19).

Unfortunately, however, the issue is less straightforward. Burer was strongly influenced by an age in which scholars 'did not distinguish between collating and correcting a text: the one operation embraced and assumed the other'.[2] This comes out clearly in the ambiguous page-headings of Burer's appendix, '*Emendationes* Velleianae *ex* codice uetusto' (my italics); and it also emerges clearly from another peculiarity. Burer took advantage of his role as collator to introduce into his notes some emendations of his own, usually prefaced by the formula, again regrettably ambiguous, *mihi legendum uidetur*. Such emendations, sometimes made in the face of the stated reading of the codex,[3] are easily isolated;[4] but there are other occasions on which

be exact, these small mistakes (which often look like printing errors) confirm the simple fact that no transcript is infallible. It is therefore quite wrong of Halm, Rockwood and Stegmann to denote Burer's readings by *M* rather than by *B*. Ellis at one time adopted the same misleading practice (*Hermath.* 10 (1897–9), 2), but fortunately not in his edition.

[1] See below, pp. 21, 25.

[2] Kenney 8–9.

[3] So e.g. at 1.13.5 'tamet si sic [sc. as his lemma from P] habeat uetustum exemplar, tamen uidetur legendum...'.

[4] Those of Burer's emendations which I mention in my app. crit. are ascribed to *Burer* in full: in this way they are distinguished from his readings of the codex, which I, like everyone else except Halm, Rockwood and Stegmann, denote by *B*. The merit of Burer's emendations varies greatly and cannot be gathered from a perusal of the app. crit., which naturally includes only his more plausible efforts. Sometimes Burer's emendations are clearly right (e.g. 130.3 *Druso suo*), sometimes almost certainly right (e.g. 123.1 *firmanda*). But many of them are pure nonsense (e.g. 119.4 *pectore* for *petere*), which he is capable of defending with such statements as the following (on 128.1): 'ipsus uideat lector quid sibi lectu optimum uideatur, nam mihi haec lectio non admodum displicet.' It is

Burer combines his two standard formulae to produce hybrids like *exemplar uetustum sic habet ut potius legendum existimem.* In such cases it is naturally impossible to deduce what exactly Burer thought the reading of (M) to be;[1] but more important is the fact that in such cases his sole testimony contains at least some conjectural element. It could perhaps be argued from this evidence that Burer regarded as *uera* a reading which was not necessarily that of (M) but in his opinion that of V. himself;[2] it could also be argued that Burer did not always record the readings of (M) if he himself had been anticipated by Rhenanus in restoring to the text what he considered to be V.'s own words.[3] Again this conclusion, if true, is of great importance.

Two passages throw further light on the problem. At 72.5 Burer follows his normal practice of quoting a lemma from P which we know is an emendation of Rhenanus, *ad quem et e Brutianis castris*; Burer then says of this lemma, 'lectio Velleiana bene habet', after which he proceeds to observe: 'In uet. cod. sic scriptum erat, adque me T e brutianis castris &c'.[4] Here an emendation of Rhenanus, by no means one of his more spectacular efforts, has been indicated by Burer to be true. Again at 118.1 Rhenanus in a marginal note had conjectured *prouocantes* for *procaces*, the reading in the text of P. Burer quotes P's lemma and then says: 'ex. uet. non habet procaces, sed procataes. Hinc lectionem marginalem ut ueram, in ordinem redigendam puto.' Here Burer wishes to restore to the text an emendation of Rhenanus on the grounds that it is true. On the basis of these examples it looks as though Burer tended not to pass over in

---

thus essential, for critical purposes, not to confuse Burer's own emendations with his readings of the codex. The latter are as reliable as the former are unreliable.

[1] E.g. 102.3 'exemp. uetustum sic habet, ut nescias an diu reluctatus, seu potius de reditu luctatus, legendum sit: mihi tamen prior lectio non usquequaque displicet.'

[2] Thus he calls one of his own conjectures *uera* at 1.14.6.

[3] So Fechter 47; Halm (1875), 541.

[4] Since B's reading of (M) is confirmed by A, we can be certain that P is an emendation of Rhenanus. See below, p. 23.

silence even those emendations of Rhenanus which he considered to be true. There is thus no need to assume that Burer did not record as many divergences of P from (M) as he noticed.

AMERBACH'S APOGRAPH: A

In 1835 J. C. Orelli produced an edition of V. based on a text which he had earlier discovered in the library of the Academy in Basel and which had been copied in Basel by Rhenanus' young friend Bonifacius Amerbach (the copy is dated 11 August 1516).[1] Orelli decided that it was not identical with the copy which Rhenanus described as having been made 'properanter ac infeliciter'. In the first place the *editio princeps*, which is based on this latter copy, contains various passages, including the first eight chapters of Book 1, which are omitted from Amerbach's copy.[2] In the second place Froben's printers were presumably using the 'anonymous' copy in 1520 and doubtless littered it with printers' marks in addition to those marks already made by Rhenanus; but from a letter which Rhenanus wrote to Amerbach in that same year, we know that Amerbach had his own copy, which is devoid both of printers' marks and of Rhenanus' corrections, with him at Avignon.[3] We must therefore conclude that while Amerbach's apograph has survived, the copy upon which the *editio princeps* was based has not. The latter evidently

---

[1] The copy, comprising 72 pages at 38 × 26 cm, is now to be found in the Öffentliche Bibliothek of Basel University (MSS AN. II.38), to whose Keeper of Manuscripts, Dr M. Burckhardt, I am most grateful for sending me a microfilm. For a more detailed description of the apograph see Ellis xiii, Bolaffi vii–ix. Its subscription *apparently* reads, in part, 'Tertio Eid. Aug. $\overline{\text{MDXVI}}$ Basileiae In edib. tuis Bo. Amorbacch' (so too Fechter 9). Amerbach was then 21 years old (cf. Fechter 5).

[2] Cf. Orelli viii–ix. A fair idea of A's omissions may be gathered from the long list in Kritz cx–cxi; but Kritz wrongly follows Orelli in stating that A omits *uidemus...deinde ego* at 104.4, *non enim...occidit* at 119.5, and *triumphosque* at 127.1. The numerous other deficiencies of Orelli's collation are noted by Fechter in his (12–32).

[3] 'apud illum [sc. Froben] aedimus Vellei fragmenta quae nosti, nam habes exscripta': cf. Fechter 35ff. (the text of the letter on p. 38).

met the same fate as the Murbach codex itself, which disappeared after being last heard of in 1786.[1]

The question whether Amerbach's apograph was copied directly from the Murbach MS or from its anonymous copy has been answered differently by different scholars.[2] Ellis argued from the nature of the apograph that Amerbach 'in describendo saepissime haesitasse quidnam potissimum eligeret; nimirum codicem exscribebat adeo non planum ut nulla in pagina... non haesitaturus esset' (xv). If true, this would indicate that A is a transcript of the original codex. But Fechter and Halm argued from the same evidence that Amerbach was able to read his exemplar easily.[3] Certainly the apograph's characteristic errors seem best explained by this latter view,[4] with which, after an examination of a microfilm, my own impression concurs. If true, this would indicate that A derives from the same source as P, namely the copy of the codex made by Rhenanus' anonymous friend.[5]

COMPARISON OF A AND P[6]

We have seen that the text of V. depends upon a lost archetype, a lost apograph, and three extant authorities, all of which, on the present hypothesis, are related to each other as follows:

---

[1] A letter written on 10 August of that year refers to a sale which was to include 'une collection des Épîtres de St. Jérôme de VIII siècle, un Velleius Paterculus du même temps et l'unique qui existe'. Cf. A. Allgeier, *Miscellanea Mercati* (1946), 457–8, referred to by Kenney 82–3, q.v. for the disappearance of other *codices unici*.

[2] Ellis and Kritz think A is a direct copy of (M); the opposite view, first put forward by Fechter, is held by Halm, Bolaffi and Stegmann. Laurent believed that A was the copy made 'properanter ac infeliciter ab amico quodam' but that it was not the copy handed to Froben's printers.

[3] Fechter 51–2; Halm (1875), 537f., 547.

[4] See below, pp. 19–20.

[5] I follow Halm (1875), 534, in denoting this copy as (R).

[6] In this section examples are drawn mainly, but by no means exclusively, from chh. 94–131. My general observations and conclusions are of course applicable to V.'s text as a whole.

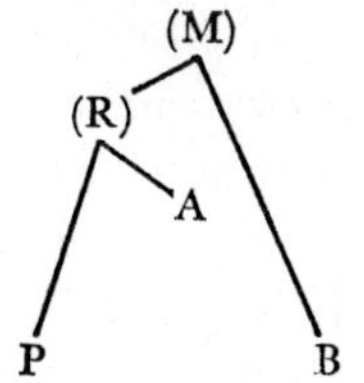

As we have also seen, (M) was extremely corrupt, difficult to read, and lacking both punctuation and word-divisions. It was copied by (R), and even if the anonymous copyist was able to improve the text in a few places,[1] we scarcely need Rhenanus' criticism of him to tell us that his main contribution would be the introduction of still further errors in addition to those already present in (M).[2] 'The number of errors corrected must always be less than the number made, and the overall trend will necessarily be towards a less correct text.'[3]

Thus at 56.3 B tells us that (M) read *tam clementer omnibus uictoribus suis uso*, but the words *uictoribus suis* are missing from both A and P. It follows that these words were omitted by their common exemplar (R) and that Rhenanus failed to fault his paradosis because the text makes sense without the omitted

---

[1] Such improvement can be hypothesised only where PA exhibit a true or improved reading as compared with B. Halm (1875), 535–6, points to 11 such places in V.'s text, of which the following allegedly occur in the Tiberian narrative: 103.2 *legerat* B: *legeret* PA; 128.1 *uirtutem aestimationem* B: *uirtutum aestimatione* PA; 130.4 *Vinicii* B: *Vinici* PA. In fact, however, the first two exs. are false since in each case A clearly agrees with B; and the third is hardly convincing. If B really does intend to read *integritas* at 115.2 (see above, p. 8 n. 5), we could add the joint reading of PA, *integras*. In the 11 examples which he mentions, Halm says that the improvements are such 'wie ein jeder des Lateinischen etwas kundige Abschreiber machen konnte'; but whether (R) was actually responsible for them is uncertain. We infer from 38.4, where A reads *initio Beat* / *in otio* and P reads *initio*, either that Rhenanus and Amerbach had discussed V.'s text together or that Rhenanus had already inserted variants into (R) by the time it was copied by A. Such circumstances would explain at least some of the occasions on which A and P offer the same alternative readings: cf. 100.3, 102.1, 118.1, 118.4, 127.1, 131.1, and also 2.14.3 mentioned in the text below.

[2] See also below, p. 14 n. 2. For Rhenanus' criticism of his friend see above, p. 7.

[3] West 12.

words.[1] Analogous is 2.14.3 where B says that (M) read *immunisque ab omnibus arbitris esset*: here P has substituted *hominibus* for *arbitris*, while A presents no noun at all, although *hominibus* is written above the line. It follows that (R) omitted *arbitris* and that A and P, realising the defectiveness of the sentence, made the easiest supplement after *omnibus*, namely *hominibus*. Again we know from B that (M) correctly read *eo die* at 27.2 and *se per* at 41.3, but both A and P read *eodem die* and *semper* respectively, doubtless deriving the errors from (R). At 112.3–4 B says that (M) read *aciem* and *at ea*, which are correct; but the text of P wrongly offers *etiam* and *antea*, readings which are sufficiently close to A's *aciam*/*aciem* and *altera* to suggest that the errors derive from their common exemplar. Finally at 130.3 B reports that (M) read *Drusuo*, but both A and P agree in offering simply *Druso*. It is highly unlikely that Rhenanus, had he been presented with *Drusuo*, would have failed to see that the true reading should be *Druso suo*, which B, with (M) before him, correctly conjectured. It follows that both A and P were confronted with *Druso*, an erroneous simplification attributable to (R).[2]

[1] In fact the words *uictoribus suis* are themselves corrupt; Gelenius proposed *uictoriis suis*, doubtless correctly.

[2] Halm (1875), 536–7, believes that the errors of (R) occur in cases where B exhibits a true or nearly true reading as compared with PA. His examples in 94–131, excluding those already mentioned above, are: 94.1 *ei* B, om. PA (but see below, p. 17 n. 1); 102.3 *Lymira* (= *Limyra*, corr. Ruhnken) B: *Limyram* P: *Limira* A (not a good ex.: see my n. ad loc.); 104.3 *fructus* B: *fruitus* P: *functus* A; 106.2 *Langobardi* B: *Longo-* PA; 109.2 *LXX* B: *LX* PA (but since B here says that in (M) the final *X* was erased, this is a false ex.); 113.3 *Sisciam* B: *Sistiam* P: *Sisci iam* A (again false, since P often has *t* for *c*); 115.4 *Delmatae* B: *Dalm-* PA; 120.1 *hostium* PA, om. B (but in this controversial case it is by no means certain that B does omit the word: see my n. ad loc.); 131.1 *ac stator* B: *et stator* PA. We might add 114.1 *uni genitio* (= *uni negotio*, corr. Gelenius) B: *uni* P: *unigenito* A; A's error doubtless derives from the influence of the Nicene Creed, and (R) may be responsible for it: P realised the error and – wrongly, as it happens – omitted *genito* (this case, analogous to 130.3 above, is further support for the view that Rhenanus did not work directly from (M)). Also 120.4 *uiti* (= *uicti*, corr. E. Thomas) B: *usi* P: *niti* A. Halm found 30 exs. belonging to this category in V.'s text, a total which he considered small: he thus questioned Rhenanus' criticism of his anonymous friend. We should however note that

In 1516 (R) was itself copied by A. When this apograph came to light more than three hundred years later, its many discrepancies from P caused editors for the first time to doubt whether (M) could be reconstructed simply from the readings of P and B alone. Reconstructing the lost archetype became of overwhelming importance: 'quaerendum enim ante omnia est', wrote Haase in 1851, 'quid scriptum fuerit in codice Murbacensi.'[1] Halm, who believed that A was not directly copied from (M), and Ellis and Orelli, who believed that it was, were all of the opinion that A was far more important than P for the reconstruction of (M).[2] Kritz, on the other hand, who like Orelli and Ellis believed that A was a direct copy of (M), and Fechter, who believed that it was not, maintained the view that for the reconstruction of (M) paramount importance should be given to P.[3] In this belief they were followed by Haase, who however expressed no opinion upon the immediate provenance of A.[4] Thus the apograph, once discovered, engendered a controversy

---

Rhenanus' remarks were made on the spur of the moment when he had been informed by Burer of the discrepancies between P and (M); but whereas Burer had presumably meant not only P's erroneous divergences from (M) but also Rhenanus' own tacit divergent corrections, Rhenanus, doubtless assuming that Burer was referring only to the former type of divergence, naturally blamed (R) for such discrepancies. And even if (R) was as accurate as Halm believed, it will nevertheless have been extremely corrupt in so far as it preserved the extensive corruption of (M). It is understandable if Rhenanus in these circumstances believed that (R) was less faithful than in fact it was. We should also observe that in at least some of the cases where A differs from P, A may have preserved an error introduced by (R) which P was able to correct. Naturally the loss of (R) makes it impossible for us to know how often this happened; but Rhenanus certainly effected such changes at 112.3–4 (see below, p. 21), and cf. also 102.3 above; 116.4 *ciui* BP: *ciuis* A; 119.1 *qua* BP: *quae* A. But in each of these last three cases the error *may* have been introduced by A alone, as certainly at 120.4 *prouidentia* BP: *prudentia* A. See below, p. 23 and n. 1.

1 Haase iv, cf. Kritz cxvi 'ad emendanda auctoris verba plurimum interesse, ut ante omnia, quid in cod. Murb. scriptum fuerit, perspiciatur'.

2 Halm iii–iv and (1875); Ellis xvi sqq.; Orelli ix sq.; Kreyssig also belongs to this school of thought.

3 Kritz lxxvi sqq., a really excellent discussion (see esp. cxv–cxvii); Fechter 52–69.

4 Haase iv. He is wrongly considered to be a supporter of A by Hellegouarc'h, *ANRW*.

which in its small way resembled the controversy over the Leidensis of Tacitus since its rediscovery in 1950.[1]

Supporters of A argued that in places where A and P differ, A almost always = (M) on the grounds that B, when available, almost always agrees with A. Ellis, for example, who gave to his edition the subtitle 'Ex Amerbachii praecipue apographo', grandly states as follows in his preface. 'uetustatem incorruptae lectionis qualis in codice Murbacensi fuit ex Amerbachii apographo multo magis quam ex Rhenani ed. pr. repetendam esse; ed. Pr. a Bureri lectionibus ex ipso Murbacensi ductis saepenumero discrepare, Am. apographon rarissime.'[2] Now it is certainly true that where A and B agree, as they very often do on the occasions when they are both available,[3] a reading of (M) has been preserved: it follows that B almost always = (M) and that Burer's accuracy has been generally confirmed by the discovery of A.[4] But it is quite wrong to argue that, because B almost always = A and because B also = (M), then *a fortiori* A = (M). Such an argument takes no account of the vital fact that B is only a *partial* witness:[5] if we were to accept the formula A = (M), we should have to assume, as of course do the supporters of A,[6] that B regularly fails to record P's divergences from (M).

As a general rule A, in virtue of its being an apograph, derives

[1] From 1840 onwards there appeared a cluster of articles with such titles as 'Ueber den Werth der Amerb. Handschrift des Vell.', of which the last is by Halm (1875). I have taken Halm and Ellis as the main targets for my comment because they have been A's two most influential supporters. Halm's work has the additional advantage of assuming exactly the same provenance of A (and of P) as the present chapter.

[2] Ellis xvii. I say 'grandly' because Ellis prints this statement in spaced type, signifying its presumed importance. Yet it is doubly misleading. By *incorruptae* Ellis means not 'not corrupt' but 'preserved intact'; and anything other than the almost total divergence of B from P could hardly have been expected, since it was B's primary intention to do just that.

[3] In 94–131, for example, B agrees with A on roughly 65 % of the occasions on which they are both available.

[4] See above, p. 8.

[5] In the Tiberian narrative, e.g., B is available on less than a third of the occasions on which A differs from P.

[6] Thus e.g. Orelli x; Halm iv and (1875), 539, 541.

from (M) almost all of the correctness which it exhibits;[1] and it must be admitted that A occasionally preserves excellent readings which, being absent from P and B, are therefore likely to derive from (M). In chapters 94–131, for example, such readings are 100.5 *pependissent pependere* (*pependissent* om. P), 105.2 *ingenio* (om. P), 120.1 *ultro* (*ultra* P).[2] On occasion A also preserves true readings of a far more mundane nature, usually confirming the corrections of scholars whose work antedates the apograph's discovery: thus Gelenius had correctly restored 130.2 *monte Caelio* (*Caeli* P), Aldus 103.3 *abhinc annos* (*annis* P), and Vascosanus 110.3 *abdito* (*addito* P).[3] But while in such cases we are naturally indebted to A's discovery, their number is comparatively very small indeed:[4] most of A's good readings

[1] This is only a general rule, for we have already seen (p. 13 n. 1) that A does include some emendations in his transcript. Another example is perhaps 94.1 where A correctly reads, but above the line, *Ti.* (*ei* B, om. P). Other possible examples are given by Halm (1875), 547ff., who however rightly concludes 'dass Amerbach nicht darauf ausgegangen ist während seiner raschen Abschrift eine Reform des Textes vorzunehmen' (549). See also below, n. 4.

[2] *ultro* was brilliantly conjectured by Freinsheim before the discovery of A.

[3] Vascosanus also emended *quia* to *quin* at 110.6, but surprisingly no one then emended P's word order *tantus etiam huius belli* to what was correctly found later in A, *etiam tantus huius belli*. Kritz indeed believed that A's word order was wrong (cxv). Of the above errors, *addito* and *Caeli* are perhaps due to faulty proof-reading.

[4] Orelli (x) was able to list only 6 places in the whole of V.'s text where in his opinion A independently preserved a true reading, and only 7 where an emendation was confirmed. Halm (1875), 539–41, has a longer list. It must in any case be emphasised that such lists are often subjective, depending as they do upon what each editor believes a true reading to be and upon how he believes that true reading was arrived at – whether by transmission, conjecture (above, n. 1 and p. 13 n. 1), or even by error. Thus Halm (1875), 541, believes A's *urbis* to be correctly transmitted from (M) at 124.1, whereas I do not; but on p. 548 he rejects *pependissent* at 100.5 as a wrong emendation by Amerbach, whereas I believe it is one of A's three really good transmitted readings in the whole Tiberian narrative. Again, at 95.2 and 112.3 A reads respectively *derecta acie* and *derigentibus quae aciem*, but P reads *di-*: *de-* is undoubtedly what V. wrote, but B on 112.3 tells us that (M) read *di-*; Halm (1875), 539, is thus quite wrong to imply that A derived these two true readings from (M). A's *de-* is due either to error or conjecture, and it is P which faithfully reproduces (M).

were already familiar to scholars from their earlier appearance in B.[1] And in each of the above cases the nature of A's discrepancy from P is not, in my opinion, sufficient grounds for impugning the general thoroughness of B.[2] We must therefore, I believe, assume that in almost every case the silence of B implies its agreement with P and hence also with (M), an assumption at which we have already arrived by a different route (above, pp. 8–11). And since the number of occasions on which P and B implicitly agree in their difference from A is many times greater than the number of occasions on which A and B explicitly agree in their difference from P, as we have just seen,[3] it follows that we are less able to reconstruct (M) from A than from P with B.[4] And since P and B were of course both available to scholars long before Orelli made his discovery, we must

---

At 95.3 A's correct *nec* may be due to error, since A has omitted the four phrases immediately preceding the word; at 104.4 A's *recipimus*, which is perhaps preferable to P's *recepimus* (although I have printed P's reading), may be due to attraction to the preceding *uidemus*; attraction may also have caused A's correct *magnam* at 112.4 before *Thracum*, in the same way as A writes *iunctis* before *praedictis* in the same sentence: in the latter case, however, A realised the error and correctly wrote *iunctus* afterwards. See too A's correct *accensaque plebe* at 121.1, where B tells us that (M) read *accensaque plebis*, and P reads *accensasque plebis*; also my notes on 120.1, 3. These examples go to show how vital it is (and here I merely state the obvious) that one's general judgement upon a MS must depend upon the judgements one has already made concerning its individual readings. I cannot help feeling that many of A's supporters have put the cart before the horse – perhaps 'quasi scripto libro per se maior fides esset, quam typis impresso, aut veritas non ex cura atque scientia describentis, sed ex materia libri penderet' (Kritz lxxxiv).

[1] See below, p. 21 n. 1, p. 22 n. 1.

[2] Most of the discrepancies involve only a single letter. Halm (1875), 548, thinks it unlikely that Burer would have missed 'eine so starke Abweichung' as *pependissent* omitted at 100.5; but I think the mistake is quite natural. Only at 105.2 do I feel that Burer has let us down.

[3] In 94–131 PB implicitly agree to differ from A in over 80 % of the occasions when A differs from P, while AB explicitly differ from P in less than 20 % of such occasions.

[4] Fechter also concludes 'dass die *editio princ. in Verbindung mit der Burerischen Collation* eben immer in die erste, die Amerbachische Abschrift in die zweite Linie zu stellen sei' (69). This conclusion, which seems to me inevitable and at which I had independently arrived from similar assumptions before I was able to see Fechter's work, is conveniently ignored by

conclude that A has made only a limited contribution to the debate which its discovery started. 'The mere fact of recent discovery', observes Kenney, 'might invest a MS with a quite spurious or inflated importance.'[1]

This conclusion may be approached from a different angle. It was Fechter who first showed that in all probability A and P were *both* derived, not from (M), but from (R).[2] But not even Halm, who (unlike Ellis) accepted Fechter's proposition, made the inevitable deduction that P was more important than A for the reconstruction of (M). Yet if Fechter is right, as I too believe, then in theory both A and P have an equal chance of preserving the readings of (M) from which (R) was copied. And that A is the less likely candidate to perform this function seems clear from the incompetence of its copyist.[3]

It would appear that Amerbach was more interested in making a quick transcript than an emended or careful copy and that he more often transcribed what he thought (R) contained than what it actually did contain. He thus introduced into V.'s text still further errors in addition to those already introduced by (R). The extent and number of these errors may easily be appreciated by examining the evidence set out below,[4] but some characteristic examples here will lend support to the belief that Amerbach made his transcript at great speed. A's version of 1.10.3–4 is typical: *nihil...praeter speciem nominis sui* (del.)[5] *uigoremque eloquentiae retinentem* (del.) *retinenti in adoptionem dederat*

---

the supporters of A, who consistently quote Fechter as if his evidence supported their case.

1 Kenney 127.

2 Fechter 52ff.

3 Writing before Fechter and thinking that both P and A were derived directly from (M), Kritz noted: 'Quum autem Rhenanus atque Burerius Amerbachium non solum doctrina et ingenio, verum etiam codicum antiquorum legendorum peritia multum superarent, recta ratio postulat, ut...editioni principi primus in usu critico locus, Amerbachio secundus assignetur' (cxvii). (In the reprint of his edition in 1848 Kritz made no reference to Fechter's work.)

4 Viz. in my app. crit. and on pp. 89–92. A true picture of A's character cannot be gathered from Fechter, Ellis or Stegmann.

5 '(del.)' here and elsewhere refers only to the word which immediately precedes it.

...*ante triumphum triumphi* (del.) *diem in ordinem*...*commemoraret*, where the text is disfigured not only by the crossings out but also by the erroneous *in* before *ordinem*. A regularly substitutes for its deletions words written above the line, e.g. 100.3 *libide* (del.), suprascr. *libidine*; *uindicans* (del.), suprascr. *iudicans*; 5 *uxorem* (del.), suprascr. *coniugem*.[1] In these three instances, all taken from the same chapter, the first and third suprascripts are correct, the second incorrect. A transposes words wrongly (e.g. 119.3 *successor exempli* for *exempli successor*),[2] and frequently makes the wrong divisions between words, e.g. 119.2 *Marco reducis* for *marcore ducis*, 127.4 *ex omnem* for *exsomnem*, 129.1 *singulare censeamus* for *singula recenseamus*.[3] A often omits, including a quite sizeable passage at 95.3,[4] and often produces nonsense, e.g. 116.3 *super* for *semper*,[5] 127.1 *dominus* for *quominus*, 130.4 *egreditudinem* for *aegritudinem*. A is particularly at fault in the divisions between sentences: these are so often wrong or non-existent that one could with justice apply to Amerbach the criticism which Rhenanus made of the copyist of (M) (above, p. 4).

While Amerbach had aimed almost entirely, and not very successfully, at copying (R), Rhenanus two or three years later aimed to let (R) stand whenever it seemed correct but to correct it whenever it seemed in error. This vital difference between editor and mere copyist means that Rhenanus was more likely than Amerbach to produce a correct text; but does it also mean that P is less or more likely than A to preserve the readings of (M) which have survived through (R)? It must be admitted

[1] Further exs. in Bolaffi xi.

[2] I quote this particular ex. because we know from B as well as from P that *exempli successor* was the reading of (M). *successor exempli* is wrongly retained by Orelli, Ellis and Stegmann, the two latter unscrupulously concealing the contradictory testimony of B. Halm to his credit declines to follow A here. Other occasions where BP explicitly agree are 102.3, 104.3, 112.3, 113.3, 116.4, 119.1, 120.4 (see above, p. 14 n. 2, p. 17 n. 4). On such occasions BP may have preserved a reading of (M), or else P may have restored a reading of (M) which (R) corrupted and A did not emend (see p. 14 n. 2). The former is usually the more likely: see below, p. 23 n. 1.

[3] Further exs. in Kritz c–ciii, Bolaffi x.

[4] See above, p. 11 n. 2.

[5] *super* is retained by Ellis, Bolaffi and Stegmann!

that Rhenanus sometimes failed to see the correctness of the paradosis with which he was confronted, and wrongly resorted to emendation. Thus at 110.4 we know from BA that (M) and (R) correctly offered *parentis*. . .*pars petere Italiam*, but Rhenanus misunderstood the sentence and wrongly conjectured *pars*. . . *properare in Italiam*. Similarly at 111.4 Rhenanus wrongly emended *furentes eorum uires* to *furentes in eum uires*. Sometimes it seems more likely that it was Froben's printers who introduced error into P, by transposition (e.g. 124.2 *ratione magis quam* for *magis ratione quam*), addition (e.g. 99.4 *est*) or omission (e.g. 130.4 *erubescere*).[1] But P's errors, whatever their provenance, must be seen in context. P fails to preserve a correct reading of (M) on roughly half the occasions on which B and A together preserve such a reading; but we know from B's silence that P hardly ever fails to preserve a correct reading of (M) on the occasions when A alone differs from P. On balance, therefore, P is more likely than A to preserve correct readings of (M). This conclusion may be corroborated if we remember that in his editorial efforts at restoring what V. actually wrote, Rhenanus stood a chance of restoring a correct reading of (M) which had been corrupted by (R). We have already seen him fail to do this on five occasions (above, pp. 13f.); but he succeeded in so restoring *aciem* and *at ea* at 112.3–4.[2] Thus on the occasions when Rhenanus' primary role as an editor happens to coincide with a secondary role as preserver of the correct readings of (M), he is again more likely than A to preserve (M).

But what of the occasions on which P fails to preserve a corrupt reading which derived from (M) through (R)? Is it not possible, as Ellis and Halm believe, that on such occasions (M) is preserved more exactly by A than by P and that A is thus of more use for the purposes of criticism?[3] On a number of occa-

[1] Other exs. in the Tiberian narrative are: 102.3 *Massiliae* BA: *-ia* P; 108.2 *parentium* BA: *-tum* P; 112.6 *quibus* BA: *qui* P; 113.1 *principem* BA: *-es* P; 116.4 *nihil non* BA: *nihil* P; 121.1 *accensaque* BA: *accensasque* P; 122.2 *adornari* BA: *-are* P; 126.2 *sepultaeque* BA: *sepultae* P; 127.4 *semperque* BA: *semper* P; 128.1 *Coruncanium* BA: *-num* P.

[2] See above, p. 5 n. 5, p. 14. Other possible exs. on p. 14 n. 2.

[3] Ellis xvii–xix; Halm (1875), 541ff. Again one can quarrel with some of

sions where P has failed to preserve a corrupt reading of (M), for whatever reason, such a reading is preserved by B as well as by A.[1] But in the majority of cases where A corruptly differs from P, B is silent.[2] And while it is true that in a few of these cases the copyist has the advantage over the editor in the matter of preserving corrupt readings,[3] the very extent of A's erroneous divergences from P, when B is silent, is more naturally explained by assuming that A's speed led to faulty transcription of (R) than by postulating that Rhenanus corrected (R) on quite so

their examples. At 94.3 P reads *mandato uictrici*, A *mandatum uictrici*: Aldus emended the latter error correctly to *uitrici*, but was Orelli right in assuming that A is nearer the truth with *mandatum* (he proposed *mandatu*, and has been followed by most edd.) than is P? In fact the noun *mandatus* is used nowhere else by V., whereas he does use *mandatum*. B is here silent, and it looks to me as though A has written *mandatum* (sc. *est*) in view of the 'dative' *uictrici* which follows. See too my nn. on 111.4 and 114.2.

[1] The majority of such cases are insignificant except in so far as they demonstrate the corrective labours of Rhenanus (see next paragraph). Significant cases in 94–131 are: 101.1 *adsidendum* BA: *ad sedandum* P; 105.1 *gentis et inamminus* BA: *gentis et inamninus* P; 110.6 *formatum* BA: *fortunatum* P; 112.5 *fuga* BA: *fugata* P; 122.1 *praepositi* BA: *pro-* P; 122.2 *totius* BA: *ocyus* P; 125.2 *ultimam* BA: *ultimum* P; 125.4 *timere* BA: *tam re* P. In these cases, of course, as in those above (p. 21 n. 1), we have derived no absolute benefit from A's discovery since these readings were already familiar from B: A's role has been to confirm them.

[2] There is an interesting case at 116.2 where B happens not to be silent but where A preserves a superior reading to both B and P. A reads *diligenti quib. ius postumus*, P reads *diligenti. quibus Iulius Posthumius*; Burer observes 'ex. uet. habet Iul. Postumus'. Halm (1875), 554, choosing this case to conclude his long article, goes to town. 'Dass Iul. in M stand, ist sicherlich falsch: denn die erst durch Rhenanus verderbt gewordene Stelle hat Pighius evident so verbessert: Celebri etiam opera diligentique Vibius Postumus..., wie buchstäblich in A zu lesen ist diligenti quib. ius Postumus, d. i. mit richtiger Abtheilung diligentiq. uibius postumus. Eine Abschrift, die so viele klare Spuren ächter und unverfälschter Ueberlieferung zeigt, verdient sicherlich grössere Beachtung, als ihr der Unverstand so mancher Kritiker zuerkennen wollte.' But since *l* and *s* were often confused in minuscule script (Havet 162 § 621), there is no reason why the same word in (M) should not have been read as *iul* by B but as *ius* by (R). A copied (R); and either P in turn misread (R) as *iul*, which is credible, or else 'emended' *ius* to *Iulius*. This case is thus closer to those in the preceding note than Halm is prepared to admit. For other confusions of *s* and *l* cf. 2.4.1 *ex Asia* P: *ex alia* A; 86.2 *at Sosium* Puteanus: *ad folium* P: *ad solium* A.

[3] Cf. e.g. 104.3n.

widespread a scale.[1] This in no way detracts from Rhenanus' statements concerning the corruptness of V.'s text, for many of the corruptions in A are also to be found in P and hence derive from (M). Nor does it detract, as we shall see, from Rhenanus' statement, which is anyway doubtless exaggerated, concerning the time and labour he expended on correcting the corrupt text.

On roughly half the occasions on which A and B agree in their divergence from P, AB preserve a corrupt reading of (M): in such cases P's reading represents an emendation or correction by Rhenanus,[2] who very often succeeded in restoring what V. had actually written. Thus, to take a straightforward example, in the passage 118.4–120.2 we know from AB that (M) – and also, by implication, (R) – offered the following series of wrong readings: 118.4 *et etiam*, *in culpa*, 119.1 *Cassi*, 3 *auique*, 4 *fugatum*, 5 *hosti*, 120.1 *minabatur*, 2 *obulos*. In each case except the first Rhenanus has correctly emended the text:[3] *etiam*, *in culpam*, *Crassi*, *auitique*, *fuga cum*, *hostium*, *minabantur*, *obuios*. On other occasions Rhenanus' emendation is more substantial, as when he correctly emended the reading of (M) at 131.1 *nominum honor omni* to *numinum hanc Romani*.[4] Such examples could be multiplied many times, and testify to the labour which on his own admission he devoted to V.'s text. 'His conjectures are not

---

1 In the cases where B, P and A are all available, the number of A's corrupt variants from P is roughly equal to that of its correct variants from P (with B usually agreeing with A in each case). But in the cases where P and A alone are available, the number of A's corrupt variants from P far outweighs that of its correct variants. The increased ratio of error is such that I believe A to be almost entirely responsible for it. I also believe that the very number of errors in A is a serious deficiency: so too Kritz cxvi, 'in unum congestis omnibus iis Amerbachiani locis, quibus vel deteriorem Rhenaniana lectionem, vel meliorem exhibet, primo aspectu in oculos incurrit malarum scripturarum numerum bonas tantopere superare, ut de maiore auctoritate Amerbachii libro tribuenda cogitari non possit.'

2 Nevertheless in my app. crit. such emendations are ascribed simply to *P*, since they appear in the text of the *ed. pr.* Only in the case of Rhenanus' marginal corrections have I ascribed emendations to *Rhenanus* in full.

3 118.4 is one of those cases where A, while wrong, is closer to the truth (*ei etiam*) than P.

4 This is one of those cases (for others see above, p. 13 n. 1) where Rhenanus' emendation has found its way into the margin of A. That it is an emendation is confirmed by the agreement of B with the text of A.

often, one must admit, brilliant and exciting, but they possess the more valuable quality of often being right.'[1]

Of course P contains many errors which, as we have just seen, derive from (M). But no one was more aware than Rhenanus that the author of an *editio princeps* cannot hope to eliminate all the errors in his exemplar. He engagingly states that his intention in publishing the book has been to allow others to continue the work of correction and emendation which he himself began: 'protulimus, inquam, ut ab aliis illi quoque subueniatur'.[2] In the final analysis Rhenanus' edition is less successful than it might have been for no other reasons than that he lacked sufficient evidence for establishing the truth and that he failed to make proper use of what evidence he had. The former reason he acknowledged himself. 'Nec propterea nullam mihi gratiam habebis amice lector, quod non omnia restituerim. Id enim absque emendatiori codice non erat possibile. at meus & unicus erat, & mendosissimus.'[2] The latter was compensated for by his inclusion of Burer's appendix. We can only be thankful that the *editio princeps* achieved the degree of success which has been outlined here.

I shall conclude this comparison with a summary. The absolute value of A's discovery has been to preserve a few excellent readings of (M) of which we would otherwise be ignorant, and to preserve some corrupt readings of (M) which are not present in P and from which we stand a chance of retrieving what V. wrote. Its secondary value has been to confirm the accuracy of B. But A must be deplored for the quick and careless way in which it was executed, and for the introduction of innumerable errors which scholars have wrongly persuaded themselves were also to be found in (M).[3] The value of

[1] Goodyear, *Comm. Tac.* 1.7.

[2] *ed. pr.* p. 69.

[3] Whatever the defects of his text, Bolaffi to his great credit rightly gave more weight to P than to A (x–xi). Others rightly sceptical of A were Novák (1906) and (1907), and Castiglioni. It is because the Oxford text of Ellis and the Teubner texts of Halm and Stegmann have unanimously and heavily sided with A that the apograph's importance is still overestimated today.

P, which for these purposes includes B, lies in its preservation of the readings of (M), both correct and corrupt, and in the sound corrections which Rhenanus effected upon a very corrupt text. I must however reaffirm that the picture which has been drawn in this section depends to a large extent upon the assumption that B's silence implies the agreement of P with (M).[1] This assumption, which on present evidence I can see no justification for denying, could be quite wrong, in which case the picture would doubtless require alteration. But such alteration must await the production of further evidence: the rediscovery of (M).

ESTABLISHING THE TEXT

The controversy over the reconstruction of (M), while entertaining, has perhaps diverted editors from their primary task, which is to establish, as far as possible, *ipsissima uerba Velleii.* 'Codicology and textual criticism', as M. L. West has aptly reminded us, 'are very different things.'[2] Naturally this task depends in the first place upon our three extant authorities, as follows. Where AB differ from P, P is as likely as AB to preserve V.'s own words; but where A alone differs from P, P almost always preserves V.'s own words; on the extremely rare occasions where B differs from both A and P, B is quite likely to preserve V.'s words.[3] Since therefore each of these authorities is capable of transmitting a true reading independently of the others, an editor must first decide which of them, in any given case, preserves the truth.[4] But what confronts the editor with equal regularity is joint corruption in P and A, with B silent.

1 'Ubicunque enim hic [sc. Burer] nihil annotavit, ea res documento est verba editionis Rhenanianae cum cod. Murb. congruere, ita ut Bureri silentio non minor auctoritas sit, quam diserto testimonio' (Kritz lxxxiii).

2 West 62.

3 I must repeat that these collective judgements are of course based upon innumerable individual judgements.

4 'rectam emendandi viam is ingreditur, qui non praeiudicata opinione ductus alteri libro omnem fidem derogaverit, alteri tamquam oraculo confisus, sed qui hoc tenuerit...unumquemque eorum [sc. Rhenanus, Burer, Amerbach] hic illic quaedam rectius legisse, quam ceteros duos' (Kritz cxvii).

These are cases where (M) itself was corrupt, and here one must resort to correction, conjecture, or despair.

Although Rhenanus' successors willingly accepted his invitation to correct V.'s text, the note of despair on which he ended his *editio princeps* was echoed two hundred years later by Bentley. 'In profane authors (as they are called), whereof one manuscript only had the luck to be preserved, as Velleius Paterculus among the Latins, and Hesychius among the Greeks, the faults of the scribes are found so numerous, and the defects so beyond all redress, that notwithstanding the learnedest and acutest critics for two whole centuries, these books are still, and are like to continue, a mere heap of errors.'[1] The proliferation of conjecture, as was noted at the beginning of this Section, has scarcely abated since Bentley's day. But the improvement of V.'s text has been in no way commensurate with the volume of these conjectures, many of which have been misplaced and misguided.[2] Yet that should be no argument in favour of adopting a so-called 'conservative' approach, which for a text of this heritage is frankly impossible. No editor of V. can refrain from placing in his text a very large number of conjectures, although I have indicated in my commentary those places where I have little confidence in the result.

I have not, however, gone so far as some other editors. There are numerous occasions when conjecture seems to reach nowhere near the truth, and here I have resorted to obelising (e.g. 99.4, 101.1, 107.1, 109.1, 111.1, 119.2, 124.1, 125.5, 127.2). Comparable are the occasions where the corruption seems to arise from the lacunose state of the text. Like Lipsius, Krause

[1] *Remarks upon a late discourse of Free-thinking* (1713), § 32, quoted by Ellis xxiii.

[2] A fair idea of the great number and varying quality of earlier Velleian emendations may be gathered from Kritz's invaluable notes; for subsequent emendations one must rely mainly upon Stegmann's apparatus and appendix, although Stegmann (as is clear to me from Prater's notes) not unnaturally omitted to mention a great many. My own app. crit. is intentionally selective, although further scholarly suggestions are sometimes mentioned in the commentary. To list all modern Velleian emendations (even if one could track them down, which I doubt) would be impossible and would serve no useful purpose.

and Haase I believe such occasions to be fairly frequent, but I have usually been content simply to indicate lacunae rather than follow Haase in supplementing them.[1] My practice in these matters may appear negative; but it has the positive value of reminding scholars of the general uncertainty of V.'s text. In the past we have found that even the most distinguished historians have built their theories upon a paradosis which is manifestly corrupt or a conjecture which cannot be confirmed.[2]

Historians and literary scholars alike, perhaps misled by V.'s frequent parentheses, have imagined that he was a careless dilettante whose history was written in no sort of order. 'It might appear presumptuous', says Syme, 'to seek for system... in an incoherent writer like Velleius.'[3] The closer one studies V.'s narrative, however, the more one recognises that it has been written according to a dramatic and logical structure: this I have attempted to clarify by my paragraphing, another aspect in which the present edition deviates from its predecessors.[4] A small matter perhaps, but one which serves to remind us that V. cannot be divorced (as some would like) from the tradition of Latin historiography, whose masters devoted great attention to the *exaedificatio* of their narratives. Here, however, I am encroaching upon subjects more germane to Section 2.

NOTE ON ORTHOGRAPHY

The spelling of certain words is inevitably inconsistent in P and A. I here give some examples of the most notable cases, indicating by capital letters the forms which I have printed. In this I follow Winterbottom 35–59, whose

[1] See Lipsius on 94.4; Krause xviii, 56; Haase iii–iv. These scholars are in my opinion right in thinking that lacunae are endemic in the transmission of V.'s text. By contrast I have not followed Haase in his other favourite form of emendation, transposition. Though some of his suggestions of this nature are ingenious, none of them is certainly right, and in general this method of emendation has not commended itself to me as an appropriate way of elucidating the difficulties presented by V.'s text.

[2] See e.g. below, 101.1n., 125.5n.

[3] Syme, *DP* 48.

[4] I should however mention that the paragraphing (of Ellis' text) by H–W is superior to that found in other works. The traditional chapter-divisions in V.'s text are, according to Krause 81, attributable to Gruter, who is generally thought to have performed the same service for Tacitus.

discussion of Quintilian's orthography should be consulted and whose opening statement I most heartily endorse. 'An editor must spell words somehow. If he tells us what he does, that is perhaps as much as can be expected from him.'

96.3 *DALMATARVM* P: *Delm-* A but 115.1 *DALM-* A: *Delm-* P and 115.4 *DALM-* PA; 95.2 *DERECTA* A: *directa* P (also 112.3); 111.1 and 130.2 *DILECTVS* A: *delectus* P; 114.5 *INTELLEGERE* A: *intelligere* P but 128.4 *INTELLEGIT* P: *intelligit* A; 105.2 *NAVVM* P: *gnauum* A (also 120.3); 2.16.2 *QVICQVAM* PA but 95.3 and 123.3 *quidquam* PA; 100.3, 124.2 and 131.1 *QVICQVID* PA but 126.3 *QVICQVID* P: *quidquid* A; 95.2 *RAETOS* A: *Rhetos* P; 114.3 *RETTVLI* P: *retuli* A; 103.4 *TEMPTEMVS* A: *tentemus* P but 106.3 *tentatum* PA; 95.3 *OBIICERE* PA but 102.1 *OBIISSE* A: *obisse* P^{mg} and 114.3 *aditiam* A: *ADIICIAM* P. Similarly with the endings of words: 103.4 and 104.2 *IMPERII* PA but 97.1 *imperi* PA; 98.1 *LVCII* PA but 102.1 *Lolli* PA and 123.2 *TIBERII* A: *Tiberi* P; 125.4 *OBSIDENTES* P: *obsidentis* A (acc. plur.). In particular A tends to make no distinction between *e*, *ae* and *oe*; and both P and A often write *c* for *t* (e.g. 98.3 *negocio* P): most of these cases I have refrained from recording.

2 HISTORY, BIOGRAPHY OR PANEGYRIC?

Modern Velleian scholarship, excluding that which has concerned itself with the transmission and establishing of the text, may be said to have begun with the essay which Sauppe first published in 1837 and in which the following was said about V.'s work. 'Wir haben in seiner Geschichte nicht sowohl eine Entwicklung der Begebenheiten in ruhiger Zeitfolge, als den Katalog einer chronologisch geordneten Gallerie von Porträts aus der römischen Geschichte.'[1] At the turn of this century Leo also commented upon the same biographical feature, adding that it 'merkwürdig wird...durch ihre Anwendung auf Caesar, Augustus und Tiberius'; from chapter 94 onwards, continued Leo, 'ist der grösste Theil des Buches ein Enkomion des Tiberius'.[2] And as recently as 1970 M. Rambaud produced

[1] Sauppe 57. His essay originally appeared in *Schweiz. Mus. f. hist. Wiss.* 1 (1837).

[2] Leo 240–1.

a similar observation. 'Tous les événements politiques sont expliqués par des interventions individuelles, l'histoire consiste à passer d'un personnage au suivant, l'abrégé historique procède par portraits, chacun expliquant une tranche du récit, d'ailleurs écourté, et le livre devient un catalogue d'hommes connus jusqu'à ce qu'il s'élargisse en panégyrique de Tibère. C'est un cas limite où le portrait supplante l'histoire.'[1] The received opinion among scholars is clear:[2] V. concentrates abnormally upon the personalities of Roman history, a procedure which in the later chapters means that his work, in the words of Syme, 'has degenerated into a biography and a panegyric of Tiberius'.[3]

Since these observations have had the effect of qualifying V.'s usefulness as an historian, it seems appropriate to test their validity against the tradition within which he was working:[4]

---

1 Rambaud 437.

2 Others who have made similar remarks include P. S. Laurentie, *Études sur les historiens latins* (1838 edn), 225ff. (a ref. I owe to Prater); F. Burmeister, *De Fontibus V.P.* (1894), 21ff.; Rockwood ix–x; Peter, *GL* 1.386; Steffen 3–4; R. Rieks, *Homo, Humanus, Humanitas* (1967), 51ff.

3 Syme, *DP* 48, 33, cf. 45. This scholar demands special comment. No one studying the first century A.D. can fail to be indebted to Syme's work: there is hardly any aspect, historical or historiographical, upon which he has not shed light or provoked thought. If in this volume I frequently record my disagreement with his opinions, it is, I hope, a tribute to the cogency and eloquence with which he has expressed many of the criticisms levelled by others also against V.'s history.

4 The method I have chosen seems natural in the circumstances. It has the disadvantage of briefly repeating some familiar material, for which I gladly acknowledge a debt to the distinguished work of E. Badian, A. H. McDonald, R. M. Ogilvie, and P. G. Walsh. But it has the advantage of placing V. in a literary tradition from which he has been deliberately excluded by Klingner 194–5 and Syme (*Tac.* 200, 358), and unthinkingly dismissed by M. Grant (*The ancient historians* (1970)) and D. Flach (*Tacitus in der Tradition der antiken Geschichtsschreibung* (1973)), in their respective discussions of first-century A.D. historiography. To the best of my knowledge no comparable treatment exists, the dissertation by Michels on V.'s *ars biographica* being poor and largely irrelevant. I am of course aware that some scholars have argued from the 'biographical' nature of V.'s narrative that at least one of his sources must have been a biography proper (see Dihle 642–4). That may be so, although almost everything argued about V.'s sources seems incapable of proof; but my concern is rather with the way in which V. handled his material, however it was obtained (some

in this way we may hope to discover whether his work is as unusual in these respects as scholars have claimed. The question is especially relevant to the present volume, not only because it has attracted scholarly comment, but also because it concerns both V.'s work in general and his Tiberian narrative in particular.

PERSONALITIES AND PATRIOTISM IN LATIN HISTORIOGRAPHY

Ancient historians were expected to choose for their works an elevated and noble theme,[1] which for many early Roman historians was the origin and development of Rome itself. Men such as Fabius Pictor and the elder Cato, who represent the historical tradition between 200 and 150 B.C., pursued this theme with a bias which subsequently became notorious and which may be traced throughout the early years of Roman historical writing.[2] The Gracchan annalist Sempronius Asellio, for example, believed that one of the functions of history was to encourage patriotism (fr. 2 'alacriores ad rem publicam defendundam'). It is, however, notable that these writers seem to have avoided an interest in the individual protagonists of history. Cato, and probably Pictor too, excluded from their works even the names of military commanders, recording their actions under a veil of anonymity.[3] The explanation of this

---

good remarks on this in Hellegouarc'h, *ANRW*; cf. also Dihle 652). I have naturally said nothing in this volume about V.'s sources as such, which for chapters 94–131 are generally, and I believe rightly, agreed by scholars to have been his general knowledge and personal observation.

[1] Cf. Lucian, *Hist. Conscr.* 53–4, Dion. Hal. *Ep. Pomp.* 3.2 (p. 232 Us.–Rad.) πρῶτόν τε καὶ σχεδὸν ἀναγκαιότατον ἔργον ἁπάντων ἐστὶ...ὑπόθεσιν ἐκλέξασθαι καλὴν καὶ κεχαρισμένην τοῖς ἀναγνωσομένοις. Dion. elsewhere (*Ant. Rom.* 1.2.1) equates this with τὴν 'Ρωμαίων ἡγεμονίαν.

[2] See Badian 2ff.; Walsh, *Livy* 115ff.; Ogilvie (1965), 5–17. This patriotic bias was also to be expected, cf. Dion. Hal. *Ep. Pomp.* 3.9 (p. 235 Us.–Rad.) διελθόντα δὲ ταῦτα μετὰ πολλῆς εὐνοίας ὡς ἄνδρα φιλόπολιν.

[3] For Cato cf. frr. 86, 87; Nep. *Cato* 3.4 'bellorum duces non nominauit sed sine nominibus res notauit', Plin. *NH* 8.11 'imperatorum nomina annalibus detraxit'; for Pictor cf. fr. 19 = Liv. 10.37.13.

practice, which has its parallel in Aeschylus' *Persae*, is most likely to be found in the political attitudes of their time.[1] Cato, we should remember, supported the measure that no man should be consul more than once, and it was he too who summed up the general feeling of the mid-second century in language that was still remembered many years later: 'ob hanc causam praestare nostrae ciuitatis statum ceteris ciuitatibus quod in illis singuli fuissent fere qui suam quisque rem publicam constituissent legibus atque institutis suis...nostra autem res publica non unius esse ingenio sed multorum, nec una hominis uita, sed aliquot constituta saeculis et aetatibus.'[2] The bias of Pictor and Cato extended only to the people of Rome as a corporate entity and not to the individuals involved. 'Nicht der Einzelne kämpft und gewinnt den Sieg', observed Eduard Meyer, 'sondern das gesammte Volk.'[3]

When Polybius' history was first published around 150 B.C., its regular character sketches of individuals will perhaps have made readers dissatisfied with the impersonal narratives of Pictor and Cato. By 101 B.C., fifty years after Cato's death, Marius had enjoyed six successive consulships, thereby acclimatising people to the reality of individual power which for centuries men like Cato had done their best to prevent. These respective developments in Greek historiography and Roman political life could not fail to combine in producing an effect on Latin historical writing. Certainly Cicero, whose lifetime had witnessed Marius followed by Sulla, Pompey and Caesar, recognised the role now played in the state by the individual –

---

[1] So too E. Meyer (below) and D. Kienast, *Cato der Zensor* (1954), 109–10. Following Nipperdey–Witte on Nep. (l.c.) F. Bömer believed the practice to be a feature of the early annalistic style, but agreed that this does not preclude the explanation favoured here (*SO* 29 (1952), 39 n. 4). For Aesch. cf. e.g. G. Murray, *Aeschylus* (1940), 125f.; A. Lesky, *Greek tragedy* (1965), 61f., 'We now understand why individuals are kept in the background, and no Greek hero is mentioned by name: it was the community which had triumphed.'

[2] ap. Cic. *Rep.* 2.2. For Cato's *ne quis iterum consul fieret* cf. *ORF*² p. 75; H. H. Scullard, *Roman politics*² (1973), 270–1.

[3] *RhM* 37 (1882), 613, cf. id., *Kleine Schriften*² (1924), 2.456.

whether himself or anyone else.[1] It may be for this reason, quite as much as his education at Athens, that he took such an interest in the great men of the past.[2] Not surprisingly, when he came to discuss historical writing in 55 B.C., Cicero expressed himself dissatisfied with the treatment accorded by earlier historians to the individuals of history.[3] He believed that the causes of historical events could be traced to the characters of the individuals involved in them, and thought it was the historian's duty to provide characterisation of such men (*De Or.* 2.63): 'causae explicentur omnes uel casus uel sapientiae uel temeritatis, hominumque ipsorum non solum res gestae sed etiam, qui fama ac nomine excellant, de cuiusque uita atque natura.' Cicero never got round to writing history himself, although Atticus had tried to persuade him 'ut (patria)...per te eundem sit ornata' (*Leg.* 1.5). Had he done so, we may infer that he

---

[1] Three illustrations must suffice: *Att.* 8.11D.7 'ut mea persona semper ad improborum ciuium impetus aliquid uideretur habere populare', *Phil.* 8.29 'o di immortales, quam magnum est personam in re publica tueri principis!', *Marc.* 22 'cum res publica immortalis esse debeat, eam in unius mortalis anima consistere'. See further Weinstock 219–20.

[2] For which cf. *Fin.* 5.19 'quid cum uolumus nomina eorum qui quid gesserint nota nobis esse, parentes, patriam, multa praeterea minime necessaria?'; for his education cf. *Fin.* 5.2–6. In general see Rawson 34, 39–40. According to Jerome (*Vir. Ill. praef.*), whose information is assumed to derive from Suetonius, Cicero's contemporaries Varro, Santra and Nepos were the first Roman biographers. If true, this would suggest that Cicero's lifetime saw the first public recognition of individual personalities. But the Roman tradition of *laudationes funebres* may tell against this notion. Nevertheless biography was a late starter at Rome, especially when compared with historiography. Such works as Gaius Gracchus' letter to M. Pomponius about his father, brother and himself (Peter, *HRR* 1^2. clxxix, 119), or the memoirs *de uita sua* of Rutilius (Bardon 1.111f.; Peter, *HRR* 1^2. 189), do not seem to fall into the class of biography proper.

[3] *De Or.* 2.53. Scholars occasionally dismiss Cicero's evidence on the grounds of his prejudice, but it is remarkable that whereas the portraits sketched by, say, Sallust or Livy became famous and often served as models for later historians, no such portrait is found amongst the fragments even of the post-Sullan historians. The only exceptions are Claud. Quadr. fr. 8, apparently a brief sketch of Manlius, and fr. 12 on Corvinus, which as extant begins *adulescens tali genere editus* and from which we infer that a character sketch may have preceded (Rambaud 434). Yet Badian (19) describes even Claudius' lack of interest in personalities as 'phenomenal'.

would have taken a lively interest in characterisation and would patriotically have celebrated the Roman state and those whom he considered to be its heroes (*Leg.* 1.8 'Cn. Pompei laudes inlustrabit').[1]

Sallust's reaction to historical writing was in this respect identical with that of his older contemporary Cicero, whether directly influenced by him or not.[2] His first monograph concerns the conspiracy of Catiline (*C.* 4.3 'de Catilinae coniuratione'): as soon as the theme is thus stated, Sallust launches into a full-length portrait of the villain (4.5): 'de quoius hominis moribus pauca prius explananda sunt quam initium narrandi faciam'. Throughout the subsequent narrative even the lesser figures are described, either briefly, as Aurelia Orestilla (15.2 'quoius praeter formam nihil umquam bonus laudauit'), or at more length, as Sempronia (25.1–5). The same practice obtains in Sallust's second monograph on Jugurtha.[3] Describing character thus by means of a portrait is known as the 'direct' method,[4] and is naturally appropriate to works of a restricted nature such as monographs. But the evidence is not exclusive to Sallust's shorter works. A familiar statement of the elder Seneca testifies that Sallust introduced into his work obituary notices of certain individuals (*epitaphia*): since there is no example of this practice anywhere in the monographs, we must assume that Seneca was referring to the now fragmentary *Historiae*.[5] It is thus clear, as Syme has emphatically observed,

[1] See further *Rep.* 2.4ff., *De Or.* 3.1ff., *Fam.* 5.12; Rawson 36, 43–4.

[2] M. Rambaud believed that Sallust was Cicero's ideal historian (*Cicéron et l'histoire romaine* (1953), 123ff.), but mentioned neither character sketches nor geographical digressions (on which see below, 96.3n.).

[3] In this monograph, after the theme is stated (5.1), a full character sketch of Jugurtha follows at once (6.1–7.1). Other figures are described with varying degrees of elaboration as the narrative progresses, e.g. Sulla at 95.2 ('sed quoniam nos tanti uiri res admonuit, idoneum uisum est de natura cultuque eius paucis dicere').

[4] The distinction between this and the 'indirect' method, for which see below, was first made by I. Bruns, *Die Persönlichkeit in der Geschichtsschreibung der Alten* (1898).

[5] Seneca states 'hoc...in paucissimis personis usurpatum a Sallustio' (*Suas.* 6.21), but the fact that Sallust apparently introduced the technique to Latin historiography is evidence of his continuing interest in personality.

that 'Sallust puts the individual at the centre of the stage and portrays him acting under the sway of the passions'.[1] Sallust resembled Cicero in seeing history in terms of the personalities who took part in the action.

The same may be said of Livy, although his technique is more varied than Sallust's. With more space at his disposal, he prefers what is known as the 'indirect' method of describing individuals whereby characters are allowed to emerge gradually from the actions and words attributed to them during the course of their lives. But that is not to underestimate the importance which Livy attached to individuals: he opened his massive work by exhorting his readers to observe the *mores*, *artes* and *uiri* that had produced the greatness of Rome (*praef.* 9). Like Sallust he does not neglect the lesser lights (such as Pacuvius Calavius, 23.2.2 'nobilis idem ac popularis homo, ceterum malis artibus nanctus opes'), whose characteristics Livy often delineates upon their introduction to the narrative. As for the more significant figures, Livy's third decade begins with a famous portrait of Hannibal (21.4.3ff.); and it can be shown that all the later decades are 'structured round the careers of the dominant personalities'.[2] Thus Marius dominates the eighth decade (which concludes with his *epitaphion*, cf. *per.* 80), Sulla the ninth, and Pompey the tenth and eleventh. These later books of Livy, like Sallust's works, reflect exactly the political realities of the first century B.C., so different from its predecessor and from the world of Pictor and Cato.

The last book in Livy's original plan seems to have been Book 120,[3] which included an *epitaphion* for Cicero: the elder Seneca has preserved this obituary, with the comment that Livy was more liberal than Sallust in his use of this technique.[4] Throughout these first one hundred and twenty books Livy traced the rise and decline of the Roman state. Books 1–50 deal with its rise, for which Livy has an unbounded admiration. He

---

[1] *Sall.* 269.

[2] Walsh (1974), 9, following Stadter 303. See also Rambaud 432.

[3] See Stadter 299.

[4] *Suas.* 6.21 'T. Liuius benignus omnibus magnis uiris praestitit', cf. 6.22.

sees the Roman people as 'princeps terrarum populus' (*praef.* 3), and his theme is that of wars against foreign peoples and of the men who waged them (ib. 9):[1] 'per quos uiros...domi militiaeque et partum et auctum imperium sit'. Using the rhetorical techniques of *exaedificatio* and *exornatio*,[2] Livy constructs a narrative of successive episodes which is designed to illustrate the greatness of Rome and which is clearly an inheritance from the earlier historians mentioned above.

The rhetorical nature of ancient historiography, though well known, will bear re-emphasis at this point. To the ancients the writing of history was a literary process directly comparable with oratory or poetry: using the material which was handed down or otherwise available to them, they aimed at embellishing and inflating their subject matter, and at surpassing their predecessors in stylistic achievement.[3] They had no conception of scientific history, which is mainly a nineteenth-century notion,[4] with the result that the modern historian, to whom historical research is scientific, needs to keep these considerations continually in mind. If he is using the evidence of ancient historians to try and discover 'how things actually happened',[5] he must 'de-rhetorise' the narrative with which he is dealing; that is, he must disentangle the factual substratum from the

[1] Walsh (1974), 9, refining Stadter, e.g. 303. Books 1–50 take us up to the Third Punic War; thereafter, so far as may be judged from historical evidence, imperialism lost its popularity at Rome: cf. E. Badian, *Roman imperialism in the late republic* (1968), 1ff., 29ff.; Brunt 170f.

[2] For which cf. A. H. McDonald, *JRS* 47 (1957), 155ff.

[3] For the former cf. Plin. *Ep.* 7.33.10 'haec, utcumque se habent, notiora, clariora, maiora tu facies; quamquam non exigo ut excedas actae rei modum; nam neque historia debet egredi ueritatem et honeste factis ueritas sufficit'; Front. p. 132 Naber = p. 125 Van den Hout 'meae res gestae tantae sunt quantae sunt scilicet, quoiquoimodi sunt; tantae autem uidebuntur quantas tu eas uideri uoles' (both passages are of course reminiscent of Cic. *Fam.* 5.12, and cf. *Leg.* 1.8 quoted above, p. 33). For the latter cf. Liv. *praef.* 1 'scribendi arte rudem uetustatem superaturos'.

[4] See R. H. Martin in *Tacitus* (ed. T. A. Dorey, 1969), 117–18, with a timely reminder of the views of J. B. Bury and Mommsen.

[5] In his notorious statement that the historian 'will bloss sagen, wie es eigentlich gewesen' Ranke was anticipated by Lucian, *Hist. Conscr.* 39 τοῦ δὴ συγγραφέως ἔργον ἕν, ὡς ἐπράχθη, εἰπεῖν, as pointed out by Peter, *WK* 431 n. 2.

rhetorical manner in which it is expressed. There is no point in constructing an historical hypothesis when its foundation is dramatic elaboration or a literary topos. Modern historians have of course become accustomed to these considerations in the case of some of their ancient counterparts, such as Livy; what must be stressed is that these considerations apply to all ancient historians without exception.

Livy, as is well known, was extraordinarily successful in adapting his rhetoric to the theme of the development of Rome. Walsh has noted that in every book 'undisguised chauvinism can be exemplified'.[1] Livy's work is of the type criticised by Josephus when he complained of the way Jewish history had been handled as compared with Roman;[2] and this tendency of works such as Livy's was described by the theorist Lucian as ἐγκώμιον, by which he appears to mean the general enthusiasm to which the patriotic historian is prone.[3] Yet Livy's bias is partially counteracted by his belief that after the fall of Carthage in 146 B.C. there was a gradual decline in the Roman state. This belief, borrowed from Sallust and outlined in Sallustian language in the preface (9),[4] is elaborated in the course of Books 51–120,[5] the nadir coming in 43 B.C. which is the date at which Book 120 closes.

Now it has long been fashionable among scholars to describe

---

[1] Walsh, *Livy* 65.

[2] Jos. *BJ* 1.7 βούλονται μεγάλους μὲν τοὺς 'Ρωμαίους ἀποδεικνύειν, καταβάλλουσι δ' ἀεὶ τὰ 'Ιουδαίων.

[3] Lucian, *Hist. Conscr.* 7: see Avenarius 13–16.

[4] For the parallels see Ogilvie ad loc. In fact the notion of decline goes back to the earlier days of Latin historiography (cf. C. O. Brink and F. W. Walbank, *CQ* 4 (1954), 102–7; Earl 42–5), and it continues later, e.g. in V. himself (2.1.1) and Florus (1.33.1 etc.). But that does not prevent such historians from patriotically emphasising the general excellence of Rome, however illogical this might appear to be. They always had the choice of stressing one side or the other. Florus is an excellent example, for despite his theory of decline (*praef.* 4–8), he explicitly says that his work as a whole is composed *ad admirationem principis populi* (ib. 3, echoing Livy). That seems to me to sum up the general tradition exactly: it certainly holds good for Livy and V. – and for Polybius. Sallust and Tacitus are, as often, the exceptions (see further below, pp. 52–4).

[5] See Walsh (1974), 9.

Livy as the last of the republican historians.[1] Had Livy stopped with Book 120 and the events of 43 B.C., much could be said in favour of that description. But Livy did not stop there: he proceeded at some unknown point to add Books 121–42 covering the years up to 9 B.C. Livy's resumption to deal with this later period places him firmly at the head of what scholars have seen as imperial historiography. The later books are themselves lost, but their character, so far as we may judge it, is of essential importance if we are to understand the direction taken by historiography after Livy's time.[2]

It is reasonable to assume that Livy's last twenty-two volumes would be dominated by the personality of Augustus to an even greater extent than the earlier books had been dominated by Sulla and Pompey respectively. The domination of successive individuals during the late republic reached its logical conclusion when Augustus, in his eleventh consulship, established the absolute autocracy of the principate in 23 B.C. The resultant change from the republican ideal could hardly be better illustrated than in these words of Tacitus which, intentionally or not, are a bitter refutation of Cato quoted earlier: 'unum esse rei publicae corpus atque unius animo regendum' (*A.* 1.12.3, cf. above, p. 31). It was inevitable that this development in the constitution of the state should be reflected in the works of those historians who, like Livy, recorded the activities of the state. In view of the loss of Livy's evidence, we must wait until we come to Tacitus to have this point explicitly confirmed (below, pp. 44–5).

The domination of Augustus produced for historians difficulties which have long been recognised. Discussing the problems of writing about the events of 27 B.C. and after, Dio said this (53.19.2–4): 'The events occurring after this time cannot be recorded in the same manner as those of previous times... Most things that happened began to be kept secret and concealed... and much that happens beyond doubt is unknown.' Of those events which were widely known, many provided awkward

---

[1] Thus Norden, *AK* 1.234ff.; Klingner 195; Syme, *Sall.* 289.

[2] On the lost books see Syme (1959), 57ff., Walsh (1961), 33–5.

material: it would, for example, have been tactless to dwell upon Augustus' controversial moral legislation, which was derided at the time and best forgotten later.[1] Historians were required to demonstrate their patriotism by describing the principate of the living emperor as a period of progress, harmony and success.[2] Thus Tacitus, who is critical of the whole imperial era up to his own time, on two occasions feels obliged to describe the reign of his contemporary emperor Trajan in euphoric terms: 'rara temporum felicitate' (*H.* 1.1.4, *Agr.* 3.1). Florus too, having adopted the traditional theory of decline and indicted all the post-Augustan rulers in his preface, concludes by stating that his own time is a period of rejuvenation (*praef.* 8). Of course these two historians avoided the pitfalls of contemporary history by writing about earlier periods. But Livy accepted the challenge, which will have been at its keenest for the years after Actium, 31–9 B.C.

Livy covered these years in Books 133–42: what theme did he choose? Walsh, judging from the surviving *periochae*, has observed that their 'most striking characteristic' is the absence of reference to political history at Rome.[3] Livy concentrates on wars against foreign peoples, thereby returning to the theme of the first fifty books which we have already seen outlined in *praef.* 9 (above, p. 35). The implication, although we naturally cannot know whether Livy at any point made it explicit, is that Augustus' principate is to be seen primarily in terms of what for Livy was the expansionist period of the republic.

Livy's concentration upon military events is hardly surprising. There is ample evidence that Augustus throughout his reign up to A.D. 9 intended himself to be seen as a great military leader and conqueror of foreign peoples.[4] That at least is how he

[1] Cf. Hor. *C.* 3.6, Prop. 2.7, Tac. *A.* 3.54.2; G. Williams, *JRS* 52 (1962), 28ff.

[2] This is doubtless true even as early as Augustus' reign, at least in its later period: cf. Sen. *Contr.* 10 *praef.* 8 'cum recitaret (Labienus) historiam, magnam partem illum libri conuoluisse et dixisse: haec quae transeo post mortem meam legentur.' General remarks in Williams 630–1.

[3] Walsh (1961), 34; see also Syme (1959), 66f.

[4] The evidence is impressively assembled by Brunt 170–6; see also Wells 1–13. There is considerable argument whether Augustus' *actual* ambitions

describes himself in the opening words of the *Res Gestae* ('Rerum gestarum diui Augusti, quibus orbem terrarum imperio populi Romani subiecit'), and such a conclusion is inescapable to anyone who reads the climax of this work (26–33). Extremely impressive is the cumulative effect of such statements as: 'Panoniorum gentes, quas ante me principem populi Romani exercitus numquam adit, deuictas per Ti. Neronem, qui tum erat priuignus et legatus meus, imperio pop. Rom. subieci, protulique fines Illyrici ad ripam fluminis Danui' (30.1). Furthermore, when the Forum Augusti and Temple of Mars Ultor were finally completed in 2 B.C., Augustus adorned the Forum with the *tituli* of the races he had conquered, as V. tells us (39.2), and on either side of the Temple he erected statues of the military men 'qui imperium populi Romani ex minimo maximum reddidissent' (Suet. *Aug.* 31.5).[1] There can be no doubt that Augustus wished himself to be seen as the latest, and greatest, in a long line of Roman imperialists.

Thus historians of Augustus were presented with splendid material and themes which they could elaborate with all the patriotic fervour traditional, as we have seen, to Roman historiography. If these foreign campaigns were contemporary, as they were for Livy, there was an additional benefit: by concentrating in this direction the historian need not compromise himself by dwelling upon events of a delicate political nature. But it should not be thought that, by concentrating thus, Livy would have been able to restrict the domination of his narrative by Augustus. On the contrary, as *princeps* Augustus was com-

---

were aggressive and expansionist (Brunt, Wells) or defensive and aimed merely at secure frontiers (everyone else). But this controversy is irrelevant to the present argument, which is that Augustus purposely projected an *image* of expansion. There can be little doubt about that. In addition to Livy see the contemporary Nicol. Dam. fr. 125 (*FGrH* 2.1, p. 391).

[1] This phrase has a purely military application, as the following words *triumphali effigie* confirm. The similarity to Liv. *praef.* 9 (quoted above, p. 35) is striking. For some other examples of comparable phraseology cf. H. Volkmann, 'Mos Maiorum als Grundzug des augusteischen Prinzipats', *Das neue Bild der Antike* (1942), 2.257 n. 1.

mander-in-chief of the armed forces and it was to him that the glories and triumphs were accorded.[1]

In his discussion of the *epitaphion* to which we referred earlier (above, p. 33), the elder Seneca proceeds to observe that Livy's successors employed it with increasing frequency: 'sequentes historici multo id effusius fecerunt'. Although most of the historians of this later period have perished, we find when we come to Tacitus that his works make regular use of *epitaphia*, and we may legitimately assume that this is due at least as much to the tradition which he inherited as to his own personal predilections.[2] Tacitus' use of obituaries is merely one example of his well known concentration upon the characters of history, whom he describes by either the direct or indirect methods.[3] Yet there is nothing remarkable about this feature of Tacitean writing apart from the skill with which it is executed: Tacitus is simply the culmination of a tradition which goes back through Livy and Sallust to Cicero and which had increasingly, as we have noted, come to see history in terms of the individuals involved.[4]

V.'s work, published sixteen years after the last books of Livy and roughly eighty years before Tacitus' *Histories*,[5] is an integral part of that tradition. Many of the lesser characters are briefly described exactly in the manner of Sallust and Livy: Fulvia at 74.3 ('nihil muliebre praeter corpus gerens') is an excellent illustration on account of her affinities with the

---

[1] See below, 96.2n.

[2] Seneca quotes examples of *epitaphia* also from Cremutius Cordus, Aufidius Bassus, and Asinius Pollio; we certainly have no reason to doubt his statement. For Tacitus see Syme, *TST* 79–90; for V. see below, p. 43 and n. 2.

[3] Cf. S. G. Daitz, *AJPh* 81 (1960), 30–52.

[4] For some useful general remarks see Williams 619–33. The trend seems confirmed by the evidence collected in the appendices of E. C. Evans, 'Descriptions of personal appearance in Roman history and biography', *HSCP* 46 (1935), 43–84.

[5] V.'s work was published in A.D. 30. This we know both from its dedication to M. Vinicius, the consul of that year, and because it is not openly hostile to Tiberius' minister Sejanus, whose downfall in the following year meant an instant and total *damnatio memoriae*. For the fashion of such dedications and further discussion of V.'s dates see Woodman (1975), 273–82.

Sallustian ladies mentioned above (p. 33). The more famous personalities are given, upon their first introduction to the narrative, full-length character sketches which make the traditional references to their *genus*, *ingenium*, *forma* etc. (e.g. Tiberius Gracchus at 2.2.1–2, Scipio Nasica at 2.3.1, Marius at 2.11.1, Cato Uticensis at 35.2).[1] Many of the later republican figures, thus introduced, dominate the subsequent narrative (e.g. Pompey from 29.2–5 onwards, Caesar from 41.1–3, Octavian from 59.1–4). In an attempt to show that V. sought 'die Geschichte der Republik mit der der Kaiser so zu verbinden, dass man die überschrittene Kluft gar nicht gewahrte', H. Peter commented upon this aspect of V.'s history as follows: 'wie unter den Kaisern, so werden in der früheren Zeit die Geschicke Roms von einzelnen Männern geleitet, und seine Geschichte besteht ihm in ihren Charakteristiken'.[2] But this is more an inevitable reflection of political reality evident also in Livy (above, p. 34) than a conscious desire on V.'s part that the empire should be seen in terms of the republic. It may be that in choosing the direct method of describing character V. was impressed by Sallust who so explicitly demonstrated the importance of individuals and whose sketches V. often echoes;[3] but it may be that he preferred this method simply because, again like Sallust (above, p. 33), he was writing a work of a restricted nature.[4] This matter requires some brief comment.

Sallust's *Catilina* and *Iugurtha*, being monographs, are restricted in their subject matter rather than in the elaboration which Sallust felt able to devote to that subject matter. V.'s

[1] For such traditional elements see e.g. Leo 180–1.

[2] Peter, *GL* 1.391 and 385. A similar view is taken by D. Timpe, *Untersuchungen zur Kontinuität des frühen Prinzipats* (1962), 21–3. Yet V. himself seems to imply the opposite at 86.1 'ex quo in quem statum peruenerit fortuna publica'; and I do not accept Peter's quotation (also in *WK* 365) of Suet. *Aug.* 31.5 in this connection, which seems to me to have a purely military significance (for the reasons see above, p. 39 and n. 1). It is most doubtful whether Augustus would have *wished* himself to be seen, in general terms, as the last in a line which included Caesar and Sulla; but that he was their successor in terms of actual power, and could be seen as such by others (e.g. Tac. *A.* 1.1.1), is undeniable.

[3] See Woodman (1968), 794–6.

[4] Thus Michels 7–8.

work, on the other hand, is a summary universal history of Rome, a genre which had not been represented for more than eighty years.[1] Having adopted this genre V. was required, not only to restrict his subject matter to the more important events of Roman history, but also to restrict his treatment even of those events which he does mention. It is for this reason that he so regularly refers to the *breuitas* and *festinatio* of his narrative,[2] and it is these qualities which determine much of the character of his work and which have misled scholars into believing that his treatment of individuals is unusual. A comparison of two examples will illustrate this.

V.'s account of the *Variana clades* opens with a character sketch of Varus spotlighting the man's sloth (117.2–3 *mitis*, *quietus*, *immobilior*, *otio*): this vice is underlined by a contrasting sketch (σύγκρισις) of Varus' German opponent Arminius (118.2 *fortis*, *celer*, *promptus*).[3] Now the importance which V. attaches to these characters is clear from his introduction to the episode (117.1 'et causa ⟨et⟩ persona moram exigit'), from the Livian manner in which Varus' vice runs as a refrain throughout the episode (e.g. 118.1 *socordiam*, 2 *segnitia*, 119.2 *marcore*), and from the conclusion to the episode where V. points the moral, again exactly in the manner of Livy (120.5 'ex quo apparet Varum...magis imperatoris defectum consilio quam uirtute destitutum militum, se magnificentissimumque perdidisse exercitum').[4] But the character sketches themselves seem in no way disproportionate because this is one of the rare occasions on which V. expands his narrative along

---

1 The last universal summarists of Roman history had been Cornelius Nepos, Varro, and Atticus: see Woodman (1975), 286 n. 4. In that same article (pp. 282–7, 303) I discuss fully the genre to which V.'s work belongs, and defend the statements which are made in the present paragraph.

2 For V.'s references to his *breuitas* and *festinatio* see below, 96.3n. and 108.1n. respectively.

3 For the technique of σύγκρισις in historical writing cf. F. Focke, *Hermes* 58 (1923), 348ff.; for other exs. in V. cf. 1.13.3–4, 33.3–4, 72.2. The first two of these examples rely upon an anecdotal technique, for which cf. Plut. *Alex.* 1.2; Momigliano 68–76.

4 For Livy's technique see Ogilvie (1965), 18.

Ciceronian or Livian lines (the episode stretches to four chapters).[1]

A strong contrast is seen in V.'s account of Drusus' campaigns in Germany which begins as follows (97.2): 'cura deinde atque onus Germanici belli delegata Druso Claudio'. The account then continues for a mere 8½ lines of which the first 6 are devoted to Drusus' character, the next 1½ to the campaign itself, and the final line to his death (97.3): 'fatorum iniquitas consulem agentem annum tricesimum rapuit'. Thus two thirds of the account have amounted to an *epitaphion* for Drusus.[2] Had V. been writing in the Ciceronian or Livian mould here, with more scope for elaboration, the *epitaphion* would have seemed far less disproportionate.[3] But on this occasion – and the same is true of almost every other occasion in his history – his *breuitas* was the most urgent consideration. Faced with the problem of what to omit and what to include, V. naturally refused to omit details of personality because, as we have seen, these were of preeminent importance in the historiographical tradition. V. is unusual, not in the time he spends on character, but in his choice of writing summary history in the first place.

The extent to which character dominates the development of Latin historiography from Livy to Tacitus prompts a further and more general consideration. It has often been observed that by far the largest portion of Tacitus' *Agricola* is historical rather than biographical, from which some scholars have speculated

---

[1] On this episode see further below, pp. 188–209.

[2] Leo (235) remarked upon the scarcity of *epitaphia* in V., but wrongly classed the present example as an introductory sketch (p. 240); and cf. 26.3, 48.6, 53.3, 116.4. No summary historian who is prepared to commemorate Cicero as does V., at 66.3–5, can be said to be unaware of the popularity of the tradition.

[3] We might compare the present state of Pompeius Trogus' work. He wrote an elaborate universal history from the earliest times down to Augustus' reign in forty-four books; but the work has not survived except in the epitomised form made much later by Justin. This summary is studded with *epitaphia* and with examples of direct characterisation (cf. Rambaud 436–7) which doubtless seemed much less conspicuous when they occupied their original place in Trogus' lengthy work. For the general similarity of V.'s work to such works as Justin's see Woodman (1975), 283–5.

that the 'historical' chapters were originally intended for a different, purely historical, work.[1] Yet the *Agricola* is to be defined as a biography because the 'distinctive feature' of such works is that 'they relate the achievements of a man as illustrations of his character and not as part of a wider, more complex historical framework'.[2] We have however seen that exactly the same could be said about the works of history so far discussed. Although Roman writers conventionally drew a distinction between history and biography,[3] it was a distinction which operated more in principle than in practice. When comparing Tacitus' *Agricola* with Sallust's monographs, Leo produced an observation which could reasonably be extended to cover many other products of Latin historiography: 'Sallust hat biographische Elemente in die Historie, Tacitus historische Elemente in die Biographie hineingearbeitet.'[4] The years which separate Cicero and Tacitus witnessed a 'Kreuzung der Gattungen' of which V.'s own work is a characteristic example. This fusion is even more evident when we consider historians' treatment of imperial personalities.

It was impossible to gauge the extent to which Augustus dominated the later books of Livy because of lack of evidence (above, pp. 37–40); but Tacitus provides a clear guide from which inferences may be drawn. In his first strictly historical work, the *Histories*, the narrative is introduced by a character-sketch of the emperor Otho (1.13.3–4) who is the dominant figure until his death at 2.48–9, which is followed by an obituary notice (2.50). Within this framework Tacitus delineates Otho's character by means of the indirect method.[5] Tacitus' practice here, which is so clearly an extension of Livy's

---

[1] Cf. F. R. D. Goodyear, *Tacitus* (*Greece & Rome* New Surveys in the Classics 4, 1970), 4.

[2] Ogilvie (1967), 12.

[3] Nep. *Pelop.* 1.1 is the standard ref., as is Plut. *Alex.* 1.2 for the Greeks; see also Momigliano 84 n. 19 and 99 n. 40 on *Rhet. Herenn.* 1.13 and Cic. *Inu.* 1.27. For this perennial debate from classical through to modern times cf. e.g. W. Steidle, *Sueton u. d. antike Biographie* (1951), 185 (index); Momigliano 1–7; E. H. Carr, *What is history?* (1964 edn), 45–9.

[4] Leo 232.

[5] Cf. Rambaud 436.

in his later decades, is continued in the *Annals*. His account of Tiberius' reign opens with a portrait of the new emperor (1.4.3–5) and concludes with a lengthier obituary notice (6.51): within this framework Tacitus again constantly delineates Tiberius' character by means of the indirect method. Tiberius dominates the six books which Tacitus devotes to his reign.

Whereas historians of an earlier period had come to see history in terms of a variety of individuals, as we have noted, imperial historians saw history primarily in terms of one individual, the emperor of the day. 'By the nature of the principate a very limited number of persons were of dominant influence on events for long periods: consequently not only their actions, but also their personalities, must claim the fullest attention of historians.'[1] This summary of Tacitean practice by his latest English editor does no more than repeat the analysis which Tacitus had himself provided mid-way through his account of Tiberius' reign (4.33.2): 'sic conuerso statu neque alia re Romana quam si unus imperitet, haec conquiri tradique in rem fuerit'. Such was the pattern of imperial historiography, and it is hardly surprising that, as the Roman empire developed, biography came to be regarded, in Momigliano's words, as 'the natural form of telling the story of a Caesar'.[2] No one, however, would describe the first six books of the *Annals* as a 'biography of Tiberius'; and those who, like Syme, attach this label to the later chapters of V.'s work have for the most part failed to take account of the development in historiography outlined here, and of the nature of the period which these chapters cover. In the years after A.D. 14, as Syme himself has recently confessed, 'the life and personality of the ruler is not separable from the processes of government'.[3]

---

[1] Goodyear, *Comm. Tac.* 1.40–1.

[2] Momigliano 99. Cf. Syme, *Amm.* 94–108.

[3] 'History or biography: the case of Tiberius Caesar', *Historia* 23 (1974), 481.

VELLEIUS' TIBERIAN NARRATIVE

Now although the preceding argument and the parallel with Tacitus dispose of the charge that V. was writing a biography of Tiberius in the narrative devoted explicitly to the latter's reign (i.e. chapters 124ff.), they do not dispose of a fundamental objection brought against chapters 94–123 by Leo in order to support the view, held (as we have seen) by others also, that here too V. has written a biography of Tiberius. Leo stated that from chapter 94 onwards, in a narrative nominally allotted to the reign of Augustus, the activities of Tiberius are described 'mit eingestreuten Schilderungen der Persönlichkeit und persönlichen Erlebnissen, so dass Augustus völlig hinter Tiberius zurücktritt'.[1] To put the matter in perspective it should be noted that Augustus has already dominated the narrative from chapter 59 to chapter 93: the Augustan narrative is thus only three chapters shorter than the Tiberian narrative. But nevertheless Leo's charge seems to me sufficiently serious to merit investigation.

V.'s theme in these troublesome chapters is primarily that of wars and campaigns against foreign peoples.[2] There is little point in our objecting to this selection of material for we have already considered the reasons which drew Livy, a notorious lover of peace, towards a similarly patriotic theme (above, pp. 38–40). Those reasons were still equally valid for V.: they were in fact of increased validity, for since his late teens V. had himself actually taken part in many of these campaigns,[3] and his imperialist instincts, doubtless sharpened by experience, emerge clearly from these chapters.[4] V. has followed Livy's

---

[1] Leo 241.

[2] Such material is to be found at 94.4–98.3, 101–2, 104.2–122.

[3] For the details see Sumner 265–74.

[4] See Hellegouarc'h (1974), esp. 82; also below, 117.3n., 119.2, 122.2n. The motives for adhering to military material for the years A.D. 4–14 were considerably increased: 'friction at Rome, disasters abroad, and scandal in the dynasty – that was the last decade of Caesar Augustus' (Syme, *Tac.* 427, cf. 373; *RR* 522; (1959), 72; Plin. *NH* 7.149). But disasters abroad were overcome and could, in the time-honoured Roman fashion, easily be

example for the period up to 9 B.C. (i.e. to 98.3), and continued where Livy left off: that Augustus was still much concerned about his military reputation may be seen from the fact that almost two thirds of his imperial salutations belong to the period which V. begins to discuss in chapter 94, that is 23 B.C. onwards.[1] It is thus hardly surprising that these two historians, Livy and V., should traverse in their narratives precisely the ground on which above all Augustus wished to be remembered.

Yet although it was Augustus who cultivated a military image for his own purposes, and although it was he to whom the victories were accorded, the campaigns themselves were actually won by his commanders in the field. The principal among these, for the relevant period, was without question Tiberius; but on account of Augustus' various plans for the succession and his apparent persistence in slighting Tiberius, it is easy to forget both the position which Tiberius held during Augustus' principate and the length of time for which he held it.

During the decade which followed Marcellus' death, 23–12 B.C., there was no doubt that Agrippa was the leading man in the state next to Augustus himself.[2] It is true that by adopting Agrippa's sons Gaius and Lucius Caesar in 17 B.C. Augustus marked them out early for the succession; but their extreme youth left the power itself potentially in the hands of Agrippa. Thus Agrippa's death in 12 B.C., when still in his early fifties, was a shattering but significant event, for the young Caesars were still mere children. 'With Agrippa dead, Tiberius was the empire's leading general, the only man who could step into Agrippa's shoes as the princeps' deputy.'[3] V. himself is more cautious in his assessment of Tiberius' position at this moment (96.1 'mors deinde Agrippae...admouit propius Neronem Caesari'), but Dio rightly describes Tiberius in 12 B.C. thus

represented as triumphs. Aufidius Bassus wrote a book on the German wars which is generally thought to have done just that (cf. Bardon 2.164–6; Syme, *Tac.* 697).

[1] See Barnes 26.

[2] See Kornemann 12ff. As often, one may accept his evidence without necessarily accepting the rigid interpretation which he places upon it.

[3] Seager 25.

(54.31.1): πολὺ τῶν ἄλλων καὶ τῇ τιμῇ καὶ τῇ δυνάμει προφέροντος. Henceforward Tiberius' career falls into three clearly separate periods. The first is 12–6 B.C., during which his position was confirmed by continuous and successful campaigns in Illyricum (12–9 B.C.) and Germany (8–7 B.C.). At first Augustus characteristically refused public acknowledgement of Tiberius' preeminence but, again characteristically, was soon compelled to do so by events.[1] Tiberius' younger brother and fellow-campaigner Drusus, who might possibly have been conceived of as a rival, died in 9 B.C., leaving (in Syme's words) 'Ti. Claudius Nero patently the first man in the State next to Caesar Augustus'.[2] Public recognition eventually came two years later when Tiberius was made consul for a second time and was granted a triumph. Finally in 6 B.C. he was given *tribunicia potestas*, the honour which had last been bestowed on Agrippa as a sign of his unapproachable position. V.'s assessment of Tiberius at this moment is exactly true (99.1): 'ciuium post unum (et hoc quia uolebat) eminentissimus, ducum maximus...uere alterum rei publicae lumen et caput'.

Meanwhile Augustus had also been granting to Gaius and Lucius Caesar honours of which the implication was all too obvious: 'while Tiberius governed for the Princeps abroad, maintained the stability and augmented the prestige of the dynasty, the rule of the young princes was to be consolidated in his absence'.[3] Tiberius retired to Rhodes for seven years, and when he returned in A.D. 2 he played no part in public life for two further years. But since he naturally fades from V.'s narrative of these nine years,[4] the details of this second period of his career are irrelevant to the present argument.

Lucius Caesar had already died in A.D. 2; by February A.D. 4 Gaius too was dead. Augustus, again overtaken by events, was compelled to return to honouring Tiberius, who in A.D. 4 was once more given *tribunicia potestas* and was adopted by the emperor. 'That year designated the ruler of Rome', writes Syme,

[1] Cf. Sutherland 65, 67.

[2] *Tac.* 368.

[3] Syme, *RR* 416.

[4] That is, in chapters 100–2, on which see below, pp. 116, 120–9.

who then proceeds to argue, firmly and persuasively, that the following decade was as much a prologue to Tiberius' principate as an epilogue to Augustus'.[1] Just as in the first period 12–6 B.C., this third period of Tiberius' career saw his position consolidated by military successes in Germany (A.D. 4–6), Illyricum (6–9), and then Germany again (10–11). 'In these difficult and dangerous years Tiberius sustained the entire military burden – and sustained it well.'[2] But, again as in 12–6 B.C., Tiberius was compelled to wait for several years before Augustus gave him public recognition of the power which he undoubtedly possessed.[3]

The position which Tiberius was acknowledged to hold at the end of Augustus' life was not only the position which he had held since A.D. 4 but also, somewhat paradoxically, that which he had held during the first period of his career as we have been considering it. It is arguable that Tiberius' position in the state in A.D. 14 was similar to that which he had held, *de facto* but not *de iure*, as early as 12 B.C., twenty-five years before. Apart from the interlude on Rhodes, Tiberius throughout this time was Augustus' deputy and principal military commander, each position reinforcing the other. No clearer evidence of this can be found than in a comparison of the imperial salutations accorded to each man. Between A.D. 4 and 14 Augustus 'advanced from imp. xvi to imp. xxi, his destined successor from imp. ii to imp. vii. The progression was clearly simultaneous.'[4] But this progression had already started before Tiberius' retirement to Rhodes: his first two salutations came in 9 and 8 B.C. respectively. Allowing for the notorious lack of political recognition given to Tiberius by Augustus, particularly in the period 12–6 B.C., this is an impressive and significant series of military honours.

Now in the chapters which troubled Leo, 94–123, V. reaches

[1] *Tac.* 369, cf. 364–74, esp. 369–71. [2] Sutherland 75.

[3] Although there were some manifestations of Tiberius' power in the years after A.D. 4 (e.g. positions of influence for his friends: Seager 46–7), there seems little doubt that Augustus delayed full recognition till the latest possible moment: see Sutherland 73 and Goodyear on Tac. *A.* 1.3.3.

[4] Barnes 23.

the year 12 B.C. as early as the beginning of chapter 96; and from that moment until Augustus' death his theme is mainly military. V.'s concentration on Tiberius in these chapters must be admitted; but it is due to his recognition, born of long years of experience in close contact with Tiberius on the frontiers of the empire, that Augustus' chosen reputation depended almost entirely upon the exploits of his eventual successor.[1]

It is another question whether modern historians gain or lose by V.'s treatment of Tiberius in chapters 94–123. But on any theory the quarter-century between 12 B.C. and A.D. 14 is of inestimable importance for the interpretation of Tiberius' principate. Even Tacitus admits that the first years of Tiberius' government were excellent (*A.* 4.6); but by A.D. 26, perhaps the very year in which V. began to write his history,[2] the emperor's retirement to Capri and the domination of Sejanus indicated a change. Between that moment and the beginning of A.D. 30, by which time V. had stopped writing, there were signs of disquiet which V. does not refrain from acknowledging.[3] 'To understand what had happened', writes Syme, 'an historian would have to go back, not only to the first period of Tiberius' government, but even further, and investigate the original predicament of the man in relation to his surroundings, family and career.'[4] V.'s narrative in chapters 94–123 goes at least some way towards providing the kind of account desired by Syme.[5]

---

[1] A modern classical scholar and shrewd military historian, F. E. Adcock, came to a similar conclusion when he surveyed the long reign of Augustus (*CAH* 10.597): 'It may be suspected that the strategy of his early principate sprang from the brain of Agrippa, and it is possible that in Tiberius Agrippa found a worthy inheritor of his plans.'

[2] For the possible moment when V. began his history see Woodman (1975), 275–82. The view which I there put forward is not that which has usually been supposed by others: for an example of this latter, traditional, view see Sumner 284–8.

[3] See below, pp. 53–4, 245–8, 272, 275–82.

[4] *Tac.* 424, adding that 'Tiberius was in his fifty-fifth year when he came to power'.

[5] Some comparative statistics indicate that this was perhaps V.'s intention. The recent study of Tiberius by Seager devotes roughly fifty pages to the years up to A.D. 14, and roughly three times that total to the years A.D. 14–29 /30. V.'s narrative for the same period, by contrast, devotes almost six times more space to the years up to A.D. 14 than to A.D. 14–29. But since V. was

It could however be objected that V.'s account in these chapters is deprived of its potential value by a failing which is universally held to vitiate his whole Tiberian narrative, the failing which Leo and Syme mentioned when they described V.'s later chapters as a 'panegyric of Tiberius' (above, pp. 28–9). This accusation lies at the heart of all problems concerning V.'s history. Thus W. C. Summers, to take a single but typical example, described V.'s attitude towards Tiberius as that of an 'obsequious royalist', and on that basis proceeded to indict the rest of his work as a whole: 'to the scientific historian it is of course anathema'.[1] Now though Summers' latter statement has been proved correct by the way in which modern scientific historians have neglected V.'s work,[2] his reasoning is based upon a fallacy.

It was earlier observed that there is a tradition of patriotic or chauvinistic historiography which may be traced back to the earliest times and which greatly inflated the achievements of the Roman *res publica*. This tradition is particularly clear in the case of Livy, whose narrative exhibits *par excellence* a tendency which Lucian described as ἐγκώμιον (above, pp. 30–6). We have also seen that imperial historiography came to concentrate to a large extent upon the person of the emperor. The reason is that the emperor has now become identified with the state: 'res est publica Caesar', as Ovid acknowledged (*Tr.* 4.4.15). It was therefore only natural that the Roman historian's traditional enthusiasm for the *res publica* should now be transferred to the *princeps* himself. And the most effective method of communicating such enthusiasm was by panegyric, which is thus the direct successor to the chauvinism of earlier history.[3] When V.

---

writing in the years when Tiberius' popularity was steadily declining, it may be, as Seager has himself remarked (269), that V.'s 'favourable picture of Tiberius' life as a whole takes on a deeper political significance'.

[1] *The Silver Age of Latin literature* (1920), 139, 147.

[2] For examples of this neglect see Woodman (1975), 289; also above, p. 29 n. 4.

[3] The aims of panegyric, in which 'ad personarum dignitatem omnia referrentur' (Cic. *De Or.* 1.141), were directly comparable with those of patriotic historiography (see above, pp. 30 and n. 2, 35). Momigliano

resorts to the techniques and *amplificatio* of panegyric, or when he writes miniature examples of actual panegyrics as in chapters 114.1–3 and 126, he does no more than carry to its logical conclusion the practice in which Livy had indulged when he employed the *exornatio* and *exaedificatio* of rhetorical historiography.[1]

It is therefore mistaken to object to V.'s Tiberian narrative as 'panegyric', for exactly the same could be said about Livy and many of his predecessors. It is equally mistaken to conclude from that objection that V.'s work should be 'anathema' to scientific historians, for exactly the same could be said about Sallust, Livy, Tacitus or Ammianus, each of whom was writing within the same rhetorical tradition.

Yet in one respect there is a basic difference between Livy and Ammianus on the one hand and Sallust and Tacitus on the other. The former historians concentrate with enthusiasm upon the optimistic aspects of their subject matter, while the latter are concerned with the depressing nature of theirs. V. of course belongs to the former class,[2] and has thus invited comparison with Tacitus, whose account of the same period leaves one with an impression of gloom and alarm. The various explanations of V.'s position are available elsewhere for those whose minds are not already closed to the issue;[3] here I prefer to make

---

notes that today 'we expect factual information rather than subjective effusions in biography', but that in the ancient world 'biographers were free to be encomiastic' (15 = *Quarto Contributo* (1969), 82–3).

[1] Individual instances of such *amplificatio* are discussed throughout my commentary (for the theory see Avenarius 14f.). Chapter 126 has already been discussed in Woodman (1975), 290–6, where it was not my purpose to place the chapter in a wider perspective such as that which has now been supplied by the present discussion.

[2] Illustrated most vividly by Steffen, whose valuable work clearly demonstrates the *Einseitigkeit* of V.'s Tiberian narrative (see e.g. pp. 77, 95, 99, 111); yet no Roman reader would have expected anything else. It is of course a feature of panegyrics that they omit items which would do no credit to the *laudatus* (cf. e.g. J. Straub, *Vom Herrscherideal in der Spätantike* (1939), 153; S. MacCormack, 'Latin prose panegyrics', *Empire and aftermath: Silver Latin II* (ed. T. A. Dorey, 1975), 154 with nn. 72–3).

[3] See e.g. the clear summary in Paladini 477. Briefly, the most important explanations are as follows. (1) Having spent many years on campaign with Tiberius, V. naturally developed an affection for him which he

only two observations upon the discrepancy between V. and Tacitus.

First, modern historians have invariably tended to accept the criteria which Tacitus laid down for judging the early empire and its rulers. There is no reason why these should be the only valid criteria. The writing of history is an interpretation of various items of evidence: V.'s own lifetime coincided with the period which he covers in the Tiberian narrative, and it is almost always possible to corroborate from other ancient sources the statements which he makes concerning contemporary events. What objection can there be to an historian who recognised the benefits inherent in the imperial system, and who devoted his rhetorical skill to the production of a corresponding interpretation of events?

Second, we should not assume, on the basis of what is said in the previous paragraph, that V.'s attitude towards the rise of Tiberius was wholly uncritical. It has already been seen that imperial historians, if their work concluded with the reign of the living emperor, were traditionally supposed to end on a high note (above, p. 38). Yet this is precisely what V. has not done. Had his work ended with the familiar panegyrical slogan of *liberalitas* mentioned at 130.2, his account of Tiberius' reign might have been regarded as almost unqualified.[1] By way of a reference to conscription, however, V. modulates to a list of some of the disappointments of the reign, including cases of

---

retained in later years and which is manifest in his history. (2) It is admitted even by Syme (*Tac.* 420 n. 2) that Tiberius' reign falls into two halves, of which the former is mainly admirable but the latter not; V.'s work describes only the first of these. (3) The accounts of Tiberius' whole reign by Tacitus and Dio are inevitably coloured both by the second half of that reign and by the apparent excesses of some later emperors whom Tiberius was thought to foreshadow. (4) Finally, one should distinguish carefully between what V. says and the way in which he says it. Doubtless these points were made in one or other of the numerous dissertations entitled *De Vell. Pat. fide historica* which appeared during the nineteenth century and of which the first (so Dihle 654, 658) was by C. Morgenstern in 1798.

[1] I say 'almost unqualified' because we should still have had to take into account V.'s treatment of Sejanus, on which see below, pp. 245–8.

maiestas (130.3–5). Although it would be easy to dismiss this brief section as a totally inadequate representation of the darkness found in Tacitus' account of Tiberius' principate, due weight must be given to V.'s striking rejection of the traditional pattern.

A parallel is to be found, again in the lost books of Livy. Livy brought his history to its conclusion with a final decade which Syme has aptly described as a 'crown or epilogue carrying the tale down to 9 B.C.'.[1] But although Livy thus appears to conform to the traditional pattern, it should be noted that the final words of the final *periocha* are 'clades Quinctilii Vari'. This anachronistic reference to the disaster of A.D. 9 has plausibly been taken to indicate Livy's criticism of the activities of Augustus in Germany which his preceding books had gone to some lengths to describe.[2] That V. was similarly disturbed by the events of A.D. 26–9 cannot be doubted: it is of the greatest significance that he, loyal supporter of Tiberius as he was, should bring his narrative to the ambivalent and anxious conclusion mentioned above. It is this anxiety which prompts the final chapter of his work (131). V.'s prayer here to the gods of Rome is both a testimony of his personal feelings and a recognition of the crisis which was soon to confront the Roman state.[3]

CONCLUSION

I therefore conclude that V.'s work, given its place in the literary tradition and the period with which it deals, is no more biographical than might have been expected. Crucial for this argument are chapters 94–123, where V., during a narrative still nominally allotted to Augustus' reign, allows Tiberius to emerge and dominate events; yet given the military subject matter of these chapters, for which there is ample precedent and reason, V.'s concentration on Tiberius is rather a true reflection of reality than an attempt at writing a biography of the future emperor. Besides, an account of the earlier years of

---

[1] *Tac.* 366. [2] Cf. Walsh (1961), 35. [3] See below, pp. 275–6.

Tiberius' career is of great importance to those who wish to study the later years. It cannot be denied that the whole Tiberian narrative is enthusiastic in tone; but V. has simply and naturally channelled towards the person of the emperor the patriotism which was expected of the ancient historian and which may be traced back to the earliest days of the Latin historiographical tradition. In all these respects V.'s history is a characteristic product of its time.[1]

Since this conclusion was prompted by the criticisms made of V.'s work by the scholars quoted at the beginning of this Section, I have said little here of V.'s positive value as a contemporary historian of the rise of Tiberius. This value will, I hope, emerge from the commentary which follows.[2] I nevertheless propose to end this Section with a practical example which, I would like to think, will provoke thought.

quia igitur res magnae quas per Gallias uirtute felicitateque correxit, multis ueterum factis fortibus praestant, singula serie progrediente monstrabo, instrumenta omnia mediocris ingenii (si suffecerint) commoturus. quicquid autem narrabitur, quod non falsitas arguta concinnat, sed fides integra rerum absoluit, documentis euidentibus fulta, ad laudatiuam paene materiam pertinebit.

Here we see the techniques of panegyric with which we become so familiar in our reading of V.: the slogans, the comparisons with the past, the pleas of the author's inability. But is the modern scientific historian to discount this ancient counterpart

---

1 A main respect in which his history is not characteristic of its time is its summary form: see above, p. 42 and n. 1, with ref. there.

2 However, I may be permitted to quote two verdicts which sum up the matter exactly. Sumner says of V. (279): 'He came to the writing of history with some, at least, of the equipment that is commonly preferred in a Roman historian. He belonged to the upper classes, was a Roman senator, and had held offices of state. He had commanded with the Roman armies and was acquainted with many parts of the Empire. He had been close to the sources of power.' Steffen says of his work (201): 'Vielmehr hat uns der Zufall mit der "Hist. Rom." ein Werk hinterlassen, das als *zeitgenössisches* Dokument von beträchtlichem Wert ist, da es wie kein anderes Zeugnis der römischen Literatur einen genauen Einblick in die zur Zeit des Tiberius herrschenden offiziellen politischen Auffassungen und Anschauungen bietet.'

as a 'panegyrist'? By no means. 'His portrayal...verges on panegyric, but conveys pertinent criticism and permits a balanced estimate. In general, emotion (of the more honourable sort), the importance of the theme, and the style he has elected impel him to exaggeration. That has happened to other historians. The History (as extant) depends largely on his own experience and meditation: the memoirs of an old soldier developed, adorned, and reinforced by other information. His own testimony is firm, valid, and not to be discounted.' Syme's verdict on Ammianus Marcellinus could with equal justice be applied to the Tiberian portion of V.'s narrative.[1]

---

[1] Syme, *Amm.* 94! The passage quoted is Amm. 16.1.2–3.

TEXT AND CRITICAL APPARATUS

SIGLA

P editio princeps quam Rhenanus imprimendam curauit anno 1520
B lectiones quas Burer e codice Murbacensi se testatur hausisse anno 1520
A apographon quod Amerbach scripsit anno 1516

Coniecturae quas Rhenanus in marginibus editionis principis, Burer in eiusdem appendice fecit, ipsorum nominibus in apparatu critico indicantur.

VELLEII PATERCVLI HISTORIARVM AD M. VINICIVM CONSVLEM

LIBER SECVNDVS

94 Hoc tractu temporum Ti. Claudius Nero – quo trimo (ut
praediximus) Liuia, Drusi Claudiani filia, despondente Ti.
2 Nerone (cui ante nupta fuerat), Caesari nupserat – innutritus
caelestium praeceptorum disciplinis, iuuenis genere, forma,
celsitudine corporis, optimis studiis maximoque ingenio in-
structissimus, qui protinus quantus est, sperari potuerat, uisuque
3 praetulerat principem, quaestor undeuicesimum annum agens
capessere coepit rem publicam, maximamque difficultatem
annonae ac rei frumentariae inopiam ita Ostiae atque in urbe
mandato uitrici moderatus est ut per id quod agebat, quantus
euasurus esset, eluceret.

4 Nec multo post missus ab eodem uitrico cum exercitu ad
uisendas ordinandasque, quae sub oriente sunt, prouincias,
praecipuis omnium uirtutum experimentis in eo tractu editis,
cum legionibus ingressus Armeniam, redacta ea in potestatem
populi Romani, regnum eius ⟨Tigrani, filio⟩ Artauasdi⟨s⟩,
dedit, cuius ***. rex quoque Parthorum tanti nominis fama
95 territus liberos suos ad Caesarem misit obsides. reuersum inde
Neronem Caesar haud mediocris belli mole experiri statuit,

1 Ti. *Gelenius*: T *A*: Titus *P* trimo *Aldus*: primo *PA* 2 Drusi... fuerat *secl. Ruhnken* (*cf.* 75.3, 79.2) despondente *Gelenius*: resp- *PBA* Ti. *suprascr. A, om. P*: ei *B* 6 esset *Halm* 6–7 uisuque praetulerat *Ursinus*: uisusque -erit *PA* 8 capescere *P* 9 ac...inopiam *secl. Bothe* Ostiae atque *Rhenanus*: ostia eratque *PA* 10 mandato *P*: -ū *A*: mandatu *Orelli* uitrici *Aldus*: uict- *PA* (*item* 12) 13 ordinandasque *P*: ordinandas *A* 14 omnibus *A* tractu *Gelenius*: tractatu *PA* 16 ⟨Tigrani, filio⟩ Artauasdi⟨s⟩ *Woodman*: Artauasdi *P*: Artauzdi *BA* 17 cuius *PA*, *post quod lacunam posui*: cum *Lipsius*: quin *Ruhnken* 19 mole *Heinsius*: -em *P*: morem *A*

adiutore operis dato fratre ipsius Druso Claudio, quem intra
2 Caesaris penates enixa erat Liuia. quippe uterque diuisis parti-
bus Raetos Vindelicosque adgressi, multis urbium et castellorum
oppugnationibus nec non derecta quoque acie feliciter functi,
gentes locis tutissimas, aditu difficillimas, numero frequentes,
feritate truces maiore cum periculo quam damno Romani
exercitus, plurimo cum earum sanguine perdomuerunt.

3 Ante quae tempora censura Planci et Pauli acta inter discordiam neque ipsis honori neque rei publicae usui fuerat, cum alteri uis censoria, alteri uita deesset, Paulus uix posset implere censorem, Plancus timere deberet nec quicquam obiicere posset adulescentibus, aut obiicientes audire, quod non agnosceret senex.

96 Mors deinde Agrippae, qui nouitatem suam multis rebus nobilitauerat atque in hoc perduxerat ut et Neronis esset socer, cuiusque liberos nepotes suos diuus Augustus praepositis Gaii ac Lucii nominibus adoptauerat, admouit propius Neronem Caesari: quippe Iulia, filia eius, quae fuerat Agrippae nupta, Neroni nupsit.

2 Subinde bellum Pannonicum, quod inchoatum ⟨ab⟩ Agrippa
Marcoque Vinicio, auo tuo, consul, magnum atroxque et per-
quam uicinum imminebat Italiae, per Neronem gestum est.
3 gentes Pannoniorum Dalmatarumque nationes situmque re-
gionum ac fluminum numerumque et modum uirium excelsissi-
masque et multiplices eo bello uictorias tanti imperatoris alio
loco explicabimus; hoc opus seruet formam suam. huius uicto-
riae compos Nero ouans triumphauit.

---

3 et *om. A* 7–8 perdomuerunt. ante *P*: -uere. tantae *A* 9 ipsis *Gelenius*: ipsi *PA* fuerat *Orelli*: foret *PA*: ⟨ut⟩ neque ipsis...foret *Burman* 9–11 cum...timere deberet *om. A* 10 censoria *Burman*: -ori *P*: -oris *Gelenius* deesset ⟨et⟩ *Pluygers* 11 nec *A*: ne *P* 12 aut...audire *secl. Ruhnken, post* senex *olim transposuit Haase* (audire *in* audiret *mutato*) non ⟨ipse in se⟩ *Ellis* 13 ⟨in se⟩ senex *Heinsius* 16 diuus *uulg.*: D. *PA* (*ut saepe*) 16–17 Gaii...Lucii *Gelenius*: Gai...Luci *PA* 18 Iulia filia eius *Haase*: f. Iul. eius *PA*: f. eius Iul. *Gelenius* Agrippa nuptae *A* 20 ⟨ab⟩ *Lipsius* 21 consul (*uocat.*) *Woodman*: c̄os *A*: COSS. *P*: consulari *Kritz*: consule *Lipsius* 21–2 pro quam *A* 23 gentes *PA*: gentīs *Laurent* 26 colo, *suprascr.* loco *A*

97 Sed dum in hac parte imperii omnia geruntur prosperrime,
accepta in Germania clades sub legato M. Lollio, homine in
omnia pecuniae quam recte faciendi cupidiore et inter summam
uitiorum dissimulationem uitiosissimo, amissaque legionis
2 quintae aquila uocauit ab urbe in Gallias Caesarem. cura
deinde atque onus Germanici belli delegata Druso Claudio,
fratri Neronis, adulescenti tot tantarumque uirtutum quot et
quantas natura mortalis recipit uel industria perficit. cuius in-
genium utrum bellicis magis operibus an ciuilibus suffecerit
3 artibus, in incerto est: morum certe dulcedo ac suauitas et ad-
uersus amicos aequa ac par sui aestimatio inimitabilis fuisse
dicitur (nam pulchritudo corporis proxima fraternae fuit); sed
illum magna ex parte domitorem Germaniae, plurimo eius
gentis uariis in locis profuso sanguine, fatorum iniquitas consu-
4 lem agentem annum tricesimum rapuit. moles deinde eius belli
translata in Neronem est, quod is sua et uirtute et fortuna ad-
ministrauit; peragratusque uictor omnes partes Germaniae sine
ullo detrimento commissi exercitus, quod praecipue huic duci
semper curae fuit, sic perdomuit eam ut in formam paene
stipendiariae redigeret prouinciae. tum alter triumphus cum
altero consulatu ei oblatus est.

98 Dum ea, quae praediximus, in Pannonia Germaniaque gerun-
tur, atrox in Thracia bellum ortum, omnibus eius gentis nationi-
bus in arma accensis, L. Pisonis, quem hodieque diligentissimum
atque eundem lenissimum securitatis urbanae custodem habe-
2 mus, uirtus compressit: quippe legatus Caesaris triennio cum his
bellauit gentesque ferocissimas plurimo cum earum excidio nunc
acie, nunc expugnationibus in pristinum pacis redegit modum;
eiusque patratione Asiae securitatem, Macedoniae pacem
3 reddidit. de quo uiro hoc omnibus sentiendum ac praedicandum
est, esse mores eius uigore ac lenitate mixtissimos, et uix quem-
quam reperiri posse qui aut otium ualidius diligat aut facilius

---

2 Lolio *PA* 4 uictorum *A* 8 perficit *Lipsius*: percipit *PA* 11 sibi *Heinsius* 14 genitis *A* 15 eius *P*, *suprascr. A* 17 peruagatusque *Ruhnken* 20 regeret *A* 22 praediximus *P*: diximus *A* 26 his *PA*: iis *Orelli* 31 mixtis iustissimos *Heinsius*

sufficiat negotio et magis quae agenda sunt curet sine ulla ostentatione agendi.

99 Breui interiecto spatio Ti. Nero, duobus consulatibus totidemque triumphis actis, tribuniciae potestatis consortione aequatus Augusto, ciuium post unum (et hoc quia uolebat) eminentissimus, ducum maximus, fama fortunaque celeberri-
2 mus, et uere alterum rei publicae lumen et caput, mira quadam et incredibili atque inenarrabili pietate (cuius causae mox detectae sunt cum Gaius Caesar sumpsisset iam uirilem togam, Lucius item maturus esset uirili, ne fulgor suus orientium iuuenum obstaret initiis), dissimulata causa consilii sui commeatum ab socero atque eodem uitrico adquiescendi a con-
3 tinuatione laborum petiit. quis fuerit eo tempore ciuitatis habitus, qui singulorum animi, quae digredientium a tanto uiro omnium lacrimae, quam paene ei patria manum iniecerit, iusto
4 seruemus operi. illud etiam in hoc transcursu dicendum est, ita septem annos Rhodi moratum ut omnes, qui pro consulibus legatique in transmarinas profecti prouincias, uisendi eius gratia †ad quem† conuenientes semper priuato, si illa maiestas priuata umquam fuit, fasces suos summiserint fassique sint otium eius
100 honoratius imperio suo. sensit terrarum orbis digressum a custodia Neronem urbis: nam et Parthus desciscens a societate Romana adiecit Armeniae manum, et Germania auersis domitoris sui oculis rebellauit.

2 At in urbe, eo ipso anno quo magnificentissimis gladiatorii muneris naumachiaeque spectaculis diuus Augustus abhinc annos XXXI, se et Gallo Caninio consulibus, dedicato Martis templo, animos oculosque populi Romani repleuerat, foeda

---

10 uirili *Withof*: uiris *PA, secl. Novák* (*1907*): uir; is *Laurent, Schoepfer*: uiribus *ed. Bipont.*: *alii alia* 14 digrediente tanto *Novák* (*1884*) a tanto *P*: & anto *A* 17 moratum *BA*: mor. est *P* 18 ⟨sunt⟩ profecti *Halm* 19 ad quem *PA, obelis notaui*: ad eum *Aldus*: ⟨Rhodum deuerterint⟩ atque eum *Halm*: atque conueniendi *Rhenanus*: undique conuenientes *Heinsius*: *alii alia* priuato *Lipsius*: (19–20) si illa...umquam *Aldus*: priuatos illa... numquam *PA* 22 urbis *secl. Herel* 23 manum *PA*: animum *Burman* 25 magnificentissimis *Cuper*: -imi *PA* 27 XXXI *Woodman*: XXX *PA* $\overline{\text{cos}}$ *A* 28 animo *A* foeda *P*: foedã (*ut uid.*) in *A*

dictu memoriaque horrenda in ipsius domo tempestas erupit.
3 quippe filia eius Iulia, per omnia tanti parentis ac uiri immemor,
nihil, quod facere aut pati turpiter posset femina, luxuria ⟨ac⟩
libidine infectum reliquit, magnitudinemque fortunae suae
peccandi licentia metiebatur, quicquid liberet pro licito uindi-
4 cans. tum Iullus Antonius, singulare exemplum clementiae
Caesaris, uiolator eius domus, ipse sceleris a se commissi ultor
fuit (quem uicto eius patre non tantum incolumitate donauerat
sed sacerdotio, praetura, consulatu, prouinciis honoratum,
etiam matrimonio sororis suae filiae in artissimam adfinitatem
5 receperat); Quintiusque Crispinus, singularem nequitiam
supercilio truci protegens, et Appius Claudius et Sempronius
Gracchus ac Scipio, aliique minoris nominis utriusque ordinis
uiri, quas in cuiuslibet uxore uiolata poenas pependissent,
pependere cum Caesaris filiam et Neronis uiolassent coniugem.
Iulia relegata in insulam patriaeque et parentum subducta
oculis, quam tamen comitata mater Scribonia uoluntaria exilii
permansit comes.

101 Breue ab hoc intercesserat spatium cum C. Caesar, ante aliis
prouinciis †adsidendum obitis, in Syriam missus, conuento prius
Ti. Nerone qui omnem honorem ut superiori habuit, tam uarie
se ibi gessit ut nec laudaturum magna nec uituperaturum
mediocris materia deficiat. cum rege Parthorum, iuuene †ex-
celsissimae insulae† quam amnis Euphrates ambiebat, aequato
2 utriusque partis numero coiit. quod spectaculum stantis ex
diuerso hinc Romani illinc Parthorum exercitus, cum duo inter
se eminentissima imperiorum et hominum coirent capita, per-
quam clarum ac memorabile sub initia stipendiorum meorum
3 tribuno militum mihi uisere contigit (quem militiae gradum

3 ⟨ac⟩ *Orelli* 4–5 magnitudineque...licentiam *Cornelissen* (*1877*) 5–6 uindicans *PA*: iudicans *Rhenanus et suprascr. A* 6 Iullus *Bacherler, P. Thomas* (*1921*): Iulius *PA*: Iulus *Schegk* 14 quas in *Purser*: quasi *PA*: quas *Orelli* pependissent *A, om. P* 17 uoluntaria *Lipsius*: -ii *PA* 20 adsidendum *BA, obelo notaui*: ad sedandum *P*: ad uisendum *Lipsius* 21 qui *Lipsius*: cui *PA* 23–4 excelsissimae insulae (-e -e *A*) *P, obelis notaui*: excelsissimo in insula *Gelenius*: excelsissimae ⟨indolis in⟩ insula *Orelli*: excelsissimo ⟨in ora⟩ insulae *Ellis* 25 colit *A* 27–8 perquem *A* 28 meorum (*prima littera deleta*) *A*

ante sub patre tuo, M. Vinici, et P. Silio auspicatus in Thracia
Macedoniaque, mox Achaia Asiaque et omnibus ad orientem
uisis prouinciis et ore atque utroque maris Pontici latere, haud
iniucunda tot rerum, locorum, gentium, urbium recordatione
perfruor). prior Parthus apud Gaium in nostra ripa, posterior
102 hic apud regem in hostili epulatus est. quo tempore M. Lollii,
quem ueluti moderatorem iuuentae filii sui Augustus esse uoluerat, perfida et plena subdoli ac uersuti animi consilia per Parthum indicata Caesari fama uulgauit. cuius mors intra paucos dies fortuita an uoluntaria fuerit, ignoro; sed quam hunc decessisse laetati homines, tam paulo post obiisse Censorinum in iisdem prouinciis grauiter tulit ciuitas, uirum demerendis hominibus genitum.
2 Armeniam deinde ⟨Gaius⟩ ingressus prima parte introitus
prospere ⟨rem⟩ gessit; mox in conloquio, cui se temere crediderat, circa Artageram grauiter a quodam (nomine Adduo) uulneratus, ex eo ut corpus minus habile, ita animum minus
3 utilem rei publicae habere coepit. nec defuit conuersatio hominum uitia eius adsentatione alentium (etenim semper magnae fortunae comes adest adulatio), per quae eo ductus erat ut in ultimo ac remotissimo terrarum orbis angulo consenescere quam Romam regredi mallet. deinde reluctatus inuitusque reuertens in Italiam, in urbe Lyciae (Limyra nominant) morbo obiit, cum ante annum ferme L. Caesar frater eius Hispanias petens Massiliae decessisset.
103 Sed fortuna, quae subduxerat spem magni nominis, iam tum
rei publicae sua praesidia reddiderat: quippe ante utriusque horum obitum patre tuo P. Vinicio consule Ti. Nero reuersus
2 Rhodo incredibili laetitia patriam repleuerat. non est diu

3 uersis *Halm* 8 perfida *P*: perfidiã *A* acuersuliq (q *del.*) *A* (*ut uid.*) 9 Caesari fama uulgauit *Lipsius*: Caesaris iam auulgauit *PA* 10 ignoro *P*: dignior *A* 11 obiisse *A*: obisse *Rhenanus*: odisse *P et* (*teste Ellis*) A^{mg} 14 ⟨Gaius⟩ *Krause* 15 ⟨rem⟩ *Heinsius* conloquio *Gelenius*: -um *PA* 20 comes est *A* 20 ductus erat *PA*: d. est *Scriner* 22 deinde reluctatus *P*: diu de re luctatus *A*: diu deinde reluctatus *Ruhnken*: diu reluctatus *Lipsius*: de⟨inde⟩ diu *E. Thomas*: *alii alia* 23 Limyra *Ruhnken*: Limyram *P*: Lymira *B*: Limira *A* cum *Gelenius*: quom *P*: quo *A* 24 L. *Gelenius*: quinquagesimum *PA* 24–5 Massiliae *BA*: -a *P*

cunctatus Caesar Augustus: neque enim quaerendus erat quem
3 legeret sed legendus qui eminebat. itaque quod post Lucii mor-
tem adhuc Gaio uiuo facere uoluerat eoque uehementer repug-
nante Nerone erat inhibitus, post utriusque adulescentium
obitum facere perseuerauit, ut et tribuniciae potestatis consor-
tionem Neroni constitueret (multum quidem eo cum domi tum
in senatu recusante) et Aelio Cato ⟨Gaio⟩ Sentio consulibus VI
Kal. Iulias, post urbem conditam DCCLV, abhinc annos
XXVI, adoptaret.

4 Laetitiam illius diei concursumque ciuitatis et uota paene
inserentium caelo manus spemque conceptam perpetuae securi-
tatis aeternitatisque Romani imperii uix in illo iusto opere
abunde persequi poterimus, nedum hic implere. temptemus id
5 unum dixisse, quam ille omnibus fauerit: tum refulsit certa spes
liberorum parentibus, uiris matrimoniorum, dominis patri-
monii, omnibus hominibus salutis, quietis, pacis, tranquillitatis,
adeo ut nec plus sperari potuerit nec spei responderi felicius.

104 Adoptatus eadem die etiam M. Agrippa, quem post mortem
Agrippae Iulia enixa erat; sed in Neronis adoptione illud
adiectum his ipsis Caesaris uerbis: 'hoc', inquit, 'rei publicae
causa facio.'

2 Non diu uindicem custodemque imperii sui morata in urbe
patria protinus in Germaniam misit, ubi ante triennium sub M.
Vinicio, auo tuo, clarissimo uiro, immensum exarserat bellum.
erat id ab eo quibusdam in locis gestum, quibusdam sustenta-
tum feliciter, eoque nomine decreta ei cum speciosissima inscrip-

---

2 legerat *BA* 2–3 L. . . . C. *PA* 3 eoque (*uel* eo quod) *B*: atque *P*: quae eo *A*: atque eo *Orelli* 4 adulescentium *P*: -tum *A* 7 recusante *om. A* ⟨Gaio⟩ *Woodman*: ⟨C.⟩ *uulg.*: ⟨Sex.⟩ Aelio, C. Sentio *Aldus* COSS. *P*: cos *A* VI *Rau*: V *PA* 8 DCCLV *Woodman*: D.CCLIIII *P*: ACC·L·IIII· *B*: aCCLIIII *A* annos *A*: -is *P* 9 XXVI *Aldus*: XXVII *PA* 11 conceptam *Boeclerus*: -ae *PA* 13 hic *Gelenius*: hinc *PA* implere temptemus *PA*, *quae uerba interpunxit Heinsius*: implere. contenti simus *Burman*: *alii*, *puncto post* temptemus *posito*, *supplementum post* dixisse *excogitant* (⟨contenti⟩ *Rhenanus*: ⟨habeo⟩ *Vossius*: ⟨sat est⟩ *Laurent*) 14 fauerit *Madvig*: fuerit *PA*: ⟨omnia⟩ omnibus fuerit *Lipsius*: qualis ille . . . fuerit *Laurent*: *alii alia* 17 respondere felitius *A* 18 adoptatus *om. A* 23 ubi *P*: uti *A* 25 id *Lipsius*: & *PA* 26 ei *P*: & *A*

3 tione operum ornamenta triumphalia. hoc tempus me, functum
ante tribunatu, castrorum Ti. Caesaris militem fecit: quippe
protinus ab adoptione missus cum eo praefectus equitum in
Germaniam, successor officii patris mei, caelestissimorum eius
operum per annos continuos VIIII praefectus aut legatus
spectator, tum pro captu mediocritatis meae adiutor fui. neque
illi spectaculo, quo fructus sum, simile condicio mortalis recipere
uidetur mihi, cum per celeberrimam Italiae partem ⟨et⟩ trac-
tum omnem Galliae prouinciarum ueterem imperatorem et
ante meritis ac uir⟨tut⟩ibus quam nomine Caesarem reuisentes
4 sibi quisque quam illi gratularentur plenius. at uero militum
conspectu eius elicitae gaudio lacrimae alacritasque et saluta-
tionis noua quaedam exultatio et contingendi manum cupiditas
non continentium protinus quin adiicerent, 'uidemus te, im-
perator? saluum recepimus?', ac deinde 'ego tecum, imperator,
in Armenia, ego in Raetia fui', 'ego a te in Vindelicis, ego in
Pannonia, ego in Germania donatus sum', – neque uerbis ex-
primi et fortasse uix mereri fidem potest.

105 Intrata protinus Germania, subacti Canninefates, Attuarii,
Bructeri, recepti Cherusci (gentes utinam minus mox nostra
clade nobiles), transitus Visurgis, penetrata ulteriora, cum
omnem partem asperrimi et periculosissimi belli Caesar uindica-
ret sibi, iis, quae minoris erant discriminis, Sentium Saturninum
(qui tum legatus patris eius in Germania fuerat) praefecisset,
2 uirum multiplicem [in] uirtutibus, nauum, agilem, proui-
dum, militariumque officiorum patientem ac peritum pariter,
sed eundem, ubi negotia fecissent locum otio, liberaliter laute-

5 $\overline{\text{VIIII}}$. *P*: VIII *A* 6 spectator *Gelenius*: tum *Orelli*: spectatum *A*: spectatus *P* 7 fructus *B*: fruitus *P*: functus *A* 8 ⟨et⟩ *Haase*: (8–9) tractum⟨que⟩ *Cludius* 10 uir⟨tut⟩ibus *Lipsius*: uiribus *PA* 11 quisque quam *P*: quisquam *A* at *om. A* 12 elicitae *P*: felicitate *A* 15 recepimus *P*: recip- *A* 19 subacta *A* 19–20 Caninifaci (*em. Rhenanus*), Attuari (*em. Popma*), Bruteri (*em. Rhenanus*) *P*: cam ui faciat Tuari Bruoteri *A* 20 ceruisci *A* gentes *P*: gentis *A*: gens *Fröhlich* 20–1 et (*om. Friebel*) utinam minus...nobiles *Vossius*: et inamminus *B*: & inamminus (*uel* mamminus)... nobilis *A*: et inamninus...nobilis *P* 21 transitus *Rhenanus*: -u *PA* Viturgis *A* 23 sibi *Burman, Cludius*: in *PA*, *secl. Krause, Herel* 24 quitū legatum *A* 25 in *secl. Raphelengius*

que eo abutentem, ita tamen ut eum splendidum ac hilarem
potius quam luxuriosum aut desidem diceres. de cuius uiri claro
3 ingenio celebrique consulatu praediximus. anni eius aestiua
usque in mensem Decembrem perducta immanis emolumentum
fecere uictoriae. pietas sua Caesarem paene exstructis hieme
Alpibus in urbem traxit, at tutela imperii eum ueris initio re-
duxit in Germaniam, in cuius mediis finibus ad caput Lupiae
fluminis hiberna digrediens princeps locauerat.

106 Pro dii boni, quanti uoluminis opera insequenti aestate sub
duce Tiberio Caesare gessimus! perlustrata armis tota Germania
est, uictae gentes paene nominibus incognitae, receptae Cau-
chorum nationes: omnis eorum iuuentus infinita numero,
immensa corporibus, situ locorum tutissima, traditis armis, una
cum ducibus suis saepta fulgenti armatoque militum nostrorum
2 agmine, ante imperatoris procubuit tribunal. fracti Langobardi,
gens etiam Germana feritate ferocior. denique – quod numquam
antea spe conceptum, nedum opere temptatum erat – ad
quadringentesimum miliarium a Rheno usque ad flumen Al-
bim, qui Semnonum Hermundurorumque fines praeterfluit,
3 Romanus cum signis perductus exercitus, et eodem, mira felici-
tate et cura ducis, temporum quoque obseruantia, classis, quae
Oceani circumnauigauerat sinus, ab inaudito atque incognito
ante mari flumine Albi subuecta, ⟨cum⟩ plurimarum gentium
uictoria, cum abundantissima rerum omnium copia exercitui
Caesarique se iunxit.

107 Non tempero mihi quin tantae rerum magnitudini hoc, quale-
cumque est, inseram. cum citeriorem ripam praedicti fluminis

---

1 eo *om. A* ac hilarem *P*: Athilā *A*: aut hilarem *Ruhnken* 2 aut desidem *P*: Audesidem *A* 2–3 claroq. (q *del.*) ingenio celebriq. ingenio (*del.*) consulatu *A*: claro celebrique consulatu *P* 4 producta *Lipsius* 5 extructis *PA*: obstructis *Gelenius* 6 at tutela *Lipsius*: ad tutelam *PA* initio *Rhenanus*: initi *PA* 7 Lupiae *Lipsius*: Iuliae *PA* 12 infinito *A* 13 tutissimam traditus (*corr. in* -is) *A* 14 armatoque *secl. Bothe*: armatorum *Laurent* 15 Langobardi *B*: Longo- *PA* 16 gene *A* 19 Semnonum *Puteanus*: Senonum *PA* Hermundurorumque *Miller*: Hermundorumque *PA* 20 eodem *PA*: eadem *Kritz* 23 maris flumine labi *A* ⟨cum⟩ *Ellis*: ⟨a⟩ *Acidalius*: ⟨laeta⟩ *Castiglioni* 25 Caesarisque seiunxit *A*

castris occupassemus et ulterior armata hostium iuuentute fulgeret †sub omnem metumque† nostrarum nauium protinus refugientium, unus e barbaris aetate senior, corpore excellens, dignitate (quantum ostendebat cultus) eminens, cauatum (ut illis mos est) ex materia conscendit alueum solusque id nauigii genus temperans ad medium processit fluminis et petiit, liceret sibi sine periculo in eam, quam armis tenebamus, egredi ripam
2 ac uidere Caesarem. data petenti facultas. tum adpulso lintre [et] diu tacitus contemplatus Caesarem, 'nostra quidem', inquit, 'furit iuuentus quae, cum uestrum numen absentium colat, praesentium potius arma metuit quam sequitur fidem. sed ego beneficio ac permissu tuo, Caesar, quos ante audiebam, hodie uidi deos, nec feliciorem ullum uitae meae aut optaui aut sensi diem.' impetratoque ut manum contingeret, reuersus in nauiculam, sine fine respectans Caesarem ripae suorum adpulsus est.

3 Victor omnium gentium locorumque quos adierat, Caesar cum incolumi inuiolatoque et semel tantummodo magna cum clade hostium fraude eorum temptato exercitu, in hiberna legiones reduxit, eadem qua priore anno festinatione urbem petens.

108 Nihil erat iam in Germania quod uinci posset praeter gentem Marcomannorum, quae Maroboduo duce excita sedibus suis atque in interiora refugiens incinctos Hercynia silua campos
2 incolebat. nulla festinatio huius uiri mentionem transgredi debet. Maroboduus, genere nobilis, corpore praeualens, animo ferox, natione magis quam ratione barbarus, non tumultuarium neque fortuitum neque mobilem et ex uoluntate parentium constantem inter suos occupauit principatum, sed certum imperium uimque regiam complexus animo, statuit auocata procul

1 ulteriora *A* iuuentute *P*: uirtute *A* 2 sub omnem metumque *B*, *obelis notaui*: sub omnem motūq. qi *A*: sub omnem motum *P*: sub omnem motum ⟨impetum⟩que *Damsté*: *alii alia* auium *A* 7 tenebamus *P*: tendebamus *BA* 8 data *BA*: data a Caesare *P* 9 et *secl. Vascosanus* 10 ⟨non⟩ colat *Madvig* 12 ac *P*: et *A* 14 impetratoque *P*: imperatoque *BA* 23 interiora *Gelenius*: inf- *PA* Hercynia silua *Heinsius*: -ae -ae *PA* 27 atque fortuitum *Herel* sed ex *Heinsius* parentium *BA*: -tum *P*

a Romanis gente sua eo progredi ubi, cum propter potentiora
arma refugisset, sua faceret potentissima.
Occupatis igitur, quos praediximus, locis, finitimos omnes aut
109 bello domuit aut condicionibus iuris sui fecit. corpus suum custo-
dientium imperium, perpetuis exercitiis paene ad Romanae
disciplinae formam redactum, breui in eminens et nostro quo-
que imperio timendum perduxit fastigium; gerebatque se ita
aduersus Romanos ut neque bello nos †lacesseretur superesse
2 sibi uim ac uoluntatem resistendi ⟨ostenderet⟩. legati, quos
mittebat ad Caesares, interdum ut supplicem commendabant,
interdum ut pro pari loquebantur. gentibus hominibusque a
nobis desciscentibus erat apud eum perfugium, totumque ex
male dissimulato agebat aemulum; exercitumque (quem LX
milium peditum, quattuor equitum fecerat) adsiduis aduersus
finitimos bellis exercendo, maiori quam quod habebat operi
3 praeparabat; eratque etiam eo timendus quod cum Germaniam
ad laeuam et in fronte, Pannoniam ad dextram, a tergo sedium
suarum haberet Noricos, tamquam in omnes semper uenturus
4 ab omnibus timebatur. nec securam incrementi sui patiebatur
esse Italiam, quippe cum a summis Alpium iugis, quae finem
Italiae terminant, initium huius finium haud multo plus CC
milibus passuum abesset.
5 Hunc uirum et hanc regionem proximo anno diuersis e parti-
bus Ti. Caesar adgredi statuit. Sentio Saturnino mandatum ut
per Cattos excisis continentibus Hercyniae siluis legiones ***
Boiohaemum (id regioni, quam incolebat Maroboduus, nomen

1 propter *secl. Madvig* 3 quos *P*: quis *B*: his (*del.*) quos (*corr. in* quis) *A* 4–5 corpus suum custodientium imperium *Madvig*: c. suum custodia tum imperium *PA*: c. sui custodia tutum imperii *Heinsius*: c. sui custoditum imperi *Kritz* (custoditum *iam Burer*): (4–6) c. suorum custodia tutum, imperium...redactum, ⟨eum⟩ breui *Burman*: *alii alia* 8 lacesseretur *PA, obelo notaui*: lacesseret ac *Rosenheyn*: ⟨lacesseret, at si⟩ lacesseretur *Rhenanus* 9 ⟨ostenderet⟩ *Burman* 10 supplicem ⟨eum⟩ *Cludius* 12 totusque *Heinsius*: tutum, qui *Scheffer* 13 LX *PA*: 'ex uestigiis uet. cod. apparet LXX. fuisse, eraso X posteriore' *Burer* 15 habebat *PA*: obibat *Heinsius*: agebat *Burman*: tractabat *Friebel* 21 huius *Heinsius*: cuius *BA*: eius *P* 25 Catthos *PA* *post* legiones *lacunam posui*: duceret *post* est (*p.* 70.1) *suppl. Lipsius* 26 Boiohoemum *P*: Botohaemum *A*

est); ipse a Carnunto (qui locus Norici regni proximus ab hac
parte erat) exercitum, qui in Illyrico merebat, ducere in
Marcommanos orsus est.

110 Rumpit interdum, ⟨modo⟩ moratur proposita hominum
fortuna. praeparauerat iam hiberna Caesar ad Danubium, ad-
motoque exercitu non plus quam quinque dierum iter a primis
2 hostium, Saturninum *** admoueri placuerat: paene aequali
diuisae interuallo ab hoste, intra paucos dies in praedicto loco
cum Caesare ⟨se⟩ iuncturae erant, cum uniuersa Pannonia,
insolens longae pacis bonis et adulta uiribus, Dalmatia omni-
busque tractus eius gentibus in societatem adductis consilii,
3 arma corripuit. tum necessaria gloriosis praeposita, neque
tutum uisum abdito in interiora exercitu uacuam tam uicino
hosti relinquere Italiam.

Gentium nationumque, quae rebellauerant, omnis numerus
amplius DCCC milibus explebat: CC fere peditum colligeban-
4 tur armis habilia, equitum VIIII. cuius immensae multitudinis,
parentis acerrimis ac peritissimis ducibus, pars petere Italiam
decreuerat iunctam sibi Nauporti ac Tergestis confinio, pars in
Macedoniam ⟨se⟩ effuderat, pars suis sedibus praesidium esse
destinauerat. maxima duobus Batonibus ac Pinneti ducibus
5 auctoritas erat; in omnibus autem Pannoniis non disciplinae
tantummodo sed linguae quoque notitia Romanae; plerisque
etiam litterarum usus, et familiaris animorum erat exercitatio.
itaque, hercules, nulla umquam natio tam mature consilio
6 belli bellum iunxit ac decreta patrauit. oppressi ciues Romani,

---

1 Acarnanto (*uel* Acarnunto), *suprascr.* Ac arnumho *A* 2 duceret *A* 4 iter dum *A* ⟨modo⟩ *Woodman*: ⟨interdum⟩ *Heinsius*: *alii alia* 7 *post* Saturninum *lacunam posui*: Saturninum admouere ⟨copias⟩ placuerat *Kritz* (admouere *iam Ruhnken*): S. admoueri placuerat. ⟨cuius copiae⟩ *ed. Bipont.* (⟨cuius copiae⟩ *iam Lipsius*): hostium ⟨aberat, et legiones etiam quas⟩ S. admouere ei placuerat *Haupt*: *alii alia* 9 ⟨se⟩ *Krause* cum *P*: tum *BA* 10 et *om. A* 11 consilii *Fröhlich*: constitit *PA*: ex constituto *Gelenius* 13 abdito *A et coni. Vascosanus*: addito *P* 14 relinquere *om. A* 16 DCCC *Gelenius*: ACCC. *P*: accc *A* 18 parentis *BA*: pars *P* pars petere *BA*: properare in *P* 20 se *suppl. hic Ruhnken, post* pars (19) *Ursinus* effuderat *Ursinus*: effugerat *PA* 21 maxima *Kritz*: proxima *PA*: porro maxima *Heinsius* 22 in *secl. Heinsius* 24 armorum *Bothe*

trucidati negotiatores, magnus uexillariorum numerus ad in-
ternecionem ea in regione, quae plurimum ab imperatore
aberat, caesus, occupata armis Macedonia, omnia [et] in
omnibus locis igni ferroque uastata.

Quin etiam tantus huius belli metus fuit ut stabilem illum et
formatum tantorum bellorum experientia Caesaris Augusti
111 animum quateret atque terreret. habiti itaque dilectus, reuocati
undique et omnes ueterani, uiri feminaeque ex censu libertinum
coactae dare militem. audita in senatu uox principis, decimo die,
ni caueretur, posse hostem in urbis Romae uenire conspectum.
senatorum equitumque Romanorum exactae ad id bellum
2 operae †pollicitati. omnia haec frustra praeparassemus nisi qui
illa regeret fuisset. itaque ut praesidium militum res publica ab
Augusto ducem in bellum poposcit Tiberium.

3 Habuit in hoc quoque bello mediocritas nostra speciosi
ministerii locum. finita equestri militia designatus quaestor
necdum senator aequatus senatoribus, etiam designatis tribunis
plebei, partem exercitus ab urbe traditi ab Augusto perduxi ad
4 filium eius. in quaestura deinde remissa sorte prouinciae legatus
eiusdem ad eundem missus.

Quas nos primo anno acies hostium uidimus! quantis pruden-
tia ducis opportunitatibus furentes eorum uires uniuersas
euasimus, ⟨exhausimus⟩ partibus! quanto cum temperamento
simul ** utilitatis res auctoritate imperatoris agi uidimus! qua

---

3 et *seclusi*: Macedonia omnis, et *Cornelissen* (*1887*) 5 quin *Vascosanus*: quia *PA* etiam tantus *A*: t. e. *P* 6 formatum *BA*: fortunatum *P*: firmatum *Burer* 7 reuocati *Gelenius*: -us *PA* 8 et *secl. Gelenius* 9 coacti *Cludius* militem *Rhenanus*: -um *PA* 9–12 audita...pollicitati *post* terreret (7) *transposuit Haase* 12 pollicitati *PA*, *obelo notaui*: ⟨ac⟩ pollicitae *Boot* (pollicitae *iam Gelenius*): ex pollicitatione *Ruhnken*: *alii alia* 13 militum *PA*: ultimum *Lipsius*: limitum *Purser*: *alii alia* 16 ministerii *Lipsius*: ministri *PA* eq. uestri *A* 17 et iam *Gelenius* 18 perduxi *Rhenanus*: -it *PA* 20 missus *P*: missum *A*: missus sum *Halm* 22 furenteis *PB*: furentis *A*: fuerit is A^{mg}: florentes *Ruhnken*: fruentes *Orelli* eorum *BA*: in eum *P* 23 euasimus *PB et* (*sed suprascr.* eius imus) *A*: elusimus *nescioquis*: exhausimus *Gruter*: *alii alia* ⟨exhausimus⟩ *Woodman*: ⟨elusimus⟩ *E. Thomas*: ⟨fudimus⟩ *Haase* partibus *PA*: artibus *Rhenanus* 24 simul *PA*, *post quod lacunam posuit Krause*: summae *Mommsen*: *alii alia* utilitatis *PA*: ciuilitatis *Ruhnken*

prudentia hiberna disposita sunt! quanto opere inclusus custo-
diis exercitus nostri ⟨hostis⟩, ne qua posset erumpere, inopsque
copiarum et intra se furens uiribus [hostis] elanguesceret!
112 Felix euentu, forte conatu prima aestate belli Messalini opus
2 mandandum est memoriae. qui uir animo etiam quam gente
nobilior, dignissimus qui et patrem Coruinum habuisset et cog-
nomen suum Cottae fratri relinqueret, praepositus Illyrico,
subita rebellione cum semiplena legione uicesima circumdatus
hostili exercitu, amplius XX milia hostium fudit fugauitque et
ob id ornamentis triumphalibus honoratus est.
3 Ita placebat barbaris numerus suus, ita fiducia uirium ut,
ubicumque Caesar esset, nihil in se reponerent. pars exercitus
eorum, proposita ipsi duci et ad arbitrium utilitatemque nos-
tram macerata perductaque ad exitiabilem famem, neque in-
stantem sustinere neque cum facientibus copiam pugnandi
derigentibusque aciem ausa congredi, occupato monte Claudio
4 munitione se defendit. at ea pars quae obuiam se effuderat
exercitui quem A. Caecina et Siluanus Plautius consulares ex
transmarinis adducebant prouinciis, circumfusa quinque legioni-
bus nostris auxiliaribusque et equitatui regio (quippe magnam
Thracum manum iunctus praedictis ducibus Rhoemetalces,
Thraciae rex, in adiutorium eius belli secum trahebat) paene
5 exitiabilem omnibus cladem intulit. fusa regiorum equestris
acies, fugatae alae, conuersae cohortes sunt; apud signa quoque
legionum trepidatum. sed Romani uirtus militis plus eo tempore

---

2 hostis *suppl. hic Ruhnken, ante* custodiis (1–2) *Novák (1907)* 3 hostis *PA, secl. Kritz*: haustis *Ruhnken* 6 dignissimus⟨que⟩ *Heinsius* 9 amplius $\overline{XX}$. hostium fudit *P*: milia *ante* hostium *uulgo ponitur*: a m $\overline{XX}$ fudit *A* 12 in se ⟨spei⟩ *Heinsius* 13 opposita *Lipsius* 14–15 instantes *Acidalius* 15 cum *Ruhnken*: ut *PA, secl. Gelenius*: uel *Purser* 16 dirigentibusque *PB*: derigentibus quae *A* aciem *B et* (*sed suprascr.* aciam) *A, et coni. Rhenanus*: etiam *P* 17 at ea *B et coni. Rhenanus*: antea *P*: altera *A* 18 Plautius *P*: plancius *A* 20–1 magnam...manum iunctus *Rhenanus*: magna...manu uinctus *P*: magnam...manu iunctis (*del.*) iunctus *A*: iunctum *B* 21 praedictus *A* Rhoemetalces *Rhenanus*: Rhomo et Alces *PBA* 23 fusa *Vossius*: fuga *BA*: fugata *P* 25 Romani uirtus militis *P et* (*ut uid.*) *A*: Romana uirtus militibus *Lipsius*: Romana u. militi *Gruter*: Romani uirtute militis *Orelli*

uindicauit gloriae quam ducibus reliquit, qui multum a more
imperatoris sui discrepantes ante in hostem inciderunt, quam
6 per exploratores, ubi hostis esset, cognoscerent. iam igitur in
dubiis rebus semet ipsae legiones adhortatae, iugulatis ab hoste
quibusdam tribunis militum, interempto praefecto castrorum
praefectisque cohortium, non incruentis centurionibus, ⟨e⟩
quibus etiam primi ordines cecidere, inuasere hostes nec sus-
tinuisse contenti perrupta eorum acie ex insperato uictoriam
uindicauerunt.

7 Hoc fere tempore Agrippa, qui eodem die quo Tiberius adoptatus ab auo suo naturali erat et iam ante biennium, qualis esset, apparere coeperat, mira prauitate animi atque ingenii in praecipitia conuersus, patris atque eiusdem aui sui animum alienauit sibi, moxque crescentibus in dies uitiis dignum furore suo habuit exitum.

113 Accipe nunc, M. Vinici, tantum in bello ducem quantum in
pace uides principem. iunctis exercitibus, quique sub Caesare
fuerant quique ad eum uenerant, contractisque in una castra
decem legionibus, LXX amplius cohortibus, †XIIII sed† pluri-
bus quam decem ueteranorum milibus, ad hoc magno uolun-
tariorum numero frequentique equite regio, tanto denique
exercitu quantus nullo umquam loco post bella fuerat ciuilia,
omnes eo ipso laeti erant maximamque fiduciam uictoriae in
2 numero reponebant. at imperator, optimus eorum quae agebat
iudex, et utilia speciosis praeferens, quodque semper eum
facientem uidi in omnibus bellis, quae probanda essent, non
quae utique probarentur sequens, paucis diebus exercitum,
qui uenerat, ad refouendas ex itinere eius uires moratus, cum
eum maiorem quam ut temperari posset, neque habilem guber-
3 naculo cerneret, dimittere statuit; prosecutusque longo et per-
quam laborioso itinere (cuius difficultas narrari uix potest) ut

---

1 uindicauit *Puteanus*: uindicatum *PA*: uindicandum *Acidalius* 1–2 a more...discrepantes *Pontanus*: amore...crepantes *PA* 4 ipse *A* 6 ⟨e⟩ *Boeclerus* 7 quibus *BA*: qui *P* ordinis *Gelenius* 8 prerupta *A* 11 et iam *Gelenius*: etiam *PA* 12 ceperat *A* 17 uides principem *BA*: uides. principes *P* 19 XIIII sed *P*, *obelis notaui*: XIIII set (*corr. in* sed) *A*: XIIII ⟨ali⟩s et *Lipsius*: X alis et *Laurent* 27 cuique *Heinsius*

neque uniuersos quisquam auderet adgredi et partem digre-
dientium, suorum quisque metu finium, uniuersi temptare non
possent, remisit eo unde uenerant; et ipse asperrimae hiemis
initio regressus Sisciam legatos, inter quos ipsi fuimus, partitis
praefecit hibernis.

114 O rem dictu non eminentem, sed solida ueraque uirtute atque
utilitate maximam, experientia suauissimam, humanitate singu-
larem! per omne belli Germanici Pannonicique tempus nemo e
nobis gradumue nostrum aut praecedentibus aut sequentibus
imbecillus fuit cuius salus ac ualetudo non ita sustentaretur
Caesaris cura tamquam districtissimus ille tantorum onerum
2 mole huic uni negotio uacaret animus. erat desiderantibus para-
tum iunctum uehiculum, lectica eius publicata, cuius ⟨usum⟩
cum alii tum ego sensi; iam medici, iam apparatus cibi, iam
⟨tamquam⟩ in hoc solum portatum instrumentum balinei
nullius non succurrit ualetudini: domus tantum ac domestici
deerant, ceterum nihil quod ab illis aut praestari aut desiderari
3 posset. adiiciam illud quod quisquis illis temporibus interfuit, ut
alia quae rettuli, agnoscet protinus: solus semper equo uectus
est, solus cum iis, quos inuitauerat, maiore parte aestiuarum
expeditionum cenauit sedens. non sequentibus disciplinam,
quatenus exemplo non nocebatur, ignouit: admonitio frequens,
interdum castigatio, uindicta rarissima, agebatque medium
plurima dissimulantis, aliqua inhibentis.

4 Hiems emolumentum patrati belli contulit, et insequenti
aestate omnis Pannonia reliquiis totius belli in Dalmatia manen-

---

4 Sisciam *B*: Sistiam *P*: Sisci iam *A* 6 orem (*ut uid.*) ductu *A* 7 utilitatem *A* 10 becillus *A* 11 districtissimus *Bentley*: distraximus *PA*: distractissimus *Rhenanus* 12 uni negotio *Gelenius*: uni genitio *B*: unigenito *A*: uni *P* 13 ⟨usum⟩ *Lipsius* (*lacuna iam ab Rhenano posita*) 15 ⟨tamquam⟩ in hoc solum portatum *Woodman*: in hoc solum importatum *P*: in h. solum um (*del.*, *suprascr.* uni) portatum *A*: huic soli portatum *Pluygers*: in h. solum una portatum *Orelli* baline *A* 18 quod (uod *del.*) *A* 19 equo *P*: eo quo *A* 23 interdum et (*om. Bothe*) castigatio *nescioquis anno 1779*: inerat et castigatio *PA*: inertium c. *Friebel* rarissima *Rhenanus*: amarissima *PA* 24 dissimulans...inhibens *Acidalius* aliquam *A* 25 contulit *PA*: non tulit *Friebel*: contudit *Novák* (*1884*) in sequenti *A*

tibus pacem petiit. ferocem illam tot milium iuuentutem, paulo ante seruitutem minatam Italiae, conferentem arma, quibus usa erat, apud flumen nomine Bathinum, prosternentemque se uniuersam genibus imperatoris, Batonemque et Pinnetem excelsissimos duces, captum alterum, ⟨alterum⟩ a se deditum iustis uoluminibus ordine narrabimus, ut spero.

5 Autumni ⟨initio⟩ uictor in hiberna reducitur exercitus, cuius omnibus copiis ⟨a⟩ Caesare M. Lepidus praefectus est, uir nomini ac fortunae Caesarum proximus, quem in quantum quisque aut cognoscere aut intellegere potuit, in tantum miratur ac diligit, tantorumque nominum, quibus ortus est, ornamentum iudicat.

115 Caesar ad alteram belli Dalmatici molem animum atque arma contulit; in qua regione quali adiutore legatoque fratre meo Magio Celere Velleiano usus sit, ipsius patrisque praedicatione testatum est et amplissimorum honorum, quibus triumphans eum Caesar donauit, signat memoria.

2 Initio aestatis Lepidus educto hibernis exercitu per gentes
integras immunesque adhuc clade belli et eo feroces ac truces
tendens ad Tiberium imperatorem et cum difficultate loco-
rum et cum ui hostium luctatus, magna cum clade obsistentium
excisis agris, exustis aedificiis, caesis uiris, laetus uictoria
3 praedaque onustus peruenit ad Caesarem, et ob ea, quae si
propriis gessisset auspiciis triumphare debuerat, ornamentis
triumphalibus consentiente cum iudicio principum uoluntate
senatus ⟨donatus⟩ est.

4 Illa aestas maximi belli consummauit effectus: quippe Perustae ac Desidiates Dalmatae, situ locorum ac montium, ingeniorum ferocia, mira etiam pugnandi scientia et praecipue

---

1 ferocem *P*: fero uocem *A* 2 quibus *P*: qui *A* 5 ⟨alterum⟩ *Rhenanus* a se *PA*: alterum *Gelenius* 7 autumno *Gelenius* ⟨initio⟩ *Ellis* 8 ⟨a⟩ *Rhenanus* Caesare M. Lepidus *Burer* (Caesare Lep. *iam Rhenanus*): Caesarem Lep. *PA* nomini *Acidalius*: -is *PA* 9 Caesarum *Scheffer*: eorum *PA*: suorum *Vossius*: Aemiliorum *Heinsius*: deorum *Laurent, Bothe* max (*del.*) proximus *A* 14 Velleiano *Gelenius*: ulli flano *P*: ulliflano *A* 17 pergentis *PBA*, *corr. Gelenius* 18 integras *P*: in integras (*uel* in integritas) *B*: in integras *A* 22 ⟨ob⟩ quae *Munker* 25 ⟨donatus⟩ *Rhenanus*: *alii alia* 27 Perustae ac *Vossius*: Desidiates *Gelenius*: Perusia aede siciales *P*: perusia aedesitiales *A*

angustiis saltuum paene inexpugnabiles, non iam ductu sed
manibus atque armis ipsius Caesaris tum demum pacati sunt
cum paene funditus euersi forent.
5 Nihil in hoc tanto bello, nihil in Germania aut uidere maius
aut mirari magis potui quam quod imperatori numquam adeo ulla
opportuna uisa est uictoriae occasio quam damno amissi pen-
saret militis, semperque uisum est gloriosum quod esset tutissi-
mum, et ante conscientiae quam famae consultum, nec umquam
consilia ducis iudicio exercitus sed exercitus prouidentia ducis
rectus est.
116 Magna in bello Dalmatico experimenta uirtutis in multos ac
2 difficiles locos praemissus Germanicus dedit; celebri etiam opera
diligentique Vibius Postumus, uir consularis, praepositus Dal-
matiae ornamenta meruit triumphalia (quem honorem ante
paucos annos Passienus et Cossus, uiri quibusdam diuersi, uirtu-
tibus celebres, in Africa meruerant; sed Cossus uictoriae testi-
monium etiam in cognomen filii contulit, adulescentis in omnium
3 uirtutum exempla geniti). at Postumi operum L. Apronius par-
ticeps illa quoque militia eos, quos mox consecutus est, honores
excellenti uirtute meruit. utinam non maioribus experimentis
testatum esset quantum in omni re fortuna posset! sed in hoc
quoque genere abunde agnosci uis eius potest. nam et Aelius
Lamia, uir antiquissimi moris et priscam grauitatem semper
humanitate temperans, in Germania Illyricoque et mox in
Africa splendididissimis functus ministeriis, non merito sed
4 materia adipiscendi triumphalia defectus est; et A. Licinius
Nerua Silianus, P. Silii filius, quem uirum ne qui intellexit
quidem abunde miratus est, [ne] nihil ⟨quod⟩ non optimo ciui,

---

1 saltum *A* 6 commissi *Herel* 7 gloriosissimum *Halm* 8 quam *om. A* fame *A* nec umquam *P*: ne cum quod *B*: necum quod *A* 11 multos *PA, obelo notauit Ellis*: incultos *Heinsius* 13 diligentique *Vossius*: Vibius Postumus *Pighi*: diligenti quib. ius postumus *A*: diligenti quibus Iulius Posthumius *P*: Iul. Postumus *B* praepositus *P*: quae positus *A* 15 quibusdam *PA, obelo notauit Ellis*: quamuis *Bothe*: quamquam *Halm*: *alii alia* diuersi *Walter*: -is *PA* 18 at Posthumi *P*: ad Postumio *BA* 21 hoc *Gelenius*: loco *PA* 22–3 Aelius Lamia *Ruhnken*: etiam *PA* 23 semper *P*: super *A* 28 ne *PB, secl. Cludius*: me *A* nihil non *BA*: nihil *P*: quod *post* nihil *suppl. Woodman, post* non *Halm* optimo ciui *PB*: optimos (s *del.*) ciuis *A*

simplicissimo duci superesset praeferens, immatura ⟨morte⟩ et
fructu amplissimae principis amicitiae et consummatione euec-
tae in altissimum paternumque fastigium imaginis defectus est.
5 horum uirorum mentioni si quis quaesisse me dicet locum,
fatentem arguet: neque enim iustus sine mendacio candor apud
bonos crimini est.

117 Tantum quod ultimam imposuerat Pannonico ac Dalmatico
bello Caesar manum, cum intra quinque consummati tanti
operis dies funestae ex Germania epistulae caesi Vari truci-
datarumque legionum trium totidemque alarum et sex cohortium
***, uelut in hoc saltem tantummodo indulgente nobis for-
tuna, ne occupato duce *** et causa ⟨et⟩ persona moram exigit.
2 Varus Quintilius, inlustri magis quam nobili ortus familia, uir
ingenio mitis, moribus quietus, ut corpore et animo immobilior,
otio magis castrorum quam bellicae adsuetus militiae, pecuniae
uero quam non contemptor Syria (cui praefuerat) declarauit,
3 quam pauper diuitem ingressus diues pauperem reliquit, – is
cum exercitui, qui erat in Germania, praeesset, concepit esse
homines qui nihil praeter uocem membraque haberent homi-
num, quique gladiis domari non poterant, posse iure mulceri.
4 quo proposito mediam ingressus Germaniam, uelut inter uiros
pacis gaudentes dulcedine iurisdictionibus agendoque pro tri-
118 bunali ordine trahebat aestiua. at illi (quod nisi expertus uix
credat) in summa feritate uersutissimi natumque mendacio
genus, simulantes fictas litium series, et nunc prouocantes alter
alterum in iurgia, nunc agentes gratias quod ea Romana iustitia
finiret feritasque sua nouitate incognitae disciplinae mitesceret

1 superesset *P. Thomas* (*1919*): perisset *PBA*: superesse *Ellis*: *alii alia* praeferens *PA*: praereptus *Gelenius* ⟨morte⟩ *Orelli* 2 amplicissimae *A* 3 imaginis *PA*: magnitudinis *olim Ruhnken* es *A* 4 horum *Burer*: honorum *BA*: quorum *P* 7 ac *P*: ad *A* 10–11 *post* cohortium *lacuna uulgo ponitur* 12 duce (*Gelenius*: -em *PA*), *post quod lacuna uulgo ponitur*: ⟨saeuiretur. sed⟩ *Lipsius* ⟨et⟩ *Orelli* 14 ut...et *PA*: et...et *Bucretius*: ut...ita *Acidalius* 20 mulcere *A* 23 ordine *PA*: torpedine *Laurent*: otiose *Cornelissen* (*1877*) 24 credat *Lipsius*: credebat *PA* 25 prouocantes *Rhenanus*: prouocantes (*del.*) *A*: procaces in exemplari A^{mg} (*sic*): procaces *P*: procataes *B* 26 in iurgia *Madvig*: iniuria *PA* eas *Gelenius* 27 mitesceret *P*: mut- *B et* (*sed suprascr.* mi) *A*

et solita armis discerni iure terminarentur, in summam socor-
diam perduxere Quintilium, usque eo ut se praetorem urbanum
in foro ius dicere, non in mediis Germaniae finibus exercitui
praeesse crederet.

2 Tum iuuenis genere nobilis, manu fortis, sensu celer, ultra
barbarum promptus ingenio, nomine Arminius, Sigimeri
principis gentis eius filius, ardorem animi uultu oculisque prae-
ferens, adsiduus militiae nostrae prioris comes, iure etiam ciui-
tatis Rom⟨an⟩ae ius equestris consequens gradus, segnitia ducis
in occasionem sceleris usus est, haud imprudenter speculatus
*** neminem celerius opprimi quam qui nihil timeret, et fre-
3 quentissimum initium esse calamitatis securitatem. primo igitur
paucos, mox plures in societatem consilii recepit; opprimi posse
Romanos et dicit et persuadet, decretis facta iungit, tempus
4 insidiarum constituit. id Varo per uirum eius gentis fidelem
clarique nominis, Segesten, indicatur; postulabat etiam *** fata
consiliis omnemque animi eius aciem praestrinxerant: quippe
ita se res habet ut plerumque cuius fortunam mutaturus ⟨est⟩
deus, consilia corrumpat, efficiatque (quod miserrimum est) ut
quod accidit, ei etiam merito accidisse uideatur, et casus in
culpam transeat. negat itaque se credere spe⟨cie⟩mque in se
beneuolentiae ex merito aestimare profitetur. nec diutius post
primum indicem secundo relictus locus.

119 Ordinem atrocissimae calamitatis, qua nulla post Crassi in
Parthis damnum in externis gentibus grauior Romanis fuit,
iustis uoluminibus ut alii ita nos conabimur exponere; nunc
2 summa deflenda est. exercitus omnium fortissimus, disciplina,
manu experientiaque bellorum inter Romanos milites princeps,
marcore ducis, perfidia hostis, iniquitate fortunae circumuentus,

---

1 decerni *Gronovius* 8 ⟨cum⟩ iure *Heinsius* 9 Romae ius *P*: 'alias Romanae ius' *Burer*: Roma eius *A*: Romanae decus *Burman* consecutus *Heinsius* 10–11 *post* speculatus *lacunam posui* 13 societatem...recepit *Rhenanus*: -e...praecepit *PA* 16 *post* etiam *lacunam posuit Ellis* 17 praestrinxerant *Gelenius*: praestruxerat *PA* 18 cuius *ed. Bipont.*: qui *PA*: cui *Vossius* imitaturus *A* ⟨est⟩ *Gelenius* 20 ei etiam *Kritz*: et etiam *BA*: etiam *P* 21 culpam *P*: -a *BA* spe⟨cie⟩mque *Burman*: spemque *PA* 22 beneuolentiae *Gelenius*: -ia *PA* 24 qua *PB*: quae *A* Crassi *P*: Cassi *BA* 29 Marco reducis *A*

cum ne pugnandi quidem egredien⟨di⟩ue occasio iis, in quan-
tum uoluerant, data esset †immunis, castigatis etiam quibusdam
graui poena quia Romanis et armis et animis usi fuissent, inclu-
sus siluis, paludibus, insidiis ab eo hoste ad internecionem trucida-
tus est quem ita semper more pecudum trucidauerat ut uitam
3 aut mortem eius nunc ira nunc uenia temperaret. duci plus ad
moriendum quam ad pugnandum animi fuit: quippe paterni
4 auitique exempli successor se ipse transfixit. at e praefectis
castrorum duobus quam clarum exemplum L. Eggius, tam
turpe Ceionius prodidit, qui, cum longe maximam partem ab-
sumpsisset acies, auctor deditionis supplicio quam proelio mori
maluit. at Vala Numonius, legatus Vari, cetera quietus ac
probus, diri auctor exempli, spoliatum equite peditem relin-
quens fuga cum aliis Rhenum petere ingressus est; quod factum
eius fortuna ulta est: non enim desertis superfuit sed desertor
5 occidit. Vari corpus semiustum hostium lacerauerat feritas;
caput eius abscisum latumque ad Maroboduum et ab eo
missum ad Caesarem gentilicii tamen tumuli sepultura hono-
ratum est.

120 His auditis reuolat ad patrem Caesar: perpetuus patronus Romani imperii adsuetam sibi causam suscipit. mittitur ad Germaniam, Gallias confirmat, disponit exercitus, praesidia munit, se magnitudine sua non fiducia hostium metiens qui

---

1 egredien⟨di⟩ue *Vossius*: egrediē *B*: egredie (*sed in* egregie *mutatum*) aut *A*: egregie aut *P*: aut egrediendi *Haase* 1–2 occasio iis...data esset *Vossius*: occasionis...d. e. *PA*: occasio nisi ⟨iniqua nec⟩...d. e. *Ellis*: occasiones... datae essent *Fröhlich*: *alii alia* in quantum uoluerant *secl. Gruter* 2 immunis *PA*, *obelo notaui*: ⟨potestas⟩ immunis *Rhenanus*: impune *Ruhnken*: ab inimicis *Heinsius*: *alii alia* 3 qui a Romanis...animi suis *A* 4 paludibus *Gelenius*: -dis *PA* 8 auitique *P*: auique *BA* exempli successor *PB*: s. e. *A* at e *P*: atque (*suprascr.* a te) *A* 9 L. Eggius tam *P*: legg. iustam *A* 10 Ceionius (*uel* Ceronius) *A*: C. Eionius *P* 12 Vala Numonius *Ursinus* (Val. Num. *iam Rhenanus*): Valnumonius *PA* ac *P*: et *A* 13 equite *Gelenius*: -em *PA* 14 fuga cum aliis *P*: fugatum aliis *BA*: fuga cum alis *Gelenius* 15 ultra *A* 16 hostium *P*: hosti *BA*: hostis *Kritz* lacerauerit *A* 17 abscissum *A* 18 tandem *Gelenius* 20 his auditis...(*p.* 80.6) reuertitur *post* exspiraret (*p.* 80.27) *transposuit Haase* 23 munit se *P*: munit et se *A et* (*ut uid.*) *coni. Burer* hostium *PA*: hostis *Haupt*

Cimbricam Teutonicamque militiam Italiae minabantur. ultro
2 Rhenum cum exercitu transgreditur ⟨et⟩ arma infert quae
arcuisse pater et patria contenti erant: penetrat interius, aperit
limites, uastat agros, urit domos, fundit obuios, maximaque
cum gloria (incolumi omnium, quos transduxerat, numero) in
hiberna reuertitur.

3 Reddatur uerum L. Asprenati testimonium, qui legatus sub
auunculo suo Varo militans naua uirilique opera duarum
legionum (quibus praeerat) exercitum immunem tanta calami-
tate seruauit, matureque ad inferiora hiberna descendendo
uacillantium etiam cis Rhenum sitarum gentium animos confir-
mauit. sunt tamen qui, ut uiuos ab eo uindicatos, ita iugulatorum
sub Varo occupata crediderint patrimonia hereditatemque
4 excisi exercitus, in quantum uoluerit, ab eo aditam. L. etiam
Caedicii praefecti castrorum, eorumque qui una circumdati
Alisone immensis Germanorum copiis obsidebantur, laudanda
uirtus est, qui omnibus difficultatibus superatis quas inopia
rerum intolerabiles, uis hostium faciebat inexsuperabiles, nec
temerario consilio nec segni prouidentia uicti, speculatique
5 opportunitatem, ferro sibi ad suos peperere reditum. ex quo
apparet Varum, sane grauem et bonae uoluntatis uirum, magis
imperatoris defectum consilio quam uirtute destitutum militum
6 se magnificentissimumque perdidisse exercitum. cum in cap-
tiuos saeuiretur a Germanis, praeclari facinoris auctor fuit Caldus
Coelius, ad uetustatem familiae suae dignissimus, qui complexus
catenarum (quibus uinctus erat) seriem, ita illas inlisit capiti
suo ut protinus pariter sanguinis cerebrique effluuio exspiraret.

121 Eadem et uirtus et fortuna subsequenti tempore ingressi Ger-

---

1 minabantur *P*: -batur *BA* ultro *A et coni. Freinsheim*: ultra *P* 2 ⟨et⟩ *Woodman* infert *Lipsius*: interfecti *PA* 3 arcuisse *Lipsius*: arg- *PA* penetrati *A* 4 obuios *P*: obulos *BA* 7 aspernati *A* 11 uacillantium etiam *PA*: uacillantes iam *Heinsius* Rhenum *Gelenius*: -o *PA* 14 occisi *A* 15 caeditii *A* 16 Alisone *Rhenanus*: a Lisone *P*: a lis- *A* 19 prouidentia *PB*: prudentia *A* uicti *E. Thomas*: uiti *B*: usi *P*: niti *A*: iuti *Heinsius* 21 graue m& bone *A* 25 Caelius *P* ad uetustatem *PA*: ad⟨ulescens⟩ uetustate *Ruhnken* 27 effluuio *Lipsius*: influuio *P*: in fluuio *A* 28 et uirtus *P*: et *om. A* sub sequenti *A* ingressi Germaniam *Bardili*: ingressa animam (-um *P*) *PBA*

maniam imperatoris Tiberii fuit quae initio fuerat. qui, concus-
sis hostium uiribus classicis peditumque expeditionibus, cum res
Galliarum maximae molis accensaque plebe Viennensium dis-
sensiones coercitione magis quam poena mollisset, senatus
populusque Romanus postulante patre eius, ut aequum ei ius in
omnibus prouinciis exercitibusque esset quam erat ipsi, decreto
complexus est. etenim absurdum erat non esse sub illo quae ab
2 illo uindicabantur, et qui ad opem ferendam primus erat, ad
uindicandum honorem non iudicari parem.

In urbem reuersus iam pridem debitum, sed continuatione
bellorum dilatum, ex Pannoniis Dalmatisque egit triumphum.
3 cuius magnificentiam quis miretur in Caesare? fortunae uero
quis non miretur indulgentiam? quippe omnes eminentissimos
hostium duces non occisos fama narrauit sed uinctos triumphus
ostendit (quem mihi fratrique meo inter praecipuos praecipuis-
que donis adornatos uiros comitari contigit).

122 Quis non inter reliqua, quibus singularis moderatio Ti.
Caesaris elucet atque eminet, hoc quoque non miretur quod,
cum sine ulla dubitatione septem triumphos meruerit, tribus
contentus fuit? quis enim dubitare potest quin ex Armenia
recepta et ex rege ⟨ei⟩ praeposito, cuius capiti insigne regium
sua manu imposuerat, ordinatisque rebus orientis ouans trium-
phare debuerit, et Vindelicorum Raetorumque uictor curru
2 urbem ingredi? fractis deinde post adoptionem continua triennii
militia Germaniae uiribus idem illi honor et deferendus et re-
cipiendus fuerit? et post cladem sub Varo acceptam, totius ***
prosperrimo rerum euentu eadem excisa Germania triumphus
summi ducis adornari debuerit? sed in hoc uiro nescias utrum

---

3 accensaque plebe *A*: accensaque plebis *B*: accensasque plebis *P* 4 coercitione *Gelenius*: coertione *PA* mollisset ⟨et⟩ *Rhenanus, retento* esset (7) 5 aequum ei ius *Rhenanus*: equum eius *PA* 6 quam *PA*: atque *Orelli* ipsi *Rhenanus*: ipse *PA* ⟨id⟩ decreto *Bothe* 7 est *Ellis*: esset *PA* 13 in diligentiam *A* 15 mihi *Burer*: militi *PA* 20 fuit *Haase*: fuerit *PA* 21 ⟨ei⟩ praeposito *Rhenanus*: praepositi *BA*: propositi *P* 26 totius *BA, post quod lacunam posui* (*fort.* ⟨militiae eius⟩): ocyus *P*: ⟨ex-spectato⟩ ocius *Halm* 27 triumphus *Heinsius*: -um *PA* 28 adornari *BA*: -re *P* nescis *A*

magis mireris quod laborum periculorumque semper excessit modum, an quod honorum temperauit.

123 Venitur ad tempus in quo fuit plurimum metus. quippe Caesar Augustus cum Germanicum nepotem suum reliqua belli patraturum misisset in Germaniam, Tiberium autem filium missurus esset in Illyricum ad firmanda pace quae bello subegerat, prosequens eum simulque interfuturus athletarum certamini ludicro quod eius honori sacratum a Neapolitanis est, processit in Campaniam. quamquam iam motus imbecillitatis inclinataeque in deterius principia ualetudinis senserat, tamen obnitente ui animi prosecutus filium digressusque ab eo Beneuenti ipse Nolam petiit; et ingrauescente in dies ualetudine, cum sciret quis uolenti omnia post se salua remanere accersendus foret, festinanter reuocauit filium: ille ad patrem patriae ex-
2 spectato reuolauit maturius. tum securum se Augustus praedicans circumfususque amplexibus Tiberii sui, commendans illi sua atque ipsius opera nec quicquam iam de fine, si fata poscerent, recusans, subrefectus primo conspectu alloquioque carissimi sibi spiritus, mox, cum omnem curam fata uincerent, in sua resolutus initia Pompeio Apuleioque consulibus septuagesimo sexto anno animam caelestem caelo reddidit.

124 Quid tunc homines timuerint, quae senatus trepidatio, quae populi confusio, quis orbis metus, in quam arto salutis exitiique fuerimus confinio, neque mihi tam festinanti exprimere uacat neque cui uacat potest. id solum uoce publica dixisse †habeo: cuius orbis ruinam timueramus, eum ne commotum quidem sensimus, tantaque unius uiri maiestas fuit ut nec bonis ***
2 neque contra malos opus armis foret. una tamen ueluti luctatio ciuitatis fuit, pugnantis cum Caesare senatus populique Romani ut stationi paternae succederet, illius ut potius aequalem ciuem

---

3 ad *P*: ab *A* 6 firmanda *Burer*: formanda *PBA* 7 eumque simul *A* 7–8 certamini *Cellarius*: -is *PA* 13 post se *P*: posse *A* accersendum *A* 14 patriae *secl. Acidalius* 14–15 expectatore uolauit *A* 19 spiritus *secl. Cludius* 20 consulibus *Burer*: COS. *PB*: $\overline{\text{cos}}$ *A* 21 et sexto *A* caelo *P*: deo *A* 23 orbis *P*: urbis *A et coni. Acidalius* 25 habeo *PA*, *obelo notaui*: aueo *Boot*: ⟨satis⟩ habeo *Ruhnken* 27 nec *P*: ne *A* *post* bonis *lacunam posui*: nec bonis contra malos opus armis foret *Orelli* 28 forent *A*

quam eminentem liceret agere principem. tandem magis ratione
quam honore uictus est, cum quicquid tuendum non suscepisset,
periturum uideret, solique huic contigit paene diutius recusare
principatum quam, ut occuparent eum, alii armis pugnauerant.
3 Post redditum caelo patrem et corpus eius humanis honoribus,
nomen diuinis honoratum, primum principalium eius operum
fuit ordinatio comitiorum quam manu sua scriptam diuus
4 Augustus reliquerat. quo tempore mihi fratrique meo, candi-
datis Caesaris, proxime a nobilissimis ac sacerdot⟨al⟩ibus uiris
destinari praetoribus contigit, consecutis ut neque post nos
quemquam diuus Augustus neque ante nos Caesar commendaret
Tiberius.

125 Tulit protinus ut uoti et consilii sui pretium res publica, neque
diu latuit aut quid non impetrando passuri fuissemus aut quid
impetrando profecissemus. quippe exercitus qui in Germania
militabat praesentisque Germanici imperio regebatur, simulque
legiones quae in Illyrico erant, rabie quadam et profunda con-
fundendi omnia cupiditate nouum ducem, nouum statum,
2 nouam quaerebant rem publicam; quin etiam ausi sunt minari
daturos senatui, daturos principi leges: modum stipendii, finem
militiae sibi ipsi constituere conati sunt. processum etiam in
arma, ferrumque strictum est, et paene in ultimam ⟨cladem⟩
gladiorum erupit impunitas, defuitque qui contra rem publicam
3 duceret, non qui sequerentur. sed haec omnia ueteris impera-
toris maturitas, multa inhibentis, aliqua cum grauitate polli-
centis, ⟨et⟩ inter seueram praecipue noxiorum ultionem mitis
4 aliorum castigatio breui sopiit ac sustulit. quo quidem tempore
ut pleraque ignouit Germanicus, ita Drusus (qui a patre in id

---

1 magis ratione *BA*: r. m. *P* 5 reditum *A* 6 numen *Krause* 8–9 candidatis *Gelenius*: candidatos *P*: candi (*del.*) candidatos *A* 9 sacerdot⟨al⟩ibus *Scheffer*: sacerdotibus *PA* 10 consecutis *P*: consecutisque *A*: consecutis quoque *Orelli*: c. quidem *Ellis* post annos *A* 13 ut...et *PA*: et...et *Gelenius*: ut...ita *Burman* 17 rabiem quandam *A* 20 ⟨se⟩ senatui *Orelli* 22 ultimam (*BA*: -um *P*) ⟨cladem⟩ *Woodman*: ultima *Vossius*: ultimam ⟨uim⟩ *Cornelissen* (*1887*) 26 ⟨et⟩ *Krause* noxiorum *Gronovius*: nostrorum *PA* 28 ignouit *ed. Bipont.*: ignaue *PA*: ⟨non⟩ ignaue *Ellis*: gnaue *Boeclerus*: egit naue *Ruhnken*: ign⟨oscendo egit gn⟩aue *E. Thomas* Drusus *Gelenius*: Brutus *PA*

ipsum plurimo quidem igne emicans incendium militaris tumultus missus erat) prisca antiquaque seueritate usus ancipitia sibi ⟨sus⟩tinere ⟨maluit⟩ quam exemplo perniciosa, et his ipsis militum gladiis, quibus obsessus erat, obsidentes coercuit,
5 singulari adiutore in eo negotio usus Iunio Blaeso, uiro nescias utiliore in castris an meliore in toga, qui post paucos annos proconsul in Africa ornamenta triumphalia cum appellatione imperatoria meruit.

†Ad Hispanias exercitumque† uirtutibus celeberrimaque in Illyrico militia praediximus, cum imperio obtineret, in summa pace ⟨et⟩ quiete continuit, cum ei pietas rectissima sentiendi et auctoritas quae sentiebat obtinendi superesset. cuius curam ac fidem Dolabella quoque, uir simplicitatis generosissimae, in maritima parte Illyrici per omnia imitatus est.

126 Horum XVI annorum opera quis cum inhaereant oculis animisque omnium, [in] partibus eloquatur? sacrauit parentem suum Caesar non imperio sed religione, non appellauit eum sed
2 fecit deum. reuocata in forum fides; summota e foro seditio, ambitio campo, discordia curia, sepultaeque ac situ obsitae iustitia, aequitas, industria ciuitati redditae; accessit magistratibus auctoritas, senatui maiestas, iudiciis grauitas; compressa theatralis seditio; recte faciendi omnibus aut incussa uoluntas
3 aut imposita necessitas: honorantur recta, praua puniuntur; suspicit potentem humilis non timet, antecedit non contemnit humiliorem potens. quando annona moderatior? quando pax laetior? diffusa in orientis occidentisque tractus et quicquid meridiano aut septentrione finitur pax augusta per omnes ter-

---

3 ⟨sus⟩tinere *Woodman*: timere *BA*: tam re *P*: tenere *Madvig*: tentare *Novák* (*1883*): sumere *Boot*: *alii alia* maluit *ante* quam *suppl. Woodman*, *post* sibi *Madvig* 9 ad Hispanias *B*: ac H. *P*: At H. *A* ad...exercitumque *obelis notaui*: ac ⟨quum⟩ Hispanias *Cludius*: at H. exercitumque ⟨in iis cum M. Lepidus, de cuius⟩ uirtutibus *Madvig* 11 ⟨et⟩ *Orelli*: ⟨ac⟩ *Rhenanus* 15 inhaereant *Orelli*: inserta sint *P*: insera *BA* 16 in *secl. Vossius* 17 eum *secl. Gruter* 19 curia *uulg.*: -iae *PA* sepultaeque *BA*: sepultae *P* obsitae *Gelenius*: oppositae *PBA* 20–1 magistratibus *Gelenius*: militibus *PA* 22 infusa *Ruhnken* 27 per *secl. Haase*: per ⟨omnia⟩ *Ruhnken*

rarum orbis angulos * a latrociniorum metu seruat immunes.
4 fortuita non ciuium tantummodo sed urbium damna principis munificentia uindicat: restitutae urbes Asiae, uindicatae ab iniuriis magistratuum prouinciae; honor dignis paratissimus, poena in malos sera sed aliqua. superatur aequitate gratia,
5 ambitio uirtute: nam facere recte ciues suos princeps optimus faciendo docet, cumque sit imperio maximus, exemplo maior est.

127 Raro eminentes uiri non magnis adiutoribus ad gubernandam fortunam suam usi sunt, ut duo Scipiones duobus Laeliis, quos per omnia aequauerunt sibi, ut diuus Augustus M. Agrippa et proxime ab eo Statilio Tauro, quibus nouitas familiae haud obstitit quominus ad multiplices consulatus triumphosque et
2 complura eueherentur sacerdotia. etenim magna negotia magnis adiutoribus egent †neque in parua paucitas ministeria defecit† interestque rei publicae quod usu necessarium est, dignitate
3 eminere utilitatemque auctoritate muniri. sub his exemplis Ti. Caesar Seianum Aelium, principe equestris ordinis patre natum, materno uero genere clarissimas ueteresque et insignes honoribus complexum familias, habentem consulares fratres, consobrinos, auunculum, ipsum uero laboris ac fidei capacissimum, sufficiente etiam uigori animi compage corporis, singularem principalium onerum adiutorem in omnia habuit atque habet,
4 uirum priscae seueritatis, laetissimae hilaritatis, actu otiosis simillimum, nihil sibi uindicantem eoque adsequentem omnia,

---

1 *post* angulos *lacunam posui*: angulos ⟨nos⟩ *Heinsius* ⟨homines⟩ immunes *Cornelissen* (*1887*) 5 aliqua *PA*: aequa *Lipsius*: *alii alia* 6 principes *A* optime *Mommsen* 10 usi *P*: uisi *A* 12 proxime *Scheffer*: maxime *PA* 12–13 haud obstitit *P*: haut o. A^{mg}: aut stilit *A* 13 quominus *P*: dominus *A* consulatos *A* 14 eueherentur *Vascosanus*: enumerentur *B*: enumerarentur *P*: nominentur (*del.*) numerentur *A*: eniterentur *Gelenius* 15 neque in parua (-o *A*)...defecit (def&it *A*) *PA*, *obelis notauit Ellis*, *secl. Vossius, Boeclerus*: atque impar capacitas ministeria deficit *Madvig*: neque in parua paucitas ministerii sufficit *Kreyssig*: *alii alia* 16 est *Ruhnken*: et *P*: e *A* 17 muniri *Gelenius*: -re *PA* 18 equestris (*ult.* s *del.*) *A* 20 familiās (s *del.*) *A* 22 uigore *A* 24 priscae seueritatis, laetissimae hilaritatis *Bothe*: s. l. h. p. *PA* 25 eoq. (q *del.*, *suprascr.* quod) *A*

semperque infra aliorum aestimationes se metientem, uultu
uitaque tranquillum, animo exsomnem.

128 In huius uirtutum aestimatione iam pridem iudicia ciuitatis
cum iudiciis principis certant, neque nouus hic mos senatus
populique Romani est putandi quod optimum sit, esse nobilissi-
mum. nam et illi antiqui ⟨qui⟩ ante primum bellum Punicum
abhinc annos CCC Ti. Coruncanium, hominem nouum, cum
aliis omnibus honoribus tum pontificatu etiam maximo ad
2 principale extulere fastigium; et ⟨qui⟩ equestri loco natum Sp.
Caruilium et mox M. Catonem, nouum etiam Tusculo, urbis
inquilinum, Mummiumque Achaicum in consulatus, censuras
3 et triumphos prouexere; et qui C. Marium ignotae originis usque
ad sextum consulatum sine dubitatione Romani nominis ha-
buere principem; et qui M. Tullio tantum tribuere ut paene
adsentatione sua quibus uellet principatus conciliaret; quique
nihil Asinio Pollioni negauerunt quod nobilissimis summo cum
sudore consequendum foret, profecto hoc senserunt, in cuius-
cumque animo uirtus inesset, ei plurimum esse tribuendum.
4 haec naturalis exempli imitatio ad experiendum Seianum Cae-
sarem, ad iuuanda uero onera principis Seianum propulit, sena-
tumque et populum Romanum eo perduxit ut quod usu optimum
intellegit, id in tutelam securitatis suae libenter aduocet.

129 Sed proposita quasi uniuersa principatus Ti. Caesaris ⟨ima-
gine⟩, singula recenseamus. qua ille prudentia Rhascupolim,
interemptorem fratris sui filii Cotyis consortisque eiusdem
imperii, Romam euocauit, singulari in eo negotio usus opera
Flacci Pomponii consularis, uiri nati ad omnia quae recte fa-

---

1 semperque *BA*: semper *P* se metientem *P*: sencientem *A* 2 exomnem *A* 3 uirtutum aestimatione *P*: -em -em *BA* 6 illi antiqui ante primum bellum *P*: ⟨qui⟩ *Halm*: illi primi ante bellum *A* 7 Ti. Coruncanium *BA*: T. Coruncanum *P* 8 honoribus pontificatum *A* 9 et equestri *P*, *inter quae uerba* qui *supplendum*: et eque aequestri *A*, *ex quibus* et qui equestri *perperam coni. Fröhlich* 14 Tullio *Lipsius*: Fuluio *PA* 15 consiliaret *A* 20 propulit *Acidalius*: -tulit *PA* 21 perduxit *P*: prod- *BA* 23 quasi *PA*: imagine *Friebel* Caesaris ⟨imagine⟩ *Sinko*: C. ⟨forma⟩ *Rhenanus*: *alii alia* 24 singulare censeamus *A* Rhascuporim *Stegmann* 25 Cotyis *Heinsius*: Cotys *P*: cotyss *A* 26 Romam *Ursinus*: formam *PBA*, *secl. Rhenanus olim et Burer* opere *A*

cienda sunt, simplicique uirtute merentis semper quam captan-
2 tis gloriam. cum quanta grauitate ut senator et iudex, non ut
princeps *** et causas pressius audit ***! quam celeriter in-
gratum * et noua molientem oppressit! quibus praeceptis in-
structum Germanicum suum imbutumque rudimentis militiae
secum actae domitorem recepit Germaniae! quibus iuuentam
eius exaggerauit honoribus, respondente cultu triumphi rerum,
3 quas gesserat, magnitudini! quotiens populum congiariis hono-
rauit senatorumque censum, cum id senatu auctore facere
potuit, quam libenter expleuit, ut neque luxuriam inuitaret
neque honestam paupertatem pateretur dignitate destitui!
quanto cum honore Germanicum suum in transmarinas misit
prouincias! qua ui consiliorum suorum, ministro et adiutore
usus Druso filio suo, Maroboduum inhaerentem occupati regni
finibus (pace maiestatis eius dixerim) uelut serpentem abstru-
sam terra salubribus consiliorum suorum medicamentis coegit
egredi! quam illum ut honorate ita secure continet! quantae
molis bellum principe Galliarum ciente Sacrouiro Floroque
Iulio mira celeritate ac uirtute compressit, ut ante populus
Romanus uicisse se quam bellare cognosceret nuntiosque peri-
4 culi uictoriae praecederet nuntius! magni etiam terroris bellum
Africum et cotidiano auctu maius auspiciis consiliisque eius
breui sepultum est.

130 Quanta suo suorumque nomine exstruxit opera! quam pia
munificentia superque humanam euecta fidem templum patri
molitur! quam magnifico animi temperamento Cn. quoque
Pompei munera absumpta igni restituit, qui quicquid umquam
2 claritudine eminuit, id ueluti cognatum censet tuendum! qua

1 quam *PA*: ⟨num⟩quam *Orelli*: ⟨magis⟩ quam *Vascosanus* 3 *post* princeps *lacunam posuit Kritz*: princeps et ⟨Caesar⟩ causas *ed. Bipont.*: princeps causas *Aldus* pressius *PA*: praesens *Lipsius*: princeps et praeses causas *Acidalius* *post* audit *lacunam posui* 3–4 *post* ingratum *lacunam posui*: ⟨Archelaum⟩ ingratum *Krause*: ⟨Clementem⟩ ing. *Vossius*: ⟨Libonem⟩ ing. *Gelenius* 7 respondente *P*: -em *BA* 16 terra *Cludius*: -ae *PA* consiliorum suorum *secl. Ruhnken* 17 quam *P*: quō (*uel* quib) *A* (*ut uid.*) ita *Novák* (*1906*): nec *PA*: sic *Burman*: et hon. nec *Gelenius* 18 sacro uiro floreque *A* 20 se *om. A* 24 suo *Acidalius*: sua *PA* 27 qui quicquid umquam *Rhenanus*: qui quidem quam *PA*

liberalitate cum alias tum proxime incenso monte Caelio omnis
ordinis hominum iacturae patrimonio succurrit suo! quanta
cum quiete hominum rem perpetui praecipuique timoris, sup-
plementum, sine trepidatione dilectus prouidet!

3 Si aut natura patitur aut mediocritas recipit hominum, audeo
cum deis queri. quid hic meruit primum ut scelerata Drusus
Libo iniret consilia, deinde ut Silium Pisonemque tam ***
alterius dignitatem constituit, auxit alterius? ut ad maiora
transcendam (quamquam et haec ille duxit maxima), quid ut
4 iuuenes amitteret filios? quid ut nepotem ex Druso suo? dolenda
adhuc rettulimus; ueniendum ad erubescenda est. quantis hoc
triennium, M. Vinici, doloribus lacerauit animum eius! quam
diu abstruso (quod miserrimum est) pectus eius flagrauit in-
cendio quod ex nuru, quod ex nepote dolere, indignari, erubes-
5 cere coactus est! cuius temporis aegritudinem auxit amissa
mater, eminentissima et per omnia deis quam hominibus simi-
lior femina, cuius potentiam nemo sensit nisi aut leuatione
periculi aut accessione dignitatis.

131 Voto finiendum uolumen est. Iuppiter Capitoline, et auctor
ac stator Romani nominis Gradiue Mars, perpetuorumque
custos Vesta ignium, et quicquid numinum hanc Romani imperii
molem in amplissimum terrarum orbis fastigium extulit, uos
publica uoce obtestor atque precor, custodite, seruate, protegite
2 hunc statum, hanc pacem, ⟨hunc principem⟩, eique functo
longissima statione mortali destinate successores quam serissi-
mos, sed eos quorum ceruices tam fortiter sustinendo terrarum
orbis imperio sufficiant quam huius suffecisse sensimus, con-
siliaque omnium ciuium aut pia ***

---

1 Caelio *A*: -i *P* 5–6 audeo cum deis *Heinsius*: auro deo cum de his *PA* 7 *post* tam *lacunam posuit Rhenanus*: tam ⟨infestos haberet, quorum⟩ *Burman* 9 duxit *Rhenanus*: dixit *PA* 10 Druso suo *Burer*: Drusuo *B*: Druso *PA* 11 est *BA*, *om. P* 12 Vinicii *B* 14 dolore *A* 14–15 erubescere *BA*, *om. P* 15 egreditudinem *A* 19 est *Orelli*: sit *PA* 19–20 Capitoline et auctor ac (*B*: et *PA*) stator *PA*: Capitoline et stator, et auctor *Puteanus*: Cap., et auctor ac sator *Ursinus* 21 numinum hanc Romani *P* (hanc Romani A^{mg}): nominum honor omni *BA* 24 pacem *P*: pacemq. (q *del.*) *A*: patrem *Damsté*: ducem *Perizonius* ⟨hunc principem⟩ *Lipsius* 26 eos *P*: eorum *A* 28 'Videtur hic parum deesse in hac perorationcula uoticia' *Rhenanus*

LECTIONES ADDENDAE

To page 59

1 temporm (*del.*) temporū *A* 18 caerem (*del.*), *suprascr.* Caesarem *A* 18 deinde (*del.*), *suprascr.* $\overline{\text{in}}$ *A*

To page 60

3 Rhetos *P* 4 d& (*del.*) derecta *A*: dir- *P* 8 planci & pauli *A* 14 Agrippe *A* 17 Admomit (*ut uid.*, *del.*) Admouit *A* 23 pannoriorum (*del.*), *suprascr.* pannonicorum *A* Delmatarumque *BA*

To page 61

10 armis (*del.*) artibus *A* 17 omneis parteis *P*: -is -is *A*

To page 62

3 *post* breui *nescioquid deletum est in A* $_8$Tib. *P*: T. *A* 12 uictrico *A* 14 quae digredientium A^{mg} 18 legatique *A*

To page 63

1 In (*del.*), *suprascr.* in *A* 4 libido (*del.*), *suprascr.* libidine *A* 5 pecandi *A* 10 arctissimam *P* 14 uil (*del.*) uiolata *A* 15 uxorem (*del.*), *suprascr.* coniugem *A* 21 T. *A* 23 sufficiat (*del.*) deficiat *A* 27 imperatorum (ratorum *del.*) riorum *A*

To page 64

5 Caium *P* 6 Lolli *PA* 7 iuuaentae *A* 10 uoluntaria uolu (*posterius del.*) *A* 15 cum (*del.*), *suprascr.* cui *A* 18 *post* habere *nescioquid deletum est in A* 21 ^{orbis} (*del.*) terrarum orbis *A* 28 COS. *P*: $\overline{\text{cos}}$ *A*

To page 65

6 eum (*del.*), *suprascr.* eo *A* 11 celo manuq. spem quae *A*

To page 66

2 tribunatū (*postr. litt. del.*) *A* 4 mei (*del.*) patris mei *A* 6 medio-

critas (*corr. in* -tatis) mae (*del.*), *suprascr.* meae *A* 26 pacientem *A* 27 cōliberaliter (*del.*) otio liberaliter *A*

To page 67

9 in sequentia (a *del.*) *A* 11 egentes (*prima litt. del.*) *A* 17 ante alpes (*del.*), *suprascr.* antea spes *A* 18 quadrigentesimum *A* 18–19 Aibim *A* 24 omnium *suprascr. A* 26 Nont (*del.*), *suprascr.* Non *A*

To page 68

5 est (*del.*) est ex *A* 8 lynthre *A* 12 ho (*ut uid.*) *A* 13 ill (*del.*) ullum *A* 17 in (*del.*) inuiolatoq. *A* 22 Marcomanorum *P* que Maraboduo *A*

To page 69

1 progredi. Vbi *A* 7 *post* fastigium *deleta sunt prius nescioquid, dein* rebat *in A* 9 sibi *suprascr. A* legatos (*corr. in* -ti) *A* 10 Caesarem (*corr. in* -es) *A* 15 opi *A* 17 dexrram *P* 19 tuebatur (*del.*) timebatur *A* ingrementi *A* paciebatur *A* 22 passum *A* 25 Herciniae *A*

To page 70

3 Marcomanos *P* 25 maturae *A*

To page 71

5 il (*del.*) huius *A* 7 delectus *P* 22 uires *B*: uireis *P*: uiris *A*

To page 72

3 se *suprascr. A* 4 forte *suprascr. A* 13 arbitrium ducis (*posterius del.*) *A* 19 craum (*suprascr.* circum-) fusa *A* 24 aput *A* 25 Militis (*ut uid., del.*), *suprascr.* militis *A*

To page 73

2 ducis (*del.*), *suprascr.* imperatoris *A* 5 castrorumq. (q *del.*) *A* 14 suo *suprascr. A* 19 $\overline{\text{LXX}}$. *P*: LXX *A* 20 adhoc *P*

To page 74

3–4 et ipse asperrime...egressus *A*[mg] 13 laetitia (*del.*), *suprascr.* lectica *A*

18 aditiam *A* 19 que retuli *A* 25 Hyems *P*: hiemps *A* 26 reliquis (*del.*), *suprascr.* reliquiis *A*

To page 75

4 uniuersam *suprascr. A* Pinetem *PA* (*cf. p.* 70.21) 10 intelligere *P* 12 Delmatici *P* 15 donorum (onorum *del.*) honorum *A* 23 auspitiis *A* 26 consumauit *A* 27 Delm- *B*

To page 76

11 Delm- *BA* ne (*del.*) in *A* 12 difficileis *P* 13–14 Delm- *BA* 26 $\overset{\text{dl}}{\text{apiscendi}}$ *A* Alicinius (*del.*), *suprascr.* Alicinius *A* 27 nequi *A* 28 minatus (n *del.*, *corr. in* r) *A*

To page 77

16 declarauerat (uerat *del.*) uit *A* 22 pacis *uel* paces (*del.*) pacis *A* iuris ditionibus *A*

To page 78

3 mediis (*del.*) mediis *A* 12 'securitatis *inducto* -is *et* -eis *substituto, mox, toto hoc inducto,* securitatis *suprascript. A*' (*Ellis*) 18 habet *suprascr. A*

To page 79

11 suplitio *A* 17 Meroboduum *A* 18 Gentilitii *A* 23 mentiens (*del.*) metiens *A*

To page 80

3 $\overline{\text{prt}}$ (*del.*) pater *A* contentierant *A* 4 *post* uastat *nescioquid deletum est in A* 8 gnaua *A* 18 intolerabileis...inexuperabileis *P*: -is...-es *A* 20 pepererunt (*del.*) peperere *A* 27 expiret (*corr. in* expiraret) *A*

To page 81

1–2 concussis (*del.*), *suprascr.* concussis *A* 14 ut (*del.*) fama *A* 17–18 T. Caesaris *A* 23 Vind (*del.*) Vindelicorum praetorumque, *suprascr.* Rhaetorum (h *del.*) *A* 26 a (*del.*, *suprascr.* sub) Varo *A*

LECTIONES ADDENDAE

To page 82

2 aut (*del.*) an *A* 6–7 sub (*del.*) subegerat *A* 18 subref& tus *A*
B a
22 trepidatio senatus *A* (*sic*) 23 si (*ut uid.*, *del.*) exitiique *A*

To page 83

13 qsilii fui (*posterius del.*) sui *A* 15 proficissemus *A* 18 omnia (*del.*) confundendi omnia *A*

To page 84

5 Bleso *PA* 7 apellatione *A* 12 optinendi *A* 17 apellauit *A* 19 am (*del.*) ambitio *A* discordia (*del.*) discordia *A* 21 maiestatis *suprascr.* maiestas *A* 26–7 quidquid...semptentrione *A*

To page 85

14 complurae (*corr. in* -ra, *ut uid.*) *A* 17 auctoritaten (*del.*) utilitatemque *A* 17–18 T. Caesar *A* 22 conpage *A* 24–5 uitio (*del.*) otiosis similimum *A*

To page 86

10 tusulo (*del.*) Tusculo *A* 20 uero (*del.*) adiuuanda uero *A*

To page 87

6 actis (*del.*) actae *A* 9 a (*del.*) senatu *A* 22 m *uel* in (*del.*) auctu *A*

To page 88

3 cum inquiete (in *del.*) *A* 10 Dolenda (Do *del.*, *suprascr.* Do) *A*
t
14 quod ex nuru *A*

COMMENTARY

Velleii Paterculi V.'s *praenomen* is unknown. Rhenanus inconsistently offers *P.* on the title page of the *ed. pr.*, but *C.* on the first page of his text; A offers no *praenomen* at all, while Priscian introduces a stray quotation from V.'s work with *M. Velleius Paterculus* (*Inst.* 6.63). For discussion see Sumner 277–8 n. 124; also Bolaffi v (n. 1).

Historiarum ad M. Vinicium consulem Rhenanus gave to V.'s work the title *Historia Romana ad M. Vinicium consulem*, but the aptness of *Romana* has been questioned by Lipsius and Sauppe 47 on the grounds that the work, esp. its early part, contains also non-Roman material. (This objection is discounted by Kritz xix–xx.) At the end of Book 1 A writes *Vellei Paterculi ad M. Vinitium liber primus explicit*, and at the beginning of Book 2 *Vellei Paterculi ad Q. Vinicium liber secundus*; but the omission of *consulem* is unfortunate, since it is clearly important that the work was dedicated to M. Vinicius as consul (cf. 101.3n., below). Whether V. chose a title which proclaimed the particular genre of historiography to which his work belongs, the genre of the summary universal history (see Woodman (1975), 282–7), is unknown; if so, it is difficult to conjecture what that title might have been (ib. 284 nn. 4–5). In the absence of any ancient evidence, Bothe's suggestion, printed here, at least has the merit of avoiding the objections which may be brought against what is found in P and A respectively.

94–98 THE YEARS 23–7 B.C.

The primary purpose of this section is to portray Tiberius as a young man whose exceptional promise was fulfilled by early successes at home and, particularly, abroad. Ch. 94 is full of such expressions as 'qui protinus quantus est, sperari potuerat' (2), while two later chapters are structured to stress the happy outcome of Tiberius' activities (pp. 105 f., 110). The present emphasis on hope and achievement makes Tiberius' subsequent retirement to Rhodes all the more dramatic (99.2–4).

We should however note that V. does not concentrate exclusively upon Tiberius. The credit for the Alpine war is given equally to Tiberius and his brother (95.2 'uterque...perdomuerunt'); the extraneous item on Plancus and Paulus (95.3) indicates V.'s readiness obliquely to criticise Augustus' activities despite the veneration in which he was held by Tiberius (pp. 103–4); the account of the German wars gives pride of place to Drusus (p. 110), and Tiberius' own mission to Germany is correctly acknowledged to have been the completion of what Drusus had begun (97.4n.); finally, V. gives as much space to L. Piso and Thrace in ch. 98 as he did to the combined activities in both Pannonia and Germany of Tiberius.

The year 12 B.C. was of great significance in Tiberius' career (above, p. 47), and it may be felt that V. reaches it all too quickly (96.1). But we should remember that Dio (53.19.4–5), discussing the difficulties of writing imperial history, singled out the magnitude of the empire and the multiplicity of simultaneous events which took place. The difficulty is increased for a summary historian such as V., whose terms of reference demand that he should give only an *imago* of Augustus' principate (89.6: see Woodman (1975), 282–7, esp. 284f.). It is true that his narrative becomes more expansive when it eventually deals with those things in which he took part himself (101ff.); but its present highly restricted nature requires that he should deal with these earlier events not chronologically but by areas of activity. Hence the contemporaneous wars in Pannonia, Germany and Thrace are each allotted separate chapters (96.2–3, 97, 98);[1] and in the same way other significant events of the period up to 12 B.C. have already been mentioned in earlier chapters (e.g. Augustus' refusal of dictatorship at 89.5, the pacification of Spain in ch. 90, the conspiracy of Caepio and Murena at 93.1).

94.1–3 TIBERIUS' CHARACTER AND QUAESTORSHIP

94.1 Hoc tractu temporum 24/23 B.C. (below, 3n.). *tractus*, usually a 'tract' of land, was first used metaphorically by Lucr. of a period of time (1.1008, 5.1216), and so again by Val. Max. 8.13 *ext.* 2 and, as Professor D. A. West points out, by Sen. *Oed.* 851 'obducta longo temporum tractu moues'. For V. the phrases *hoc tractu temporum* (also at 1.6.4, 78.1, cf. 1.7.2) and *eodem tractu temporum* (2.9.1, 10.2, cf. 1.15.3) are mannerisms. Klebs (290 and n. 14), observing that *tractus* in this sense occurs in no subsequent historian except Sulp. Sev., who closely follows V.'s set phraseology, reasonably concludes that Sulp. has been influenced by V. (cf. *Chron.* 1.13.6, 2.5.1, 2.9.3 etc.).

Ti. Claudius Nero... On this, the first occasion on which the future emperor is formally introduced into the narrative, he is given his full name as it was before his adoption by Augustus (cf. *PIR*² 2.219), and also a full-length character sketch which comprises the conventional elements *genus, pueritia, forma, ingenium* etc. This is in line with V.'s practice elsewhere (see above, p. 41).

quo trimo (ut praediximus) Liuia... At 79.2. Octavian married the nineteen-year-old Livia on 17 January 38 B.C. (EJ p. 46 top). For her see *PIR*² 5.73–9, no. 301; *RE* 13.900–24 = Livius 37 (Ollendorff); also below, 130.5n.

[1] Thus the latest date in this section, 7 B.C., occurs not at 98.3 but at 97.4. For V.'s tendency to write by topics cf. 1.14.1, 38.1; Woodman, *EA* 8–9.

Drusi Claudiani filia, despondente Ti. Nerone...nupta fuerat Ruhnken would reject these words as interpolated from 75.3 and 79.2, but Kritz rightly follows Fröhlich in noting that a reference to Tiberius' mother is most appropriate at the beginning of a character sketch of the future emperor (see above): she had, after all, married the most powerful individual in the Roman world. Compare the brief and relevant remarks of G. T. Griffith on similar repetitions in Thucydides' character sketches (*PCPS* 7 (1961), 22).

For M. Livius Drusus Claudianus, Livia's father, cf. *PIR*² 5.71–2, no. 294; *RE* 13.881–4 = Livius 19 (Münzer); for Ti. Claudius Nero, Tiberius' father, cf. *RE* 3.2777–8 = Claudius 254 (Münzer).

94.2 innutritus caelestium praeceptorum disciplinis *praeceptorum* is the gen. pl. of *praeceptum* (so H–W), not of *praeceptor* (Shipley, Michels 13, Lana 270). This is the 'heavenly advice' which the infant Tiberius received in the home of his newly adoptive father, the emperor Augustus. Horace confirms: 'quid mens rite, quid indoles | nutrita faustis sub penetralibus | posset, quid Augusti paternus | in pueros animus Nerones' (*C.* 4.4.25–8). Time and again Horace may be used to illustrate V. (see e.g. 97.2n.) – and vice versa, a fact which Nisbet–Hubbard rightly recognise in their commentary on the *Odes*. The resemblance between the two authors makes V.'s exclusion of Horace from his literary survey all the more remarkable (36.3).

For *innutritus* cf. Sen. *Cons. Pol.* 2.5 'liberalibus disciplinis...innutritus'; *celsitudo*, which occurs in the next colon, is previously unknown in extant Latin.

quantus est, sperari potuerat For the indic. in subord. clauses in or. obl., found particularly in historical writing, cf. K–S 2.542ff., L–H–S 547–8. Cornelissen (1877), 51, objected to *sperari*, but cf. Prop. 4.7.13 'perfide nec cuiquam melior sperande puellae'.

uisuque praetulerat principem The appearance or 'look' of a ruler was particularly important (cf. Eur. fr. 15.2N² quoted by Ursinus, πρῶτον μὲν εἶδος ἄξιον τυραννίδος). The classic instance is Alexander, whose special relationship with the divine powers is symbolised on statues by his beauty of countenance and eyes gazing heavenwards, and who was seen as the sun (cf. H. P. L'Orange, *Apotheosis in ancient portraiture* (1947), 11ff., 34ff.). In Rome Sulla was remarkable for his blonde hair (Plut. *Sulla* 6.12f.), and V. himself states of him that 'quidam magi ex notis corporis respondissent caelestem eius uitam et memoriam futuram' (24.3). Subsequent leaders, notably Pompey and Caesar, found a convenient model in Alexander (cf. D. Michel, *Alexander als Vorbild für Pompeius, Caesar u. Marcus Aurelius* (1967); also Weinstock 37f.). There is a corresponding symbolism in the Roman literary tradition, esp. with ref. to Augustus. In *Ecl.* 1 Virgil's herdsman sees Aug. as a god (7 'erit ille mihi semper deus') and will remember his *uultus* for ever (63 'quam nostro illius labatur pectore uultus'); in *Aen.* 1 Virgil describes Aeneas/Augustus as 'os umerosque deo similis', whose mother Venus 'laetos oculis adflarat honores' (589–91: see Weinstock 24–6). Horace describes Aug. as the sun (*C.* 4.2.46–7), and his *uultus* (in contrast to that of the tyrant, *C.* 3.3.3) shines upon his people: 'uultus ubi tuus | adfulsit populo' (*C.* 4.5.6–7).[1] Tacitus records that at Actium 'diuus Augustus *uultu et aspectu*... legiones exterruit' (*A.* 1.42.3, cf. Liv. 28.26.14); Suet. describes Aug. as having 'oculos...claros ac nitidos, quibus etiam *existimari uolebat inesse quiddam diuini uigoris*, gaudebatque si qui sibi acrius contuenti *quasi ad fulgorem solis* uoltum submitteret' (*Aug.* 79.2). See further Grant, *FITA* 357f.; Gutzwiller on *Pan. Lat.* 3.6.4.

Suet. also tells us (*Tib.* 68.2) that Tiberius had *praegrandes oculi* which had the unusual ability of seeing in the dark when first awakened from sleep; and on the coins and statues of the emperor which have survived, the eyes are in fact often given unusual treatment (cf. R. P. Hinks, *JRS* 23 (1933), 34f.; E. H. Swift, *AJA* 25 (1921), 248ff., with plates viii and ix). Moreover, although Tiberius notoriously refused to promote his own divinity (126.4n.) and rigidly controlled the erection of statues to himself (Suet. *Tib.* 26.1, Dio 57.9.1), nevertheless his portraits regularly depict his eyes as having a 'distinctive upward cast' (Swift, art. cit. 251, 253). In addition, most extant portraits of Tiberius represent the emperor as youthful, which is remarkable since we expect such portraits to have been set up mainly during his reign as *princeps* – i.e. between his fifty-fifth and seventy-ninth years. Yet Swift has explained this phenomenon by referring to Tiberius' early achievements in Armenia, the Alps and Pannonia.[2] Tiberius 'thereby established, as it were,

---

[1] These last two exs. happen to illustrate a further ancient belief, that the look of a ruler could signify his favour or displeasure: cf. Isoc. *Evag.* 24, Headlam on Herod. 4.73. The idea derives from the identical belief concerning the look of a god, e.g. Hes. *Theog.* 81f., Hor. *C.* 4.3.1–2, Calp. Sic. 7.76ff.; K. Meuli, *MH* 12 (1955), 208 n. 5. For biblical exs. cf. Anderson on Psalms 31.17, 67.1; T. Blatter, *Macht u. Herrschaft Gottes* (1962), 118.

[2] Swift, art. cit. 257. He there also asserts that in 20 B.C. Tiberius personally received back the standards which Crassus had lost to the Parthians at Carrhae. This action, for which the only evidence is Suet. *Tib.* 9.1, would naturally strengthen his suggestion. But whether Tiberius in fact achieved this success must, I think, remain doubtful: K. Krämer rightly observes that V. 'hätte es als Geschichtsschreiber des Tiberius sicher nicht unterlassen, von der Übernahme der Feldzeichen durch diesen zu berichten, wenn Tiberius sie wirklich in Empfang genommen hätte' ('Zur Rückgabe der Feldzeichen im Jahre 20 v. Chr.', *Historia* 22 (1973), 363). It is of course possible that, if there is to be a lacuna at 94.4 (see n.), V. there

his prospects for the succession to the throne' and 'there can be no doubt that his victories were celebrated by the erection of many statues in his honor. In all probability, therefore, it was at this time that the prevailing youthful type of Tiberian portrait was established.' If Swift's hypothesis is true, then V.'s statement that early in his career Tiberius *uisu praetulerat principem* is also true – not only symbolically but also iconographically.

For the continuance of the tradition after Tiberius' reign see e.g. Sen. *Apoc.* 4.1 (line 22) where Apollo is made to describe Nero as 'mihi similis uultu similisque decore'; later still, an inscription describes Gallienus as 'dis animo uultuque compar' (*CIL* 3.8193).

For V.'s phraseology cf. 118.2 'ardorem animi uultu oculisque praeferens'; Burman quotes Mart. 5.61.9 'procuratorem uultu qui praeferat ipso'. For a general study of the emperor's iconography cf. L. Polacco, *Il volto di Tiberio* (1955).

94.3 quaestor undeuicesimum annum agens capessere coepit rem publicam Tiberius was elected quaestor in 24 B.C. (Dio 53.28.3–4), and started his political career in that office in December of that year (cf. 111.4n.) when he was 'in his nineteenth year': he did not attain the age of nineteen until 16 November 23. Thus B. Levick is correct in saying that V. writes 'with precision' ('The beginning of Tiberius' career', *CQ* 21 (1971), 480 with n. 4); but she confuses the issue by referring to her earlier paper (1966), 238f., where she claims that the phrase *annum agens* is ambiguous. It is not, at least in V.'s usage: at 61.4 'in his twentieth year ⟨but not yet 20⟩', and 97.4 'in his thirtieth year ⟨but not yet 30⟩', are correct references to Octavian and Drusus in 43 and 9 B.C. respectively.

As to which quaestorship Tiberius held, Mommsen (*Staatsr.* 2^3.571 n. 1) and others suggested that he was *quaestor Ostiensis*; and Levick, in agreement, claims that 'the language of Vell. seems to answer the question', presumably with ref. to the word *Ostiae* in the next clause. But in fact V.'s language implies the opposite. If Tiberius had been *quaestor Ostiensis*, he would have dealt with the corn supply *ex officio* and not, as V. explicitly states, *mandato uitrici*. If, on the other hand, Tiberius had been some other quaestor but was delegated by Aug. to alleviate the corn supply (which is what Suet. *Tib.* 8 implies, as Levick is compelled to admit), then V.'s language *mandato uitrici* has point.

In a cogent and ingenious article ('The quaestorship of Ti. Nero', *Mnem.* 27 (1974), 160–72), E. Badian has argued that Tiberius began the year as *quaestor consulis*, the consul being of course Aug. himself (for the 11th time).

---

confirmed Suetonius' statement. But if so, we should expect him also to have mentioned Tiberius at 91.1 'ab oriente ac rege Parthorum signa Romana...Augusto remissa sunt'.

In this role Tiberius would act in co-ordination with the *quaestor Ostiensis* by command of the consul, who was his step-father (hence *mandato uitrici*); he would also administer *in Rome* the twelve distributions of corn to which Aug. himself refers at *RG* 15.1 'consul undecimum xii frumentationes frumento priuatim coempto emensus sum' (hence 'Ostiae *atque in urbe*', as V. says). Such an appointment would also explain, as Badian points out, how Tiberius also found time to investigate the *ergastula* in the same year (Suet. *Tib.* 8).

Half-way through 23 B.C. Aug. resigned from the consulship, more or less for ever. What became of Tiberius, the consul's quaestor? His duties did not terminate on that account. Badian argues, in my opinion decisively, that Tiberius thereupon became *quaestor Caesaris*, an office which carried much distinction in later years and of which Tiberius was, suitably, the first holder.

ac rei frumentariae inopiam Bothe would reject these words as spurious after *difficultatem annonae*, but V. is fond of such 'Ciceronian' fullness (97.2n.), and indeed Cicero himself has 'difficultatem annonae summamque inopiam rei frumentariae' at *Dom.* 12. Cornelissen (1877), 55, repeated Bothe's suggestion without quoting him (see too 127.4n.).

Rockwood wrongly notes that *moderor*+acc. is post-Aug.: cf. Cic. *Flacc.* 12, Sall. *J.* 82.2.

quantus euasurus esset, eluceret V. sometimes alludes to the continuity of the 'ruling house' by describing its successive members in similar or identical phraseology (97.4n.). Here Tiberius clearly belongs to the tradition of Aug. (59.6 'tanti mox uiri') and Caesar (42.1 'tanti mox euasuri uiri'). For impers. *elucet*+interrog. clause cf. Cic. *Part.* 41.

94.4–95.2 TIBERIUS IN ARMENIA (20 B.C.), AND WITH DRUSUS IN RAETIA AND VINDELICIA (15 B.C.)

94.4 uirtutum experimentis in eo tractu editis *tractu* is clearly right (so Gelenius): V. uses the noun four times elsewhere of the provinces (1.2.3, 104.3, 110.2, 126.3). PA's *tractatu* presumably arose through a copyist's objection to its occurrence so soon after 1 and in a different sense. Ellis observes a similar corruption at Cic. *Rep.* 2.11.

For *uirtutum experimenta* cf. 116.1, Flor. 1.7.2, *Pan. Lat.* 12.7.7, Sulp. *Chron.* 1.21.7, to which F. adds Just. 7.1.1, 30.4.15.

regnum eius ⟨Tigrani, filio⟩ Artauasdi⟨s⟩, dedit, cuius *** If we believe the paradosis (*Artauasdi dedit*), V. is saying that Tiberius gave Armenia to Artavasdes as a client kingdom. Yet every other source (Suet. *Tib.*

9.1, Tac. *A.* 2.3.2, Dio 54.9.4–5, and esp. *RG* 27.2) states that Tiberius gave Armenia to Tigranes. Most modern scholars therefore assume that V. has simply made a mistake (so e.g. Baumgartner in *RE* 2.1326; Stein in *PIR*² 1.234; Koestermann on Tac. 2.3.2), Kritz adding the refinement that V. may have confused Tigranes with a later Artavasdes who was placed on the Armenian throne *iussu Augusti* (Tac. 2.4.1). Vossius suggests that V. simply omitted Tigranes in favour of this later king since Tacitus tells us that Tigranes' rule was brief (loc. cit.).

Such hypotheses will not work. (1) As many of the older edd. saw, it is highly unlikely that V., a contemporary observer, should be the only source to make this mistake. (Besides, V. had an interest in the 'eastern question', being present on Gaius' mission there more than 20 years later: cf. 101.) (2) Other sources go out of their way to associate Tiberius with the imposition of Tigranes (see *RG*, Tac., locc. citt.), and propaganda celebrated the event widely (Seager 18 n. 1), esp. on the coinage in legends which V. is later able to reproduce exactly (122.1 *Armenia recepta*, cf. *BMC Emp.* 1.109 *Armenia Recepta*). (3) The later Artavasdes was associated with Roman military defeat in Armenia (Tac. 2.4.1), and Aug. pointedly omitted reference to him in *RG* (Syme, *Tac.* 390 n. 3). It is thus impossible that V. made a mistake or confused Tigranes with the later Artavasdes.

Realising the difficulties raised by the passage, Lipsius suggested a lacuna which he proposed to fill thus: 'regnum eius Artauasdi ⟨ereptum, Tigrani tra⟩didit'. I think that Lipsius was on the right lines, but I cannot accept his supplement since Tigranes took over the kingdom from Artaxias, not from Artavasdes. I therefore propose: 'regnum eius ⟨Tigrani, filio⟩ Artauasdi⟨s⟩, dedit', compare *RG* 27.2 'regnum id Tigrani regis Artauasdis filio... per Ti. Neronem tradere' (and note that V. echoes *RG* elsewhere).[1] V. would then be alluding to an Artavasdes who had already figured in his narrative by name at 82.3.

The imposition of Tigranes in 20 was by no means the end of the Armenian problem (see Tac. *A.* 2.3–4, *RG* 27.2; Magie 1.476, 484ff.); and the submission of Phraates IV, to which V. refers in the next sentence (*rex quoque Parthorum...*), did not take place until about 10 B.C., ten years later (cf. Schur, *RE* 18.4.2000–1; Gagé on *RG* 32.2).[2] I am therefore inclined to believe that *cuius*, which other edd. either emend or obelise, is correct, and that V., like Tac., provided some brief information on the intervening years which is lost through a further lacuna. (On lacunae see also above, pp. 26f.).

tanti nominis fama territus The panegyrical flavour of this sentence is

---

1 On V. and *RG* see Canfora 134–5.

2 K. Krämer however believes, I think wrongly, that V. is here referring to 20 B.C. (*Klio* 55 (1973), 247).

clear. (1) R. G. M. Nisbet has noted that it was a panegyrical motif to describe the fear of foreign princes and their seeking the ruler's friendship (*CR* 19 (1969), 175): cf. Hor. *CS* 54–6, *RG* 31–2 (the present instance at 32.2), *Pan. Lat.* 4.38.3. (2) W. S. Maguinness has noted that another motif was to stress what was achieved by the ruler's *name* (*Hermath.* 47 (1932), 56f.): cf. Cic. *Leg. Man.* 13, 45, Plin. *Pan.* 14.1, adding Luc. 2.465, Vict. *Vir. Ill.* 78.7 'Pharnacem Mithridatis filium fama nominis fugauit', *Pan. Lat.* 2.22.2, 4.3.5, 6.11.1 (F. notes other exs. of *fama nominis* at Liv. 3.2.3, 38.58.5, Curt. 8.13.2, Luc. 9.91f., Tac. *A.* 5.10.1). For *fama territus* cf. Liv. 28.7.17, Stat. *Theb.* 4.346. For the submission of Phraates IV, see refs. to Schur and Gagé (last n.), and Just. 42.5.12 'plusque Caesar *magnitudine nominis sui* fecit'.

95.1 belli mole This phrase, which first occurs in Acc. *Trag.* 610, is frequent in V. (79.1, 97.4, 115.1, cf. 129.3): cf. Ogilvie on Liv. 2.19.5, Heubner on Tac. *H.* 1.61.2, 2.6.1.

adiutore operis dato...Druso Claudio *adiutor* has an official ring, cf. Tac. *A.* 3.12.1 'adiutoremque Germanico datum a se auctore senatu rebus apud orientem administrandis'; also below, 127.3n. For Nero Claudius Drusus (Germanicus) cf. *PIR*[2] 2.194–9, no. 857; *RE* 3.2703–19 = Claudius 139 (Stein).

95.2 diuisis partibus J. Stanger (*De Vell. fide*, 1863) proposed to read here *e diuersis partibus*, comparing 109.5 where that phrase occurs. Tiberius and Drusus did indeed attack from different directions (Dio 54.22.4), but Drakenborch on Liv. *Epit.* 136 saw rightly that V. is here concerned with division of labour (cf. *adiutore operis dato*). *partes diuidere* is technical ('having divided the operations/responsibilities', cf. Liv. 25.30.6, 37.21.8, 39.23.8, 44.11.4 etc.) and does not of course preclude an attack on two fronts (cf. Liv. 8.25.9, 37.29.5).

Raetos Vindelicosque For the campaign cf. K. Christ, *Historia* 6 (1957), 416ff.; Wells 66ff.

nec non derecta quoque acie feliciter functi *fungor* + noun qualified by a perf. pass. partic. is uncommon, but cf. Cic. *Tusc.* 1.109, Ov. *Fast.* 4.824, *Her.* 8.109. For the technical *derigere aciem* cf. 47.1, 112.3, *Bell. Alex.* 37.4, Liv. 2.49.10, Tac. *A.* 6.34.3, etc.; for *nec non* (*...quoque*) cf. K–S 1.826 Anm. 7, L–H–S 778–9; A. Önnerfors, *Pliniana* (1956), 99ff., esp. 104ff.

gentes locis tutissimas...truces For the conventional nature of such descriptions cf. 106.1–2nn. For *locis* (*-o*) *tutus* cf. also Liv. 23.26.2 (and Gronovius ad loc.), Tac. *H.* 3.9.1, Flor. 1.19.4, and often in Ov. For *numero frequentes* cf. also Sulp. *Chron.* 1.48.1, *Dial.* 2.4.4.

maiore cum periculo quam damno V. is often accused of being uncritically eulogistic, yet he here provides a realistic touch of danger (Professor F. R. D. Goodyear compares Tac. *H.* fr. 4 Koest. 'nouae gentes saepe ex usu et aliquando cum damno quaeruntur') which is missing from every other account of the campaign except Horace's. At *C.* 4.14 Hor. also balances the phrase *sine clade* (l. 32) with the more sinister *graue proelium* (l. 14), a correspondence missed by Kiessling–Heinze in their interesting comparison of Hor. and V. (ad loc.).

For the contrast between *periculum* and *damnum* cf. Sen. *Ben.* 4.12.2; for *plurimo cum sanguine* (below) cf. Liv. 2.64.5: *multo sanguine* is at Vell. 90.2.

pērdŏmŭērūnt A so-called 'heroic clausula'. It is generally recognised that such clausulae are more common in the historians (Sall.: 12%, Liv.: 11.3%) than in Cic. (1.9%: figures from W. H. Shewring, *CQ* 25 (1931), 13ff.), although E. Fraenkel showed that dactylic rhythms are less unusual in Cic. than had been previously thought, and that such hexameter endings regularly involve words of four or five syllables, as here (*Leseproben aus Reden Ciceros u. Catos* (1968), 198ff.). In the Tiberian portion of V.'s narrative there is a striking deviation from normal 'historical' practice, the average of such clausulae being 2.4%. Yet this figure is to some extent misleading, since V.'s heroic clausulae tend to cluster in episodes which deal with wars in foreign lands. The exs. are: 109.4 'passu(um) abesset', 110.5 'de/creta patrauit', possibly 111.1 (text uncertain), 112.5 'legion/um trepidatum', 125.2 'qui sequerentur', 5 'obtinend/i superesset'. Quadrisyllabic endings are relatively rare in 'classical' hexameter poetry, and pentasyllabic endings even rarer (statistics in C. Bailey's edn of Lucr., vol. 1, p. 115). For a similar elision to 109.4 cf. *Aen.* 1.599 'omni(um) egenos' (and cf. 2.325, 3.109, 6.64).

95.3 CENSORSHIP OF PLANCUS AND PAULUS (22 B.C.)

'The appointment of a pair of censors in 22 B.C. (Paullus Aemilius Lepidus and L. Munatius Plancus) announced a return to Republican practices and a beginning of social and moral reform' (Syme, *RR* 339). 'The Munatii and the Aemilii were on good terms with each other, and thus one could expect smooth co-operation from the censors...Augustus would hardly have elected them censors if they had not been loyal and suitable persons' (J. Suolahti, *The Roman censors* (1963), 503). V.'s paragraph is a bitter comment on the emperor's hopes: *acta inter discordiam neque ipsis honori neque rei publicae usui.*

Even the omens had been wrong (Dio 54.2.2). The office of censor lapsed thereafter for seventy years (Suet. *Claud.* 16.1).

95.3 Planci et Pauli Respectively *RE* 16.1.545–51 = Munatius 30 (Hanslik); and *RE* 1.565–6 = Aemilius 82 (v. Rohden), *PIR*[2] 1.62–3, no. 373. Unlike Paulus, Plancus has already been mentioned several times in V.'s work: he is one of the few individuals whose character is allowed to emerge gradually from his words and deeds (the 'indirect' method of characterisation, see above, p. 34). He is disloyal (63.3–64.1, 83.1), a fratricide (67.3–4), obscene (the brilliant description of his nude dance at 83.1–3); and V. invariably treats him with an irony or sarcasm (cf. esp. 63.3, 74.3, 83.1) which is otherwise untypical. The censor by tradition was supposed to be 'non luxui aut uoluptatibus adsuefactus, sed qui prima ab iuuenta legibus obtemperauisset' (Tac. *A.* 12.5.3); his position demanded *grauitas* (Cic. *Dom.* 130, *Cael.* 35), and embraced the guardianship of public morals (Suolahti, op. cit. 47–52). V. doubtless means us to relish the appointment of such a man as Plancus to such a position. It was the final irony.

uis censoria Burman's *censoria* for *censori* (PA) is superior to Gelenius' *censoris* because of the plausible haplography and because *uis censoria* is at Liv. 23.23.2.

Paulus uix posset implere censorem, Plancus timere deberet nec... 'Paulus was scarcely able to do justice to the censor's office, Plancus ought to have been afraid ⟨of it⟩: there was no accusation he could bring against young men, or hear ⟨others⟩ bringing, which he as an old man did not recognise as applicable to himself.' I agree with Ruhnken that the sentence is extremely odd, but, like Kritz, I can see no justification for emendation. The text makes sense, however awkwardly.

For *implere* Ruhnken compares Amm. 27.6.15 '(indoles) imperatorem implesset', Solin. 1.81 'oratorem L. Plancum Rubrius histrio sic impleuit ut et ipse Plancus uocaretur', Sidon. *Ep.* 7.15.2; also ib. 8.9.5, Veg. *Mil.* 1.6. The use of *agnosco* is rightly given by *OLD* s.v. as 'to recognise as applicable to oneself or as existing in one's own character', cf. Sen. *Dial.* 3.12.3, Quint. 8.3.71.

96.1 DEATH OF AGRIPPA (12 B.C.)

96.1 Mors deinde Agrippae M. Vipsanius L.f. Agrippa (*RE* 9A.1.1226–75 = Vipsanius 2 (Hanslik); Wiseman 275, no. 497) died early in 12 B.C. (Dio 54.28.3). He became Tiberius' father-in-law when the future emperor married his daughter Vipsania (date unknown: 20 according to Seager 14 and n. 1; 16 acc. to Massauer). See also 79.1, 88.2, 90.1, 127.1n. Gaius and

Lucius Caesar, Agrippa's sons by his third wife, Augustus' daughter Julia, were born in 20 and 17 B.C. respectively: they were adopted by Aug. in 17 (Dio 54.18.1). For Gaius cf. *RE* 10.1.424–8 = Julius 134 (Gardthausen); *PIR*² 4.165–8, no. 216; for Lucius cf. *RE* 10.1.472–3 = Julius 145 (Gardthausen); *PIR*² 4.185–7, no. 223.

nouitatem suam multis rebus nobilitauerat The subtle wording of Agrippa's epitaph is an interesting comment on the change from republic to empire. During the middle and late republic, a man of *nouitas* could 'ennoble' his family only by becoming consul (128.1n.), an achievement of such difficulty that it happened rarely (Wiseman 1ff.). Thus during this period *nouitas* and *nobilitas* were effectively opposed to one another, and in republican parlance *nouitatem nobilitare* is an oxymoron (cf. also Wirszubski 55 on Vell. 34.3 'Cicero...uir nouitatis nobilissimae'). Yet with the dissolution of the republican constitution, many more *noui* than previously became consuls (Wiseman 203); and subsequently Aug., through his absolute power, was able to guarantee the consulship for those of his supporters who deserved it, regardless of their status (Syme, *RR* 372). Thus Agrippa himself rose from proverbial obscurity (cf. Sen. *Contr.* 2.4.13) to three consulships (in 37, 28, 27 B.C.). Now though Agrippa had thereby technically ennobled himself and his family, his three consulships were nevertheless due solely to the gift of Augustus. Since this fact might depreciate Agrippa's honour, V. here does not say (as he might have done) that Agrippa was ennobled by the three consulships, but by *multis rebus* – a reference to his outstanding feats in war, engineering and administration. V. has tactfully shifted the emphasis away from the political honour itself to the achievement which won that honour. Yet he has retained the language of republican politics, the paradoxical phrase (pointed by assonance) emotively crediting Agrippa with a feat which had in fact long since become obsolete.

For *in hoc perduxerat ut* (below) cf. 128.4n.

Iulia, filia eius Julia married Tiberius in 11 B.C. (Dio 54.35.4), having been betrothed in the previous year before Tiberius went to Pannonia (ib. 31.2). For her cf. 100.3n.

Haase's transposition of the paradosis seems to me more likely than Gelenius', despite 100.3.

96.2–3 THE 'BELLUM PANNONICUM' (13–9 B.C.)

The episode is written to a dramatic pattern, glorifying Tiberius: a threatening crisis is followed by the intervention of Tiberius who, after notable successes, is awarded a triumph. An identical pattern is used in the following chapter; and a far more elaborate version occurs in chh. 117–20, the *Variana clades* (see p. 188).

96.2 bellum Pannonicum For a clear account of the campaign see Wilkes 62–6; for the problems involved cf. Syme, *DP* 13ff., 43ff., 135–42. Dio tells us (54.31.3) that in 12 B.C. Tiberius used the Scordisci tribe as allies, though in 16 they had been enemies of Rome (54.20.3). V. has already told us (39.3) that it was Tiberius who reconciled these natives to Rome, presumably around 15 after his Alpine campaigns; but Syme treats this and other evidence with some scepticism (*DP* 44–5).

inchoatum ⟨ab⟩ Agrippa Marcoque Vinicio, auo tuo, consul The passage is not as hopeless as some edd. have believed. P's *COSS*, presumably = *consulibus* as if giving a date, is impossible since Agrippa (last cos. 27) and Vinicius (suffect. 19) never held office together. Rhenanus was doubtless misled through finding no *ab* before *Agrippa* in his exemplar (see below). Lipsius interpreted the same reading as *consule*, to which A's $\overline{cos}$ might also point: this would give a date of 19 B.C., but since the war began either in 14 (Syme, *DP* 35, ref. to Dio 54.24.3) or in 13 (Dio 54.28.1–2), Lipsius' notion is incorrect. Kritz interpreted the paradosis to mean *consulari*, which is most attractive (cf. a similar abbreviation at 2.12.2). But is 'auo *tuo*' a sufficiently explicit allusion to the younger M. Vinicius, V.'s dedicatee? It is true that such inexplicit allusions also occur at 103.1 and 104.2, but each of these has been immediately preceded by the explicit reference 'sub patre tuo, *M. Vinici*' at 101.3 (see n.). In the present case we have had no explicit reference to the younger Vinicius since 65.2, thirty chh. earlier. I suspect that V. wrote *consul*, a vocative addressed to the younger Vinicius (cf. Cic. *Phil.* 5.53).

Lipsius supplied *ab* before *Agrippa*, probably rightly. Although there are parallels for the abl. of agent without *ab* (K–S 1.380, L–H–S 122), the two supposed exs. in V. are not certain (39.1, 63.1: probably dative), and *inchoare* is in fact always followed by *ab* + abl. (*TLL* 7.1.971.51–2). The omission would of course be easy.

For the elder M. Vinicius cf. 104.2n.: he went to Pannonia as *leg. pro praetore* (Syme, *DP* 35).

per Neronem gestum est 'Under the new régime it was the Princeps to whom the *auspicia* belonged and who had the supreme command of all troops in the Empire; he alone, with a few exceptions in special cases, was entitled to the triumph' (Fraenkel 431; cf. Weinstock 112, and refs. to Mommsen in both places: also above, pp. 39f.). V., despite his enthusiasm for Tiberius, reflects the political and military reality as scrupulously as did Aug. himself (*RG* 30.1 'Pannoniorum gentes...deuictas per Ti. Neronem, qui tum erat priuignus et legatus meus'; also 4.2).

96.3 situmque regionum ac fluminum Geographical descriptions, either of an idealised landscape with groves and a winding stream, or of foreign lands with their wild and exotic scenery, occur in widely different types of literature. Thus each type of landscape is alluded to at Hor. *AP* 16–18 'cum lucus et ara Dianae | et properantis aquae per amoenos ambitus agros | aut flumen Rhenum...describitur' (see Brink ad loc.; for the ideal scene cf. also Curtius 183ff., esp. 202ff., Norden on *Aen.* 6.179ff., G. Schönbeck, *Der 'locus amoenus' von Homer bis Horaz* (1962)).

Naturally enough it was the unusual terrain of foreign lands which most occupied historians, for whom such descriptions became an essential component of their works. Cicero recommended them (*Orat.* 66 '(historia) in qua...regio saepe...describitur', *De Or.* 2.63 'rerum ratio...desiderat regionum descriptionem'), and Lucian pilloried those who took the fashion to excess (*Hist. Conscr.* 19). Roman historians subscribed to the convention: Sallust described Africa (*J.* 17.1 'Africae *situm* paucis exponere') and the Black Sea in a famous digression (*H.* 3.61–80, cf. Syme, *Sall.* 194–5); Livy described Gaul and Germany (*per.* 103 '*situm* Galliarum continet', 104 'prima pars libri *situm* Germaniae moresque continet'); Trogus' 41st book described 'Arabiae *situs*' (Just. *prol. lib.* 41); Tacitus described Britain (*Agr.* 10.1 'Britanniae *situm* populosque...referam') and Judaea (*H.* 5.2–10, cf. Syme, *Tac.* 125–6). Moreover, it is clear from these examples (and many more are given by Norden, *Tac. Germ.* 452–4) that historians came to use the word *situs* almost as a technical term for such descriptions, underlining the conventional place which they occupied in historiography. Thus when Tacitus admits that his account of Tiberius' reign contains no '*situs* gentium' which might 'retinent ac redintegrant legentium animos' (*A.* 4.33.3), it is clear from the phraseology – as well as from the context, q.v. – that he is apologising for the absence of a conventional element which the readers of history had become accustomed to expect. The same is true of V. in the present passage: he is prevented from a geographical description by his brevity (*hoc opus seruet formam suam*).

Yet τοπογραφίαι were employed not merely *delectandi causa*: they often played an important part in panegyric (cf. Menand. rhet. 373.17–20 διαγράψεις δὲ ἐν ταῖς πράξεσι ταῖς τοῦ πολέμου καὶ φύσεις καὶ θέσεις χωρίων [θέσις = *situs*, cf. Norden, *Tac. Germ.* 12 n. 1] ἐν οἷς οἱ πόλεμοι, καὶ ποταμῶν δὲ καὶ λιμένων καὶ ὀρῶν καὶ πεδίων, Plin. *Pan.* 15.3 'cognouisti per stipendia X mores gentium, regionum *situs*'; also below, 105.3n.). The reason is obvious: the more difficult the foreign terrain in which the *laudatus* won his victories, the more the victories are themselves magnified (cf. Luc. 3.310 'ignoto si quos petis orbe triumphos').

Now Horace was prevented from elaborating his poetry along these lines by the brevity of his genre (*Epist.* 2.1.250–9): 'nec sermones ego mallem | repentis per humum quam res componere gestas | *terrarumque situs et flumina* dicere et arces | montibus impositas et barbara regna tuisque | auspiciis totum confecta duella per orbem | ...sed neque paruum | carmen maiestas recipit tua nec meus audet | rem temptare pudor quam uires ferre recusent.' But he makes a virtue out of this necessity by implying that the real reason for his incapacity is the magnitude of Augustus' achievements, which are too great to be encompassed by Horace's *paruum carmen*. This device, the 'panegyrical *recusatio*', allows Horace to panegyrise Aug. by allusion rather than by elaboration. See Wimmel 30–4, 293–5; Fraenkel 428–30; esp. Doblhofer 67–79.

V. too capitalises on his brevity (on which see below) by using it for oblique panegyric. He in fact goes one further than Horace, promising to deal with these topics – which of course he mentions in the conventional language (*situm*) to whet our appetites – in another work which we already know will be more elaborate (cf. 48.5, 89.1: see below on *alio loco*).

numerumque et modum 'the number and type of their forces'. *numerus* and *modus* are also combined at Virg. *Aen.* 11.328, Luc. 1.562; but in each case scholars are uncertain whether *modus* = 'type' or 'size'. If V. had meant the latter, I suspect he would have used an adj. to eliminate the interpretation of *modus* = 'limited size' (cf. 73.3 'magnum modum legionum').

multiplices...uictorias Hardly exaggerated for a campaign which lasted four years, in all but one of which Tiberius' victories were duly acknowledged in one form or another (Dio 54.32.3, 34.3, 55.2.4) – and that during a period when Aug. was trying to eclipse Tiberius' achievements (above, pp. 48–9; Seager 26–8).

alio loco V. several times refers to his intention of writing a *iustum opus* (89.1, 99.3, 103.4) or *iusta uolumina* (48.5, 114.4, 119.1). For various reasons some scholars (Sauppe 47; Peter, *WK* 366) have doubted whether V. is to be taken seriously. In view of the number of times both the Augustan poets and later historians also advertise elaborate future works, apparently not with sincerity but simply in order to magnify their hypothetical subject matter (e.g. Jer. *Chron.* 2 *praef.* 4 'reliquum tempus Gratiani et Theodosii latioris historiae stilo reseruaui'; cf. Janson 75–6; Peter, *WK* 414 and n. 2), it may be that V.'s references are merely conventional.[1] But such a suggestion, while in keeping with the oblique eulogy of *situm regionum ac fluminum* above (see n.), cannot be proved (cf. Woodman (1975), 287–8 for full discussion); and Sumner has rightly observed that 'there is nothing casual or perfunctory about the way Vell. announces the project' (283).

[1] See too C. W. MacLeod, *CR* 24 (1974), 294, on the ending of Philo's *Legatio ad Gaium*.

Other scholars have inferred from the refs. to *iusta uolumina* that V. intended to write several further works (e.g. Manitius 467), and Syme, discussing the present passage, claims that V. alone recognised the importance of the Pannonian war because he 'reserved it for a separate monograph' (*DP* 141). But I agree with those (e.g. S–H 582, Sumner 282 n. 137) who believe that such an inference is utterly unrealistic. If V.'s intention is to be taken seriously, we must in my opinion envisage only one future work, of uncertain scope.[1] A single large history would doubtless take up more than one *uolumen*, and hence V.'s references to *iusta uolumina* may be subsumed under his references to a *iustum opus*.

Does this mean that we must reject Syme's view that V. was alone in recognising the importance of the Pannonian war? I think not. In 2 above he describes it in language which is strong for an area which did not provoke the same emotional response as Parthia or Britain (*bellum...magnum atroxque et perquam uicinum*); and at 90.1 he regards the final year of the war to be the end of Dalmatian independence, a belief which is seen as significant by Wilkes 65.

hoc opus seruet formam suam V. several times refers to the brevity or restricted form of his work: 1.16.1, 29.2, 38.1, 52.3, 55.1, 66.3, 86.1, 89.1, 99.4, 103.4. I have argued at length elsewhere that V.'s work is a summary universal history of Rome, and that these references are a feature of that genre (Woodman (1975), 277–87). See also below, 108.2n.

ouans triumphauit *ouare* = 'to celebrate an *ouatio*', *triumphare* = 'to celebrate a (curule) triumph'; but when the two words are used together, as here and 122.1, *triumphare* loses its technical significance and the phrase is simply a grandiose way of saying 'celebrate an *ouatio*': cf. *RG* 4.1 'bis ouans triumphaui', Val. Max. 2.8.7 'neque ouans aut curru triumphauit'.

V. is referring to Tiberius' first ever *ouatio* on 16 Jan. 9 B.C., 'probably the most hard-earned second category triumph in Roman history' (Wilkes 65): cf. EJ p. 45 'Ti. Caesar ex Pan[nonia ouans urbem intr]auit', convincingly restored and referred to this *ouatio* by L. R. Taylor, *AJPh* 58 (1937), 186. Yet Sutherland (67) and Seager (27) have stated on the basis of Dio 54.34.3 that Tiberius had already celebrated an *ouatio* in 11 B.C. (τῶν ἄθλων [Bekker: ἄλλων codd.] τῶν αὐτῶν τῷ Δρούσῳ τυχεῖν). This would bring Tiberius' total of triumphs (counting ovations as triumphs, as V. obviously intends) to three by 7 B.C. and four by A.D. 12; yet V. twice states that Tiberius had only two triumphs by 7 B.C. (97.4, 99.1), and later states that he celebrated only three triumphs in all (122.1). V. is unlikely to be wrong in such a matter:

[1] On this last point see Woodman (1975), 278 nn. 4, 5.

Dio is presumably referring to the *ornamenta triumphalia*, which we know Tiberius had already received in 12 B.C.

For *uictoriae compos* (above), cf. 1.10.3, Liv. 9.43.14, 29.10.8, Val. Max. 1.1.1.

97 WAR IN GERMANY (16–7 B.C.)

The episode is written to the same dramatic pattern as its predecessor in order to glorify Tiberius (see above, p. 105). Yet the central and lengthiest section is not concerned with Tiberius at all: it comprises an extended *epitaphion* for his brother Drusus (above, p. 43), providing further evidence that V. does not concentrate exclusively on Tiberius (above, p. 95).

The *clades Lolliana*, with which the chapter begins, was generally considered by scholars to have been a grave disaster until Syme (1933), 17–19, argued that it was no more than 'a trifling defeat' (also *RR* 429). Syme, whose view has had much influence on subsequent scholarship, contended that V. has magnified the disaster in order to discredit Lollius; but the following annotations suggest that this is not the case.

97.1 accepta in Germania clades *accipere cladem* is a common, colourless and technical phrase (*TLL* 3.1245.20ff.) which can in no sense be said to dramatise or magnify the situation. V.'s statement is bald in the extreme when compared with those of later writers: Tac. *A.* 1.10.4 'pacem... cruentam: Lollianas Varianasque clades', Suet. *Aug.* 23.1 'graues ignominias cladesque duas omnino nec alibi quam in Germania accepit, Lollianam et Varianam, sed Lollianam maioris infamiae quam detrimenti' (Syme (1933), 18, naturally omits the first half of this sentence), Dio 54.20.4 ὁ δὲ δὴ μέγιστος τῶν τότε... πολέμων, Obseq. 71 'Romani...grauiter uexati'.

M. Lollio, homine in omnia pecuniae...uitiosissimo Two points must be made about the charges of peculation, treachery and deceit which V. lays against Lollius here and at 102.1. (1) The charges are in no way connected with Lollius' military ability or the lack of it, about which V. makes no comment whatsoever. (2) The charges are confirmed by Plin. *NH* 9.118, Suet. *Tib.* 13.2, Tac. *A.* 3.48.2.

The picture of Lollius to be drawn from this evidence is seemingly contradicted by Horace, *Odes* 4.9, which contains such lines as: 'abstinens | ducentis ad se cuncta pecuniae' (37–8). Yet Horace's ode was published (13 B.C.) long before Lollius was in a position to accept bribes in the east or to endanger the young Gaius there (1 B.C. at the earliest). There is nothing to prevent both Horace and the other authors from being right in their respective estimations of Lollius: the man had simply become corrupted in the interval. Even so, some modern scholars believe that Horace did not find Lollius a congenial topic in 13 B.C. (Fraenkel 425–6, Williams 79–80, 88; against, H. P. Syndikus, *Die Lyrik des Horaz* (1973), 2.375–6). There is certainly a tremendous difference between the first half of the ode, where Horace talks of the power of poetry (1–28), and the second, where he addresses Lollius and seems continually apologetic (29–52): the final couplet is esp. suggestive, 'non ille pro caris amicis | aut patria timidus perire'. Fraenkel doubted whether Lollius 'was greatly pleased in reading the ode', while Syme says that 'the charges of rapacity and avarice...may perhaps be held confirmed rather than refuted by this poem' (*RR* 429). For Lollius cf. *RE* 13.2.1377–87 = Lollius 11 (Groag); *PIR*² 5.83–4, no. 311.

For *summa dissimulatio* cf. 88.3, Val. Max. 7.4.4, Sulp. *Dial.* 1.5.3: F. adds Sen. *Dial.* 10.18.6. For *in omnia* cf. 2.13.1, 83.2, 127.3, Cic. *Inu.* 2.177, Liv. 28.17.10, Sen. *Contr.* 2.1.20, Sen. *Ben.* 3.20.2, Flor. 3.20.1 (F.). The word play *uitiorum...uitiosissimo* is typically Velleian: e.g. 1.12.5, 32.6, 52.6, 100.3, 106.2, 119.4 (other exs. in Verhaak 77–8).

amissaque legionis quintae aquila Unlike some modern scholars whom Syme (1933), 17–18, quotes, V. nowhere claims that the legion was lost, only its eagle. And 'the loss, even temporary, of an eagle was a disgrace which was not obliterated by its recovery' (Syme). But once again V. prefers bald statement.

uocauit ab urbe in Gallias Caesarem Dio 54.20.4–6 agrees with V. that the *clades* brought Aug. from Rome to Gaul; but Syme (1933), 17 and n. 24, dismisses this joint evidence and claims that V., in order to magnify the *clades*, simply pretends it was the reason for Augustus' trip to Gaul (so too Wells 95 and n. 1). If this were true, Syme would have some justification for his opinion of V.'s account. And we might well ask how V. could possibly have known that the *clades* was Augustus' reason for going to Gaul, since modern scholars have been able to suggest a wide variety of quite different reasons (cf. e.g. Seager 23). Yet Syme and Wells have apparently overlooked an earlier passage of Dio, according to which Aug. himself let it be known that wars in Germany were the reason for his journey (54.19.1): ἐς τὴν Γαλατίαν...ὥρμησε, πρόφασιν τοὺς πολέμους τοὺς κατ' ἐκεῖνο κινηθέντας λαβών. Conclusion: V.'s statement is not a fabricated magnification of the *clades* but an accurate reflection of what Aug. had himself said. (Naturally Augustus' real reason may have been quite different, but that consideration is irrelevant to the present issue.)

Since Aug. travelled to Gaul in 16 B.C. (Dio 54.19.6), it is likely that the *clades* had occurred earlier that same year, which is what Dio certainly implies (ib. 20.4–6). Syme, however, prefers 17 B.C. (Obsequens' date) since it better suits his thesis.

97.2 cura deinde atque onus...belli delegata Freitag has fully demonstrated V.'s love of phraseology incorporating two words of the same, similar or related meaning: e.g. 26.3 'gloriae famaeque', 35.1 'conspicuam atque praenitentem', 47.3 'gladios caedesque', 50.4 'uigore acfulgore', 57.1 'praesagia atque indicia', 70.2 'multitudo ac uis', 85.2 'otio ac mollitiis', 89.4 'prisca illa et antiqua' (125.4), etc. For *cura belli*, frequent in Livy, cf. Heubner on Tac. *H.* 2.82.1; for *cura delegata* cf. Sen. *NQ* 4.7.2, Colum. 11.2.72, Tac. *G.* 15.1, Quint. 4 *praef.* 2.

tot tantarumque uirtutum quot et quantas natura mortalis recipit uel industria perficit The question whether virtue can be taught or not was debated frequently in the fifth century B.C. (P. Shorey, *TAPA* 40 (1909), 185ff., W. K. C. Guthrie, *The Sophists* (1971), 250ff.), but by Cicero's time had become merely a topic of the rhetorical schools (*Part. Or.* 64, *Top.* 82). Cicero alludes to the topic on several occasions (J. Dziech, 'De V.P. virtutis aestimatore', *Eos* 24 (1919–20), 18–23, quotes *Fin.* 4.21, *Amic.* 6, and the *locus classicus* at *Arch.* 15, to which add *De Or.* 1.38 quoted by Kritz, *Fin.* 5.43, *Top.* 76), and V. may have had such passages in mind: his language seems to echo that of Cicero (e.g. for *natura mortalis* cf. *Diu.* 1.1, *Tusc. Disp.* 1.62; for *uirtutem perficere* cf. *Acad.* 2.26, a parallel which confirms Lipsius' *perficit* for *percipit* (PA) here; and cf. also 130.3n.). But the conventionality of the topic makes this inference uncertain (see further Hor. *AP* 408 and Brink's n., Sen. *Ep.* 108.8, Quint. 1 *praef.* 26, 2.19, 12.2.1 etc.). A fascinating example is the famous couplet of Horace, 'doctrina sed uim promouet insitam, | rectique cultus pectora roborant' (*C.* 4.4.33–4), which, by a striking coincidence, also refers to Drusus (and to Tiberius himself): see above, 94.2n. For the wording of V.'s phrase cf. also 2.2.2.

cuius ingenium utrum bellicis...an ciuilibus...in incerto est On this and the following sentiments cf. *Cons. Liu.* 13–20, written on the death of the same man: the ideas appropriate to a *consolatio* (e.g. *mores, res gestae*: cf. Esteve-Forriol 57, 134–5) are naturally appropriate also to a historical *epitaphion* (see further below, p. 215). To describe Drusus' excellence in war and peace, V. uses the panegyrical formula of the 'unresolved alternative' (122.2n.), his uncertainty being elaborated in the clauses which follow: *morum certe* (μέν) *dulcedo* is balanced by *sed* (δέ) ...*domitorem Germaniae*.

For *ingenium sufficit* cf. Ov. *Ex P.* 2.5.26; for *bellicis operibus* cf. Val. Max. 9.3.2, Curt. 8.1.20; for *morum...suauitas*, below, F. quotes Cic. *Amic.* 66.

97.3 aduersus amicos aequa ac par sui aestimatio 'his judgement, which was fair to his friends and equal to ⟨the judgement which he made of⟩ himself'. Although I realise that there are other ways of interpreting the phrase, this seems to me the likeliest. It follows that *aduersus* depends upon *aequa* (as Sen. *Ep.* 93.1, 120.1, Tac. *A.* 16.4.2) and that *sui* depends upon *par* (cf. Cic. *Senect.* 78; K–S 1.448h): hence *aduersus...sui* is chiastic.

agentem annum tricesimum i.e. 9 B.C. (cf. Dio 55.2.1). For *agentem*, which is to be taken ἀπὸ κοινοῦ with *consulem* (cf. 92.2) and *annum*, cf. 94.3n.

97.4 moles deinde eius belli Ellis' misguided belief in A led him to suggest the deletion of *eius*, which the apograph has written above the line. But Freitag has noted that the frequent and often redundant use of *is* is a feature of V.'s prose: to her exs. at 2.4.4, 22.2, 40.4, 59.5, 79.2 and 94.4 we may add two in the immediate context here: *eius gentis* above and *quod is* below. For discussion of this phenomenon elsewhere cf. E. Laughton, *Eranos* 49 (1951), 35ff.; E. Fraenkel, ib. 50ff.; P. T. Eden, *Glotta* 40 (1962), 78–89; Ogilvie on Liv. 5.34.3–8. For *moles belli* cf. 95.1n.

sua et uirtute et fortuna By tradition *uirtus* and *fortuna* were mutually opposed to one another ('plerumque dissidentes', Amm. 14.6.3; cf. *TLL* 6.1.1195.55ff.), since *fortuna* was capricious where *uirtus* was reliable (Tac. *G.* 30.2, *H.* 4.29.2, Sen. *Ben.* 3.18.2). But on the basis of *fortes fortuna adiuuat* (Otto 144), it was recognised that an outstanding person could equal the achievement of Pompey: 'cum uirtute fortunam adaequauit' (Cic. *Arch.* 24); that is, he was 'cum fortis tum etiam felix' (Cic. *Mur.* 38, cf. Sall. *J.* 95.4). The most likely persons to achieve this reconciliation of opposites were naturally those who were believed to be blessed with their own personal *fortuna.* This latter notion, in origin Greek, was popularised at Rome especially through Sulla (cf. J. P. V. D. Balsdon, *JRS* 41 (1951), 1ff.) but above all through Caesar (Weinstock 112–27). V. reflects the view that was held of Caesar during the latter's lifetime (51.2 'sua et celeritate et fortuna C. Caesar usus', 55.1 'sequens fortunam suam Caesar', 'mox pugnauit sua (fortuna)', 3 'sua Caesarem in Hispaniam comitata fortuna est'), and his recurrent phraseology makes it clear that he regarded Augustus (74.4 'usus Caesar uirtute et fortuna sua') and Tiberius (here and 121.1 'eadem et uirtus et fortuna...imperatoris Tiberii fuit') as belonging to the same tradition. See further, in addition to works cited above, H. Erkell, *Augustus, Felicitas, Fortuna* (1952, with earlier bibliog.); Hellegouarc'h (1964) and esp. 'La fortune du prince', *Hommages à M. Renard* (1969), 1.421–30; Lana 221–30 (a list of V.'s refs. to *fortuna* on p. 221 n. 2). On the associated notion of *felicitas* see 106.3n.

peragratusque uictor omnes partes Nowhere else in classical Latin is *peragro* a deponent verb. Like Kritz I prefer to accept the anomaly than to emend (*peruagatusque*, Ruhnken; Professor F. R. D. Goodyear suggests *peragransque*): there are numerous verbs in Latin which come to acquire an additional deponent form, just as there are numerous deponent verbs which come to acquire an additional active form (cf. Draeger, *Hist. Synt.* 1.155–6, K–S 1.110–11, L–H–S 292–3). The lack of a precise parallel does not necessarily mean that the paradosis is not what V. wrote. (For an opposite approach to a similar problem cf. Ogilvie on Liv. 4.24.2.) For *peragro* combined with *uictor* elsewhere cf. e.g. Lucr. 1.74–5, Flor. 1.33.12.

commissi exercitus Perhaps more likely 'once it had been engaged ⟨in battle⟩' (cf. Liv. 3.4.7 etc.) than 'entrusted ⟨to him⟩' (cf. 72.4 'commissa *sibi* parte exercitus'). *sine ullo detrimento...exercitus* is also at Nep. *Hann.* 5.2.

curae For this characteristic of Tiberius cf. 106.3n., 113.1n.

perdomuit Tiberius thus completed the conquest ('*per*domuit') begun by Drusus ('magna ex parte domitorem', above): see Wells 156f. For Tiberius' triumph and second consulship cf. *ILS* 95 = EJ 39.

98 WAR IN THRACE (13–11 B.C.)

98.1 quae praediximus A relative pronoun + *praediximus* occurs seven times elsewhere in V. (Sauppe 69), and other forms of the verb are at 105.1, 107.1: hence Velleian usage favours P's reading.

in Thracia bellum For discussion of the war cf. Syme, *DP* 65ff. For *in arma accensis* below cf. Flor. 2.6.4, Oros. 6.7.3, to which F. adds Liv. 44.36.4 'in pugnam accendebat'.

L. Pisonis L. Calpurnius Piso (Pontifex), *RE* 3.1.1396–9 = Calpurnius 99 (Groag); *PIR*² 2.61–7, no. 289; Syme (1934), 127–31; *JRS* 50 (1960), 12ff. Also below, 3n.

hodieque = *etiam hodie*, a favourite word of V. (1.4.2, 3, 1.11.3, 2.8.3, 25.4, 27.5, 61.3, 81.2), found also in Livy (according to Ogilvie on 5.4.13), Tacitus and other authors: cf. L–H–S 475, K–S 2.15, Krebs–Schmalz 1.654f. For the use of *eundem* below, emphasising the apparently contradictory qualities of a person, cf. Fordyce on Catull. 22.14.

securitatis urbanae custodem habemus Piso, who held office for 20 years until his death in A.D. 32 (Tac. *A.* 6.10.3), became almost the archetypal Urban Prefect. Though he was technically *praefectus urbi*, an office instituted by Aug., V.'s choice of the word *custos* is not so much 'Tacitean' avoidance of official terminology as an echo of late republican phraseology: e.g. Cic. *Cat.* 3.24 'Marium custodem huius urbis', *Dom.* 40, [Sall.] *In Tull.*

3. The usage continued afterwards, both with ref. to Piso (e.g. Sen. *Ep.* 83.14, Porph. on Hor. *AP* 1) and to others (e.g. Liv. 6.6.15, Sil. 12.63, Juv. 13.157 with Mayor's n.). For *custodem habere* cf. Plaut. *Capt.* 394 (F.), Curt. 7.8.30, Quint. *Decl.* 254 p. 43.28.

(bellum) uirtus compressit *bellum comprimere* is common, e.g. 129.3 (and n.), Cic. *Sest.* 67, Just. 5.10.6; for the abstract subject cf. Plaut. *Merc.* 340, Caes. *BC* 3.65.2 (F.), Liv. 10.11.5.

98.2 triennio V.'s evidence alone tells us of the duration of the war, and, when coupled with Liv. *per.* 140 on 11 B.C., 'Thraces domiti a L. Pisone', indicates that the traditional dates of the war are correct (13–11 B.C., cf. also Dio 54.34.6–7). Syme, however, argues for 12–10 B.C. (*DP* 65, and (1934), 130).

Stegmann and Freitag regard the present sentence as a parenthesis since it is introduced by *quippe* (cf. e.g. 112.4); but the word, which Sauppe 70 notes as occurring more than forty times in V., here = *enim* (as e.g. 100.3, 121.3).

eiusque patratione These words have caused confusion, perhaps not surprisingly. Kritz referred *eius* to *bellum* in 1 above, thus avoiding the sequence *pacis patratio*...*pacem reddidit*: this is certainly possible (*bellauit* in 2 eases the hiatus). But since it is clear from Dio 54.34.6 that the restoration of peace to Thrace would also mean its restoration to Macedonia, I think Ruhnken was right to refer *eius* to *pacis* just preceding. The repetition *pacis*–*eius* (= *pacis*)–*pacem* is no objection (cf. 100.5n.).

patratio is found nowhere else in this sense, but of course both *pacem patrare* and *bellum patrare* are common: the former, however, is not in V. For *in pristinum*...*redegit modum* above cf. 89.3, *SHA Hadr.* 22.5.

98.3 de quo uiro hoc omnibus sentiendum ac praedicandum est Note the striking emphasis with which V. demonstrates his approval of Piso's character, which is of the same type as Maecenas' (88.2) and Sentius Saturninus' (105.2). Piso is described in very similar terms by Seneca (*Ep.* 83.14); and Tac. sums him up as a man of *sapiens moderatio* (*A.* 6.10.3). As I hope to show elsewhere, the *otium* of these three men is an indication of their loyalty to the emperor, which explains V.'s approval of them. (Syme, *RR* 424, rightly attributes to Piso 'good sense and the firm avoidance of desperate ambition or party spirit'.)

The superl. *mixtissimos* below is not found elsewhere.

99–104.1 THE YEARS 6 B.C.–A.D. 4

'The most obscure decade of the Principate of Augustus', complains Syme (*DP* 31). 'There is a singular lack of historical evidence for the nine years in which Tiberius was absent from the service of Rome' (*RR* 392–3). One reason for this obscurity is the fragmentary state of Dio's text; but Syme and his followers believe another reason is the prejudice of V., who they claim is writing a biography and panegyric of Tiberius. 'He therefore records the guilt of Julia, the unsatisfactory behaviour of Gaius Caesar, the perfidy and deserved end of Tiberius' enemy, Marcus Lollius, the guide and counsellor of Gaius. But he does not record the successes won by the men who held the commands on the Rhine and in Illyricum, the rivals and successors of Tiberius' (Syme, *DP* 48).[1] Although the justice of these individual allegations will be discussed below, a general point deserves to be made here. Tiberius' retirement from public life coincided with V.'s own introduction to military service in the eastern provinces. It is hardly surprising that he prefers to discuss this area rather than the Rhine or Illyricum. And it is certainly unreasonable for modern historians to object to his preference, since he provides us with information found in no other ancient source.

V.'s account of these years is framed by two passages in which he illustrates the honours given to Tiberius. The first (99.1) is an accurate assessment of Tiberius' position in 6 B.C. (see above, p. 48), the second (103.4–104.1) a panegyrical treatment of Tiberius' adoption by Augustus.

99–100.1 TIBERIUS' RETIREMENT TO RHODES

99.1 ciuium post unum (et hoc quia uolebat) eminentissimus V. means that Tiberius did not wish to rival Augustus; he is not implying that Tiberius had either the opportunity or ability to do so. Tiberius was a man like Agrippa, whose position (see above, p. 48) he was now acknowledged to hold: cf. 79.1 'parendique, sed uni, scientissimus', Dio 54.29.2 ὅσον τε γὰρ τοὺς ἄλλους ἀρετῇ κατεκράτει, τοσοῦτον ἐκείνου ἐθελοντὴς ἡττᾶτο. V. has here hit on an essential feature of Tiberius' psychology which is illustrated by various events in his life, including his great reluctance in A.D. 14 to accept the full burden of the empire (124.2n.). He had played second fiddle too long: cf. J. H. Thiel, *Mnem.* 3 (1935–6), 191ff., G. Marañón, *Tiberius* (1956), e.g. 183–6.

---

[1] So too e.g. Wells 158 and Wilkes 67. Wilkes' statement that V.'s account of these years is 'devoted largely to the misdeeds of Julia and her circle' is simply untrue: V. spends twice as long on the activities of Gaius Caesar. Syme returns to his attack on V. in 'The crisis of 2 B.C.', *SBAW* (1974), 7.5–6. (I owe this last reference to Mr I. M. Le M. DuQuesnay.)

eminens, eminentissimus (the superl. not registered before V.), and *eminere* are favourite words of V. and between them occur at least 29 times in his work (Sauppe 70–1). For the natural application of such superlatives to imperial personalities cf. Frei-Stolba (1969), 30 n. 91.

fama fortunaque For this alliterative collocation, common in Cic. Sall. Tac., cf. Wölfflin 258. For V.'s fondness of alliterating *f* cf. 72.3 'fugae fortunaeque', 112.1 'felix...forte', 1.11.6 'felicitatem fortunae', 2.11.3 'florere fortunam', 95.2. This is a selection of various types: others in Milkau 17–25.

uere alterum rei publicae lumen et caput An image as striking as it is surrealistic. Since the state may be looked upon as a body (*corpus*, cf. 90.1; Béranger 218ff.), it is metaphorically consistent to say that it has either a *caput* (viz. the *princeps*, cf. 101.2n.) or, as the case may be, two *oculi* or *lumina* (cf. Cic. *Senect.* 35 'alterum illud exstitisset lumen ciuitatis', Val. Max. 4.3.3 'duobus rei publicae diuinis oculis'). But to say that one of two men is both a single eye *and* a single head of the state is, at the least, imagistically confusing. Yet V. equates *lumen* and *caput* similarly, though not quite so spectacularly, at 52.3 'conlisa inter se duo rei p. capita effossumque alterum Romani imperii lumen'. Cornelissen (1877), 51, suggested ⟨*co*⟩*lumen et caput*, comparing Colum. 3.4.3 (the phrase is also at Liv. 38.51.4, Arnob. *Nat.* 1.29, and cf. Cic. *Sest.* 19). But 52.3 suggests that there is nothing wrong with the text.

99.2 incredibili atque inenarrabili pietate For *incredibili pietate* cf. Cic. *Red. Quir.* 5, *Sest.* 145, *CIL* 11.1368.4; *inenarrabilis* is a favourite adj. of Livy and the elder Pliny. For the alliteration cf. 2.13.2 'inescandae inliciendaeque', 2.14.1 'immensa illa et incondita', 23.1 'infestissimus...impatientissimus', etc.; Milkau (as above, 1n.). For Tiberius' *pietas* cf. 105.3n.[1]

cuius causae mox detectae sunt... '...the reasons for which were revealed later when Gaius had already assumed the *toga uirilis* and when Lucius' coming of age was likewise recognised, namely that his brilliance should not stand in the way of the careers of the rising young men.' *causae* looks forward to the following *ne*-clause; *mox* looks forward to the following *cum*-clause (for *mox...cum* cf. 61.2, 123.2, Suet. *Tib.* 14.3, Curt. 10.3.12; J. C. Jones, *ALL* 14 (1906), 528). Thus *cum* dates Tiberius' explanation of

---

1 It is clear from 102.2–3 below, as Miss D. J. Monk points out to me, that V. inconsistently sees Gaius' oriental retirement as a dereliction of *pietas*. V. was writing his history in the shadow of Tiberius' later retirement to Capri – what view would he have taken of that?

his retirement and not (as Levick (1972), 787 n. 1, says) the retirement itself. The train of thought is clarified by Suet. *Tib.* 10.1–2, 11.5, which also confirms that V. here relates Tiberius' official explanation: 'ne aut obstare aut obtrectare praesens uideretur; quam causam et ipse, sed postea, reddidit...transacto autem trib. pot. tempore [1 B.C.], confessus tandem nihil aliud secessu deuitasse se quam aemulationis cum C. Lucioque suspicionem.'

I have followed Burman in parenthesising *cuius...initiis* since these words form a self-contained unit within an otherwise rambling sentence; but Kritz's excellent note rightly observes that *causae mox detectae* is integral to the logic of the whole sentence and is to be contrasted with *dissimulata causa* below.

uirili Withof's brilliant but neglected emendation of the paradosis *uiris* seems to me far superior to those of other edd.:[1] the corruption may have been caused by the confusion of *s* with *l* (see above, p. 22 n. 2). For the ellipse of *toga* cf. 101.3 'in hostili [sc. ripa]'. Lucius had presumably assumed the *toga uirilis* in 3 or 2 B.C.

dissimulata causa 'Tiberius' motives have been hotly debated, in antiquity and later' (Seager 30, with further discussion). For the phraseology cf. Curt. 10.1.28, Suet. *Tib.* 37.3, *Claud.* 15.3; for *fulgor* metaphorically used, above, cf. 1.5.1, 2.4.6, 50.4; *TLL* 6.1.1516.84–1517.1ff.; for *initia* = 'beginnings of a career', above, cf. *TLL* 7.1.1654.73ff.

commeatum...adquiescendi a continuatione laborum petiit Suet. again confirms, *Tib.* 10.2: 'tunc autem honorum satietatem ac requiem laborum praetendens commeatum petit'. For *adquiescere a* cf. Sen. *Ep.* 7.3.

99.3 manum iniecerit A standard legal phrase for laying claim to a person (cf. 41.1; *OLD* s.v. *inicio* 6): the metaphor is here most effective. The sentence of which this phrase forms part resembles Tac. *H.* 1.4.1, where Heubner quotes V.

iusto...operi Cf. 96.3n.; the phrase is also at Plin. *NH praef.* 20.

99.4 illud etiam in hoc transcursu... This long sentence, while following naturally after the reference to *iustum opus*, disturbs an otherwise logical section: 99.2 reasons for Tiberius' departure, 3 the departure itself, 100.1 effects of his departure. The sentence is thus a brief digression, signposted by the ring composition of 99.3 *digredientium*/100.1 *digressum*: for this technique elsewhere cf. 103.3 *adoptaret*/104.1 *adoptatus*, 113.3 *hibernis*/ 114.4

[1] *Krit. Anmerkungen über Horaz u. and. röm. Schriftsteller* (1793), 3.102ff. I know of the emendation only through Prater's notes.

hiems; Woodman, *EA* 8 n. 31. V. refers to his work as *transcursus* also at 55.1, 86.1.

uisendi eius gratia †ad quem† conuenientes An exceptionally difficult passage which many edd. have attempted to emend, often in the light of Suet. *Tib.* 12.2 'nemine cum imperio aut magistratu tendente quoquam quin deuerteret Rhodum'. Much depends upon the meaning of *conuenientes.* (1) The verb might mean 'coming together to one place', cf. Cic. *Verr.* 6.66 'ex finitimis *uisendi causa conuenirent*'. If so, we need to emend only *ad quem*: Heinsius' *undique*, though otherwise persuasive, is implausible since the proconsuls and legates of the previous clause presumably set out for their provinces from Rome, not *undique.* Aldus' *ad eum* avoids this difficulty but is weak. (2) V. however uses the same verb in what seems to be a similar context at 101.1 'conuento prius Ti. Nerone', where the meaning is 'Tiberius having been met first'. If on this analogy we assume that in our present passage *uisendi* and *conuenientes* are synonymous, it follows that these two words must belong to different clauses and that a verb of motion has been omitted. Halm's conjecture, improving on those of earlier scholars, meets these requirements: 'uisendi eius gratia ⟨Rhodum deuerterint⟩ atque eum conuenientes...'. (3) Yet there is a difference between 99.4 and 101.1. In the former Tiberius is being met by other people; in the latter, though V. leaves it ambiguous, Tiberius himself went to meet Gaius (cf. Suet. *Tib.* 12.2, Dio 55.10.19). Since a different action is involved in each case, it may be wrong to place too much weight upon the reappearance of the same verb at 101.1. I have obelised only *ad quem*, but do not thereby wish to imply that corruption is to be found only within these limits.

si illa maiestas priuata umquam fuit Tiberius' *maiestas* (also at 124.1) was acknowledged by the lowering of the *fasces* referred to in the main clause: cf. Liv. 2.7.7 'submissis fascibus...confessionemque factam maiestatem uimque maiorem esse', Val. Max. 4.1.1; H. Drexler, *Aevum* 30 (1956), 197. Although I have, like most edd., printed Aldus' emendation of the paradosis here, Purser's *sed illa...numquam fuit* deserves mention.

100.1 sensit terrarum orbis digressum a custodia Neronem urbis How can the *terrarum orbis* feel the effects of Tiberius' departure *a custodia urbis*? *urbis* is seemingly illogical, and was deleted by Herel. Yet V. is reflecting a concept which gained currency in the late republic and which is well expressed in Ov. *Fast.* 2.683 'Romanae spatium est urbis et orbis idem', where see Bömer (and cf. Prop. 3.11.57 'septem urbs alta iugis, toto quae praesidet orbi'). For *sentire*+abstract subject cf. e.g. Liv. 2.46.5, Cic. *Fam.* 4.9.3.

The interlaced word order of *digressum a custodia Neronem urbis* is typically

Velleian: cf. 1.11.4, 2.14.3, 48.5, 117.4 etc.; Kritz lxxiii sqq.; see further J. D. Denniston, *Greek prose style* (1952), 54–5 (adding e.g. Eur. *HF* 1139 μιᾶς ἅπαντα χειρὸς ἔργα σῆς τάδε, Dem. *Cor.* 143 πάντων εἷς ἀνὴρ μεγίστων αἴτιος κακῶν, Gorg. *Palam.* B11*a*.37 DK τοὺς δὲ πρώτους τῶν πρώτων Ἕλληνας Ἑλλήνων) and Goodyear on Tac. *A.* 1.10.1.

nam et Parthus...et Germania... It is quite clear from *nam et...et* that only these two events explain *sensit...urbis* above: the Julia affair, introduced by *at in urbe* below, is designed to make an altogether different point (2n.). Even so, Syme (*DP* 31, 48) and Lana (179–80) take the present sentence as an example of V.'s falsification of history. It is true that the disturbances in Germany (cf. 104.2) cannot be attributed to Tiberius' absence; but the continued troubles in the east could very naturally be seen as a result of it since it was Tiberius whom Augustus had chosen to settle them (Dio 55.9.4). Tiberius had simply refused to be sent.

adiecit Armeniae manum Burman preferred *animum.* Certainly *inicere manum* (99.3n.) and *adicere animum* are the more usual combinations, but cf. Val. Max. 7.5.4 'manum...adiecit'.

100.2–5 THE DÉBÂCLE OF JULIA (2 B.C.)

100.2 At in urbe...erupit The language of this opening sentence portrays Aug. as emulating the *liberalitas* of Julius Caesar described at 56.1: 'Caesar...*magnificentissimisque gladiatorii muneris, naumachiae* et equitum peditumque, simul elephantorum certaminis *spectaculis...repleuit* (urbem).' The link is even closer if we recall that no *naumachia* had been staged between Caesar's in 46 B.C. and the present one in 2 B.C. And just as 56.1 begins by referring to Caesar's famous *clementia* ('omnibus, qui contra se arma tulerant, ignouit'), so the present section soon refers to that of Augustus (4–5nn.). For similar links elsewhere between members of the ruling house cf. 94.3n., 97.4n.

V.'s language here leaves little doubt that his purpose in this section is to highlight the irony of the year 2 B.C. At the precise moment when Aug. was above all displaying his *liberalitas* to the people of Rome (*eo ipso anno quo*), his very own daughter (*in ipsius domo*), together with one who was a living example of his *clementia* (*singulare exemplum clementiae*), operated against him. And V. takes advantage of Augustus' reaction to the scandal by reaffirming the emperor's *clementia* (5n.).

For games as an ex. of *liberalitas* cf. Cic. *Mur.* 77; Yavetz 48. For Aug.'s *naumachia* cf. *RG* 23, for his gladiators ib. 22.1, and Gagé ad locc. For the *liberalitas* of Caesar and Aug. in general cf. Kloft 58–64, 73–84.

In view of the close parallel with 56.1, G. Cuper was probably right to read *magnificentissimis* here (*-imi* PA). Burman however noted that *magnificentissimo munere* is at 93.1; but Cuper's slight change avoids the juxtaposition of two adjj. in the genitive.

abhinc annos XXXI The dedication by V. of his work to M. Vinicius (101.3n.) presupposes that the work would be published in Vinicius' consulship, A.D. 30. Naturally therefore V. dates events from that year (*abhinc*).[1] But the paradosis here (*XXX*) gives a date of 1 B.C. which is one year too few, just as at 103.3 it gives one too many. On such occasions we must decide whether the error is due to V. himself or to the transmission of the text. I do not think V. would get the present date wrong since (1) he specifically refers also to the famous dedication of Mars Ultor in 2 B.C. and to the consuls of that year, and (2) the '*abhinc* period' is comparatively short. As transmitted numerals are almost infinitely corruptible, I have printed *XXXI* as being what V. wrote. J. M. C. Laurent (*Fasti Consulares Capitolini* (1883), 2.79ff.) believed that here V. was simply giving a 'round number': certainly this must also be the belief of V.'s edd., none of whom has altered the figure.

dedicato Martis templo See *RG* 21.1 with Gagé's nn. (also his edn, pp. 175–6).

foeda dictu memoriaque horrenda...tempestas erupit *foedus* and *erumpere* are equally applicable to real (e.g. Liv. 25.7.7, 29.18.5, Pacuv. *Trag.* 415R, Hirt. *BG* 8.5.2) and to metaphorical storms (e.g. Ov. *Met.* 8.156f., Val. Max. 8.1 abs. 3). For *foeda dictu* cf. Sen. *NQ* 1.16.2, *Ep.* 17.7, Plin. *Ep.* 3.14.2.

100.3 filia eius Iulia For her see *RE* 10.1.896–906 = Julius 550 (Fitzler); *PIR*[2] 4.298–301, no. 634; Goodyear on Tac. *A.* 1.53.1; P. Sattler, 'Julia und Tiberius', *Stud. aus dem Gebiet der alt. Geschichte* (1962), 1–36 (= W. Schmitthenner (ed.), *Augustus* (1969), 486ff.); Levick (1972). The last two works contain full bibliographies.

per omnia As 31.1, 33.1, 35.2, 40.2, 69.6, 79.1, 91.3, 125.5, 127.1, 130.5. 'Eine Lieblingswendung des Vell.', says Klebs (297), but wrongly adding that the phrase is found elsewhere only in Colum. (e.g. 4.2.3), Quint. (e.g. 1.6.12, 10.1.28, 2.24) and Sulp. Sev. (e.g. *Chron.* 1.23.5, *Dial.* 1.10.1): Hand, *Turs.* 4.447, adds Liv. 10.39.8, Just. 19.1.13, 42.5.9, cf. also Liv. 1.34.12, Manil. 1.213, Cels. 3.4.3, 4.6, 5.7, 8.1.25, Sen. *Ep.* 18.3, 31.8, *Laus Pis.* 130

[1] Dating from Vinicius' consulship is at 1.8.1, 4, 1.12.6, 2.7.5, 49.1, 65.2; plain '*abhinc* dating' is at 90.2, 4, 93.1, 103.3. In general see Woodman (1975), 273–6.

(F.); E. Wölfflin, *ALL* 5 (1888), 144. For V.'s comparable but less frequent *in omnia* cf. 97.1n.

quod facere aut pati turpiter posset femina The combination of *facere* and *pati* is conventional, e.g. *Rhet. Herenn.* 1.16, Cic. *Pis.* 11 'qui nihil sibi umquam nec facere nec pati turpe duxit', *Att.* 14.13.6, 14.14.2, Liv.2. 12.9, 3.65.11, 23.9.2, 24.38.2, Hor. *C.* 3.24.43, Sen. *Contr.* 7 *praef.* 7, Val. Max. 2.6.12 'quae multa et facere et pati turpiter cogit', Sen. *Dial.* 4.3.1, Apul. *Met.* 9.18.

(nihil)...luxuria ⟨ac⟩ libidine infectum reliquit The two abll. *luxuria* and *libidine* cannot depend upon *infectum*: there appears to be no example of this construction in Latin, and it would be hard to see its meaning if there were. The two abll. must therefore qualify *reliquit* and are likely to be causal, as Mr I. M. Le M. DuQuesnay points out to me (cf. e.g. Cic. *Fin.* 1.33 'temporibus autem quibusdam et aut officiis debitis aut rerum necessitatibus saepe eueniet ut...', 1.42 'utilitate non arte laudatur', *Mur.* 23 'aliis...te uirtutibus...consulatu...dignissimum iudicaui' (F.), Sall. *J.* 10.4 'officio et fide pariuntur', Tac. *G.* 18.1 'non libidine sed ob nobilitatem plurimis nuptiis ambiuntur', *A.* 4.48.1; K–S 1.379, 394–6; Draeger, *Hist. Synt.* 1.543ff.). The meaning is: 'on account of her *luxuria* and *libido* she left undone nothing which...'.

One alternative method of solving this problem may be mentioned.[1] *luxuria* was emended to *furiosa* by P. Thomas (1919) and to *luxurians* by F. Krohn (*BursiansJB* 217 (1928), 86). Yet although these suggestions produce unexceptionable sense, they cannot be right, since the alliterative collocation of *luxuria* and *libido* is standard (cf. Wölfflin 265).

It will be seen that I have followed Orelli in supplying *ac*, thus avoiding the asyndeton of two paired nouns which is found in the paradosis. In such cases it is often very difficult to decide what the correct reading should be, especially since some writers of the 'silver' age were fond of this type of asyndeton (see Winterbottom 70–1); but none of Wölfflin's examples of the doublet *luxuria/libido* exhibits 'asyndeton bimembre', and a scribe could very easily have omitted *ac* between these two nouns. See also 125.5.

For *infectos* (*-a*) (*re*)*linquere* cf. Virg. *Aen.* 10.720, Ov. *Met.* 6.202, Val. Fl. 3.317.

magnitudinemque fortunae suae peccandi licentia metiebatur Cornelissen (1877), 51, suggested *magnitudineque...licentiam*, which is attrac-

[1] Herel's *intactum* for *infectum* produces excellent Latin (cf. Sen. *Thy.* 221 'quid enim reliquit crimine intactum?') but intolerable sense: there is no point in saying that Julia touched with *luxuria* and *libido* that which is stated to be *already* disgraceful (*turpiter*).

tive but not necessary.[1] For *magnitudo fortunae* cf. Liv. 39.50.2, Sen. *Ben.* 5.5.1, Tac. *A.* 2.72.3. For the standard word-play of *liberet pro licito* below cf. C. Weyman, *ALL* 13 (1904), 387.

100.4 Iullus Antonius, singulare exemplum clementiae Caesaris *clementia* had been one of the outstanding virtues claimed by Julius Caesar: cf. 50.4, 55.2, 56.1; Weinstock 233ff., adding Hellegouarc'h, *VL* 261–3; T. Adam, *Clementia Principis* (1970), 84–5. From him Aug. had 'inherited' it: cf. 86.2, 87.2 and esp. *RG* 34.2.

Iullus Antonius was the second son of Mark Antony and Fulvia. Unlike his elder brother Marcus, whom Octavian killed, he was (as V. says) spared by Octavian and subsequently honoured: praetor (13 B.C.), consul (10), and proconsul (? of Asia, 7/6); in 21 he had married Marcella, Aug.'s niece. He was a 'singular example of Augustus' clemency' not (as Levick (1975), 127, believes) because he was allowed to commit suicide but because his hitherto distinguished career had contrasted so sharply with his unfortunate parentage. On him see *RE* 1.2.2584–5 = Antonius 22 (Groebe); *PIR*² 1.153–4, no. 800. Nothing is known of his priesthood.

For *exemplum clementiae* cf. Ov. *Tr.* 5.4.19, Curt. 8.14.41, Plin. *NH* 8.56, Amm. 17.12.12 etc. For *incolumitate donauerat* below cf. Suet. *Aug.* 51.1 (F.), a similar passage to ours here.

100.5 Quintiusque Crispinus T. Quinctius T.f. Crispinus Sulpicianus, *RE* 24.1106 = Quinctius 69 (Hanslik); M. J. McGann identifies him with the addressee of Hor. *Epist.* 1.16 (*CQ* 10 (1960), 207 and n. 6).

singularem nequitiam supercilio truci protegens One of V.'s typically effective vignettes, modelled (so Ruhnken) on Cic. *Pis.* 12 'istius insignem nequitiam frontis inuolutam tegumentis', *Prou. Cons.* 4 'libidines eius illae tenebricosae quas fronte et supercilio...contegebat' (cf. too *Red. Sen.* 16, *Quint. fr.* 1.1.15). I can find no parallel for *supercilio truci*, but *triste supercilium* is at Lucr. 6.1184, Mart. 1.24.2, 11.2.1, and *graue supercilium* at Val. Max. 7.2. *ext.* 1, 9.1.6, Plin. *Pan.* 41.3 (F.). For the use of *protego* cf. Just. 38.1.10 'risu protectis insidiis' (F.).

singularem here recurs quickly after *singulare* in 4 above. V. often repeats the same word or phrase in close proximity, and Kritz lxvii–lxx gives a long list of exs. Here are some others: 1.2.2 *usurpabat*/1.3.2 *usurpauerit* (1.5.3 *usurpat*); 2.6.2 *regalis potentiae*/4 *regalis...potentiae*; 2.7.3 *iudicio publico*/4 *iudiciorum publicorum*; 31.4 *dissuadebat*/32.1 *dissuadens*; 34.2 *singularis uirtus*/3 *singulari uirtute*; 60.3 *insidiis eius petitus*/5 *petebatur insidiis* (64.1 *insidiis eiusdem*

---

1 *magnitudine fortunae...licentiam* had already been suggested by E. Wilhelm (*Quaestiones Velleianae*, 1866).

petitus); 69.6 *exercitus traiecerant*/70.1 *traiecerunt exercitus*; 124.2 *contigit*/4 *contigit*. Such subconscious iterations, which of course must be distinguished from effective iterations (128.1n.), are found in many other authors besides V.: see the refs. in E. J. Kenney, *CQ* 9 (1959), 248 n. 1; Woodman (1975), 278 n. 3; L–H–S 820–2.

Appius Claudius *RE* 3.2.2668 = Claudius 15 (Münzer); *PIR*[2] 2.239, no. 985.

Sempronius Gracchus *RE* 2A.2.1371–4 = Sempronius 41 (Groag).

Scipio *RE* 4.1.1427 = Cornelius 319 (Groag); *PIR*[2] 2.354, no. 1435.

quas in cuiuslibet uxore uiolata poenas pependissent 'Augustus acted with astonishing mildness in 2 B.C.' (Levick (1972), 812). I believe that *pependissent*, which is not in P, is one of A's relatively few excellent readings (see above, p. 17): either Rhenanus deleted the word on account of *quasi*, which is in both P and A, or his printer omitted it through haplography (*pependere* follows). I thus assume that *quasi* is an earlier error, for which Purser's *quas in* ('in the case of') neatly accounts. Kritz argues that, if *pependissent* had been in (M), Burer would have spotted its omission from P; but in view of *pependere* I doubt this, and in any case the addition of words is not one of the characteristic errors of A.

patriaeque et parentum subducta oculis Since *patria* and *parentes* are regularly found together (1.7.1; Wölfflin 270, adding Lucil. 1337–8M), *patriae* is probably genitive: for *oculi* of things cf. e.g. 84.2, Cic. 2 *Verr.* 2.81. For *subducta oculis* cf. Lucr. 2.70, Curt. 3.3.3, 9.4.18 (F.); for *comes exilii* below cf. Liv. 6.3.4, 34.35.7, 43.16.15, Tac. *A.* 3.15.3, 4.13.3 (Fletcher); for *uoluntaria comes* cf. Val. Max. 6.8.7.

101–2 THE MISSION OF GAIUS CAESAR (1 B.C.–A.D. 4)

101.1 ante aliis prouinciis †adsidendum obitis This phrase has recently been attacked by Barnes (23) on the grounds that it does not square with *ILS* 140 = EJ 69.9–10 'consulatum quem (C. Caesar) ultra fines extremas p. R. bellum gerens feliciter peregerat'. This inscription, taken with other evidence (for which cf. J. E. G. Zetzel, *GRBS* 11 (1970), 259ff.; G. W. Bowersock, *JRS* 61 (1971), 227), reveals that Gaius won a victory in Arabia (that is, *ultra fines p. R.*) in A.D. 1 which V. is alleged to have disguised as 'mere tourism' (Barnes, reading *ad uisendum*). V. has of course done nothing of the sort. Since he explicitly says *prouinciis*, he can only be referring to activities *within* the boundaries of the empire. The allusion is presumably to

Gaius' preliminary trip to the Balkans in 1 B.C. (Dio 55.10.17). Massauer suggests Gaius' even earlier trip to Gaul in 8 B.C. (Dio 55.6.4), but this seems far less likely.

Gaius' activities in the Balkans are perhaps able to elucidate the textual problem, of which Barnes is evidently unaware. Dio (loc. cit.) says that there were dangerous disturbances on the Danube at the time, but that they were entrusted to others on account of Gaius' age and inexperience. But since Gaius was nominally commander-in-chief, it would be quite proper for V. to ascribe the mission to Gaius himself. Thus P's *ad sedandum*, a correction of Rhenanus, seems on the right lines. Lipsius suggested *ad uisendum*, strongly supported by Heinsius who claimed that the word is technical for provincial missions (e.g. 94.4, Liv. 27.35.3, Tac. *A.* 15.21.1). Of the two, I prefer Rhenanus'; but am not convinced that it is what V. wrote.

The upshot of this discussion is that V. has not mentioned the victory in A.D. 1 at all. But this can hardly be attributed to his Tiberian bias. His *breuitas* compelled him to omit certain items, and the victory in Arabia finds no mention even in Augustus' *RG*. V. simply prefers to deal with Gaius' far more important mission to Syria and Armenia (cf. *RG* 27.2), providing us with eye-witness evidence of a spectacular summit conference of which we would otherwise be ignorant (1–2).

For *prouincias obire* cf. 74.1, Cic. 2 *Verr.* 5.80.

in Syriam missus, conuento prius Ti. Nerone Gaius was sent to Syria in 1 B.C. (Dio 55.10.18–19), reaching it by way of Athens, Samos where Tiberius went to meet him (Suet. *Tib.* 12.2: Dio says Chios), and Asia Minor, and then Egypt and Arabia (*CAH* 10.274–5; Magie 1.481–2, 2.1343). Gaius had arrived at his destination by A.D. 1, but we do not know exactly when.

qui omnem honorem ut superiori habuit I have kept Lipsius' easy but tentative change to *qui* on account of Dio 55.10.19 ὁ Τιβέριος... αὐτὸν ἐθεράπευσε. Kritz's objection that this conjecture is less favourable to Tiberius seems to me misguided. Gaius had the *maius imperium*, and Tiberius respected convention: V.'s acknowledgement of the fact redounds to Tiberius' credit. For the resulting ellipse of *ei* cf. 109.2 'ut supplicem commendabant'.

ut nec laudaturum magna nec uituperaturum... V.'s assessment is restricted to Gaius' activities in Syria (*ibi gessit*, i.e. to 102.1), and, taken in conjunction with the splendid scene next described, is a far more appreciative version than that of Dio (55.10.19 ἀπελθὼν δὲ εἰς τὴν Συρίαν καὶ μηδὲν μέγα κατωρθωκὼς ἐτρώθη). Syme naturally overlooks the fact (above, p. 116).

For (*nec*) *mediocris materia* below cf. Sen. *Dial.* 9.17.1, Suet. *Gramm.* 24.

iuuene †excelsissimae insulae† This reading of PA is clearly wrong. Orelli suggested *iuuene excelsissimae ⟨indolis in⟩ insula*, Ellis *iuuene excelsissimo, ⟨in ora⟩ insulae*. Professor F. R. D. Goodyear notes that a combination of these conjectures would explain the corruption: *iuuene excelsissimae ⟨indolis, in ora⟩ insulae*. The scribe expected a genit. agreeing with *excelsissimae*, and his eye slipped from *indolis* to *insulae*. But certainty is far off, and I have obelised.

The young Parthian king was Phraataces (Phraates V), on whom see Magie 1.483–4. The date of the meeting, usually said to be A.D. 2, is in fact uncertain (Magie 2.1345 n. 46).

quam amnis Euphrates ambiebat *amnis* had been a favourite word of the poets, and was used by Livy of important rivers, of those in the east, or of those with mythical connections (K. Gries, *Constancy in Livy's Latinity* (1949), 21–6). Its flavour is here heightened by the pointing of its etymology: cf. Varro, *LL* 5.28 'Tiberius amnis quod ambit Martium campum et urbem: nam ab ambitu amnis', Virg. *Aen.* 6.550 'quae...ambit torrentibus amnis', Plin. *NH* 4.40, Tac. *A.* 15.4.2, Amm. 14.8.10; G. J. M. Bartelink, *Etymologisiering bij Vergilius* (1965), 94. V. seems here consciously to aim at such effects in order to bring an almost epic quality to the scene: note further the precision of detail for vividness (*aequato, utriusque, ex diuerso hinc...illinc*), and the solemn and sumptuous *epulatus est* (3, cf. *TLL* 5.2.704.23ff.).

101.2 eminentissima imperiorum et hominum...capita For *caput* = 'chief person' or, as appropriate, *princeps*, cf. e.g. 52.3, 99.1 (and n.), Liv. 6.3.1 'caput rei Romanae Camillus', Corn. Sev. ap. Sen. *Suas.* 6.26, Tac. *A.* 1.13.4 (of Tiberius), Luc. 9.123f. (of Pompey); Wilhelm 16. Following J. G. C. Anderson (*CAH* 10.276),[1] Magie (1.484) notes that by this summit meeting 'the Parthian empire was recognised as the equal of Rome', a fact which V. admits by his use of the plural *imperiorum* (cf. Plin. *NH* 5.88 'inter duo imperia summa Romanorum Parthorumque', Tac. *A.* 2.56.1).

For *clarum ac memorabile* below cf. Liv. 40.39.9, Sen. *Dial.* 1.2.12; for *memorabile spectaculum* cf. Plin. *Ep.* 2.1.1, Sen. *Dial.* 10.13.6.

101.3 militiae gradum ante sub patre tuo, M. Vinici, et P. Silio auspicatus For the first time since 65.2 V. explicitly addresses the younger M. Vinicius, the man to whom he dedicated his history, who was consul in A.D. 30, and whose consulship he uses for dating purposes (100.2n.). Other such apostrophes to Vinicius are at 1.13.5, 113.1, 130.4, and cf. 96.2, 103.1, 104.2. Why V. should have dedicated his work to Vinicius is uncertain. It is possible, but unprovable, that V.'s father had served in Germany under Vinicius' grandfather, the elder M. Vinicius (cf. 104.3n.); but

[1] Anderson quotes Strabo 11.515, Just. 41.1 'Parthi penes quos uelut diuisione orbis cum Romanis facta nunc Orientis imperium est'; but not V.

even that would provide only a tenuous link between V. and the Vinicii. Kritz, following others, argued that V. 'vel huic [the younger] M. Vinicio vel patri eius aliquo beneficio obstrictum fuisse' (xxi); but again there is no proof. All we can say for certain is what derives from the present passage: that V. began his career under P. Vinicius, and dedicated his history to this man's son. In so dedicating his work, V. follows a tradition which had been established by the minor historians Coelius Antipater, Lutatius Catulus, Sulla and Hirtius, but which was eschewed by Sallust, Livy and Tacitus. It was a mark of honour for a consul to be addressed during his term of office by an author (cf. Virg. *Ecl.* 4 to Pollio, Hor. *C.* 1.4 to Sestius), and Vinicius doubtless appreciated the regular mention of his name in a history which gives such strong support to Tiberius. V. for his part is able to dignify his work by constant references to an illustrious consul which at the same time provide the work with a pleasantly informal tone. On the whole question of V.'s dedication to Vinicius see Woodman (1975), 273–5; on M. Vinicius himself cf. *RE* 9A.1.116–19 = Vinicius 7 (Hanslik); Sumner 288ff.

For P. Vinicius cf. *RE* 9A.1.119–20 = Vinicius 8 (Hanslik), but note that his position was *legatus Aug. pro praetore* (R. Syme, *Historia* 11 (1962), 148f.; *DP* 68–9; Sumner 288). For P. Silius cf. *RE* 3A.1.72–4 = Silius 9 (Nagl). The respective dates of the Thracian and Macedonian commands of these men are not exactly known. Syme (*RR* 400 n. 6), Hanslik and Massauer put Vinicius' command in 1 B.C., thus placing Silius' in A.D. 1: V. could not then join Gaius' retinue until late A.D. 1 or A.D. 2. Sumner however has suggested that these commands fell a year earlier respectively, allowing V. to join Gaius earlier. But I am doubtful of Sumner's suggestion (next n.).

For *militiam...auspicatus* cf. Suet. *Aug.* 38.2; *militiae gradus* is technical and common, e.g. *CIL* 11.5693 = *ILS* 2666.

mox Achaia...maris Pontici latere We simply do not know in what capacity V. undertook this impressive journey. Dihle (639) suggested that V. had by now joined the staff of Gaius Caesar and was thus with Gaius on the first part of his journey when he travelled from Athens to Asia Minor (above, 1 n.). That is clearly possible; but I feel that, if it were true, V. would have given us some indication of his contact with Gaius' staff. Hence I prefer the suggestion that in A.D. 1 he was still in Thrace and Macedonia (last n.). However that may be, we might recall that Polybius prided himself on his experience of military affairs and on his journeys through Africa, Spain, Gaul, and by sea (3.59.7). Like Polybius, V. is not the armchair ancient historian with whom modern scholars are often required to contend.

haud iniucunda...recordatione perfruor V.'s enthusiasm is communicated by elegant Ciceronian language: *perfruor* is a favourite of Cic., and cf. *Brut.* 9 'recordatio...iucunda', *Fam.* 5.13.4 'iucundas recordationes'.

102.1 perfida et plena subdoli ac uersuti animi consilia In 1 B.C. Augustus had been sufficiently convinced of Lollius' worth to send him east as Gaius' *comes* (Suet. *Tib.* 12.2). 'Was such an acute judge of character so long deceived?', asks Syme (1933), 18 n. 31. V. clearly thought so, as did Gaius himself (Plin. *NH* 9.118 'interdicta amicitia a C. Caesare'). Either that or Lollius' character had changed (cf. 97.1n.). For *subdoli ac uersuti animi* cf. Sall. *Cat.* 5.4 'animus...subdolus uarius' (F.); for *moderatorem iuuentae* above cf. Mart. 2.90.1.

fama uulgauit Lipsius' emendation restores the normal phraseology, cf. *TLL* 6.1.219.75ff. For *mors...fortuita an uoluntaria* below cf. Plin. *Ep.* 3.9.5.

obiisse Censorinum...grauiter tulit ciuitas On Hor. *C.* 4.8 Kiessling remarked upon the 'wunderbaren Zufall' whereby Horace had devoted two successive, and similar, odes to Censorinus and Lollius (4.8, 9), while here V. gives successive, but contrasting, obituaries of the same two men. 'Die Erinnerung daran wird dem Vell. die Antithese nahegelegt haben', added Heinze. For C. Marcius L.f. Censorinus, who died while proconsul of Asia, cf. *RE* 14.2.1551–2 = Marcius 44 (Miltner); Magie 2.1581.

For the two acc. + infin. constructions used by V. here cf. K–S 1.691–2. *decedere* (1.11.1, 2.4.7, 21.4, 87.3, 93.1, 102.4) and *obire* (47.2, 59.2, 87.3, 102.3; with *mortem* at 1.9.3, 61.4, 91.4) are V.'s two commonest words for dying: for his other varied terms see Georges 5. For *genitus* + dat. gerundive, below, cf. Sall. *H.* 3.3 'M. Antonius perdundae pecuniae genitus' (and cf. 116.2, 129.1n.).

102.2 ⟨Gaius⟩ ingressus Krause's supplement is supported by Kritz, who notes that the abbreviation *C* might easily have dropped out after 'deind*e*'.

prospere ⟨rem⟩ gessit *rem* is essential: Novák (1907), 143, placed it before *prospere* to preserve the clausula, one of V.'s favourites; yet the word is more likely to have been omitted after *prospere* (Heinsius). V. ends sentences with a double spondee elsewhere in this part of the narrative: 94.3, 96.1, 2, 102.3.

ex eo ut corpus minus habile, ita animum minus utilem rei publicae V. is not to be criticised for a judgement which is confirmed by Dio (55.10*a*. 8): ἐκ τοῦ τραύματος ἠρρώστησε, καὶ ἐπειδὴ μηδ' ἄλλως ὑγιεινὸς ἦν, ὑφ' οὗπερ καὶ τὴν διάνοιαν ἐξελέλυτο, πολλῷ μᾶλλον ἀπημβλύνθη. And Gaius would not have gone to meet the native at all if he had read Plb. 5.75–6 (adduced by Boeclerus). For *corpus habile* cf. Cic. *Leg.* 1.26, Cels. 2.1.5, Sen. *Dial.* 9.8.9, Veg. 2.14. Note V.'s typical jingle *habile...habere.*

102.3 nec defuit conuersatio hominum uitia eius adsentatione alentium The difference between friendship and flattery was a topic of the rhetorical schools (Cic. *Top.* 85); it inevitably occurs frequently in imperial literature, since 'praecipuum est principis opus amicos parare' (Plin. *Pan.* 85.6, cf. Xen. *Cyr.* 8.7.13, Sall. *J.* 10.4, Tac. *H.* 4.7.3). Exs. are: Cic. *Lael.* 89, 91, Caes. *BC* 1.4.3, Curt. 8.5.6, Tac. *H.* 1.15.4, *Pan. Lat.* 3.26.1 (and Gutzwiller ad loc.). E. Badian has suggested (in Sumner 267 n. 67) that V. may here be alluding to Sejanus, who was perhaps with Gaius in the east (see below, p. 248 n. 1).

conuersatio = 'company' is not found before V.; for *uitia alere* cf. 82.4, Sen. *Dial.* 3.1.5, 4.20.2; for *fortunae comes* below cf. 1.9.6, Sen. *Phaedr.* 206. *consenescere* below has been defined as meaning 'to live in lifelong retirement, to live in exile, to which only death puts an end' (P. Trèves, *AJPh* 63 (1942), 134, paralleling Livy): certainly that is the tone of the word in this context.

deinde reluctatus This reading of P, and A's *diu de re luctatus*, are both in my opinion attempts to make sense of what appeared in the anonymous copy of (M). And P is superior to A because we need a word to indicate that, between here and the preceding sentence, Gaius has changed his mind about oriental retirement. It is true that at first sight Burer's note would seem to support A: 'Exemp. uet. sic habet, ut nescias an diu reluctatus, seu potius de reditu luctatus, legendum sit: mihi tamen prior lectio non usque quaque displicet.' But unfortunately this is one of those occasions where Burer's terminology is confusing: the phrase *legendum sit* is his usual method of putting forward a conjecture of his own (see above, pp. 9f.), and that he is so doing here would seem confirmed by his last statement *mihi...displicet.* I thus do not believe that B is here reporting a reading of (M) or that his note has any bearing upon what appears in A.

(Limyra nominant) The names of towns in Asia could often be either fem. sing. or neut. plur.: thus PA correctly record *Artageram* in 2 above, for this form is also found on an inscription (EJ p. 39); Dio however, equally correctly, makes it plural (τὰ Ἀρτάγειρα, 55.10*a*.6). In the present case Rhenanus, while correcting the remainder of the name, has made the town feminine; this is doubtless possible, but the agreement of BA on the ending *-ra* indicates that it was neut. plur. in (M). Cf. *RE* 13.1.710. On such formulae as *nominant* cf. 107.1n.

ante annum ferme 'roughly a year earlier' (for which idiom cf. 104.2, 112.7; K–S 1.406; *TLL* 2.133.30ff.). The interval was in fact a year and a half (20 Aug. A.D. 2.–21 Feb. A.D. 4: cf. EJ pp. 47, 51). The intrusion into the paradosis of *quinquagesimum* after *ferme* is due to misinterpretation of the letter *L* (= 'Lucius', not 'fifty').

103–104.1 TIBERIUS' RETURN TO ROME AND ADOPTION

Tiberius was allowed to return to Rome (with Gaius' permission) in A.D. 2. Now 'the entry of a great man into the city, with the welcome he receives, is a traditional topic', which may be illustrated by innumerable examples.[1] Those writers who treated such *aduentus*, whether in prose or verse, developed certain conventions for their descriptions.[2] Thus V.'s own account of Octavian's return to Rome from Alexandria (89.1 'Caesar autem reuersus in Italiam atque urbem ⟨quo⟩ occursu, quo fauore omnium hominum, aetatium, ordinum exceptus sit') may be compared with many other accounts of similar events (e.g. Cic. *Pis.* 51–2 'quid dicam aduentus meos, quid effusiones hominum ex oppidis, quid concursus ex agris...me ita accepit ut non modo omnium generum aetatum ordinum omnes uiri...'). It is hardly likely, however, that Tiberius' return in A.D. 2 qualified for such celebration. His *trib. pot.* had expired in 1 B.C., and Gaius had made it a condition of his return that he should take no part in public life (Suet. *Tib.* 13.2). Yet by A.D. 4 Gaius was dead, and Augustus was compelled to look once more to Tiberius as his successor. Tiberius was given *trib. pot.* for the second time, and was adopted by Augustus. Again, the adoption by an emperor of his successor also became a favourite theme of later writers (cf. Plin. *Pan.* 7–8, Tac. *H.* 1.15–16, Dio 69.20): it was an extra opportunity to develop some of the topoi which would be relevant when the adopted successor eventually came to the throne. An excellent illustration of these last commonplaces is 89.3–5 (and see also below, pp. 234–45).

Now whereas in ch. 89 V. properly distinguished between Octavian's arrival at Rome and the benefits brought about by his accession to the principate (89.2 *deinde, post reditum in urbem*), in the present section he treats Tiberius' return and adoption as if they were almost simultaneous. Moreover he devotes all his literary attention towards describing the latter event (103.4–5, cf. 103.3n.), and there is at least one occasion where he uses for the *adoptio* a topos normally reserved for the *aduentus* (*concursumque ciuitatis*, cf.

---

[1] T. E. V. Pearce, *CQ* 20 (1970), 313–16, a valuable collection of exs. (the quotation from p. 314). In later times there developed the ceremony of *aduentus*, the arrival of an emperor at Rome or another city, greeted by every kind of solemnity including panegyrical speeches of welcome. For this cf. Weinstock 289–90, 295–6, 299–300, 329–39, 415; S. MacCormack, *Historia* 21 (1972), 721–52, each with refs. to extensive bibliography.

[2] The technical term for the speech of welcome was *prosphonetikon*: cf. Menand. rhet. 377.31ff., [Dion. Hal.] *Ars Rhet.* 5 p. 272 Us.–Rad. See Cairns 18ff., esp. 21–3. For the application of these conventions to a somewhat similar passage to ours, Hor. *C.* 3.14 (Aug. returns from Spain), see Cairns 179ff.

103.4n.). By this means V. avoids the awkwardness of dwelling upon Tiberius' unspectacular return.

But is V.'s enthusiastic description simply conventional? 'Of the true sentiments of Senate and People when the Claudian returned to power, no testimony exists', says Syme (*RR* 431). Massauer agrees: 'Vell. lässt sich daher leicht zu Übertreibungen hinreissen'. Yet Plutarch testifies to very similar receptions accorded to Pompey the Great (*Pomp.* 26.1, 27.2, 3, 57.1),[1] and the phenomenon is not unknown even in modern times.[2] I agree with Sumner's comment on V.'s account (269): 'there is no reason at all to doubt that these things happened, that people behaved like this'.

103.1 spem magni nominis i.e. Gaius and Lucius *Caesar*. Aug. too had attributed their deaths to *fortuna* (*RG* 14.1, Suet. *Tib.* 23), and cf. Hadrian's adoption of Antoninus Pius on the death of L. Aelius (Dio 69.20.4): ἐπεὶ δὲ ἐκεῖνον τὸ δαιμόνιον ἡμῶν ἀφείλετο, εὗρον ἀντ' ἐκείνου αὐτοκράτορα ὑμῖν ὃν δίδωμι. For *fortuna subduxerat* cf. 72.5.

(fortuna) iam tum rei publicae sua praesidia reddiderat V. implies, in view of the preceding relative clause (last n.), that it is Tiberius who will soon be called 'Caesar' (cf. Plin. *Pan.* 8.6 'simul filius, simul Caesar, mox imperator et consors trib. pot.'). V. here doubtless alludes to the Augustan cult of Fortuna Redux, the origins of which are seen in Hor. *C.* 1.35.29ff. (see Nisbet–Hubbard's intro. n.); later, Augustus' return from the east was commemorated by dedications to the goddess on the coinage (*RIC* 1.85) and on inscriptions (*CIL*^{2} 1 p. 229), and cf. *RG* 11.1 'aram Fortunae Reducis...pro reditu meo senatus consecrauit' (see Weinstock 125f.).

sua most naturally refers to *rei publicae*: Tiberius has a special relationship with the state (cf. 104.2n., 120.1n.). But the word may also refer to *fortuna*: Tiberius is her own particular concern (cf. 97.4n.) *iam tum* is emphatic (Cic. *Arch.* 11, Virg. *Aen.* 7.738 etc.), and the metaphor *praesidium* is Ciceronian (e.g. *Phil.* 3.34, 38, 10.9, 17, 13.44, *Pis.* 48).

patre tuo P. Vinicio consule A.D. 2. The exact moment is unknown (perhaps early August, cf. Magie 2.1345 n. 46). For P. Vinicius cf. 101.3n. For the genit. plur. after *utriusque* above cf. 3 below, 50.4; K–S 1.427 Anm. 4.

reuersus...repleuerat Tiberius' physical return in A.D. 2 opened the way for a return of the good life on his adoption in A.D. 4. The emphasis on 'return', also in *reddiderat* above and *refulsit* below, helps to unify both events. See also below, p. 239.

---

[1] Cf. Weinstock, as above.

[2] See *Letters of Queen Victoria* (ed. Benson and Esher, 1908), 2.317–18.

103.2 legendus qui eminebat The man who deserves to be adopted by the emperor (cf. Plin. *Pan.* 7.4, Tac. *H.* 1.15.2 'est tibi frater...dignus hac fortuna, nisi tu potior esses', 16.4; also [Ael. Arist.] 35 p. 254K.8–9 καὶ πρότερον ἢ καταστῆναι εἰς τὴν ἀρχὴν ἄξιος τῆς βασιλείας ἦν) is presumed worthy of being emperor himself (for which cf. 126.4n.).

103.3 quod...adhuc Gaio uiuo facere uoluerat There is no other evidence for this statement; but since Aug. had apparently acquiesced in Gaius' desire to retire from public life (Dio 55.10*a*.8), it would be in keeping with his character if he had already entertained thoughts, however reluctantly, of resorting once more to Tiberius.

eoque 'and for that reason', viz. that Gaius was still alive (so Kritz). Burer's hesitancy over the reading of (M) is clearly directed at what follows *eo* and not at *eo* itself ('ex uestigiis uet. cod. apparebat pro atque [= P], eoque, siue eo quod scriptum: nam uestigia literarum uix poterant uideri prae uetustate'). The meaning and precise reference of *eo* are perhaps not immediately obvious, but in view of *post utriusque...obitum* below (and cf. 99.2) there can be no doubt about the sense. V. uses *eo* with the same meaning at 60.5, 67.4, 127.4.

Aelio Cato ⟨Gaio⟩ Sentio consulibus The full praenomen is perhaps more likely to have been omitted after *Cato*. The consulship of these men in A.D. 4 is the first of three events by which V. dates Tiberius' adoption, a practice which he usually reserves for solemn occasions (49.1 outbreak of civil war, 65.2 Triumvirate and death of Cicero, 90.2 peace in Spain after 200 years). Thuc. 2.2.1 is similarly impressive.

VI Kal. Iulias 26 July. Rau, *Chronologie* 3, proposed thus to alter the paradosis in conformity with epigraphical evidence of the date (EJ p. 49).

abhinc annos XXVI *abhinc* = 'from A.D. 30' (cf. 100.2n.), but Tiberius' adoption in A.D. 4 is not twenty-seven years from A.D. 30 as the paradosis states. V. is unlikely to have got such a date wrong; and besides, the quarter-centenary of the adoption was celebrated in the very year preceding Vinicius' consulship (Grant, *RAI* 63). Aldus' *XXVI* restores correct chronology.

Kritz however notes that the two figures here transmitted, *post urbem conditam annis DCCLIIII* and *abhinc annos XXVII*, add up to 781 (p. xlii): this means that Vinicius' consulship fell 781 years after the founding of the city,[1] a figure also arrived at by adding together the corresponding dates at 49.1 and 65.2. Aldus' emendation would make the present passage anomalous, by producing a total of 780. Yet the transmitted dates at 49.1 and 65.2 are

[1] V. generally dates the founding of Rome to 751 B.C. (Kritz xli).

true, as is the present date if Aldus' emendation be accepted. If we must preserve the total 781, I would prefer to alter *DCCLIIII*: *DCCLV*, which would provide the total 781, could easily have been corrupted into *DCCLIV*, an equivalent form of which is found here in the paradosis. There is much to be said for *DCCLV*, since Tiberius' adoption is 755 years from the founding of the city and not, as the paradosis states, 754 years (cf. Rau, *Chronologie* 3).

adoptaret Note that V. ends this sentence thus, and begins with *adoptatus* at 104.1: in between we have a brief example of rhetorical *exornatio*, elaborating upon the adoption (cf. 99.4n., 114.4n.). For modern discussion of the adoption cf. H. U. Instinsky, *Hermes* 94 (1966), 324ff.; Levick (1966); Seager 37f.

103.4 Laetitiam illius diei For the significance of the day itself cf. e.g. Cic. *Pis.* 52, *Dom.* 76, Hor. *C.* 3.14.13, *Ciris* 27–8, Plin. *Pan.* 22.1, *Pan. Lat.* 5.7.6. For *laetitia* cf. Plin. *Pan.* 22.5 'tam aequalis ab omnibus ex aduentu tuo laetitia percepta est', *Pan. Lat.* 5.8.3, 7.8.7.

concursumque ciuitatis An essential element of the *aduentus* topos, cf. 87.1, Cic. *Pis.* 51 (both quoted above, p. 130), Hirt. *BG* 8.51.1–3, Liv. 24.16.16, 27.45.6, 35.43.9, Plin. *Pan.* 23.2, *Pan. Lat.* 2.37.4, 4.32.5, 5.8.1, 7.8.7, 11.10.5, 11.3; Pearce (above, p. 130 n.1).

uota paene inserentium caelo manus *uota* are to be expected in such a context (cf. Plin. *Pan.* 23.5 'in unius salutem collata omnium uota cum sibi se ac liberis suis intellegerent precari quae pro te precarentur'). The described action is often the accompaniment of prayer (cf. G. Appel, *De Romanorum Precationibus* (1909), 196). For the phraseology cf. [Sen.] *Herc. Oet.* 169, Luc. 8.551f., but the contexts are different.

spemque conceptam Boeclerus' *conceptam* restores standard phraseology, cf. 67.2, Liv. 4.15.4, 25.38.12, Ov. *Fast.* 1.485, Curt. 9.6.1, Tac. *H.* 1.13.4 etc.

perpetuae securitatis aeternitatisque Romani imperii These slogans find their parallels in the literary, epigraphic and numismatic evidence that has come down to us. They either echo the ideological thinking of the Augustan and Tiberian principates, or foreshadow that of later times. Each slogan is naturally appropriate to the theme of adoption, a device designed for security and perpetuation.

(1) The *aeternitas* of Rome and her empire seems first attested in Cicero (*Phil.* 2.51, *Marc.* 22), but was a concept especially dear to the Augustan age (Tib. 2.5.23 and Smith ad loc., Virg. *Aen.* 1.276–9, Liv. 4.4.4, Val. Max.

5.3.1): see esp. M. P. Charlesworth, *HThR* 29 (1936), 107ff.; also C. Koch, *Religio* (1960), 142ff. The legend 'Aeternitatis Augustae' first occurs during Tiberius' reign (Grant, *Aspects* 85–7), and after the fall of Sejanus an inscription recorded 'prouidentia Ti. Caesaris Aug. nati ad aeternitatem Romani nominis' (*ILS* 157 = EJ 51, cf. *ILS* 163). Later exs. of *aeternitas imperii* are at Suet. *Nero* 11.2, Plin. *Pan.* 67.3, and Henzen 110–11. See also below, 131.1n., and in general Syme, *Tac.* 208 n. 1; Heubner on Tac. *H.* 1.84.4; A. J. Toynbee, *A study of history* (1954), 7.7ff. 'The mirage of immortality'.

(2) Though clearly comparable with the preceding, *perpetuitas* carries the notion of striving or hard work (e.g. *ILS* 103 'beneficio eius [sc. Aug.] et perpetua cura'). 'Such a conception is consistent with the sober and laborious spirit of Tiberius' rule, and...we have independent evidence that his principate witnessed a considerably extended use of the epithet *perpetuus*' (Grant, *Aspects* 85f.). Cf. *ILS* 121 (= EJ 126) 'imperator perpetuus', 157 (EJ 51) 'pro perpetua salute diuinae domus', 3786 'Aug. Paci perpetuae'. See also below, 120.1n.; later history in Grant, *RAI* 156f.

(3) It is perhaps surprising that *securitas* developed later than these two other slogans. Seneca (*Ep.* 73.2) and Tacitus (*Agr.* 3.1) both refer to *securitas publica*, which occurs first on Hadrian's coinage (*RIC* 2.221) *securitas Augusti* is on Nero's coinage, having been anticipated by Gaius (Sutherland 113, 169). Plin. *Pan.* often refers to the notion (cf. Durry on 27.1), esp. 8.1 'adoptio...qua...libertas et salus et securitas fundabatur', 58.7; and cf. also *ILS* 2933, 3788, *CIL* 6.2051. The earliest evidence for this word used as a slogan seems to be V. himself, here and at 89.4, 128.4 (cf. H. Instinsky, *Sicherheit als politisches Problem des röm. Kaisertums* (1952), 15ff.). Later history in Grant, *RAI* 110–13. The word has obvious connections with *salus* (below, 5n.).

in illo iusto opere Cf. 96.3n.

...nedum hic implere. temptemus id unum dixisse Heinsius' punctuation, adopted here, means that no further alteration of the text is required and that the passage closely resembles the comparable 89.1 'ne in operis quidem iusti materia, nedum huius tam recisi digne exprimi potest'. Some scholars, however, have considered *temptemus* to be inappropriate to govern *dixisse* in view of 124.1 *id solum dixisse*, where the infinitive is apparently governed by an expression of mere contentment (but where the text is regrettably corrupt). Certainly a combination of Rhenanus' and Burman's proposals produces a good clausula and sense: *nedum hic implērĕ tēmptēmūs. ⟨contenti simus⟩ id unum dixisse...* But in view of the well known motif discussed below at 104.4n., I believe that *temptemus* is entirely appropriate to govern *dixisse*: though he cannot elaborate fully here on the day of the adoption, V. will nevertheless attempt to describe one of the joys which it brought (*spes*).

For *implere* = 'to develop a theme fully' cf. Petron. 94.1, Oros. 4.5.6: the usage is common in the elder Seneca (*TLL* 7.1.636.34ff.). For the use of the perf. infin. cf. K–S 1.133–5, L–H–S 351–2.

quam ille omnibus fauerit Since this clause is explained by the next sentence, which begins with the temporal adverb *tum*, it follows that *ille* = *dies*, resumed from the beginning of the previous sentence: cf. esp. 86.1 'quid ille dies terrarum orbi praestiterit...quis in hoc transcursu tam artati operis exprimere audeat?' *fauerit* is Madvig's emendation (1.21) of the paradosis *fuerit* and is supported by Manil. 1.11 'fauet mundus scrutantibus ipsum' (see Wageningen's n.); cf. also Hor. *C.* 3.11.50 'dum fauet nox'. Others either supply a word (e.g. ⟨*omnia*⟩ *omnibus*, Lipsius; ⟨*faustus*⟩ *fuerit*, Halm) or emend *quam* (*quantus*, Burman; *quanti*, Rosenheyn; *qualis*, Laurent).

103.5 refulsit certa spes 'These pious prayers were answered almost at once by famine, pestilence and years of warfare, with grave disasters' (Syme, *RR* 431 n. 2). But Rogers rightly points out that 'our concern is men's expectation rather than subsequent historical events' (29n.). *certa spes*, a slogan comparable to *certa possessio* (89.4) and *certa pax* (38.3), is the theme of this sentence: words for 'hope' occur four times, having been introduced by *spem* at 1 above. On *spes* see Grant, *FITA* 279–81, *RAI* 54, 74; Sutherland 132. For *refulsit...spes* cf. Pers. *prol.* 12 (F.).

liberorum parentibus, uiris matrimoniorum For this and associated topoi cf. Cic. *Marc.* 23, Hor. *C.* 4.5.23 (on Aug.'s return from Gaul), Sen. *Clem.* 1.13.5 'tollere filios cupiunt', Plin. *Pan.* 22.3 'feminas etiam tunc fecunditatis suae maxima uoluptas subiit cum cernerent cui principi ciues, cui imperatori milites peperissent', 26.5 'ad tollendos liberos...pauperibus educandi una ratio est bonus princeps', 27.1 '(maius) est educandi incitamentum tollere liberos...in spem libertatis, in spem securitatis', *Pan. Lat.* 2.37.4, 3.13.3 and Gutzwiller ad loc., 4.38.4, *ILS* 8393 (= EJ 357.36), Menand. rhet. 376.4ff.

salutis On this slogan see Weinstock 163ff., esp. 172 on Tiberius (with wealth of illustration): e.g. Val. Max. 2.9.6 'salutaris princeps', 8.13 *praef.*; Val. opens his work by calling Tiberius 'certissima salus patriae' (1 *praef.*). *tranquillitas* below does not occur on the coinage until Hadrian (Syme, *Tac.* 756), but note *tranquilliore statu* on a coin of 16 B.C. (*RIC* 1.75 = EJ 35). For *pax* below cf. 126.3n.

104.1 'hoc', inquit, 'rei publicae causa facio' Suetonius agrees (*Tib.* 21.3 'r.p. causa adoptare se eum pro contione iurauerit'), Tacitus not (*A.*

1.10.7 'ne Tiberium quidem...r.p. cura successorem adscitum'). Most modern scholars believe that Aug., in using these words (on which cf. Béranger 169–75), was being complimentary: cf. Seager 37, 38 n. 1.

104.2–109 TIBERIUS IN GERMANY (A.D. 4–6)

It has been observed by Sumner, whose excellent remarks on these chapters (268–71) constitute a useful antidote to the 'perverse and obdurate scepticism' of Syme (*RR* 431), that it takes V. as long to cover the ten years from Tiberius' adoption to Augustus' death as it took for the previous thirty-four years since Actium. This tendency, natural in any historian as he nears his own times, is particularly welcome in V. Tiberius' adoption marked a turning-point in the fortunes of the future emperor; and V., by his close association with Tiberius, 'was now at the centre of the most important and crucial events going on in the Roman world' (Sumner 270).

V.'s account of these first three years' campaigning is annalistic, but his narrative never becomes a monotonous catalogue of military facts. The first year concentrates on Tiberius' *aduentus* in Gaul,[1] his reception by his veterans (104.3–4: note the vivid direct speech), and the character of Sentius Saturninus (105.2); the second spotlights an impressive incident involving a German elder (107.1–2: direct speech again); the account of the third year is enlivened by a much admired full-length portrait of Maroboduus (108–109.4).

104.2–105 CAMPAIGNS OF A.D. 4

104.2 uindicem custodemque imperii sui Ennius in a famous line had called Romulus *patriae custodem* (*Ann.* 112V), and such phraseology was used in republican times to describe prominent men: Cic. calls Pompey 'propugnator et custos imperii' (*Dom.* 129), and Marius 'custos ciuitatis atque imperii uestri' (*Red. Quir.* 9): cf. A. Alföldi, *MH* 9 (1952), 225; W. Neuhauser, *Patronus u. Orator* (1958), 42. The title was naturally appropriate for an emperor who, like Augustus, claimed to show *cura* to his citizens (106.3n.) and who sought to secure the Roman empire by military operations along its frontiers: cf. *CIL* 11.1421 = *ILS* 140 (EJ 69.8), Hor. *C.* 4.5.2 'custos gentis', 15.17 'custode rerum'. So too V. is here moved to apply the title to Tiberius, joining to it the word *uindex* (for the combination cf. Cic. *Verr.* 5.126, *Leg. Agr.* 2.24, Liv. 2.1.8, Val. Max. 6.3.3: for *uindex imperii* cf. 75.3 (also of Tib.),

---

[1] Tiberius' *aduentus* is recorded on an inscription, *CIL* 13.1.2.3570 (cf. J. Heurgon, 'L'inscription de Tibère à Bavai', *Ant. Class.* 17 (1948), 323–30, who however wrongly numbers the inscription 1370).

Liv. 27.45.7, 28.28.14 'maiestatis imperii'). See further 105.3n., 120.1n.; Norden, *AP* 156; Premerstein 128; Béranger 183–4.

sub M. Vinicio...immensum exarserat bellum A.D. 1. The elder M. Vinicius (cos. suff. 19 B.C.) was the grandfather of V.'s dedicatee, the younger M. Vinicius: for him see *RE* 9A.1.112–16 = Vinicius 6 (Hanslik); R. Syme, *CQ* 27 (1933), 142ff. (repr. with addendum in *DP* 26–39), *Historia* 11 (1962), 148; Wiseman 274, no. 494. The exact dates of his German command are uncertain, but we have no reason to assume that he did not continue in office until Tiberius replaced him with Sentius Saturninus in A.D. 4 (105.1n.). But even this, if true, would hardly allow V. himself enough time to become acquainted with Vinicius, as Syme has implied (*RR* 384). It is however possible, but not provable, that V.'s father had served under the elder Vinicius in Germany (below, 3n.). See further Woodman (1975), 274 n. 1. For *immensum bellum* cf. Just. 14.3.8; for *bellum sustentatum* below cf. Caes. *BG* 2.14.6.

eoque nomine decreta... 'and on that account', as Tac. *A.* 14.59.4 'decretae eo nomine supplicationes'; for *cum inscriptione operum* below cf. Tac. *A.* 2.83.2.

104.3 successor officii patris mei Sumner (264–5) and others have assumed from this phrase that V.'s father had served in Germany, presumably under the elder M. Vinicius. But the phrase more naturally refers simply to the office of *praefectus equitum* rather than to the place where the office was held.

per annos continuos VIIII...spectator V. several times refers to his own participation in the events which he describes (also 101.2 'mihi uisere contigit', 3n., 111.3, 113.3 'inter quos ipsi fuimus', 114.2, 115.5, 121.3; and cf. 107.1n., 118.1n.). These references usually denote the modest pride with which he looks back on his career, although similar allusions are also found in ancient historians to whom autopsy was an important part of their work (cf. Canfora 18–19). But we should also note that V.'s references to himself are relatively sparing: he 'does not invariably obtrude himself into the narrative' (Sumner 274).

P's numeral *VIIII* is rightly defended by Sumner 274 n. 107. P's reading *spectatus* was emended by Gelenius to *spectator et*; A's *spectatum* by Orelli to ⟨*cum*⟩ *spectator, tum. spectator* seems undoubtedly right (it balances two other *-or* nouns in this sentence); as for the rest, I believe that this is one of the places where Rhenanus has wrongly emended his exemplar and that A is nearer the truth: I thus follow Orelli, but (with E. Thomas) prefer to dispense with his ⟨*cum*⟩.

pro captu mediocritatis meae The early years of autocracy at Rome encouraged a tendency, which rapidly increased, to magnify the *princeps* and, correspondingly, to emphasise one's own deference. Thus Val. Max. addresses Tiberius as *certissima salus patriae*, mentions his *caelestis prouidentia*, and refers to himself as *mea paruitas* (*praef.*; cf. E. Herkommer, *Die Topoi in den Proömien der röm. Geschichtswerke* (1968), 51; Curtius 84; J. H. Schmalz, *BPhW* 32 (1912), 556; Latte 321). Having just mentioned Tiberius' *caelestissima opera*, V. equally naturally refers to his own *mediocritas*, a word which was to become almost technical in such contexts: cf. 111.3, Gell. 14.2.25, Stat. *Silu.* 5 *praef.*; for later exs. cf. e.g. Tert. *Marc.* 2.27 (2.318.2–3 Migne) 'pro captu mediocritatis humanae', *TLL* 8.569.11ff. It is this topos which lies behind the closely related convention discussed below, 4n. See also 130.3n.

condicio mortalis The phrase, an uncommon variant on *condicio humana*, is perhaps modelled on Cic. *Tim.* 41, *Phil.* 14.33 (F.): it occurs also at 2.2.2 above in a not dissimilar context (and cf. 97.2, 130.3). For the tone of the present passage cf. Liv. 1.19.3 'quod nostrae aetati di dederunt ut uideremus'.

meritis ac uir⟨tut⟩ibus In support of Lipsius' emendation cf. Suet. *Aug.* 66.1 'uirtutes ac merita'.

104.4 neque uerbis exprimi...potest It had long been a rhetorical convention to begin one's speech with a declaration of modesty: it was a method of ensuring the listeners' goodwill (e.g. Cic. *Arch.* 1 'si quid est in me ingenii, iudices, quod sentio quam sit exiguum'; see further *Rhet. Herenn.* 3.11, Curtius 83–5). With the increasingly deferential attitude assumed by writers under the empire (above, 3n.), this convention became combined with the 'inexpressibility topos': the emperor's achievements and virtues are so miraculous, incredible etc. that the writer has scarcely the ability to discuss them. Cf. e.g. Hor. *C.* 1.6.9ff., *SHA Max. Balb.* 17.6–7 '(haec) quomodo dicam aut prosequar? praesertim cum *mediocritas mea* non modo publicam felicitatem sed ne peculiare quidem gaudium animi mei possit *exprimere* cum eos Augustos et principes generis humani uideam...', *Pan. Lat.* 3.1.1 (and Gutzwiller ad loc.), 4.2.7, 6.1.1–3 '*maiestas tua* hunc *mediocritati meae* diem... celeberrimum ad dicendum dedisset... (3) ex ingenio meo, quod *mediocre est*', 8.1.1, 10.2.1ff., 12.1.1–3, Arnob. *Nat.* 1.1 '*pro captu* et *mediocritate* sermonis (mei)'. There are of course various subdivisions of this topos: cf. 96.3n., 122.2n., 126.1n. In general see Curtius 83–5, 159ff., 411ff.; Janson 100ff., 124ff.

For *continere* used absolutely, above, cf. Tert. *Ad Ux.* 1.6 (F.); for the sentiments of the direct speech cf. Cic. *Mur.* 38 (Ruhnken); for *mereri fidem* below cf. Tac. *D.* 31.5 (F.).

105.1 recepti Cherusci (gentes utinam minus mox nostra clade nobiles) Vossius' emendation of the paradosis, if we omit the *et* which he added after *gentes* (so Friebel), requires only the slightest change (*utinam* for *et inam-*) and produces thoroughly Velleian Latin: for *mox...nobiles* cf. 2.8.3 'Cimbri et Teutoni...multis mox nostris suisque cladibus nobiles'; for *utinam* cf. 28.3 'primus ille (et utinam ultimus)'; for *utinam minus* cf. Cic. *Fam.* 14.4.1 'quod utinam minus uitae cupidi fuissemus'. In my opinion the main problem is whether we should keep the paradosis *gentes* or follow Fröhlich in preferring *gens*. Normally the singular would be used to refer to a tribe, but these German tribes were diffuse entities, with various branches (e.g. Tac. *G.* 38.1 'nunc de Suebis dicendum est, quorum non una...gens'). V., who appears to use *gens* and *natio* synonymously (38.1, 110.3), is doing the same here as at 106.1 below: 'recept*ae* Cauchorum nation*es*'.

For (*nostra*) *clade nobiles* cf. Liv. 9.1.1 (F.), 22.39.8, Curt. 4.9.9, Sil. 3.356.

cum omnem partem asperrimi...belli Caesar uindicaret sibi, iis... *sibi*, for the paradosis *in*, is usually attributed to Cludius (and in a misleading fashion by Stegmann), but it was in fact already known to Burman (see his n. on 100.3). It is true that V. often uses *uindicare* without the dative and that *praeficere* seems on occasion to be found with *in*+abl. (Kritz quotes Cic. *Sest.* 41 'inque eo exercitu...inimici mei fratrem praefecerat'). But *sibi* is to be commended (1) because it produces a tighter and more pointed sentence; (2) because the phrase *partem sibi uindicare* is Ciceronian and thus likely to appeal to V. (e.g. *Marc.* 6, *Off.* 1.22, *Acad.* fr. 20); and (3) because similar (panegyrical) contexts support it (*Pan. Lat.* 3.12.1 'laborum asperrima sibi sumens', 4.29.2 'difficillimam enim pugnae partem tibi deligis'). *sibi* may similarly have been corrupted to *in* at Juv. 8.241 (see Housman's edn, p. li).

Sentium Saturninum (qui tum legatus patris eius...fuerat) On this man, one of V.'s heroes, see *RE* 2A.2.1511–26 = Sentius 9 (Groag). Since Latin idiom permits the use of the pluperf. instead of the imperf., especially in the cases of *fueram* and *habueram* (K–S 1.140.4), we have no need to emend either *tum* (*iam*, Gruner) or *fuerat* (*erat*, Ruhnken). The relative clause simply means 'who at that time was a legate of his father in Germany', and thus does not pose the problems discussed by Groag (op. cit. 1521–2) or by Lana (157 n. 685); nor may it be used as evidence that Saturninus' Rhine command began earlier than A.D. 4 (as suggested also by R. Syme, *Historia* 13 (1964), 165). *patris eius* of course = Augustus, as e.g. Tac. *A.* 3.12.1 'patris sui legatum...fuisse'.

105.2 uirum multiplicem [in] uirtutibus I think F. Raphelengius (in Lipsius' edn) was right to delete *in*, a construction for which there seems to be no parallel in classical Latin. The corruption would be easy; and G.

Zebian, writing on the ablative of respect, has noted that V. 'almost exhausts all the conceivable nouns and adjectives which appear in the construction' (*AJPh* 86 (1965), 254–5, comparing here Hor. *C.* 1.5.5 'simplex munditiis'): for further Velleian exs. see Georges 60–1. For *nauum, agilem* below cf. Hor. *Epist.* 1.18.90 (F.); for *multiplicem...prouidum* cf. Cic. *Leg.* 1.22.

eo abutentem 'using it to the full', but misunderstood by J.-M. André as 'abusing' ('L'otium chez Valère-Maxime et Velleius Paterculus', *REL* 43 (1965), 313): cf. Cic. *Rep.* 1.14 'sumus...parati...abuti tecum hoc otio', *Tusc.* 1.6 'hominis est intemperanter abutentis et otio et litteris'. André's discussion of *otium* in V. seems to me to be generally misguided, and I hope at some time to present a reconsideration which will also embrace the character sketches of Saturninus and others. For *liberaliter lauteque* above cf. Nep. *Chabr.* 3.2 'uiuebat laute et indulgebat sibi liberalius quam ut inuidiam uulgi posset effugere' (F.).

de cuius uiri claro ingenio celebrique consulatu praediximus *ingenio*, which is in A but not P, presents a tricky problem. Kritz followed P on the not unreasonable grounds that at 92.1ff., to which reference is here being made, V. nowhere uses the word *ingenium*. But Halm (1875), 545, who follows A, countered thus: 'da er aber dort [i.e. 92] ausführlich und nach einzelnen Punkten des Sentius weise Verfügungen...schildert, so konnte er immerhin an einer späteren Stelle sagen, dass er sich über dessen clarum ingenium schon früher ausgelassen habe'. Both arguments have their merits, and the silence of B would normally tip the balance (in my opinion) in favour of P. Here, however, A's characteristic carelessness has been its saving grace. Its full reading at this point is as follows: *claroq.* (*q* del.) *ingenio celebriq. ingenio* (del.) *consulatu.* The insistence upon *ingenio,* albeit wrong on one occasion, makes it likely that the word derives from (M). We must assume that Rhenanus omitted *ingenio* either through error or because he was anticipating the point made later by Kritz. And for once Burer failed to notice the omission.

105.3 aestiua...perducta Lipsius preferred *producta*, but the paradosis is acceptable: compare Caes. *BG* 4.30.2 'rem in hiemem producere' with 5.31.3 'res...ad mediam noctem perducitur'. For the use of *immanis* below cf. 46.1, 69.6, Ov. *Tr.* 2.335 'diuitis ingenii est immania Caesaris acta'. For *emolumentum...uictoriae* below, 'l'avantage d'une immense victoire' (H–W), cf. Donat. *ad Aen.* 8.200; for *emolumentum* + defining genit. cf. 114.4, Plaut. *Trin.* 694.

paene exstructis hieme Alpibus This reading of PA was altered to *obstructis* by Gelenius but retained by Vossius, who compared Flor. 1.38.11

'hiemem quae altius Alpes leuat'. I think Vossius was right: Latin writers of this period love such rhetorical point, and indeed Florus returns to it a few chapters later (1.45.22 'hieme creuerant Alpes': the whole passage should be compared). The same point was also made by Silius, in a passage (4.743f.) which Nisbet–Hubbard quote to support a similar interpretation of Hor. *C.* 1.9.1. For *exstruere* in this sense cf. *TLL* 5.2.1940.76ff.

Tiberius' dash from one part of the Roman world to another (cf. also 120.1, 123.1n.) is a typical manifestation of his *pietas*, a virtue which became a feature of his life after his adoption by Augustus. 'Filial loyalty played a prominent part in the aristocratic tradition to which Tiberius was devoted. His consciousness of his position as Augustus' son is remarkable throughout the rest of his career, showing itself in a dedicated loyalty to Augustus' person, policies and precepts' (Seager 38).

V.'s present sentence is intended to magnify this *pietas*, by emphasising the difficulty of the winter journey. Winter snows and/or the Alps are often found as examples of panegyrical *amplificatio*: e.g. *Pan. Lat.* 2.45.4, 4.36.5 'cruda adhuc hieme iter gelu intractabile, immensum spatio, niuibus infestum incredibili celeritate confecit', 11.2.4, 9.4 'prope soli Alpium uias hibernis niuibus obstructas diuinis uestigiis aperuistis' (this last is quoted by Ruhnken to support Gelenius' *obstructis*).

at tutela imperii eum ueris initio reduxit in Germaniam Editors have been divided on whether the paradosis *ad tutelam imperii* should go with *traxit* or *reduxit*: logically it seems to go with *reduxit* (*tutela* is redundant after *pietas*), but punctuation after *traxit* is most awkward. I have therefore preferred Lipsius' easy change *at tutela*, which solves this problem and also (as Kritz notes) produces a characteristically Velleian series of antitheses. For *at* used thus cf. e.g. 2.5.3; for *tutela* + transitive verb cf. Virg. *G.* 4.111, Hor. *C.* 2.17.23.

One of the commonplaces of any form of government, especially of benevolent dictatorship, is that the people should be cared for. A vast complex of words and slogans accumulated to express this idea, including *custos* (104.2n.), *cura* (106.3n.), *patronus* (120.1n.), and *tutela* with its derivatives: e.g. Cic. *Rep.* 2.51 'quasi tutor et procurator r.p.'. Naturally such phraseology was extensively used under the empire: thus Horace, in a bold metaphorical analogy, addressed Augustus as 'o tutela praesens | Italiae dominaeque Romae' (*C.* 4.14.43–4, cf. *Epist.* 2.1.2 'res Italas armis tuteris', Strabo 17.25 (p. 1172 Meineke) τὴν προστασίαν τῆς ἡγεμονίας, Tac. *A.* 1.2.1 'ad tuendam plebem', Suet. *Aug.* 94.8). Tiberius, as often, confirmed the Augustan trend: see e.g. 124.2 below and Tac. *A.* 1.12.1 'eius tutelam suscepturum'. Tiberius' association with Sejanus is also described by V. as aiming at *tutela securitatis* (128.4): it is thus ironical that Tiberius' disposal of Sejanus was seen equally as a manifestation of *tutela* by Val. Max. 9.11 *ext.* 4.

For later exs. cf. Suet. *Tit.* 6.1, Plin. *Ep.* 10.52, 102, and in *Pan. Lat. passim.* The main discussions of the concept are Premerstein 117ff.; Béranger 204, 257–60, 266ff.; Grenade 446ff.: cf. also Grant, *FITA* 452–3 and *RAI* 89–90 (who, like Béranger, rejects Premerstein's too rigid view of the concept).

106–107 CAMPAIGNS OF A.D. 5

In 103.4–5 we were given the reaction of the *city of Rome* to Tiberius' adoption; in 104.3–4 we were given the reaction of *Italy, Gaul* and *veteran soldiers* to Tiberius' return; the most eye-catching event of the present section (107.1–2) shows us the reaction of a *barbarian prince* to Tiberius' presence. This three-part climax based on ever-widening geography is intended to emphasise the loyalty which Tiberius could command; but it also forms a dramatic structure, bridging the pauses in the narrative which are demanded by logic (104.1) and the annalistic method (105.3).

V.'s account of the incident contains vivid and realistic detail (e.g. 'armata hostium iuuentute fulgeret', 'ut illis mos est', the direct speech), but Lipsius was sceptical of its veracity and E. Kornemann has stated that 'die Szene...wohl nicht anderes ist als eine rhetorische Ausschmückung des Empfangs der Semnonengesandtschaft',[1] a bald account of which is given at *RG* 26.4. There is clearly some force in this thesis. The 'supplication of foreign princes' is a standard motif of panegyric (94.4n.), and N. Scivoletto has observed that V.'s narrative strongly resembles Martial 5.3 (see 107.2n.):[2] it might be argued that both authors are resorting to a conventional topic. But E. T. Salmon has usefully noted of Augustus that he 'was no doubt quite capable of inserting false and/or misleading statements into the *Res Gestae,* but it is most unlikely that he would render the document ridiculous by including in it statements that were not only untruthful but which would also be immediately recognised as such'.[3] Since I believe the same is almost always true of V., I would contest the view of Lipsius and Kornemann; and we should note that no scholar has questioned the veracity of a comparable incident at 101.2–3.

106.1 pro dii boni *di boni* is common, as is *di immortales*; but *pro dii boni* is not: cf. Sall. *H.* 1.77, Sen. *Contr.* 1.6.1 (F.). For the unusual use of *perlustrata* below cf. Liv. 8.36.9 'perlustrauitque hostium agros'.

gentes paene nominibus incognitae It was conventional to stress that foreign tribes and/or their names were an unknown quantity: e.g. Cic. *Prou.*

---

[1] 'Zu den Germanenkriegen unter Augustus', *Klio* 9 (1909), 445.
[2] 'Da Velleio a Marziale: sul concetto di princeps', *GIF* 8 (1955), 105–15.
[3] *Historia* 5 (1956), 462.

Cons. 33 'quas regiones quasque gentes nullae nobis antea litterae, nulla uox, nulla fama notas fecerat, has noster imperator nosterque exercitus et populi Romani arma peragrarunt', Liv. *per.* 48, Curt. 3.2.9 'ignota etiam ipsi gentium nomina' (cf. Wilhelm 64), Tac. *Agr.* 24.1. The application of this topos in panegyric is obvious: it is usually easier to conquer the known than the unknown. The numerous adjectives in this chapter formed with the negatival prefix *in-* encourage the atmosphere of daring achievement.

infinita numero, immensa corporibus, situ locorum tutissima This description, which smacks of the conventional (cf. e.g. 95.2 'gentes locis tutissimas, aditu difficillimas, numero frequentes', 115.4 'situ locorum ac montium...paene inexpugnabiles', Cic. *Marc.* 8 'domuisti gentes immanitate barbaras, multitudine innumerabiles, locis infinitas', Tac. *H.* 5.18.1 'immensis corporibus' (of Germans), Liv. 1.15.4, 5.6.9; also below, 2n., and above, 95.2n.), nevertheless squares with what Tacitus says of the Chauci (*G.* 35.2–3 'tam immensum terrarum spatium non tenent tantum Chauci sed et implent...quieti secretique'). The combination of *infinita* and *immensa* is Ciceronian (*ND* 1.26, 2.15, *Verr.* 3.149, 5.22, *Red. Sen.* 2, *Diu.* 2.91); for *infinita numero* cf. Apul. *Mund.* 2, *Pan. Lat.* 4.35.1. For the combination of simple and superlative adjj. cf. L–H–S 168; E. Löfstedt, *Late Latin* (1959), 42 n. 4.

armatoque...agmine Laurent and Bothe objected to this phraseology but cf. Virg. *Aen.* 7.648 'agminaque armat' (F.), Luc. 3.71–2 'agmina... | non armata'.

106.2 gens etiam Germana feritate ferocior It is a well known feature of ancient geographical and ethnographical writing that certain standard characteristics are attributed to foreign peoples: thus *feritas* for the Germans, e.g. 95.2, 118.1 (and n.), 119.5, Hirt. *BG* 8.25.1, Val. Max. 7.6 *ext.* 3, Tac. *G.* 43.4, Quint. *Decl.* 3.13 'mores etiam Germanis feri' (the last quoted by Ruhnken). It is equally well known that the same characteristic is often attributed to various quite separate peoples, regardless of whether it is appropriate or not (the so-called 'transference' theory). 'What one observer had said about one definite people was transferred by another to a different people...This produced a stock of commonplaces (τόποι) which were utilised in describing any given people' (J. G. C. Anderson (ed.), *Tacitus: Germania* (1938), xxix; see too Syme, *Tac.* 125ff.). Although V. had visited these areas himself and was able to make his own observations, he certainly seems to have been influenced by the literary phenomenon described above. Yet in the reminiscences of an old soldier we could hardly expect anything but a conventional reaction to foreign peoples.

V. has here embellished his impression by means of word play and double alliteration. For the use of *Germanus* as opposed to *Germanicus* see Nägelsbach 296n.

denique – quod numquam antea spe conceptum, nedum opere temptatum erat – Scholars such as Syme (*DP* 33 n. 23) and Wells (218–19), understanding V. to claim for Tiberius the honour of being the first to penetrate to the R. Elbe, have accused him of deliberate falsification since we know that Drusus and L. Domitius Ahenobarbus had reached the Elbe in 9 B.C. and A.D. 1 respectively (Flor. 2.30.26; Tac. *A.* 4.44.2, Dio 55.10*a*.2). But is this what V. means? It is strange, to say the least, that he should make so obviously false a claim. I have little doubt that the much criticised parenthesis (*quod numquam antea*...) refers not simply to the clause which ends *perductus exercitus* but to the following clause as well, i.e. to the rest of the chapter. It is clear from the words which link the two clauses, *et eodem*, that V. thought of the passage as a single sentence describing a single operation. V.'s admiration is directed not at Tiberius' reaching the Elbe but at the *joint* military and naval operation which had turned out so successfully. As nominal commander-in-chief of the expedition (Plin. *NH* 2.167 'auspiciis diui Aug.') Augustus was equally delighted, but since he did not have 'the instincts of a soldier' (Syme, *CAH* 10.340), his delight is restricted to the more spectacular naval part of the campaign (*RG* 26.4). V., on the other hand, the professional soldier, sees the joint operation as a whole, and is impressed as much by the technical expertise of his commanding officer (*temporum quoque obseruantia*) as by his success (*mira felicitate*...*ducis*). The difficulties of planning such an operation in A.D. 5 fully justify V.'s enthusiastic account.

For *concipere aliquid spe* cf. Liv. 33.33.8 (Ruhnken), 28.17.2, Amm. 30.2.7; it is equally good Latin to say *concipere spem alicuius rei* (cf. 103.4n.). *opere* here seems = 'in fact', a rare meaning; but cf. Curt. 9.2.14 'gloria plus habet nominis quam operis'.

106.3 et eodem 'and to the same place'. Kritz, who rightly and emphatically argues that V. is praising the success of Tiberius' joint operation, both naval and territorial, fails to see that the paradosis makes exactly this point (he suggests *eădem*). *eodem* is not inconsistent with, or repeated by, *flumine Albi* below: the fleet had to sail upstream (*flumine*) for a considerable distance before it reached the point (*eodem*) at which the army was.

mira felicitate et cura ducis Two slogans are here interestingly combined. *felicitas*, one of Cicero's four cardinal military virtues (*Leg. Man.* 28), had long been attributed to successful generals (cf. Cic. *Fin.* 4.22 (201 B.C.), Liv. 40.52.5 (179 B.C.); in general Cic. *Diu.* 1.102); but it was due mainly to Marius and Sulla that the concept became widely exploited, especially by

Caesar (Weinstock 113ff.), who liked to be called Felix (Grant, *FITA* 15 n. 4). *Felicitas* was naturally taken over by Augustus also: for the evidence cf. H. Erkell, *Augustus, Felicitas, Fortuna* (1952), 108ff., and see esp. Suet. *Aug.* 94.1. Tiberius maintained the tradition, even if he did nothing to enlarge upon it. The senate erected a *simulacrum Felicitatis* at Tiberius' supposed birthplace (Suet. *Tib.* 5.1), and legends such as *Felicitas Tiberi* and *Flamen Victoriae Felic. Caesar. perpetuus* are recorded (*CIL* 13.6796, *ILS* 6631, cf. 6332): see in general Erkell, op. cit. 114f.; Grant, *Aspects* 76f. That *felicitas*, originally a military virtue, came to be used in a much more general sense is shown by the development of such expressions as *felicitas temporum* (Tac. *Agr.* 3.1, *H.* 1.1.4) and by the appearance of the *caduceus* (the symbol of *felicitas*) on the coins of A.D. 34 to celebrate Tiberius' twenty years in office (Grant, *RAI* 45). See too above, 97.4n.

cura too had its republican heritage, but it was a virtue to be claimed by the politician in the execution of his duties (Hellegouarc'h, *VL* 252–3, cf. Vell. 45.3), or else it was used technically (e.g. *cura annonae*). *cura* clearly appealed to those exercising benevolent despotism: see Ovid on Augustus (*Tr.* 2.574), 'o pater, o patriae cura salusque tuae', and compare Dio 53.12.1 τὴν μὲν φροντίδα τήν τε προστασίαν τῶν κοινῶν, Vitr. 1.1.2 'te non solum de uita communi omnium curam publicaeque rei constitutione habere', Val. Max. 7.6.6. It was a term of extensive application (see the exhaustive study by Béranger 186ff.), only a very small percentage of which was military (cf. 97.2n.; Béranger 200–1): yet V. here, as at 114.1, uses it to describe Tiberius in a military context (on this see further below, 113.1n.).

For *mira felicitas* cf. Suet. *Dom.* 6.2, Flor. 1.24.17, 36.14, 2.13.59 etc.

Oceani circumnauigauerat sinus i.e. the coastline between the mouth of the Rhine and the tip of modern Denmark (cf. *RG* 26.4 'classis mea per Oceanum ab ostio Rheni ad solis orientis regionem usque ad fines Cimbrorum nauigauit', Plin. *NH* 2.167 'Germaniam classe circumuecta ad Cimbrorum promunturium'), which Tacitus describes similarly: 'cetera Oceanus ambit, latos sinus et insularum immensa spatia complectens' (*G.* 1.1, cf. 37.1 'eundem Germaniae sinum proximi Oceano Cimbri tenent'). *circumnauigare* is not found elsewhere in classical Latin, but is found later, e.g. Bede, *Hist. Eccl.* 5.9. *obseruantia* above would normally mean 'reverence' *uel sim.*, but V. has used the word in its primary sense (cf. Cic. *Tusc.* 4.21 'tempus obseruans').

ab inaudito atque incognito ante mari Drusus had in fact been the first to sail the North Sea (cf. Suet. *Claud.* 1.2, and Albinovanus Pedo's poem about the expedition in Sen. *Suas.* 1.15), but Ruhnken rightly takes to task those who accuse V. of falsification here: Drusus had gone no further than the land of the Chauci (i.e. the coastline between the rivers Weser and Elbe, cf. Dio 54.32.2), whereas Tiberius' fleet had rounded the tip of Denmark (last n.). It was of course conventional to describe the sea as 'uncharted', esp. in the familiar topos directed against seafaring (e.g. Sen. *Suas.* 1.10 'ignoti maris naturam', Sen. *Ben.* 5.6.1, Tac. *Agr.* 10.4); but, as often in V., rhetoric coexists happily with truth (cf. *RG* 26.4 on this expedition: 'quo neque terra neque mari quisquam Romanus ante id tempus adit'). For the northern naval expeditions of Augustus' reign cf. C. G. Starr, *The Roman imperial navy* (1941), 141–3. For the combination of *inauditus* and *incognitus* cf. Sen. *NQ* 1.16.4, Suet. *Nero* 42.1, Gell. 11.7.1, Arnob. *Nat.* 2.72.

⟨cum⟩ plurimarum gentium uictoria Some addition is clearly required to complete the sense. Acidalius suggested ⟨*a*⟩, which might have been omitted after *subuecta*; but E. Thomas' parallel of 104.3 is inexact since *ab* is there combined with *protinus* (for which F. compares *Bell. Alex.* 30.3, Cels. 7.8.1, 26.5, Plin. *NH* 20.226, Mart. 10.104.11), and it is awkward to understand *a* = 'after' here when the preposition has been used = 'from' in the preceding phrase. Ellis' ⟨*cum*⟩ seems to me more likely: the word, in an abbreviated form, could almost as easily have been omitted; and the phrase *cum uictoria* is at 40.1 above (cf. also Vitr. 9 *praef.* 1, Liv. 37.16.12). For *cum* repeated cf. e.g. 95.2, Cic. *Cat.* 1.33, *Vatin.* 18, Caes. *BG* 3.1.2, 5.52.3, and esp. 3.23.4 (where some MSS omit one *cum*). Kritz's support of Burman's emendation *uictori* (agreeing with *exercitui*) must be rejected: his unimaginative argument that 'non *classis* plurimas gentes vicerat, sed *exercitus*' is refuted by the way in which Dio describes the earlier naval expedition of Drusus (54.32.2).

The abl. *flumine Albi* above 'may be regarded as "space over which" or as instrumental', according to Shackleton Bailey (*Propertiana* (1956), 281): to his exs. add those in L&S s.v. *subueho.*

107.1 tantae rerum magnitudini hoc...inseram Since most ancient historians claimed to be recounting only the most important material at their disposal (cf. Avenarius 128f.), they naturally apologise when embarking upon a less significant episode. But V.'s apology here is of course disingenuous, since the episode is in fact a deliberate climax (above, p. 142). Compare esp. Sulp. *Vit. Mart.* 20.1 'adque ut minora tantis inseram', not mentioned by Klebs. The attempt by Manitius 465ff. to find Velleian influence in such phrases of Curtius as 'hoc qualecumque est' (6.10.11) must naturally be disregarded.

†sub omnem metumque† Either *-que* is an intrusion or else a noun has been lost, possibly hidden by *sub omnem*. If the latter, should we suggest a suitable partner for *metumque* (B) or *motumque* (A)? Although the latter has proved the more popular with edd., *metumque* is more appropriate to the theme of the episode (cf. 2 *arma metuit* and n.). Something like *per timorem metumque nostrarum nauium* may well be right, but certainty is far off. For *iuuentute fulgeret* above cf. perhaps Sil. 12.347 'fulgente iuuenta'; for *corpore excellens* below cf. perhaps Liv. 30.32.11 'celsus...corpore' (F.).

cauatum (ut illis mos est) ex materia... alueum Boeclerus noted that according to Pliny (*NH* 16.203) such dug-outs were in service with German pirates: see Norden, *Tac. Germ.* 308 n. 3. The parenthesis is not only an explanatory phrase analogous to *nominant* at 102.3 and to Livy's *uocant*-formula (for which cf. H. Nissen, *Krit. Untersuch. ü. d. Quellen des 4. u. 5. Dekade des Livius* (1863), 74ff.), but, like the preceding aside, is also a reminder of V.'s personal participation in the event (cf. 104.3n.). Note further V.'s air of amused superiority as he recalls the bizarre craft (*id nauigii genus*). For the precise use of *cauare* cf. Virg. *G.* 1.262, Liv. 21.26.8; for that of *temperare* below cf. Ov. *Met.* 13.366.

107.2 diu tacitus Walsh, *Livy* 205f., has noted that Livy will often heighten the drama of an episode by interposing a 'silence'; here V.'s *tacitus* performs the same function before the direct speech which follows. *linter*, above, is normally feminine; but not so here or at Tib. 2.5.34.

furit iuuentus quae, cum uestrum numen absentium colat... Scholars had long wondered what this *numen* could possibly be before Madvig proposed to solve the difficulty by supplying *non* before *colat* (2.308–9). On this radically different reading the Germans are mad (*furit*) because *potius arma metuit quam sequitur fidem*. But what could be more natural, for those with no long-standing experience of Rome, than fearing her mighty army massed on the opposite bank of their native river? (The long passage of Curtius which in some respects closely resembles our sentence (9.8.5–7: too long to quote, but ending '*furere* clamitantes et *cum dis* proelium inituros') differs fundamentally in that there the Sabarcae are contemplating an attack on the great army of Alexander and hence are mad, *furere*; but here the Germans are simply, and quite naturally, afraid.) Thus in our sentence *furit* is to be explained not by the contrast between *potius* and *quam* but by the contrast between the *cum*-clause and the rest of the sentence as a whole: the Germans are mad because, although they indeed have had some previous experience of Rome (*cum...numen...colat*), they are still afraid. Madvig's ⟨*non*⟩ must therefore be rejected; and the Roman *cultus* to which reference is made may well be an allusion to the altar which Domitius Ahenobarbus had erected on the bank of this same river three years previously (Dio 55.10*a*.2). Naturally V.'s reference to an actual *cultus*, though based on firm fact as Dio shows, may be somewhat optimistic; but such optimism is in keeping with the eulogistic nature of the episode. N. Scivoletto (above, p. 142 and

n. 2) has drawn attention to an epigram of Martial (5.3) where a native dwelling on the bank of the Ister sets eyes on Domitian and eulogises him with these very similar words (5–6): 'sors mea quam fratris melior, cui tam prope fas est | cernere, tam longe quem colit ille deum'. The notion of gazing at a quasi-divine figure is repeatedly stressed by V. in this chapter (1 *uidere Caesarem*, 2 *contemplatus*, *uidi deos*, *respectans Caesarem*, for which last cf. Plin. *Pan.* 23.2 'respectantium turba', *Pan. Lat.* 12.19.3 'oculis sequi') and is to be viewed in the light of the discussion at 94.2n.

sequitur fidem below is a phrase often found in legal contexts (cf. Ogilvie on Liv. 2.29.7), but can imply, appropriately, a condition of mutual trust (cf. E. Fraenkel, *TLL* 6.1.664.77–80, on Caes. *BG* 5.20.1, 56.3).

107.3 Victor omnium gentium...quos adierat, Caesar... Comparable descriptions of Pompey by Cicero (*Pis.* 16 'omnium gentium uictore') and by V. himself (40.2 'uictor omnium quas adierat gentium Pompeius', cf. Sulp. *Chron.* 2.26.5 '(Pompeius) uictor omnium gentium quas adierat') show the tradition of military men to which Tiberius now belonged. For such titles as *uictor* and *inuictus*, and the cult of Victoria, see Weinstock 91ff., 186–8 (p. 101 for Tiberius). It is difficult to say whether V.'s assessment of Tiberius' victories is accurate. If the campaigns of A.D. 4–5 were in fact a prelude to the more important matter of dealing with Maroboduus (see Syme, *CAH* 10.368f.; Seager 39), then his optimism is probably justified. But the issue was never put to the test: the attack on Maroboduus, which if successful would have set the seal on these earlier triumphs, was cut short by the Pannonian revolt in A.D. 6.

For *incolumi inuiolatoque* below cf. Macrob. 3.16.10 (of a fish); for *fraude temptato* below cf. Sen. *Ben.* 6.27.6 (F.).

108–109 MAROBODUUS AND THE ROMAN STRATEGY FOR A.D. 6

108.1 Maroboduo See *RE* 14.1907–10 (Stein); Dobiáš.

excita sedibus suis The Marcomanni migrated to Bohemia after their defeat by Drusus in 9 B.C.; for this and the various operations described by V. in 108–9 see the map in Wells. *exciri sedibus* is common (Liv. Sen. Curt. Luc. Amm.); *incinctus* below is commonly used of places by Mela, and is so used before V. by Ov. *Am.* 3.8.47 (F.).

108.2 nulla festinatio huius uiri mentionem transgredi debet As he is writing a history of Rome in summary form, V. is often compelled to by-pass certain topics by pleading either *breuitas* (cf. 96.3nn.) or *festinatio* (cf. 124.1): these two terms are interchangeable in ancient literary criticism and are a feature of works which belong to summary genres (see Woodman (1975), 278–87). Occasionally, however, there are topics of such importance that V., despite his literary haste (1.16.1 'quamquam...in hac tam praecipiti festinatione', 41.1 'quamlibet festinantem', cf. 117.1), is required to expand his narrative. One of these topics is Maroboduus, who is here given an extended portrait which comprises the conventional elements of his *genus*, *animus*, *facta* etc. (see above, p. 41; also below, 109.5n.).

It is thus not unreasonable to argue, as does Dobiáš 155, that the words *nulla festinatio...transgredi debet* mark 'a soldier's respect for his enemy'. But I think Rambaud goes too far when he extrapolates as follows (425–6). 'Le Romain essaie de comprendre non seulement ses compatriotes mais aussi les étrangers, élargissement de sa vision du monde et de l'humanité, d'où le portrait de Maroboduus chez Vell. Pat....Ainsi, le portrait historique, subissant l'influence des philosophies et d'un nouvel humanisme, devient l'instrument du jugement moral et de l'analyse psychologique, qui répondent au besoin intellectuel d'apprécier et de comprendre.' At any rate V.'s portrait must be seen in the light of his uncompromising words at the beginning of this chapter: 'nihil erat iam in Germania quod uinci posset praeter gentem Marcomannorum' (on which see Hellegouarc'h (1974), 82). For Norden's view of the portrait see below, 118.2n.

transgredi in this sense appears not to be found before V., but cf. Val. Max. 4.7 *ext.* 2 'grauissimo crimini sim obnoxius constantis et benignae amicitiae exempla sine ulla eius mentione transgressus' (Ungewitter and F.); hitherto writers had used *praeterire*, as Cic. *Marc.* 1 'tacitus praeterire nullo modo possum' (imitated at *Pan. Lat.* 10.6.2).

natione magis quam ratione barbarus Though Mar. possessed the traditional *ferocitas* of the Germans (*animo ferox*, cf. 106.2n.), his education, to which V. here alludes, had been at Rome (Strabo 7.1.3, p. 399 Meineke). The allusion is sharpened by word play, a useful device in character sketches (cf. Norden, *AK* 1.208), which on this occasion involves a change of vowel-quantity. Among other writers who enjoyed this refinement are Cicero (e.g. his plays on *ratio*/*oratio* at *Clu.* 6, *Sull.* 4 etc.: cf. H. Holst, *Die Wortspiele in Ciceros Reden* (1925), also Shackleton Bailey on *Att.* 1.16.5), the author of *Rhet. Herenn.* (4.29, labelling it paronomasia), and Virgil (cf. Norden on *Aen.* 6.204ff.). Quintilian, however, disapproved (9.3.69–71). For *barbarus*+abl. cf. 73.1, Cic. *Marc.* 8, Ov. *RA* 335.

non tumultuarium...occupauit principatum Dobiáš 156 notes that V. emphasises the difference between Mar.'s royalty and normal German 'kingship'. 'It was not a mere *principatus* (chieftainship), such a command as Germans normally entrusted to an able prince for a limited period (*mobilis*) in the hurried emergency of immediate war danger (*tumultuarius*).' *parentium* below = 'of his subjects', a substantival use of the present participle for which cf. 50.3: Ruhnken notes that the usage is in imitation of Sall. *J.* 3.2, 102.7.

sed certum imperium uimque regiam complexus animo, statuit... Having correctly described the nature of Mar.'s sovereignty (last n.), Dobiáš then suggests that it 'must surely have turned into a royal power *before* the Marcomannic migration' (156, my italics). That is, he takes *animo* with *statuit*, as a result of which *complexus* = 'having gained control of' (as Vict. *Epit.* 2.1 'Tiberius...imperium complexus est'). But *animo* could equally well go with *complexus*, as Rhenanus believed; and since this interpretation actually affects the meaning of *complexus*, whereas *animo* with *statuit* is simply redundant, I prefer to think that V. meant: 'having entertained visions of a stable empire and royal power' (cf. Liv. 35.42.12 'spe animoque complexum orbis terrarum imperium'). I therefore conclude that Mar. moved to Bohemia with the intention of doing these things, which is certainly what V. implies by *eo progredi ubi* below. For *potentiora arma* below cf. Liv. 31.7.14 (F.).

iuris sui fecit The phrase is also at 69.2, and Klebs 291 thus concludes that Sulp. *Chron.* 2.17.2 is a Velleian imitation; but the phrase is also at Sen. *Med.* 138, *Ep.* 77.15, Luc. 7.55, Just. 9.1.3 (F.). On *finitimos omnis aut bello domuit* above see Woodman (1968), 797–8.

109.1 corpus suum custodientium imperium The paradosis *custodia tum* presents problems of such difficulty that no solution carries complete conviction. I have printed the suggestion of Madvig (2.309), not because it is palaeographically easy, but because it takes account of two considerations which other editors have either disregarded or failed to notice: (1) the clearly intentional contrast between *suum...imperium* and *nostro quoque imperio*,[1] (2) the exclusively military reference of the phrase *perpetuis exercitiis ...redactum*. From (1) I deduce that there should be no sentence-break either immediately before or immediately after *imperium* (this disposes of many of the suggestions listed by Kritz); from (2) I deduce that *redactum* cannot qualify *imperium* and must therefore qualify *corpus* (this disposes of those who have emended to *corpus...imperii*). The sense is: 'having got them almost to Roman standards of discipline by interminable exercises, he soon

---

[1] This point is acknowledged by E. Bolaffi in his discussion of the crux, *Boll. Fil. Class.* 36 (1929), 106–7; but he nevertheless rejects Madvig's suggestion. His own emendation *corpus suum 'custodia tutum* [sc. *habebat*]; *imperium...*, which my arguments above contradict, had been anticipated by Cludius.

brought the body of states protecting *his* empire to such a peak of domination that it caused terror in *our* empire'. No one would pretend that the Latin is easy or elegant; but the interlaced word order of *corpus suum custodientium imperium* is characteristically Velleian (100.1n.), and for this use of *custodientes* cf. J. N. Adams, *Glotta* 51 (1973), 126.

ad Romanae disciplinae formam redactum *disciplinae formam* is another of V.'s many Ciceronianisms (cf. *De Or.* 3.141, *Fin.* 5.9). For the thought F. compares Liv. 4.37.7 'disciplinae Romanae plus in Volsco exercitu quam in Romano esset', and for the language Flor. 1.34.11 'redacto in disciplinam milite'. *exercitium* above is not found before V. in the sense of *exercitatio*.

ut neque bello nos †lacesseretur superesse sibi uim ac uoluntatem resistendi ⟨ostenderet⟩ Burman supplied *ostenderet*, and the sense remains clear despite the other deficiencies of the text. Kritz printed the following variation of Rosenheyn's suggestion: *neque bello nos lacesseret, et superesse sibi uim ac uoluntatem resistendi ⟨ostenderet⟩*; Stegmann prints Gelenius' version of Rhenanus' supplement: *neque bello nos ⟨lacesseret, et si⟩ lacesseretur, superesse sibi*... etc. Either is possible, but the truth is irrecoverable. For *uim*...*resistendi* cf. Liv. 2.56.4.

109.2 ut supplicem commendabant Cludius wished to supply *eum* before the verb, but cf. Cic. *Fam.* 13.13 'quare ut et meum amicum et tua dignum amicitia tibi commendo'. A similar ellipse is produced by Lipsius' emendation of 101.1 (see n.).

totumque ex male dissimulato agebat aemulum (1) Although *agere aemulum* can mean 'play the part of a rival ⟨and not actually be a rival⟩' (i.e. with a notion of pretence which makes nonsense of *ex male dissimulato*), nevertheless it can also mean 'act as a rival', 'behave as a rival', even simply 'be a rival': this latter meaning, without any notion of pretence, is at 92.2, 124.2, and cf. Goodyear on Tac. *A.* 1.4.4. Editors have also been troubled by *totum*; but the usage is not unlike such exs. as Cic. *Tusc.* 5.5 'tibi nos... penitus totosque tradimus', *Acad.* 1.34; and for the sense cf. 92.2 *in comitiis habendis praecipuum egit consulem*, 'he really behaved as consul ⟨at this point during his consulship⟩'. (2) *ex dissimulato* is an adverbial phrase on the analogy of those discussed at Hand, *Turs.* 2.656 (e.g. *ex improuiso*). Maroboduus tried to hide his rivalry (cf. Sen. *NQ* 4 *praef.* 5 'Plancus...aiebat non esse occulte nec ex dissimulato blandiendum'), but he failed (*male*, cf. Ov. *Her.* 15.7 'sed male dissimulo').

exercitumque...exercendo For the etymological word-play F. compares Dares 26, Veg. 3.10.

The apparent precision of V.'s information on enemy manpower and Roman operational planning (2–5) has led two scholars to two different hypotheses. G. M. Columba, 'Tiberiana: la storia di Maroboduo', *Boll. Fil. Class.* 8 (1901), 158–61, argued that V. derived his information, as did Tac. (*A.* 2.63) and Strabo (7.1.3, p. 399 Meineke), from the speech which Tiberius delivered about Maroboduus in the senate in A.D. 18 and which Tac. briefly reports. C. Jodry, on the other hand, argued that both V. in his history and Tiberius in his speech independently referred back to original military documents which had been preserved in the imperial archives since the abortive mission against Maroboduus; Tac. and Strabo both depend upon Tiberius' speech, as before ('Les documents militaires chez V.P.', *REL* 29 (1951), 265–84). Since Tacitus' summary of Tiberius' speech (2.63.3) bears a marked similarity to V., and since at 129.3 V. seems to echo the letter concerning Maroboduus which Tiberius read to the senate on this occasion (see n.), I think Columba has the better argument.

quod habebat Several edd. have not unreasonably questioned *habebat*, which seems odd to qualify *opus* and for which there is no exact parallel (exs. such as Cic. *ND* 1.100 are different). But since V. can use *opus* as equivalent to *bellum* (117.1, cf. *opus belli* at Prop. 3.11.70, Liv. 22.55.2), and since *bellum habere* is regular (Cic. Liv. Tac.), I think we are justified in retaining the paradosis.

109.4 finem...terminant The same pleonasm is at 37.5, Cic. *Cat.* 3.26; for the analogous and far more common pleonasm with words of 'beginning' cf. L–H–S 793; Löfstedt, *Synt.* 2.179f. For the 'heroic clausula' with which this sentence ends cf. 95.2n.

109.5 Hunc uirum...diuersis e partibus...adgredi statuit 'The campaign was a masterpiece of organisation and deserves a proud place in the annals of military art. The armies and the generals of Augustus have nothing to lose by a comparison with those of any age in the history of Rome...The invasion of Bohemia was to be the crowning achievement of Augustan strategy' (Syme, *CAH* 10.368–9).

The resumptive use of *hunc* here, a feature of portrait-writing (Leo 140, 217, 308–9), impressively sums up the man whom it has taken V. almost two chapters to describe: 'Voilà l'homme...que Tibère César décida d'attaquer' (H–W).

ut...legiones * Boiohaemum** The paradosis lacks a verb: some edd. assume ellipse, others follow Lipsius in supplying *duceret* after the parenthesis. Although there are numerous exs. in Latin of the ellipse of verbs of motion (Lindgren 52–4; K–S 2.551–2; L–H–S 424), in almost every case there is a preposition to ease the construction. Indeed P. Cluverius rightly felt that a preposition would be needed even if the verb were expressed, which explains why I have placed the lacuna before *Boiohaemum* and have not followed Lipsius.

For the projected route of advance see Wells 160–1. *excisis continentibus Hercyniae siluis* = 'having cut down the forests which adjoined the Hercynian ⟨forest⟩'. *ipse* = 'the general himself', as Caes. *BG* 7.90.7 etc.

110–116 REVOLT IN PANNONIA AND DALMATIA (A.D. 6–9)

The revolt in Pannonia, 'grauissimum omnium externorum bellorum post Punica' (Suet. *Tib.* 16.1), broke out in A.D. 6, the year in which Tiberius was planning to attack Maroboduus and in which V. was elected quaestor for A.D. 7 (111.3). Scholars are generally agreed that Augustus' immediate reaction was one of panic: he at once began conscripting a vast army (111.1), part of which was conducted to the front by V. himself in A.D. 6 (111.3). V. returned to Rome in order to take up his quaestorian appointment in December A.D. 6, but instead was sent back to Tiberius by Augustus as *legatus Augusti*, spending not only the year of his quaestorship in the front line but remaining there till the end of the war (111.4, cf. 104.3).

The war itself has been discussed in modern times by numerous scholars, most recently by Koestermann (345–78) and Wilkes (69–77 and (1965), 111–25). Each of these recognises in varying degrees the value of V.'s account, written as it is from his unique position as a participant. Koestermann's is by far the most detailed of modern discussions,[1] and he estimates V.'s contribution as follows (357):

> 'Die Feldzüge hat er als Mithandelnder und Augenzeuge erlebt, und das gibt seiner Schilderung nicht nur die persönliche Note, sondern verleiht ihr auch einen authentischen Charakter, den es unbedingt zu respektieren gilt. Freilich müssen wir dabei seine sehr ausgesprochenen Sympathien und Abneigungen immer in Anschlag bringen.'

We perhaps need not take the statutory allusion to V.'s *Abneigungen* too seriously, for there is little evidence to support it; but the most important of his *Sympathien* is naturally his appreciation of Tiberius. V. not only stresses Tiberius' kindness to his troops, which he had himself experienced (114.2),

[1] He provides a full bibliography of earlier scholarly material, amongst which note esp. Rau 313–46 and Syme, *CAH* 10.369–73. Note also Sumner 271–4; but A. Mócsy, *Pannonia and Upper Moesia* (1974), 37–9, is most disappointing.

but also gives firm support to the circumspection of Tiberius' policy (110.3n.). Although this policy did not always square with what Augustus himself thought necessary (113.2n.), the old emperor eventually came to recognise that Tiberius had been proved right (115.5n.).

It is natural that for a war of such complexity scholars do not always agree either on what the evidence (i.e. V., Dio) appears to report, or on what actually took place. Details of this nature, as they affect V.'s account, are discussed in the annotations which follow; but one point, which touches on an important controversy (cf. 111.4nn.), may conveniently be discussed here. V.'s narrative, as in the preceding chapters, is broadly annalistic. Thus, for example, the events of A.D. 7 are reported in 112.3–113.3; the winter of A.D. 7/8 is specifically mentioned (113.3 *hiemis initio, hibernis*, 114.4 *hiems*), as is the beginning of the campaigning season in A.D. 8 (114.4 *insequenti aestate*). The end of A.D. 8 is specifically given at 114.5 (*autumni ⟨initio⟩, in hiberna*), likewise the beginning of the A.D. 9 season (115.2 *initio aestatis*). It should be noted, however, that these annual divisions are marked off not only by phraseology of this type but also by a stylistic device which may be paralleled in other historians.

Sallust and Livy both employ digressions to indicate breaks in their narratives between one episode and another, while Tacitus regularly marks the end of a year by an obituary tribute to some of those who have died during that year.[1] V.'s technique in the narrative of the Pannonian revolt is comparable. The end of the war as a whole (115.5) is marked off from the next episode, the disaster to Varus (117ff.), by ch. 116 which constitutes a tribute to those who served well during A.D. 6–9. The break between A.D. 8 and 9 is marked off by tributes to M. Lepidus and V.'s brother, Magius Celer Velleianus (114.5–115.1); the break between A.D. 7 and 8 is emphasised by a digression on Tiberius as the ideal general (114.1–3). The technique is clear. But what of the break between A.D. 6 and 7? Although here there is no such explicit phraseology as found on the other occasions mentioned in the preceding paragraph, the generalised reference to *hiberna* at 111.4 is followed by a tribute to the achievements of Messalinus during A.D. 6. This tribute evidently performs exactly the same function as the other 'bridging' passages just mentioned: certainly the recognition of V.'s technique for A.D. 7/8, 8/9, and at the end of the war strongly supports such an interpretation of 112.1–2. If this hypothesis is accepted, it is a powerful argument against those who believe that V.'s account of A.D. 7 begins at 111.4 (see nn.).[2]

[1] See e.g. Ogilvie (1967), 164f., 245; Syme, *Sall.* 145; *TST* 79f.

[2] Those who hold this belief are forced to conclude that 112.1–2 is 'ein nachträglicher Einschub in die Geschichte des Jahres 7 n. Chr.' (Rau 326), which is self-evidently unsatisfactory. In the section of commentary which follows I have made use of sub-headings to emphasise the systematic arrangement of V.'s narrative.

110–112.2 THE EVENTS OF A.D. 6

110–11 Outbreak and counter-measures

110.1 Rumpit interdum, ⟨modo⟩ moratur...fortuna A more puzzling sentence than scholars have generally allowed. V. appears to draw a contrast between the two effects of *fortuna*, its total disruption (*rumpit*) and mere postponement (*moratur*). Like some others I cannot believe that V. expressed this contrast by the almost intolerable asyndeton of a single *interdum* as found in the paradosis. Heinsius' chiastic *rumpit interdum, ⟨interdum⟩ moratur* is a strong possibility and is paralleled in Sen. *Ep.* 114.8 'hominis esse interdum, interdum temporis' and Plin. *Ep.* 6.16.6. I nevertheless prefer a combination, also chiastic, of *interdum* and *modo*, found in several authors (cf. *TLL* 8.1314.8ff.; L–H–S 521, K–S 2.73; E. Wölfflin, *ALL* 2 (1885), 243–4, 253), but esp. in Sallust (e.g. *J.* 42.1, 55.8, 72.9, 74.1). It is true that the combination is usually found in the form *modo*...*interdum*, but not at Ov. *Tr.* 2.269 'eripit interdum, modo dat medicina salutem'; and *modo* in its abbreviated form *mo* could easily have been omitted before *moratur*.

The contrast itself is also strange, because apparently anticlimactic (*rumpit*...*moratur*); but the reason is as follows. Both V. (cf. 108.2–109.4) and Tiberius himself (cf. Tac. *A.* 2.63) believed that Maroboduus was a dangerous threat who should be removed. The inability to do so in A.D. 6, as planned, was a severe blow to Roman pride; but in A.D. 18 Tiberius, now emperor, subtly brought about the downfall of Maroboduus who was forced to seek refuge with Rome and live for the rest of his life in sanctuary at Ravenna. There is no doubt that, though twelve years late, the victory was regarded both by V. (cf. 129.3) and by the emperor (cf. Tac. loc. cit.) as a great achievement. Thus *moratur*, from the point of view of Roman pride, is more, not less, climactic than *rumpit*.

hiberna...ad Danubium The base was at Carnuntum (cf. 109.5), 'in prehistoric and Roman times the most important crossing of the Middle Danube' (Wells 159, referring to E. Swoboda, *Carnuntum* (4th edn, 1964), 32–3). Archaeology has not yet located the base.

admotoque exercitu...placuerat There is undeniably a lacuna to be placed somewhere between *hostium* and *paene*. Many suggestions have been advanced, but, as in the many other cruces which occur in chh. 110–16, much remains inevitably obscure. I shall indicate simply what I believe to be the extent of the corruption, and how it might be cured.

Mommsen, Haupt (1.267–8) and Stegmann each proposed similar solutions, of which Haupt's is both representative and the best: we may conveniently begin by discussing it. Haupt placed a lacuna immediately after *hostium* and proposed the following supplement: *aberat, et legiones etiam quas*.

Yet *aberat* is unnecessary: *iter* is an adverbial acc. with *admoto* no different from e.g. Liv. 43.21.9 'diei progressus iter', Caes. *BG* 4.4.4. I also believe *quas* is mistaken. Unlike Heinsius, who objected to the repetition *admotoque* ...*admoueri*, I think V. was intending here a similar effect to that at 109.1 *imperium*...*imperio* (see n.): if so, it is more likely (though of course the point is subjective and cannot be proved) that *Saturninum admoueri* occurred in a main clause.

Now if this hypothesis is accepted, the result is a phrase which not only preserves the paradosis but also makes good sense: *Saturninum admoueri placuerat*. We should then follow Lipsius and others in supplying *cuius copiae* after *placuerat* to provide the required noun for *diuisae* and *iuncturae* which follow. Yet two further points suggest themselves. (1) At 109.1 the correspondence between *imperium* and *imperio* was confirmed by the addition of *quoque* with the latter; and a word to perform the same function would undoubtedly be desirable here. And since we know that a feminine noun has been lost somewhere in the passage, it is not unreasonable to suppose that (e.g.) *etiam* was lost with it. *etiam* had of course been proposed by Haupt, but not in a position where it would assist the repetition which I believe is important. (2) The focal point of the following phrases seems to be the rendezvous with Tiberius, *cum Caesare ⟨se⟩ iuncturae erant*: it is unlikely that this was part of a relative clause. Like Kritz therefore I prefer to regard *paene*...*iuncturae erant* as a new and complete sentence, with the noun understood from the sentence at present being discussed.

Of course any supplement of a noun before *placuerat* requires that *admoueri* be changed to *admouere* (Ruhnken *et al.*) or *admouere ei* (Haupt), each of which is possible. In the light of all the preceding remarks, I would suggest the following: 'admotoque exercitu non plus quam quinque dierum iter a primis hostium, Saturninum ⟨copias etiam⟩ admouere ei placuerat' ('and having moved forward his army not more than five days' march from the first of the enemy, he had decided that Saturninus should also move forward his forces'). Something along these lines satisfies the logic and wholly Velleian style of the sentence as transmitted, and also minimises the extent of the corruption as much as possible. But no solution is demonstrably right; and in my text I have preferred simply to print the paradosis and mark a lacuna.

For the technical *admouere exercitum, copias* etc. cf. *TLL* 1.773.17ff.; for *iter ab* cf. Cic. *Planc.* 96, *Sest.* 131, Plin. *Ep.* 10.18.1; for *placet* and acc. + infin. cf. 60.1; K–S 693d, 695f, L–H–S 358.

110.2 cum uniuersa Pannonia...arma corripuit Before A.D. 9 'the Romans labelled the whole area between the Middle Danube and Macedonia as Illyricum' (Wilkes 161), and it is this nomenclature which V. often uses (e.g. 109.5, 112.2, 116.3, 123.1, 125.1, 5). After A.D. 9, however, Illyricum was divided into two separate provinces, *Superius* and *Inferius*, which soon became known as Dalmatia and Pannonia respectively. It is this later terminology which V. uses here (so too e.g. 39.3, 90.1, 114.4, 116.2). See in general Wilkes 95, 167–8.

Dio 55.29.1–2 plainly states that it was the Dalmatians, not the Pannonians, who began the revolt. But, as Koestermann remarks (347), 'der römische Autor will nicht die genetische Entwicklung kennzeichnen, sondern das Gesamtgebiet umreissen, in dem der Aufruhr tobte. Dass dabei der Hauptnachdruck auf Pannonien liegt, dessen Bevölkerung zahlenmässig weit überwog und wo sich alsdann die wichtigsten Kämpfe abspielten, ist nur natürlich.' It was not in fact until after the Pannonians revolted that Tiberius took a hand in affairs (Dio 55.30.1).

insolens longae pacis bonis et adulta uiribus The Romans were prepared to believe that peace was occasionally desirable (for the phrase *pacis bona* cf. 92.2, Liv. 21.21.4, 34.22.4, Val. Max. 7.4 *ext.* 1, Tac. *H.* 3.81.1); but, like the Greeks (cf. Theogn. 153–5, Solon 5.9 Diehl, Hdt. 8.77, Eur. fr. 437N², Thuc. 3.39.4, Plb. 6.18.5, 32.13.6, Diog. Laer. 1.59), they recognised that a desirable state of existence could go to people's heads: Cato, fr. 163 Malc. 'plerisque hominibus rebus secundis...superbiam atque ferociam augescere atque crescere', Sall. *J.* 40.5 'insolentia ex secundis rebus', 100.1, Cic. *Pis.* 23, Hirt. *BG* 8.13.4, Liv. 23.2.1, Curt. 10.1.40, Sen. *Dial.* 4.33.1, *Clem.* 1.1.7, Tac. *H.* 1.15.3 (with Heubner's parallels), 2.7.1, Stat. *Theb.* 11.448, Front. *Strat.* 1.3.3, Amm. 28.6.13, *Pan. Lat.* 3.27.1.

V. thus sees the cause of the revolt in terms of traditional political theories (cf. Dio 55.29.2 τὴν ἡλικίαν σφῶν ἀνθοῦσαν εἶδον [sc. οἱ Δελμάται]). But Koestermann (346 n. 3) agrees with another passage of Dio, 55.29.1, where the cause is given as the tribute which the natives were compelled to pay to Rome (*contra* Syme, *CAH* 10.369).

For *longa pax* cf. Heubner on Tac. *H.* 1.67.2; for *adulta uiribus* Ruhnken compares Lucr. 3.449 'adoleuit uiribus aetas' (for *adulta* of a place cf. Cic. *Brut.* 27 'Athenis...iam adultis'). Juv. plays on the phrases *longa pax* and *pacis bona* at 6.292 'longae pacis mala' (cf. Syme, *Tac.* 218 n. 6).

in societatem adductis consilii Fröhlich's excellent *consilii* restores normal phraseology, cf. esp. 118.3 'plures in societatem consilii recepit'; also 35.4, Cic. *Sest.* 8, *Vatin.* 41, Liv. 2.4.2, 38.31.5 etc. For the tribes which joined in cf. Koestermann 346 n. 4.

110.3 tum necessaria gloriosis praeposita, neque tutum uisum... So ends the first paragraph of V.'s account of the war; the last paragraph ends with a similar sentiment: 'semperque uisum est gloriosum quod esset tutissimum' (115.5). Within this framework (ring composition) V. continually stresses the painstaking care shown by Tiberius, who preferred method and efficiency to spectacular victories: 111.4 'prudentia ducis', 113.2 'utilia speciosis praeferens', 114.1 'Caesaris cura', 115.5 'ante conscientiae quam famae consultum', 'prouidentia ducis'.

The *gloriosa* to which V. refers are the *proposita* of 1 above, viz. the projected campaigns against Maroboduus. Taken with 108.1 *nihil erat... Marcomannorum*, this brief reference may support those who believe in Augustus' expansionist policy (see Brunt 175, Wilkes 69 and n. 3; in general above, p. 38 and n. 4); on the other hand, this may simply be V.'s own interpretation of that policy, whatever it was.

For *gloriosa* as subst. cf. Cic. *Fin.* 5.72; for *necessaria* cf. 1.16.1, Sall. *J.* 73.6, to which F. adds Cic. *Top.* 69, Curt. 5.12.6, Cels. 3.22.2, Front. *Strat.* 3.14.4. For the contrast *gloriosus/necessarius* cf. Calp. Flacc. 19 (F.).

omnis numerus amplius DCCC milibus explebat As the normal expr. is *numerum explere* (*TLL* 5.2.1718.38ff.), Acidalius toyed with reading *explebatur* here; but cf. Liv. 38.23.9 'numerus captiuorum...milia quadraginta expleuit', Curt. 4.12.13, 7.4.30 etc. For *armis habilia* below cf. Ov. *Fast.* 2.14 'habilis telis', Claud. *II Cons. Stil.* 365 'habiles armis umeros'.

110.4 iunctam sibi Nauporti ac Tergestis confinio 'Of the old road from Italy to the valley of the Save, across the low eastern gateway of Italy, the Julian Alps, the Romans had long been aware. Here Italy was most vulnerable, here Philip V of Macedon had planned to send over a horde of Bastarnae' (Syme, *CAH* 10. 352, cf. Liv. 39.35, 40.57). For the threat of invasion cf. also Dio 55.30.1.

maxima...auctoritas Although Heinsius in fact altered the paradosis *proxima* to *porro maxima*, most edd. credit him only with *maxima*. This latter is undoubtedly correct, the two words being often confused: cf. 114.5, 127.1; Ellis 178 (with reff.).

duobus Batonibus ac Pinneti ducibus There was a Pannonian Bato (*RE* 3.1.141–2 = Bato 4 (Henze); *PIR*[2] 1.360, no. 93: he came from the Breuci tribe, cf. Dio 55.29.3), and a Dalmatian Bato (*RE* 3.1.142–3 = Bato 5 (Henze); *PIR*[2] 1.360–1, no. 94: from the Desidiates, cf. Dio 55.29.2). Pinnes was another Pannonian leader, cf. *RE* 20.2.1712 = Pinnes 2 (Stein).

110.5 plerisque etiam litterarum usus, et familiaris animorum erat exercitatio A most peculiar statement, of whose precise significance I am not sure. Some scholars (e.g. A. Mócsy, *RE* Suppl. 9.767; P. A. Brunt, *Italian manpower* (1971), 243) have thought that V. refers to the Pannonians' knowledge of *Roman* culture; but this, though at first sight it appears to follow from the preceding phraseology, makes no significant point and does not square with the carefully arranged argument of the passage as a whole. This argument, which employs a series of correspondences, is as follows. The greatest authority (*maxima auctoritas*) rested with the leaders (*ducibus*), but in fact (*autem*) all the Pannonians were disciplined (*in omnibus disciplinae notitia*); they were all not only disciplined (*in omnibus non disciplinae tantummodo*) but also knew Latin (*sed linguae quoque notitia Romanae*); further, a considerable number of them (*plerisque*, responding to *in omnibus*) were capable of *litterarum usus* and *animorum exercitatio*. Since these last two elements balance *disciplinae* and *linguae* above but refer to a different group of people (*plerisque*), I do not think the interpretation of Mócsy and Brunt can be maintained. We must fall back, therefore, on the interpretation given by H–W: 'beaucoup d'entre eux même avaient une certaine culture littéraire et les exercices de l'esprit leur étaient familiers'. On this view V. apparently sees intellectual attainment as one reason why the diverse Pannonian tribes achieved such swift success against the might of Rome (*itaque*, below). Bothe suggested emending *animorum* to *armorum*; but this destroys the logic even more,[1] and anyway, as Burman observed, the expression is unexceptionable (Cic. *Off.* 1.123 'exercitationes animi', cf. Sen. *Ep.* 82.16).

nulla umquam natio tam mature consilio belli bellum iunxit ac decreta patrauit The speed of events is vividly emphasised in the following sentence: *oppressi*, *trucidati*, *caesus*. V.'s phraseology (cf. also 79.1 'consultisque facta coniungens' and 118.3, a similar context) is Sallustian: cf. *C.* 1.6 'nam et prius quam incipias consulto, et ubi consulueris mature facto opus est' (see Woodman (1968), 797; and for the Sallustian verb *patrare* cf. Syme, *Sall.* 261). For the 'heroic clausula' cf. 95.2n.

110.6 ea in regione, quae plurimum ab imperatore aberat Tiberius was presumably NW of his *hiberna* at Carnuntum (1n.). Koestermann 348–9 agrees with those who place the massacre of the *uexillarii* in the territory of the Desidiates (i.e. around Sarajevo: map in Wilkes 175); but he points out that the *negotiatores* are more likely to have been located to the NE, in the more congenial lowlands around Sirmium.

omnia [et] in omnibus locis...uastata No one except Cornelissen (1887) has been troubled by this clause; but how may its subject (*omnia*) be joined to an adverbial phrase (*in omnibus locis*) by *et*? It may not. The case at 83.2 is not comparable, since there *et* joins two items each of an identical nature and reference: 'in omnia et omnibus uenalis'. Cornelissen suggested

---

1 To be fair, I should add that Bothe punctuated the passage differently: '...notitia Romanae (plerisque etiam litterarum usus) et familiaris armorum [erat] exercitatio'.

occupata armis Macedonia omnis, et in omnibus locis...uastata; but this destroys the effectiveness of the polyptoton with *omnis*, of which Latin writers are very fond (in V. e.g. at 83.2, quoted, 109.3). We must either assume that another adverbial phrase has dropped out or that *et* has been wrongly added, perhaps through the influence of 83.2. The latter suggestion is the more economical; and for a similarly erroneous addition of *et* cf. 107.2.

stabilem illum et formatum tantorum bellorum experientia... animum It is extremely difficult to decide whether to read *formatum* with BA or *firmatum* with Burer. In favour of Burer's emendation are the following points: *firm(at)us* and *stabilis* are a natural combination, found elsewhere (e.g. Cic. *Fin.* 3.29; *TLL* 6.1.819.48–9); *firmatum* appropriately contrasts with *quateret*, and perhaps also with *terreret*, below; *firmatum* is perhaps supported by 78.2 'bellique experientia durabat exercitum'; *firmatus animus* is at Cic. *Clu.* 13, *Tusc.* 2.28. Yet *formare* is the *mot juste* for moulding a soldier's spirit (cf. Liv. 44.1.5 'ad militarem disciplinam...formato milite', Sil. 8.546 'laetos rectoris formabat Scipio bello'), and *animum formare* is a set expression which, occurring in Cic. *Brut.* 142, becomes popular in the 'silver' age (cf. Brink on Hor. *AP* 307). Hitherto Vossius and Kritz have been the only edd. to retain the paradosis: I think they were right. See also 123.1n., where a similar suggestion of Burer is accepted.

111.1 reuocati undique et omnes ueterani 'and everywhere all the veterans too were recalled'. *et* = *etiam*; it does not join *undique* and *omnes* (so *TLL* 5.2.873.34). Ruhnken rightly notes that *reuocare ueteranos* is technical, quoting Tac. *H.* 2.82.1 (see Heubner ad loc.). For *dilectus* above cf. 130.2n.

uiri feminaeque ex censu libertinum coactae dare militem A rare measure, cf. Suet. *Aug.* 25.2 'libertino milite...bis usus est: semel ad praesidium coloniarum Illyricum contingentium...eosque seruos adhuc uiris feminisque pecuniosioribus indictos'. These forces were apparently collected during the course of A.D. 6 and sent out with Germanicus in 7 (cf. Dio 55.31.1 under this year: στρατιώτας οἱ οὐκ εὐγενεῖς μόνον ἀλλὰ καὶ ἐξελευθέρους δούς, ἄλλους τε καὶ ὅσους παρά τε τῶν ἀνδρῶν καὶ παρὰ τῶν γυναικῶν δούλους). On *coactae*, attracted into the gender of the nearest noun rather than agreeing with *uiri*, cf. K–S 1.45, L–H–S 435.

audita in senatu uox principis... The sentences which begin thus and end with †*pollicitati* below were transposed by Haase to follow *quateret atque terreret* above. This suggestion is rendered even more attractive if the transposed passage is merely *audita...conspectum*: we should then have respective sections on the reaction of Aug. and the measures taken. But it is hard to see how the error might have arisen, and anyway writers do not always compose as logically as this transposition supposes: besides, *in senatu* might easily have led V. subsequently to mention *senatorum...operae.*

urbis Romae Kritz strangely prints *Romanae,* a quite acceptable expression (cf. D. Kuijper, *Mnem.* 21 (1968), 50 n. 9; Krebs–Schmalz 2.697), but one for which there is no authority in the paradosis.

exactae ad id bellum operae †pollicitati A absurdly but typically places a comma after *operae* and nowhere else; P places full stops after both *operae* and *pollicitati,* thus producing a semblance of sense ('The services of senators and knights were demanded for the war. They promised them'). But I cannot believe that V. wrote a sentence of such extreme obliqueness and brevity. Hottinger's punctuation after *omnia* hardly helps (reported in Krause's edn ad loc.); besides, *omnia haec* together appropriately sum up the various aspects of the war effort which have been mentioned. Of the numerous emendations which have been proposed (see Kritz), I am attracted to only two. (1) Ruhnken emended to *ex pollicitatione,* noting that *-one* could easily have been omitted before *omnia.* But the expression is unparalleled. (2) Gelenius emended to *pollicitae,* upon which *pollicitaeque* is perhaps an improvement.[1] Something of this nature is possible: for *operas* (*-am*) *polliceri* cf. 59.5, Sall. *C.* 28.1, 40.6, Liv. 5.7.7, 46.8 etc.; for *exigere* and *polliceri* together cf. Cic. *Brut.* 17; for *polliceri* in a passive sense cf. Ov. *Fast.* 3.366, Hyg. *Fab.* 100. But the truth is irrecoverable.

111.2 ut praesidium militum Since Tiberius is described by V. at 103.1 as 'rei publicae praesidium' and by Suet. *Tib.* 21.3 (in the context of the Pannonian revolt) as 'unicum populi Romani praesidium', edd. have objected to the word *militum* here. Some of their conjectures have been most ingenious: *ultimum* (Lipsius), *iam solitum* (Heinsius, cf. 120.1 'perpetuus patronus Romani imperii adsuetam sibi causam suscipit'), *limitum* (Purser), *ut praesidium milites, res publica...* (Gruner). But none of these suggestions carries complete conviction; and Kritz rightly notes that a reference to *praesidium militum* comes very naturally after *nisi qui illa regeret fuisset* (where *illa* = *milites,* in effect). I have therefore retained the paradosis, but with some hesitation.

111.3 mediocritas nostra For such humbling refs. to oneself cf. 104.3n.; for such abstract nouns as *mediocritas* as subject of the verb, a mainly imperial usage, cf. Nägelsbach 81; L–H–S 746f. For *speciosi ministerii* below cf. Liv. 4.8.6 (Heinsius), Val. Max. 8.13.1 (Kritz).

designatus quaestor Since V. has been discussing the events of A.D. 6, most scholars assume that he was designated quaestor in that year: from this

[1] *ac pollicitae* was suggested by Boot.

is deduced his date of birth, traditionally 20/19 B.C. (cf. Sumner 275 n. 111). The precise moment of V.'s designation is unknown, but quaestorian elections were usually held early in the year (the date became fixed at 24 January): see Sherwin-White on Plin. *Ep.* 4.15.6 with reff. *designatus* here merely = 'elect' and of course implies none of the procedures discussed at 124.3n., 126.2n. For *equestris militia* above cf. Mommsen, *Staatsr.* 3.543 and n. 2.

necdum senator aequatus...tribunis plebei 'and though not yet a senator I was placed on a parity with senators and even tribunes elect' (Shipley). We thus infer that 'die andern Legaten, denen mit V. diese Truppen anvertraut wurden, waren Senatoren; ja sogar designirte Volkstribunen waren darunter' (Sauppe 44n.). No evidence survives to indicate whom V. means: the only other person whom we know to have been sent out on a similar mission was Germanicus, but that was in the following year (above, 1n.).

perduxi There is no evidence that V. set out late in A.D. 6 (as assumed by Syme, *CAH* 10.371; Koestermann 357; Wilkes 71; Seager 41; Massauer). A much earlier moment is far more likely (next n. but one).

111.4 in quaestura deinde...missus V. implies that in A.D. 6 he came back to Rome in time for 5 December, the day on which quaestors traditionally took up office (cf. Mommsen, *Staatsr.* 1³.606). We have no means of knowing if he was sent back to the front at once, before the end of the year, or if he waited until the beginning of the next year's campaigning season (cf. 112.3n.). If the latter, the present sentence is strictly anachronistic, since every other event in 110–112.2 is attributable to A.D. 6; but V.'s term of office began in the last weeks of that year, as we have just seen, and in view of *designatus quaestor* in 3 above this is a most appropriate moment for him to mention the special circumstances of his actual appointment. It would certainly have been uncharacteristic if V. had dwelt upon the subject by returning to it at a later stage in the narrative (cf. 104.3n.). On *remissa sorte* and special commissions such as V.'s cf. Mommsen, *Staatsr.* 1³.516 and n. 1.

There is some doubt over P's reading *missus*, 'sicherlich eine verunglückte Conjectur Rhenan's' according to Halm (1875), 542, who himself had earlier conjectured *missus sum* on the basis of A's reading *missum*. But in my opinion Burer's silence implies that *missus* derives from (M): it would be typical of A, which makes a similar error at 89.3, to corrupt *missus* to *missum* under the influence of the preceding *eundem*. Kritz also favoured P's reading, but argued that *missus* is a participle and that the main verb is *uidimus* below; yet the change from singular to plural in the same sentence seems to me too harsh (cf. esp. *nos*). With Bolaffi, therefore, I prefer to regard *missus* as the main verb: Latin writers regularly omit parts of *esse*, including *sum*, from perf. pass. forms of the verb (see esp. Lindgren 36ff.); and Bolaffi rightly observed that this type of ellipse is particularly common in V. (*De Vell. sermone...quaest. select.* (1925), 27ff.).[1]

primo anno 'Unter dem *primus annus* das erste Jahr zu verstehen ist, das Vell. mit Tiberius gemeinsam an der Front verbrachte, also 7 n.Chr.' (Koestermann 359, following Rau 324–5). But this view, accepted also by Massauer, must be rejected for several reasons. (1) At 112.1 V. writes *prima aestate belli*, meaning A.D. 6: supporters of the Rau–Koestermann view are compelled to believe that 'diese Zeitangabe...darf nicht mit *primo anno* gleichgesetzt werden' (Massauer). But the reader can hardly do anything else, and it is impossible to believe that V., having written *primo anno* in the *preceding* section here, should expect us to understand by it the *following* year, A.D. 7. (2) V.'s narrative is broadly annalistic (above, p. 154): he has hitherto, with the single exception of the brief sentence on his quaestorship, been relating the events of A.D. 6, and he continues relating the events of the same year at 112.1–2. It is highly unlikely that he interrupted his orderly narrative of this year in order to anticipate at some length the events of A.D. 7. This argument is scarcely affected by the brief anticipation in *in quaestura... missus* above (see n.), and is strongly supported by the function of 112.1–2 below (see p. 154). (3) There is no reason why *primo anno* should not mean A.D. 6. We have already seen that V. was elected quaestor early in that year and that he was not required to be back in Rome until December of the same year: in the interval there were several months during which, once Augustus' troops had been conducted to the front, he could witness the items mentioned here under *primo anno.* (4) At 104.3 V. states that he was with Tiberius 'per annos *continuos* VIIII' starting from A.D. 4: there can thus be no doubt that he was with Tiberius during the first year of the war and that it is this year to which *primo anno* refers. (See too below on *intra se...elanguesceret.*)

prudentia ducis Cf. 115.5n.

furentes eorum uires uniuersas euasimus, ⟨exhausimus⟩ partibus Another of the many controversial phrases in V.'s account of the war. Kritz tries to argue that *euasimus* is ignominious whereas *elusimus* (= A's *eius imus*) is not; but since the two words are virtually identical in meaning, I cannot see that his distinction is valid. Haase rightly said of *euasimus*: 'sine ignominia dicitur; neque enim de audacia agitur, sed laudatur ducis prudentia',

---

1 The ellipse proposed here, since it comes at the end of a sentence, causes no ambiguity and fulfils all the conditions mentioned by Goodyear in his discussion of the subject (*Comm. Tac.* 1.346–50).

and in support of this cf. Front. *Strat.* 1.5.18 'iniquitate locorum et multitudine hostium pressus...aduersarium euasit'. It is nevertheless difficult to make sense of the paradosis *uniuersas euasimus partibus* because the last of these words is extremely obscure. Thus H–W, who print the paradosis, are forced to supply the words which I have italicised in order that it should make sense: 'D'échapper à l'assaut furieux de toutes leurs troupes *et de les vaincre en les attaquant* séparément.'

Is there a contrast between *uniuersas* and *partibus*, as most edd. assume, or is *partibus* an emendation by someone who believed there ought to be such a contrast (so e.g. Koestermann 359 n. 3)? I find the latter unattractive: the obvious solution is to suppose that V. wrote *artibus* (so Rhenanus), which seems both weak in itself and awkward after – especially so long after – *quantis opportunitatibus.* As edd. observe, V. is extremely fond of the contrast between *uniuersus* and *partes*, and I think it more than likely that he intended such a contrast here: cf. esp. 38.4 'saepe amissa partibus, uniuersa ductu Augusti facta stipendiaria est', 113.3 'ut neque uniuersos quisquam auderet adgredi et partem...uniuersi temptare non possent'. It will be noted, however, that on these and comparable occasions (cf. 38.1, 126.1, 129.1, and the quotations adduced by Heinsius on 126.1 and by Haase xii) the contrast is between two phrases, verbs or other words: here there is no such antithesis. Several edd. have thus thought that a verb has been omitted. *elusimus* has been the most popular supplement on account of A's suprascript *eius imus*; but if it is praiseworthy to avoid the '*uniuersas* uires' of the enemy, it cannot be praiseworthy also to avoid the enemy *partibus.* A different action is called for. Gruter, who objected to *euasimus* on the same grounds as Kritz above, proposed instead to read *exhausimus*: such a word would, I believe, make excellent sense alongside *euasimus*: 'we avoided the fury of the combined enemy forces, while wearing them out section by section'. *exhausimus,* which could plausibly have been omitted after *euasimus,* is an apt description of Tiberius' policy in Illyricum (see e.g *elanguesceret* below),[1] and for *uires exhaurire* cf. e.g. Val. Max. 3.4.4, Sen. *Suas.* 5.8.

furentes has also been questioned, but it seems a natural word to use of barbarians being carried along on a wave of warlike success (cf. e.g. Tac. *H.* 3.71.1 'furens miles'): for this substantival use of the pres. partic. cf. K–S 1.769.3.

quanto cum temperamento simul ** utilitatis res...agi uidimus Several problems again arise in this sentence. Some scholars (e.g. Ruhnken, Madvig) have questioned *utilitatis,* but cf. 112.3 'ad arbitrium utilitatemque nostram', 113.2 'utilia speciosis praeferens', 110.3n.; Ellis 178f. Any

---

[1] Dio 55.30.5 gives a comparable picture of the tactics in Illyricum, but attributes them to the enemy.

reference to such matters as are mentioned at 114.3 would be completely inappropriate in the present context.

Granted, then, that *utilitatis* is sound, does *temperamentum* mean 'combination' or 'moderation'? Although the latter is of course a familiar quality of Tiberius (122.1n.), the appearance in the paradosis of *simul* has led many edd. to believe that the former is more likely to be correct. But what might have been omitted? Ruhnken and Kritz suggested emending *auctoritate* to *auctoritatis*; but the phrase *res auctoritate imperatoris agi* seems not only unexceptionable but positively desirable. Heinsius, comparing 114.1 'uirtute atque utilitate', proposed ⟨*uirtutis*⟩ *simul* ⟨*et*⟩ *utilitatis*; but there the context is different. I agree with Krause: 'satius fuit monstrare lacunam quam explere'. And since Krause marked the lacuna as printed above, he must have assumed that the omission was another noun prefaced by *simul* (thus, purely for the sake of illustration, *simul* ⟨*securitatis, simul*⟩ *utilitatis*). Certainly parablepsy seems the likeliest cause of the corruption, although most edd. do not appear to have seen it in these precise terms.

qua prudentia hiberna disposita sunt An essential quality of the ideal general, cf. Xen. *Cyr.* 6.1.23, 8.5.2ff., Liv. 35.14.9, 28.6, Tac. *Agr.* 22.2, Veg. 1.22. But this is not merely a topos: Tiberius' *hiberna* were at Siscia (Dio 55.30.4), and 'die Wahl von Siscia...zum Hauptquartier zeigt die kluge Überlegung des Tiberius, da diese Stadt mitten im Aufstandsgebiet lag' (Massauer). It is of course quite possible that V. had himself witnessed the *hiberna* before he returned to Rome in time for 5 December A.D. 6.

inclusus custodiis exercitus nostri ⟨hostis⟩, ne qua posset... Following a hint from Ruhnken, who however had a different solution to the problem, Kritz transposed *hostis* from its place in the paradosis before *elanguesceret* below. There is much to be said for this suggestion. The sentence as transmitted is extremely odd if the subject is delayed until the penultimate word of the subordinate clause. If we assume, as is plausible, that *hostis* was omitted after *nostri* at an earlier stage in the transmission, it is not difficult to see why it was re-inserted but in the wrong place. In the construction which V. is using, it looks at first sight as if *ne* qualifies not only *posset* here but also *elanguesceret* below. This of course cannot be so: mentally we must supply *ut* before *elanguesceret* if the clause is to make sense (for this idiomatic omission of *ut* cf. K–S 2.211*c*). A copyist who wished to clarify the sense might very well have inserted *hostis* before *elanguesceret* in order to define the reference of the verb.

intra se furens uiribus...elanguesceret 'Coniungendum *uiribus elanguesceret*...ablativo *uiribus* non caussa significatur, sed illud in quo languor cernitur' (Kritz). Yet there is no example where *elanguesco* is constructed with an abl. of this nature (*TLL* s.v.). I thus agree with Heinsius that *uiribus* goes with *furens* (for such abll. cf. *TLL* 6.1.1625.51ff.), and that the idea is the same as at Tac. *H.* 4.17.3 'Galliam suismet uiribus concidisse', cf. Hor. *Epod.* 16.2 'suis et ipsa Roma uiribus ruit', Liv. *praef.* 4 'uires se ipsae conficiunt', 6.19.6 'suis ipse oneratus uiribus ruat', Manil. 1.912 'imperiumque suis conflixit uiribus ipsum' (cf. too Häussler, *Tac.* 273). Such an idea is entirely appropriate here. One of V.'s concerns is to show how Tiberius, using a smaller force of men but the right strategy, overcame a very large force: compare 110.2 *adulta uiribus*, 3 *numerus explebat*, 4 *immensae multitudinis* with 112.3 *ita placebat barbaris numerus suus, ita fiducia uirium ut, ubicumque Caesar esset, nihil in se reponerent* and with 113.1–2 *maximamque fiduciam uictoriae in numero reponebant* (*Romani*). *at imperator*...Above all compare *intra se furens uiribus* with *furentes eorum uires* just above.

The similarity of the present passage to 112.3 was remarked upon by Rau 326 and Koestermann 359, the latter of whom concludes as follows. 'Die Ähnlichkeit der Situation [at 112.3] mit der am Ende von Kap. 111 geschilderten legt den Schluss nahe, dass es sich um das gleiche Ereignis handelt' (360). Since 112.3 is generally agreed to refer to A.D. 7, this conclusion, if true, would support the view that *primo anno* also refers to A.D. 7 (see above). But we must remember that the present clause is one, not of result, but of purpose (*ne*): Tiberius' tactics, here assigned to late A.D. 6 (cf. *hiberna*), were designed to bring about the exhaustion of the enemy – something which does not happen until the following year (112.3). Tiberius was to operate on a similar principle in A.D. 8/9 (below, p. 179).

For *copiae* = 'supplies' etc., above, cf. e.g. Tac. *A.* 15.16.1 'inopes copiarum' (Krause).

112.1–2 Tribute to Messalinus

112.1 Felix...forte 'A solemn formula to proclaim the successful accomplishment of an undertaking, giving due weight to the respective claims of god and man' (Ogilvie on Liv. 2.49.6: for other exs. of this alliterative combination cf. Wölfflin 260). For the nature and function of the present section of V.'s narrative see above, p. 154.

Messalini M. Valerius Messalla Messalinus, *RE* 8A.1.159–62 = Valerius 264 (v. Lunzer). His father was the famous and eloquent M. Valerius Messalla Corvinus (*RE* 8A.1.131–57 = Valerius 261 (Hanslik)); his brother was M. Aurelius Cotta Maximus Messalinus (*RE* 2.2.2490–1 = Aurelius 111 (v. Rohden); *PIR*[2] 1.304–7, no. 1488).

112.2 subita rebellione cum semiplena legione uicesima circumdatus 'Bei der Analyse dieser Worte ergibt sich, dass sich der General bei dem Ausbruch der Empörung...in dem insurgierten Lande befunden hat', remarks Koestermann 350. Yet Dio's more detailed account states that Messalinus, with much of his army, was accompanying Tiberius on his projected campaign against Maroboduus; when the revolt broke out, Tiberius sent him on ahead to Pannonia, where, after an initial reverse at the hands of Dalmatian Bato, he defeated the enemy (55.29.1, 30.1–2). Koestermann, who says that V.'s account 'eine eigene Kontroverse bei den Historikern entfesselt hat', makes much of this discrepancy between the two authors, strongly favouring V.'s version. 'Messalinus aber als Statthalter Illyriens hatte seinen natürlichen Platz in seiner Provinz, nicht an der Seite des Tiberius. Ich bin daher absolut geneigt, dem Bericht des V. vor der sachlich nicht vertretbaren Darstellung Dios den Vorzug zu geben.' Yet Dio's account seems to me too detailed and explicit to be dismissed in this way, and Professor Goodyear points out that the two accounts may be largely reconciled if we interpret *subita rebellione* as 'by/in a sudden uprising', one of the many which took place in this war.

For *hostili exercitu* below cf. Heubner on Tac. *H.* 3.82.1.

112.3–114.3 THE EVENTS OF A.D. 7

112.3–6 Events in Illyricum

112.3 Ita placebat barbaris numerus suus... There is no explicit indication that a new year's campaigning begins at this point: the reason may possibly be that, in contrast to A.D. 8 and 9 (114.4, 115.2), V. had not yet returned from Rome and thus was not on hand to witness it (cf. 111.4n.). However that may be, the organisation of V.'s narrative implies that a new year begins at this point (see above, p. 154), and scholars are generally agreed that V. henceforward deals with A.D. 7 (Syme, *CAH* 10.372; Wilkes 72–3; Koestermann; for a dissenting view see below, 113.3n.). On the similarity between the present passage and 111.4 see n. on *intra se... elanguesceret* there. *fiducia uirium* below is found in several authors but esp. in Livy.

nihil in se reponerent 'they placed no reliance upon themselves'. We might have expected *nihil spei*, which indeed is what Heinsius proposed to write; but for the omission of such a word cf. Tac. *G.* 30.2 'plus reponere in duce quam in exercitu', Just. 24.8.2. Kritz's parallel from V., 32.1, is unhelpful since there the meaning is rather different.

proposita 'confronted by', a rare meaning for which cf. Cic. *Fam.* 5.16.2 'telis fortunae proposita sit uita nostra' (Burman), Liv. 28.2.16 'propositum bello se fore ratus' (Kritz). Lipsius conjectured *opposita*.

ad arbitrium utilitatemque nostram Orelli objected to the latter noun on the grounds that *ad utilitatem* is unparalleled; but cf. e.g. Cic. *Verr.* 1.119, 3.21, *Sest.* 91. For *ad arbitrium* cf. *TLL* 2.413.66ff.; for *exitiabilem famem* below cf. Symm. *Ep.* 4.21.1 (F.).

neque cum facientibus copiam pugnandi The paradosis reads *ut*, which, despite Ellis 179, is nonsense. We cannot be certain whether it is a corruption of some other word (*cum*, Ruhnken; *uel*, Purser; *nostris*, Ellis) or whether it arose through dittography after *neque* (Gelenius). I have sided with Ruhnken. Acidalius noted that the plural *facientibus* is abrupt after *instantem*, which he proposed to emend to *instantes*; but the logic of the preceding passage, and the references to *Caesar* and *ipsi duci*, both indicate that the paradosis is here likely to be correct. For *facere copiam pugnandi*, common in Sall. *J.* and Liv., cf. *TLL* 4.910.83ff.; for *derigere aciem* below cf. 95.2n.

monte Claudio 'Die Lage des *Mons Claudius* zu bestimmen, ist kaum mit Sicherheit möglich.' Thus Koestermann, who, in discussing the topography (360–1), rejects the identification of this mountain with the Mons Alma mentioned by Dio under A.D. 6 (55.30.2) and prefers instead to locate it east of Siscia in the Papuk range, 'das sich gerade während des letzteren Krieges als ein ausgezeichneter Rückhalt für die in Slavonien operierenden Partisanen bewährte'. Wilkes 72 agrees (cf. map on p. 18).

112.4 A. Caecina et Siluanus Plautius consulares These men are A. Caecina Severus (*RE* 3.1241–3 = Caecina 24 (Groag); *PIR*² 2.21–2, no. 106), who was consul in 1 B.C.; M. Plautius Silvanus (*RE* 21.30–3 = Plautius 43 (Hofmann); Syme (1934), 139ff.; K. M. T. Atkinson, *Historia* 7 (1958), 315f., 328f.), who was consul in 2 B.C. Both Caecina and Rhoemetalces, who is mentioned below, had played a successful part in Illyricum in the previous year (Dio 55.29.3–30.4), but V. made no mention of it. Caecina had returned to his province of Moesia to deal with marauding tribes (Dio, loc. cit.), but now returned with Silvanus, who had just relinquished the legateship of Galatia-Pamphylia (Syme, op. cit.). Of the five legions to which V. refers, Caecina had probably brought with him three, Silvanus two (Syme, ib. and (1933), 26–7). Their object was to march west from Sirmium along the river Bošut and past the Mons Alma, to join forces with Tiberius at Siscia (Wilkes 72). See further below, 5n., 113.1n., 2n.

circumfusa At the Volcaean Marshes (Dio 55.32.3), NW of Sirmium, in the Bošut valley. For the location, the enemy tactics, and the similarity to Trasimene, cf. Koestermann 361–2, Wilkes 72.

Rhoemetalces, Thraciae rex The brother of Rhascupolis, cf. 129.1n.; also Magie 1.513f., 2.1369 n. 53.

in adiutorium eius belli Ellis believed that *in* was 'ecclesiasticis magis dignum quam Paterculo' (180), but cf. Val. Max. 1.5 *ext.* 2 'in adiutorium eorum', 3.7.10, to which F. adds Sen. *Dial.* 3.13.5.

exitiabilem...cladem 'Almost one of the greatest disasters in the annals of Rome' (Syme, *CAH* 10.372). For the phrase F. quotes Suet. *Aug.* 23.1 (of the *Variana clades*).

112.5 fusa...acies *fuga* (BA) was emended to *fugata* by Rhenanus; but despite the frequency of word-repetitions in V. (100.5n.), I do not believe that he used the same verb both here and four words later. Like several edd., I prefer Vossius' *fusa* (for *fundere/fugare* cf. 1.9.4, 2.12.2 (where a third verb follows, as here), 32.4, [46.4], 112.2; Wölfflin 261f.). For *apud signa* below cf. *TLL* 2.337.6ff.

plus...uindicauit gloriae quam ducibus reliquit The paradosis reads *uindicatum*, an error which may be due to attraction to *trepidatum* above (as Novák (1907), 145, suggested). Puteanus' emendation restores sense,[1] and involves a smaller change than the proposals of other scholars. For the (presumably stock) contrast cf. Liv. 2.63.5 'magna accepta clade uirtus militum rem prolapsam neglegentia consulis restituit', 6.30.6, 42.49.5. For *gloriam uindicare* cf. Plin. *Pan.* 8.2 (F.).

Following Abraham 10f., Koestermann (361–2, 377) suggests that in his criticism of Caecina and Silvanus V. echoes the judgement of Tiberius himself, and that their omission from the 'Ehrenliste' in ch. 116 means that they 'nicht oder nicht unbedingt zur Partei des Kaisers gehört haben und daher das Missfallen unseres Autors erregten'. Yet Caecina played an important part in Germany after Tiberius had come to the throne (Tac. *A.* 1.63–9), a fact which surely contradicts rather than (as he seems to think) supports Koestermann's thesis. I think it more likely that we have here simply V.'s personal attitude towards the two men, never forgiving them for their disgraceful incompetence on this single, but critical, occasion.

112.6 primi ordines Gelenius wished to read *ordinis,* not realising that *primi ordines* is a technical expression for 'first-rank soldiers'. Vossius, Ruhnken and Kritz get it right, quoting betweeen them Caes. *BG* 5.30.1, 6.7.8 (see also Meusel's edn, Intro. p. 54 § 19, Anm. 2), Liv. 30.4.1, 44.33.4,

---

[1] Following Halm, Stegmann wrongly attributes also to Puteanus the correction *a more...discrepantes* below: it was in fact made by I. Pontanus.

Front. *Strat.* 1.5.12; J. N. Madvig, 'Die röm. Officiere', *Kleine Philol. Schriften* (1875), 515 and n. 1. The use of *incruentus* above is perhaps also military, cf. *TLL* 7.1.1059.58ff. (Sall. Liv. Tac. Amm.). For *perrupta...acie* below cf. Heubner on Tac. *H.* 2.44.1.

uictoriam uindicauerunt The end of the battle is heightened by the strong alliteration on *ui-* (also at 1.1.3, 2.1.1, 27.5, 34.3, 45.5, 52.6, 74.2, 82.3, 115.5, 116.2, 120.3) and by the favourite clausula – ◡ – – –. For the phrase itself cf. 34.2, Liv. 44.14.8. For *ex insperato*, another favourite expr. of Livy, cf. *TLL* 7.1.1949.5ff.

112.7 The Banishment of Agrippa Postumus

V. was not the only person despatched from Rome with reinforcements for Tiberius: in A.D. 7 Germanicus, as Dio tells us (55.31.1), was also sent out on a similar mission. The reason that Germanicus and not Agrippa Postumus was chosen, continues Dio (55.32.1–2), was that the latter had a severely deficient character, as a result of which he was banished to the island of Planasia. It is extremely interesting, as Koestermann has remarked (357 n. 2), that in his narrative of A.D. 7 V. too mentions Agrippa's fate; but in contrast to the logical progression of Dio's account, summarised above, 'erscheint das Einschiebsel bei Vell....als ein völlig unorganisch eingegliederter Fremdkörper'. Koestermann explains his remark, which is clearly justified, as follows. 'Wahrscheinlich lag der Grund dafür, die Schicksale des Agrippa schon hier zu berichten und über die Verbannung hinaus bis zu seinem gewaltsamen Lebensende zu verfolgen (dessen nähere Umstände übrigens völlig im Dunkeln gelassen werden), für ihn darin, dass er nunmehr den Vorteil hatte, bei der Schilderung des Regierungsantrittes des Tiberius gar nicht mehr die Mordtat erwähnen zu müssen.' Like most other scholars, Koestermann seems to believe that V. here deals with Postumus' death, which is not the case (see below); but in so far as V. never mentions the man again in the rest of his work, the essence of Koestermann's explanation is undeniable. In this, as in many other matters, V. has followed the example of Tiberius himself, who 'silentio rem obliterauit' (Suet. *Tib.* 22).

112.7 iam ante biennium Evidently A.D. 5 (for this use of *ante* cf. 102.3n.): the reference is presumably to Agrippa's earlier banishment to Surrentum (Suet. *Aug.* 65.1). V. seems to have been misunderstood by E. Hohl, who says that this event took place 'nicht ganz zwei Jahre nach der Adoption' (*Hermes* 70 (1935), 350 and n. 1), and neglected by S. Jameson, who says the event took place 'probably in A.D. 6' (*Historia* 24 (1975), 302). Jameson does however argue strongly that Tiberius was not responsible for

Agrippa's death (pp. 313f.); but this in no way affects V.'s silence on the matter (see above). On Agrippa and his adoption by Aug., cf. 104.1 and n.

in praecipitia conuersus Cf. Tac. *A.* 2.39.2 'ad...magis praecipitia conuersus' (Fletcher). For *prauitate animi* above cf. Cic. *Parad.* 22, to which F. adds. *Comm. Petit.* 40.

crescentibus in dies uitiis Cf. Suet. *Aug.* 65.4 'Agrippam nihilo tractabiliorem, immo in dies amentiorem'. For *animum alienare*+dative (instead of *ab* and abl.) above cf. e.g. Liv. 44.27.7, Sen. *Ep.* 82.15.

dignum furore suo habuit exitum Most scholars (e.g. W. Allen, 'The death of Ag. Post.', *TAPA* 78 (1947), 139; Syme, *Tac.* 367 n. 9; Koestermann 357 n. 2; Massauer; J. D. Lewis, *Auckland Classical essays* (ed. B. F. Harris, 1970), 170) assume that V. is here alluding to Postumus' murder, which took place in A.D. 14 after Tiberius had succeeded to the throne. V., it is argued, places the man's death here in order to dissociate Tiberius from it. Now *exitus* can of course mean 'death' (e.g. Sall. *C.* 55.6 'dignum moribus factisque suis exitum inuenit'); but the word can also mean the 'final state of a person' (*OLD* s.v. 4), as at Cic. *Verr.* 2.5.189 'Verrem...dignus exitus eiusmodi uita atque factis uestro iudicio consequatur', *Fam.* 15.11.2 'tibi uelim ei sint exitus quos mereris et quos fore confido', Sen. *Ira* 3.16.4 'habuit itaque quem debuit exitum'. Since Postumus' 'final state' was banishment to Planasia, and since this took place in A.D. 7, the precise year which V. is here discussing,[1] it is surely his banishment, not his death, to which reference is being made. V. is thus not guilty of the charge generally laid against him; but he is guilty of later passing over Postumus' death in silence (see above, p. 170).

113 Events in Illyricum continued

113.1 tantum in bello ducem quantum in pace uides principem 'Dem Verhältnis von *dux* und *exercitus* entsprach logischerweise das von *princeps* und *ciuitas*', observes Häussler on this sentence (*Tac.* 355: for *dux/princeps* cf. also Cic. *Off.* 2.16). The correlation was exploited extensively by Roman emperors, who used such military terms as *custos* (104.2n.) and *statio* (131.2n.) to refer respectively to themselves and their position. In addition it was a panegyrical convention that the ruler should display the virtues of both war and peace (Doblhofer 22–6, 92ff.). It is thus not surprising that V. here sees Tiberius as presenting a consistent image or that he can attribute to Tiberius in a military context qualities which were more

[1] Syme and Lewis mistakenly assume A.D. 6 is being discussed.

usually appropriate in a civil context (*cura*, 106.3n.: cf. *prouidentia* at 115.5n.). What is more noteworthy here is the manner in which V. expresses the correlation between *dux* and *princeps*. Modern historians have rarely questioned Tiberius' ability as a military commander since they have been far more concerned with his administrative ability as emperor. Yet V. here chooses to defend a controversial military decision of Tiberius (2n., below) by comparing it with his ability as *princeps*. Since he would hardly have adopted this line of defence if it had not been plausible, we have here some brief but valuable testimony to the character of Tiberius' government in the years before A.D. 30.

decem legionibus Five legions, incl. Legio XX (cf. 112.2), had originally been based in Illyricum and were under the command of Tiberius; three came with Caecina from Moesia, two with Silvanus from Galatia-Pamphylia. See Syme (1933), 23, 25ff.; Wilkes 92–3; also Koestermann 362 n. 3.

For *quique*...*quique* above, a construction first found in Augustan prose, cf. K–S 2.35; L–H–S 515.

†XIIII sed†... So P; A reads *XIIII set.* Lipsius argued that this is an instance of haplography and that V. wrote *XIIII alis et.* Certainly *alis* is a credible conjecture: not only the immediate context, but much of V.'s account of A.D. 7, has been full of technical military language, and a ref. to *alae* would be entirely appropriate here (so too D. B. Saddington, 'The Roman *Auxilia* in...early imperial writers', *Act. Class.* 13 (1970), 114f.). But whether haplography caused the corruption, it is unfortunately impossible to say: Laurent equally reasonably preferred *X alis et.* I have therefore obelised the phrase.

fiduciam uictoriae in numero reponebant For this and indeed the whole passage cf. Tac. *A.* 4.2.1 'cohortes una in castra conducendo ut... numeroque et robore et uisu inter se fiducia ipsis oreretur'. *fiducia uictoriae* is another military expression (Caes. Curt. etc., but not Liv.); for *fiduciam reponere in* cf. e.g. Val. Max. 3.7.7, Plin. *Ep.* 3.9.16.

113.2 optimus...iudex, et utilia speciosis praeferens V. 'here writes with understanding, intelligence, and insight, and without adulation. He penetrates to the essential Tiberius' (Sumner 272). As Koestermann says (363), it was presumably Augustus' decision to burden Tiberius with these excessive numbers of troops: Tiberius would hardly have sent them back if he had been originally responsible for requesting them. Tiberius' action thus conflicted with Augustus' estimation of the situation and doubtless caused some controversy (Sumner 272). Certainly V.'s tone is defensive: Boeclerus compared Fabius Cunctator's defence of his own military policy (Liv. 22.

39), but an even closer parallel is Horace's laboured defence of Lollius (*C.* 4.9.40–1 '*bonus*... | *iudex* honestum *praetulit utili*'). Though Horace is using pseudo-philosophical terms, his meaning is very similar to V.'s. Compare also Liv. 22.3.8 'salutaria magis quam speciosa suadentibus'.

probanda...probarentur V. is extremely fond of *traductio*, 'quae facit uti, cum idem uerbum crebrius ponatur...etiam concinniorem orationem reddat' (*Rhet. Herenn.* 4.20). Cf. e.g. 1.5.2 *imitaretur/imitari*, 1.17.3 *uisum/uiderit*, 26.2 *certatum erat/certabatur*, 34.3 *uiceramus/uinceremur*, 66.2 *defendisset/defenderat*, 85.3 *desertores/desertor* (cf. 119.4), 103.2 *legeret/legendus*, 125.4 (and n.). Other exs. in Verhaak 79–81.

exercitum, qui uenerat,...dimittere statuit The reference is to the five legions brought by Silvanus and Caecina, which, to judge from the immediate context (*hiemis initio*, below), had arrived late in A.D. 7. In fact, as we know from Dio (55.34.6–7, 56.12.2–3), Silvanus continued to operate around Sirmium with an army in A.D. 8 and 9: clearly he was not dismissed by Tiberius. Syme (1933), 27, and (1934), 140–1, has argued that two or three of the newly arrived legions returned no further than Sirmium, but remained there on active service with Silvanus until the end of the war. See too Wilkes 93.

ad refouendas ex itinere eius uires Cornelissen (1883), 418, wished to emend *eius* to *fessas*, but *ex* = 'after' is common with verbs expressing recovery (K–S 1.503–4). For *refouere uires* cf. 1.15.1, Tac. *A.* 12.66.1, Stat. *Theb.* 6.521, Sil. 11.538.

maiorem quam ut temperari posset For the military principle involved cf. Veg. 3.1 'modus a magistris quaeritur armorum. nam...euidenter apparet nimium copiosos exercitus magis propria multitudine quam hostium uirtute depressos...in locis autem asperis uel fluminibus transeundis...saepe decipitur', 26 'amplius iuuat uirtus quam multitudo'. *temperari* (cf. 107.1n.) and *gubernaculo* below combine to produce a metaphor from sailing: cf. Plin. *NH* 11.219 'gubernacula uitae temperat'.

113.3 longo et perquam laborioso itinere Koestermann (363 n. 3) states that the way back to Sirmium can in no sense merit this description. His attractive suggestion is that Tiberius escorted the army through the mountainous territory south of the Save in order to avoid the two Batos.

metu finium 'fear for their territory': for the genit. cf. Hor. *Epod.* 9.37; in prose F. quotes *Pan. Lat.* 2.25.3.

hiemis initio Late A.D. 7 (thus Koestermann 363–4, Sumner 272; and cf. Syme (1934), 141 and n. 3). I can see no reason why Dihle (640), apparently following Sauppe 44, believes that V. means the winter of A.D. 6: this is demonstrably not the case (see above, p. 154).

partitis praefecit hibernis The reason for this may be that Tiberius, as Koestermann suggests (364 and n. 1), returned to Rome for the winter. V. makes no mention of it, but Suet. states that Aug. recalled Tiberius 'saepius' (*Tib.* 16.2), and cf. Dio 55.27.5.

114.1–3 Tiberius the ideal general

After a reference to the beginning of the winter of A.D. 7/8 (113.3 *hiemis initio, hibernis*), V. separates the second year of the war from the third by interposing an account of Tiberius the ideal general (see above, p. 154). Much that he says is conventional, being based on the topos that the general treats himself and his soldiers alike (cf. e.g. Xen. *Ages.* 5.3 εἴ ποτε μοχθῆσαι στρατιᾷ συμβαίη, ἑκὼν ἐπόνει παρὰ τοὺς ἄλλους, Cic. *Mur.* 38 'numquam iste plus militi laboris imposuit quam sibi sumpsit', Amm. 25.4.12 'periculorum socius et laborum', *SHA Hadr.* 10.2 'ipse quoque...uitam militarem magistrans', Arr. *Anab.* 7.9.9, Jul. *Or.* 3.28 κοινωνεῖ μὲν ἅπασι τῶν πόνων καὶ ἔχειν ἐν αὐτοῖς τὸ πλέον ἀξιοῖ). But though several of Tiberius' characteristics as here described may be paralleled in other works such as Plin. *Pan.* and Tac. *Agr.*,[1] others may not: there can be little doubt that V. here provides an accurate and personal account of Tiberius' relationship with his troops. Indeed V. tells us as much (2): 'cuius ⟨usum⟩ cum alii tum ego sensi'. Tiberius emerges as a man of *cura* and practical humanity – qualities which, on the basis of 113.1 (see n.), are equally appropriate to the *princeps* of the Roman empire. This account is thus a prelude to the panegyric of Tiberius in ch. 126.

114.1 solida ueraque uirtute atque utilitate An elegant phrase, with reminiscences of Cicero: for *solida ueraque* cf. *Sest.* 93, *Phil.* 5.50, *Vatin.* 8; for *solida utilitas* cf. *Fin.* 1.72. *uera uirtus* is 'a cliché of Roman public moralising' according to Jocelyn on Enn. *Trag.* 254, to whose parallels add e.g. Cic. *Fin.* 5.36, Liv. 32.33.10, 35.4.7, 42.47.5, *Pan. Lat.* 6.10.4. For *solida uirtus* cf. Val. Max. 2.8.5, 5.4 *ext.* 5.

salus ac ualetudo...sustentaretur Caesaris cura It was a con-

[1] A fair number of the parallels which I quote derive from Boeclerus ad loc. and from the commentary on Plin. *Pan.* by Lipsius, whose references are unfortunately not repeated in Durry's edn.

ventional attribute of the ideal general to look after the health of his soldiers when they were ill: Cic. *Mur.* 38, Tac. *A.* 1.69.1, 71.3, Plin. *Pan.* 13.3, Front. p. 207 Naber = p. 197 Van den Hout, *SHA Hadr.* 10.6, *Sev. Alex.* 47.2 'aegrotantes ipse uisitauit per tentoria, milites etiam ultimos [cf. V.'s *gradum...sequentibus*] et carpentis uexit et omnibus necessariis adiuuit', Auson. *Grat. Act. ad Grat.* 17, Dio, *epit.* 68.8.2. *salus ac ualetudo* is a solemn phrase, appearing in a prayer at Cato, *RR* 141.3 (see Norden, *AP* 220 n. 4, comparing the same doublet on an inscription, *CIL* 1^2.2, app. numm. 355, p. 759). *ualetudo sustentari* is again Ciceronian (*Off.* 2.86); for *Caesaris cura* cf. 106.3n.

districtissimus ille tantorum onerum mole The paradosis, which makes no sense, was emended by Rhenanus to *distractissimus*. This is accepted by many edd., yet I doubt whether the word can mean 'preoccupied' (cf. *TLL* s.v.), and there seems to be no example at all of its being followed by a simple abl. In his copy of Heinsius' edition (now in the British Museum), Bentley suggested *districtissimus*. This word, which has exactly the right meaning, is often confused with *distractus* (e.g. Cic. *De Or.* 3.131, Curt. 3.3.4) and is regularly followed by the abl. I have therefore adopted it. For *districtus animus* cf. Sen. *Dial.* 10.7.3; for *districtus* contrasted with *uacare* cf. id. *Ep.* 56.9; for the superlative form cf. Ellis 181; Neue–Wagener 2.227. For *mole* cf. 131.1n.

114.2 iam ⟨tamquam⟩ in hoc solum portatum instrumentum balinei From the evidence as given in the app. crit., I suspect that at an earlier stage in the transmission the paradosis read *solum um portatum*: A guessed that the nonsensical word should be *uni*, P that it should be *im-*. Yet *uni* is wrong alongside *in hoc solum*, and *importatum* is not the right word to use of a bath (even in Illyricum): dittography after *solum* seems a more likely explanation. But the text is still awkward. *in hoc solum*, as transmitted, must refer to *succurrit ualetudini*; but this detracts from the force of *nullius non* and also makes wrong sense – it was Tiberius' bath. The similarity of our phrase to *tamquam...huic uni negotio* above can hardly be fortuitous: V. is presumably making the same point here, in which case *iam ⟨tamquam⟩ in hoc solum* would make perfect sense ('his bath, carried as if for this very purpose, aided the health of all'). I have found no parallel for *instrumentum balinei* (nor for *apparatus cibi* above) except perhaps Sen. *Ep.* 60.2 'mensae instrumentum'; for *apparatus* coupled with *instrumentum* cf. Liv. 22.14.13.

ab illis *illis* is to be taken ἀπὸ κοινοῦ with *praestari*, in which case it refers to *domestici*, and with *desiderari*, in which case it refers to the soldiers whom V. is discussing.

114.3 temporibus interfuit For this use of *intersum* cf. *Aetna* 575 *aeuo*,

Plin. *Ep.* 2.1.2 *posteritati*; Wopkens observed the imitation by Sulp. *Dial.* 3.3.6 'cui quidem tempori hic interfuit' (see too Klebs 297).

equo uectus est The ideal general either rides on horseback instead of in a carriage, or walks instead of riding on horseback: cf. Plin. *Pan.* 14.3, Front. p. 207 Naber = p. 197 Van den Hout, *SHA Hadr.* 10.4, Dio, *epit.* 68.23. The antithesis was Domitian, who 'in expeditione et agmine equo rarius, lectica assidue uectus est' (Suet. *Dom.* 19).

cenauit sedens i.e. as opposed to reclining, a characteristic of Tiberius which is confirmed by Suet. *Tib.* 18.2 'sedens in caespite nudo cibum caperet' and which he shared with Hannibal (Just. 32.4.10 'nec...cubantem cenasse'). It is clear from Amm. 25.4.4 ('stans interdum more militiae, cibum breuem uilemque sumere uisebatur') that the idea is closely related to the topos of the ideal general's diet, for which cf. Front. p. 207 Naber = p. 197 Van den Hout, Amm. 15.5.3, *SHA Hadr.* 10.2, *Pan. Lat.* 3.11.4 and Gutzwiller ad loc.

non sequentibus disciplinam, quatenus exemplo non nocebatur, ignouit The ideal general restores discipline when necessary, but allows some things to go unrebuked, provided no bad precedent is set: cf. 125.3 (also of Tib.) 'haec omnia ueteris imperatoris maturitas, multa *inhibentis, aliqua* cum grauitate pollicentis, ⟨et⟩ inter [cf. *medium* here, below] seueram praecipue noxiorum ultionem mitis aliorum *castigatio* breui sopiit ac sustulit' (cf. also 126.4n.), Xen. *Ages.* 11.6 τὰς μὲν τῶν ἰδιωτῶν ἁμαρτίας πρᾴως ἔφερε...κρίνων τοὺς μὲν ὀλίγα...κακῶς διατιθέναι, Plin. *Pan.* 18.1, Tac. *Agr.* 19.3, Suet. *Iul.* 67, Front. p. 207 Naber = pp. 196–7 Van den Hout 'tantam militaris disciplinae labem pro re Lucius coercuit, industria sua ad militandum exemplo proposita...grauiora demum peruerse facta seuere animaduertit, leuiora sciens dissimulauit: locum paenitendi reliquit', Dio 52.34 *passim.*

exemplo is abl., as at 125.4, 31.4 'ut exemplo nocet', Cic. *Leg.* 3.32 'uitiosi principes plus exemplo quam peccato nocent', [Ov.] *Hal.* 30, Quint. *Decl.* 252 (p. 34.19). For *sequi disciplinam* cf. Liv. 25.38.6 (F.).

interdum castigatio The paradosis *inerat et* makes no sense. It is remarkable that scholars have toyed with such proposals as *moderata* (Rau, *Chronologie* 48), since it is clear from the surrounding adjj. *frequens* and *rarissima* that a temporal word is required.[1] An anonymous scholar in 1779 suggested *interdum et,* which Bothe later improved by omitting *et*: we now have an appropriate sequence, for which cf. Cic. *De Or.* 3.201 'frequenter...

[1] F. Walter however noted that the combination *moderata/rara* is at Cic. *Orat.* 59, Quint. 11.3.126 (*Wien. Stud.* 48 (1930), 186).

interdum...raro'. For the combination of adjj. and adv. cf. L–H–S 172 (also 817).

agebatque medium...dissimulantis...inhibentis '*medium* must be neuter: "he pursued a moderate course [avoiding the extremes of never punishing and always punishing] of pretending very often not to see things and sometimes giving a reprimand". The genitive participles are possessive. Cf. Liv. 2.27.3 *medium se gerendo nec...nec...*' (F.).[1]

114.4–115.1 THE EVENTS OF A.D. 8

114.4 The Pannonians capitulate

114.4 Hiems emolumentum patrati belli contulit, et... The winter is that of A.D. 7/8, already referred to at 113.3: after the digression on Tiberius, V. here resumes where he left off (ring composition, cf. 99.4n.). The sense of V.'s phrase seems to be: 'L'hiver nous valut l'avantage de finir la guerre' (H–W: for the definitive genit. after *emolumentum* cf. 105.3). Kritz argues strongly in favour of Friebel's *non tulit*, saying that since the winter was not a time for fighting, the war cannot have been brought to a close during it. Yet the argument may be turned on its head. There would be no point in V.'s reporting *hiems...non tulit*, since that was normally to be expected; but it *is* worth reporting that, even without fighting, the enemy gave up. That being so, Lipsius' *et* is needed to preserve the logic of the rest of the sentence: the paradosis reads *sed*, but the two words are often confused (cf. Kritz on 2.9.6). See further next n. but one.

patrare bellum is an archaistic expression popularised by Sall. (*J.* 21.2, 75.2, 88.4, cf. Quint. 8.3.44), whence it was imitated once by Livy (28.41.8), several times by V. (2.11.2, [21.3], 30.6, 59.4, 79.3, 123.1: see Woodman (1968), 792), and by Tac. (*H.* 3.64.2, *A.* 2.26.1, 3.47.1). *emolumentum belli* is at Just. 9.1.2 but in a different sense.

seruitutem minatam Another Sallustianism, cf. *J.* 94.4 'seruitium minari' (F.). For *reliquiis...belli...manentibus* above cf. 2.17.1 'belli mane-

---

[1] It might be thought that *medium* is masc. and that *ago* is used here as at 109.2 (n.): *medium* would then be analogous to Caes. *BG* 1.34.1 *aliquem locum medium utriusque* ('a place halfway between the two'). But 'if in V. the genitives depend on masc. *medium* the words mean "halfway between a man pretending not to see many things and a man sometimes giving a reprimand"; but clearly this is not the meaning: the participial phrases are not contrasts but complements' (F.). Acidalius, realising the impossibility of just this interpretation, therefore conjectured *dissimulans... inhibens*. So too Madvig 2.310.

bant reliquiae': for *reliquiae belli* cf. *TLL* 2.1844.79ff. (Cic. Sall. Liv. *al.*); V. uses the alternative *reliqua belli* at 123.1.

conferentem arma...apud flumen nomine Bathinum On the basis of a calendar entry for 3 August (*CIL* 1^2.248 = EJ p. 50: *Ti. Aug.* ⟨*in*⟩ *Inlyrico uic*(*it*)), most scholars have assumed that the Pannonian capitulation to which V. refers must have taken place on that day in A.D. 8 (cf. Koestermann 367). But Professor Goodyear points out to me that *hiems...contulit* above, if correct, implies a date much earlier than 3 August. We must therefore assume that the calendar entry refers to some later victory over the Pannonians in A.D. 8 which V. has not recorded.[1] This is by no means impossible. We know from Dio 55.34.4–6 that the capitulation of Breucian Bato and Pinnes, to which V. here refers, was followed by the murder of this Bato by his Dalmatian namesake: as a result of this action the Pannonians subsequently revolted again, and were eventually put down by Silvanus. Only when this latter victory was assured could Tiberius, as commander-in-chief, be credited with anything like the complete conquest of Pannonia; and this may have been on 3 August A.D. 8. V. has failed to record the resurgence of rebellion amongst the Pannonians, not because it might detract from Tiberius' personal achievement, but because the action took place on the eastern front, of which he had no personal experience (cf. Wilkes (1965), 113f.).

The river Bathinus was either the modern Bošut (so Koestermann 365f.) or the Bosna (so B. Saria, *Klio* 23 (1930), 92–7; G. Alföldy, *Act. Arch. Hung.* 16 (1964), 251f.; Wilkes 73).

arma conferre is an almost technical phrase for 'handing in one's arms' (e.g. Caes. *BG* 2.15.2, 7.11.2, 12.3), but when indication is given of the place to which the arms are handed in, an expression of motion is naturally to be expected (thus Caes. *BC* 2.18.2 'arma omnia...in domum Gallonii contulit'). It looks to me therefore that *apud*, often found = 'at' with names of rivers (e.g. 1.11.4; *TLL* 2.337.17ff.), here has the force of *ad*: this rare usage is archaistic (in Lucil. 994M = 1008 Krenkel) and occurs once in Sall. (*H.* 1.119), whence Tac. doubtless imitated it at *A.* 11.8.4. Such an archaism would be in keeping with V.'s tone at this point (see last two nn.), but none of the standard works (K–S, L–H–S, *TLL*) refers to V. at all.

Batonemque et Pinnetem...captum alterum, ⟨alterum⟩ a se deditum These are the two Pannonian leaders (110.4n.). Dio 55.34.4 says that Bato had betrayed Pinnes, and presumably therefore gave himself up: hence *captum* and *a se deditum*. Rhenanus' supplement is required to complete the sense.

iustis uoluminibus ordine narrabimus Cf. 96.3n.

---

[1] It cannot refer to the victory in Dalmatia in A.D. 9 because that victory took place within days of the *Variana clades*, the probable date of which was late September A.D. 9 (cf. 117.1 and n.).

114.5–115.1 Two tributes

Although this section carries forward the narrative of events to some small extent (*autumni...exercitus*; *Caesar...contulit*), its main purpose is to pay tribute to M. Lepidus and V.'s brother Magius Celer Velleianus (see above, p. 154). This explains my paragraphing, as a result of which it is implied that Tiberius had begun to plan his Dalmatian operation (cf. 115.1) before the beginning of the new campaigning season (115.2 *initio aestatis*), i.e. in the later months of A.D. 8. This in fact is precisely what Tiberius did (below, 114.5n.): the artistic arrangement of V.'s narrative conforms exactly to what we know of the chronology of events for A.D. 8/9.

114.5 autumni ⟨initio⟩ If the final victory over the Pannonians really did occur on 3 August (above, 4n.), Ellis' supplement is perhaps more likely than Gelenius' *autumno*.

omnibus copiis ⟨a⟩ Caesare M. Lepidus praefectus est M. Aemilius Lepidus, also referred to at 115.2–3, and cf. 125.5n.; for him cf. *RE* 1.561–3 = Aemilius 75 (v. Rohden); *PIR*² 1.60–1, no. 369; Syme, *TST* 30–49; L. Hayne, *Ant. Class.* 42 (1973), 500. The reason why Lepidus was left in charge was that Tiberius, taking advantage of the success in Pannonia in A.D. 8, at once began to plan for the following year's operations in Dalmatia: see esp. Wilkes (1965), 114–21. As a result, he did not return to Rome until after A.D. 9 had begun (Dio 56.1.1). Whether V. remained with Lepidus at Siscia (as Dihle 640 and Sumner 273 assume), or whether he left at the same time as Tiberius (as is apparently assumed by Koestermann 368 and Massauer and argued by Wilkes (1965), 113), is uncertain. I suspect the former is the truth. V.'s description of Lepidus below, *quem in quantum...diligit*, resembles his stock descriptions of other men (1.9.3 'uirum in tantum laudandum in quantum intellegi uirtus potest', 2.2.2, 43.4 'uiri in tantum boni in quantum humana simplicitas intellegi potest', 97.2); but, unlike them, the present description contains the telling detail *potuit* instead of the standard *potest*. As at 116.4 this may imply that V. had personal experience of Lepidus – presumably (given the context in which the description occurs) during the winter season of A.D. 8/9. It follows from this hypothesis that V. marched with Lepidus to join Tiberius at the beginning of A.D. 9, and the description of the journey (115.2, below) is based on his own personal experience.

uir nomini ac fortunae Caesarum proximus The paradosis reads *nominis...eorum*: neither word is correct. There is no ex. in Latin of *proximus* + genit.; the closest parallel is that quoted by Kritz on 36.3 (Cic. *Clu.* 30 'propiora huiusce causae'). On the other hand it would have been more than natural for a scribe to write the genitive after *uir* (cf. e.g. 116.3 'uir antiquissimi moris'), and besides, V.'s text contains several examples of *-s* being wrongly added to a word (Kritz xciv). Acidalius correctly wrote *nomini.*

eorum is nonsense, and such emendations as *suorum* (Vossius) or *Aemiliorum* (Heinsius) are misguided because they anticipate *tantorumque nominum, quibus ortus est, ornamentum* which follows. Laurent's and Bothe's *deorum* is wrongly printed by Ellis, Stegmann and Bolaffi: there is a world of difference between the legendary martyr Cato and the quasi-divine Livia on the one hand (respectively 35.2 'ingenio dis quam hominibus propior', 130.5 'deis quam hominibus similior') and the down-to-earth Lepidus on the other. Besides, *nomini deorum proximus* makes no sense. As Kritz saw, J. Scheffer's *Caesarum* is exactly what is wanted. Lepidus' elder brother married Augustus' granddaughter Julia; Lepidus himself was a cousin of Augustus' grandchildren, one of whom, L. Caesar, was betrothed to an Aemilia Lepida; his grandmother was Scribonia, the former wife of Aug., and his daughter went on to marry Drusus Caesar. There are thus ample grounds for the description of Lepidus printed here, even without resorting to Tac. *A.* 1.13.2 'M. Lepidum...capacem [sc. principis loci]'. See Syme, *RR* Table IV.

intellegere Of knowing a person, as e.g. 116.4, Phaedr. 3.12.8, Sen. *Ep.* 79.14, Quint. 11.1.10. For *in quantum* (...*in tantum*) cf. 1.9.3, 43.4, 2.8.1, 119.2, 120.3; K–S 1.569, L–H–S 153.

ornamentum The metaphor is Ciceronian, e.g. *Sull.* 88, *Phil.* 11.36, *Mil.* 37, *Flacc.* 75. So too is *miratur ac diligit* above, cf. *Acad.* 2.115, *Rep.* 2.1, *Leg.* 2.4; also *Pan. Lat.* 7.17.4 (F.).

115.1 belli...molem Cf. 95.1n. For *animum atque arma* below cf. 119.2; Wölfflin 254; *TLL* 2.103.75ff. For *animum conferre ad* cf. *Bell. Alex.* 9.1, Curt. 8.2.28 (F.).

Magio Celere Velleiano *RE* 14.441 = Magius 14 (Fluss). For the honours to which V. refers, and their date, cf. 121.2–3 (and n.); for his praetorship cf. 124.4n.

115.2–5 THE EVENTS OF A.D. 9: THE DALMATIANS CAPITULATE

Following Rau 337 and Koestermann 368, Massauer states that 'für dieses Jahr ist Vell. nicht mehr Augenzeuge, sondern auf den Bericht seines Bruders angewiesen'. Wilkes (1965), 113f., is apparently of the same opinion. Yet even if one does not accept that V. remained with Lepidus in A.D. 8 and joined Tiberius in A.D. 9 (cf. 114.5n.), his presence in Illyricum with Tiberius is attested by 104.3 'eius operum per annos continuos VIIII praefectus aut legatus spectator...adiutor'.

115.2 per gentes integras... 'The line of Lepidus' march was probably along the Una or Vrbas valley, across the Strmica pass (Mons Ditionum) above Knin to the final destination at Burnum (Šuplja Crkva), where the camp of Legio XX was established' (Wilkes 75). For *gentes integras* cf. Cic. *Leg. Man.* 26, *Dom.* 60; for *immunes clade* below cf. 120.3, Luc. 8.704; for *educere* + abl., above, cf. K–S 1.369.

tendens ad Tiberium imperatorem Koestermann 369f. has taken exception to this phrase, inferring from Dio 56.12.2 that Lepidus had already arrived in Dalmatia before Tiberius returned from Italy. But Wilkes (1965), 116f., has shown that Dio has misinterpreted the evidence, arguing rightly that V.'s description of Lepidus' march 'suggests that it was undertaken on orders received after Tiberius had returned'. And even if Tiberius had not yet returned, V.'s phrase 'ought to be able to cover the idea "marching to where Tiberius was going to be"' (Sumner 273 n. 103, rightly). For *cum difficultate...luctatus* below cf. Sen. *Ep.* 28.7 'cum difficultatibus rerum... conluctantur', Liv. 44.7.11 (F.).

115.3 ob ea quae si... T. Munker (in Heinsius' edn) wished to supply *ob* before *quae*; Kritz argues that *quae* is to be taken with *gessissent*. Neither is correct. As Burman saw, *ob* needs to be supplied mentally with *quae*: for this type of ellipse cf. his n. on 1.7.1 'ne in id quod Homerus incideret'; also L–H–S 835.

115.4 Perustae ac Desidiates For these tribes and their location see Wilkes 173ff. and 170–1 respectively (map, p. 175); also Koestermann 375 and n. 1. For the conventional manner in which V. describes them (*situ locorum, ingeniorum ferocia*) cf. 95.2, 106.1–2 and nn.; also Wilkes 177 n. 1.

non iam ductu sed manibus atque armis ipsius Caesaris tum demum pacati sunt Tiberius had left the area early in A.D. 9 (Dio 56.1.1), and, while nominally retaining over-all command (as is clear from the fact that even Germanicus was eligible only for *ornamenta triumphalia*: Sumner 273 n. 101), had entrusted the concluding of the war to others. But the war dragged on, and Augustus was compelled to send Tiberius once more to the front to conclude operations in person (see Dio 56.12.1ff.). Hence V.'s contrast between *ductu* and *manibus atque armis ipsius* (cf. also 73.3). We should not however think that V. is here obliquely criticising Tiberius' subordinate commanders: the following phrase *cum paene funditus euersi forent* makes it clear that this is not the case. For the common combination of *manus* and *arma* cf. Ogilvie on Tac. *Agr.* 25.3.

115.5 opportuna uisa est uictoriae occasio At the end of the war V. emphasises Tiberius' policy by chiastic alliteration (cf. too 1.6.2 'mollitiis fluentem ac nimium felicem malo suo', 1.8.5 'adiutus legionibus Latinis aui', 1.10.2 'cogitationem regiam Romana disiecit constantia', 2.19.1 'exturbauit et lege lata exules fecit'), including the strong alliteration on *ui-* (112.6n.). For *opportuna occasio* cf. Val. Max. 5.4.3, Petr. 12.2, 78.8.

damno amissi pensaret militis Herel wished to read *commissi*, but cf. 21.4 'amissorum...ciuium paene damno repensata est', *Cons. Liu.* 200 'consulis erepti...damna', Ov. *Met.* 14.197 'damnum mihi lucis ademptae', Suet. *Aug.* 25.4 'cuius abrupti damnum', Sen. *Ben.* 1.2.2; F. adds Phaedr. 3.11.3, Just. 25.3.6.

semperque uisum est gloriosum quod esset tutissimum V. concludes the whole episode on the same note as he began: see 110.3n. Ruhnken spotted the echo of Sall. *H.* 1.55.8 'nihil gloriosum nisi tutum...aestimet'; for other antitheses of *gloriosum/tutum* cf. ib. 4.69.1, Sen. *Contr. exc.* 8.4, Sen. *Ben.* 3.30.3, and compare Liv. 34.14.4 'quod pulcherrimum, idem tutissimum'.

ante conscientiae quam famae consultum For this antithesis cf. Plin. *Ep.* 1.8.14, 3.20.9, 5.1.10, Tac. *A.* 6.26.1; F. adds Sen. *Dial.* 7.20.4.

prouidentia ducis Like the comparable and etymologically connected *prudentia ducis* (cf. 111.4 (twice), 129.1; Liv. 27.27.11, 29.30.9), *prouidentia ducis* (cf. Tac. *H.* 2.19.1) was a military virtue which Tiberius displayed especially in the present war. Although Aug. and he had undoubtedly differed on how the war should be conducted (113.2n.), the emperor eventually realised that Tiberius' strategy had been proved correct (cf. Suet. *Tib.* 21.5, Aug. to Tiberius, usually referred to *c.* A.D. 9: 'ordinem aestiuorum tuorum ego uero laudo, mi Tiberi, et inter tot rerum difficultates καὶ τοσαύτην ἀποθυμίαν τῶν στρατευομένων non potuisse quemquam *prudentius* gerere se quam tu gesseris, existimo'). Certainly modern scholars have also agreed with Tiberius, cf. e.g. Seager 43: 'The Pannonian revolt shows Tiberius' generalship at its best. Despite the difficulty in coming to grips with the enemy, the great advantages given to guerillas by the terrain, and the pressure from Rome for quick results, he kept calm and refused to abandon the methods that he knew would bring ultimate success.' But Augustus' allusion to the ἀποθυμία of the soldiers is confirmed by Dio (56.12.2) and shows what Tiberius had to contend with. The gnomic character of V.'s present paragraph, and particularly this last sentence *nec umquam consilia ducis iudicio exercitus sed exercitus prouidentia ducis rectus est*, indicate that V. still feels the need to defend his commander's policy many years later. See too Koestermann 373 n. 1. For a later parallel cf. Tac. *H.* 3.26.3 'miles periculi quam morae patientior: quippe ingrata quae *tuta*, ex temeritate spes'.

Yet it was not only in the military sphere that *prouidentia* operated (cf. too 113.1n.). It became one of the commonest imperial virtues, and particularly of Tiberius himself. For *prouidentia* in Tiberius' reign cf. Rogers 20–34; Grant, *Aspects* 89f., *RAI* 62–4; for the virtue in general cf. M. P. Charlesworth, *HThR* 29 (1936), 107–32; Béranger 210ff. and in *Hermes* 88 (1960), 481ff.; Frei-Stolba (1969), 37 and n. 10; Burdeau 38; Sutherland 60; Gutzwiller on *Pan. Lat.* 3.5.4.

116 A CHAPTER OF TRIBUTES

V.'s narrative of the revolt in Illyricum has now ended; that of the *Variana clades* is about to begin. To separate the two accounts V. interposes a chapter of tributes to seven individuals (on this technique see above, p. 154). The chapter has provoked the bitter condemnation of R. Syme (below, 5n.), and it is certainly true that the men whom V. mentions are friends of the future emperor Tiberius (cf. Lana 93ff.; Syme, *RR* 435f.; Koestermann 377–8). But, as Seager has aptly reminded us, 'there is no ground for supposing that they did not deserve his commendation' (269). On the omission of Caecina and Silvanus see above, 112.5n.

116.1 praemissus Germanicus *praemissus* must mean occasions when Germanicus acted on his own responsibility, even though Tiberius retained over-all command at all times (115.4n.). Such occasions are rare and are restricted to A.D. 9. He took Splonum and Seretium, and was involved in a débâcle at Raetinum, before Tiberius was sent back from Rome in that year (Dio 56.11–12.1); he also managed to take Arduba independently of Tiberius but after the latter had returned (Dio 56.15.1–3). Wilkes (1965), 117, thinks the latter is meant here; but either or both could be meant.

Koestermann has objected to V.'s brief treatment of Germanicus (377). 'Der Historiker hat, ohne ausdrücklich die Unwahrheit zu sagen, durch geschicktes Verschweigen ihm unsympathischer Dinge seinen Bericht so frisiert, dass alle Gloriole auf Tiberius fällt.' It is true that Dio gives far more scope to Germanicus' activities, but, as Wilkes 74 has shown, the later historian has, for his own purposes, greatly exaggerated Germanicus' contribution.

For Germanicus cf. *RE* 10.435–64 = Iulius 138 (Kroll); *PIR*² 4.178–85, no. 221; also below, 125.4, 129.2–3. For *experimenta uirtutis* above cf. 94.4n.

116.2 ...diligentique Vibius Postumus For the text of this phrase see above, p. 22 n. 2. For the man cf. *RE* 8A.2.1978–9 = Vibius 45 (Hanslik): he was consul in A.D. 5, and became governor of the new province of Dalmatia in A.D. 9 (Wilkes 81).

Passienus L. Passienus Rufus, *RE* 18.4.2098 = Passienus 6 (Hanslik). He was proconsul of Africa in A.D. 3–5.

Cossus Cossus Cornelius Lentulus, *RE* 4.1364–5 = Cornelius 182 (Groag); *PIR*² 2.333–5, no. 1380. He succeeded Passienus as proconsul of Africa, where in A.D. 6 he celebrated a victory over the Gaetulians (Dio 55.28.3–5, Flor. 2.31). Dio and Florus testify that as a result of this victory Cossus himself took the cognomen 'Gaetulicus'; but Groag, in the articles just mentioned, believes the name was used only by his younger son, Cn. Cornelius Lentulus Gaetulicus (*RE* 4.1384–6 = Cornelius 220 (Skutsch); *PIR*² 2.338–40, no. 1390). V.'s statement below would seem to support Groag (*etiam* presumably means 'in addition to the *ornamenta triumphalia*'). Compare the case of Cn. Claudius Severus Arabianus (*PIR*² 2.248–9, no. 1027), son of C. Claudius Severus (ib. 2.246–7, no. 1023).

quibusdam diuersi Many edd. have seen great difficulty in the paradosis *quibusdam diuersis*, but F. Walter's simple change to *diuersi* produces excellent sense (*Philologus* 80 (1925), 452). For the use of *quaedam* he compares Cic. *Brut.* 110 'in quibusdam laudandi uiri'; and for the abl., Tac. *A.* 2.33.3 'diuersi natura'. For *uirtutum exempla* below cf. Sen. *Contr.* 9 *praef.* 3; for *genitus in* below cf. *TLL* 6.2.1992.29–32 (Sen. Curt. elder Plin.), and compare 102.1n., 129.1n.

116.3 L. Apronius *RE* 2.273–4 = Apronius 4 (v. Rohden); *PIR*² 1.188–90, no. 971. His daughter was the wife of Cossus' younger son (mentioned above, 2n.). From the context it is clear that *meruit* below = 'deserved', rather than (as above) 'won'. For *excellenti uirtute* below cf. *TLL* 5.2.1215.76ff.

in hoc quoque genere For *genus* = 'respect', 'area', 'field', perhaps colloq., cf. Cic. *Att.* 4.2.7, 5.20.6, 10.11.2. For *experimentis testari* above cf. Val. Max. 3.7 *ext.* 6 (there is no ex. of *experimentum* = *documentum, argumentum* before V.); for *uis fortunae* below cf. *TLL* 6.1.1190.61ff.

Aelius Lamia This is Ruhnken's emendation of the paradosis *etiam*. 'prior syllaba *et* orta ex *el*, quod est *Aelius* nominis compendium, *e* pro *ae* posito, ut saepissime...*iam* autem, *l* in *i* corrupto, nihil aliud est quam *lam*, i.e. *Lamia*' (Kritz). As each scholar remarks, V.'s description here fits in quite well with what we know of Lamia from other sources: cf. *RE* 1.522 =

Aelius 76 (v. Rohden); *PIR*² 1.34–5, no. 200. No other source tells us of his activities in Germany or Illyricum; but his governorship of Africa in A.D. 15/16 is attested by Tac. *A.* 4.13.3. I believe we are on far surer ground here than at 125.5 (see n.): we have both external information on the man and a plausible explanation of how the corruption might have arisen.

priscam grauitatem semper humanitate temperans For *prisca grauitas* cf. 86.2, Tac. *H.* 1.83.1, Amm. 22.7.6. For the antithesis of *grauitas/humanitas* cf. Cic. *Leg.* 3.1; F. also compares Sen. *Ep.* 99.20 'tanto temperamento ut illis nec humanitas nec dignitas deesset'. For *humanitate tempero(r)* cf. Cic. *Att.* 4.6.1. For *uir antiquissimi moris* above cf. Liv. 39.11.5, 42.47.4, Tac. *H.* 1.14.2; for *functus ministeriis* below cf. Liv. 3.57.10, 8.40.3 (F.).

non merito sed materia adipiscendi triumphalia defectus est Having done splendid service in three provinces, Lamia 'lacked, not merit, but the opportunity of winning the *ornamenta triumphalia*'. V. sharpens the point by the characteristic paronomasia of *merito/materia* (for which type cf. *Rhet. Herenn.* 4.29 *fin.*). For the ellipse of *ornamenta* cf. Tac. *A.* 4.18.1, 44.1, 11.20.3, *H.* 4.4.2, Plin. *Pan.* 89.3, Suet. *Claud.* 24.3: most of these exs. are from Kreyssig, who, however, observing that V. elsewhere uses the full phrase (104.2, 112.2, 115.3, 125.5), wished to supply *ornamenta* here. For the notion of being deprived of an opportunity of glory Ruhnken quoted Liv. 45.12.9 'alterius (consulis) obscura fama quia materiam res gerendi non habuit', *Pan. Lat.* 7.4.4. For *materia...defectus* cf. Val. Max. 7.6.5.

116.4 A. Licinius Nerua Silianus *RE* 13.454–5 = Licinius 137 (Nagl); *PIR*² 5.53, no. 224. He is one of only two persons whom V. mentions by four names, the other being P. Scipio Africanus Aemilianus at 2.4.2 (cf. Bacherler 1049ff.); his father was P. Silius, under whom V. began his military career (101.3n.). For *intellexit* below cf. 114.5n.

[ne] nihil ⟨quod⟩ non optimo ciui, simplicissimo duci superesset praeferens, immatura ⟨morte⟩ et... Many emendations have been proposed for this extremely corrupt passage (see Kritz, Stegmann 176), most of which carry little conviction. I shall do no more than indicate where I think the corruption lies, and support a tentative solution.

It would appear that V. has made his description of Licinius directly parallel to that of Lamia above: 'nam *et* Aelius Lamia, *uir* antiquissimi moris et priscam grauitatem...*temperans*...*defectus est*; *et* A. Licinius Nerua Silianus...quem *uirum*...miratus est...*praeferens*...*defectus est*'. This close correspondence suggests that *praeferens*, which Gelenius emended to *praereptus*, is sound (cf. *temperans* above). If so, the participle requires an object, which is presumably to be located somewhere in *ne nihil...duci perisset*, the offering of the paradosis.

It is unlikely that *ne*, to which several edd. have objected, is correct. I believe, as did Ellis at one time (*Hermathena* 10 (1897–9), 22), that the word is an intrusion into the text under the influence of *ne...quidem* above.[1] Madvig (2.310), also dispensing with *ne*, proposed *nihil non optimo ciui* ⟨*simile, uiro*⟩ *simplicissimo, duci peritissimo praeferens*; Halm proposed *nihil non* ⟨*quod uiro*⟩ *optimo, ciui simplicissimo, duci peritissimo* ⟨*competeret*⟩ *praeferens.* E. Thomas accepted Halm's attractive proposal (an abbreviated form of the relative pronoun is always liable to omission or corruption), but preferred to read *peri*⟨*tissimo competi*⟩*sset*, which is closer to the paradosis. Ellis, however, pursuing a quite different and otherwise misguided line of his own (loc. cit.), solved this latter problem by supposing that *perisset* was a corruption of *superesse* (he compared 125.5 'cum ei pietas...superesset', cf. also 109.2 'superesse sibi...uoluntatem'). I regard this as quite credible: given a form of *superesse* in the context of an untimely death, a scribe might not unnaturally write *perisset*.

P. Thomas (1919), recognising the merit of Halm's ⟨*quod*⟩ and Ellis' *superesse*, combined them to read as follows: *nihil non* ⟨*quod*⟩ *optimo ciui simplicissimo duci superesset praeferens*. I think we must either accept this emendation, while admitting that it may still be far from what V. wrote, or obelise the whole passage, as do Halm, Ellis and Bolaffi in their texts. On balance I think the former course is justified, although I have transposed *non* and ⟨*quod*⟩ to produce the more idiomatic word order (cf. 89.2 'nihil... quod non...', Liv. 35.31.16). The passage, which as printed is unfortunately but inevitably disfigured by critical paraphernalia, means: 'qui montra toutes les vertus qui font un excellent citoyen et un général plein de simplicité' (H–W).

The retention of *praeferens* means that we have no reference to Licinius' death. But since the paradosis offers *immatura*, I agree with Orelli that V. probably wrote *immatura morte*, as at 2.3.2. The noun could easily have dropped out once *superesset* had been corrupted (as hypothesised) to *perisset*.

principis Presumably Tiberius (the other *laudati* are all 'Tiberian' men). But Aug. is obviously possible (so Nagl, last n.). For *fructus amicitiae* cf. *TLL* 6.1.1392.52ff.

consummatione euectae in altissimum paternumque fastigium imaginis 'Quomodo *imago* possit *euehi in fastigium*, aut per se *splendorem*

---

[1] Although the comparison is perhaps not exact, cf. how A has written ampl*ic*issimae' below under the influence of 'simpl*ic*issimo' here. The postulated intrusion of *ne* is of course at least as early as (M).

atque decus significare, nemo via et ratione probaverit.' Thus Kritz, in support of Ruhnken's *magnitudinis*. Yet Ruhnken contradicted himself by retaining *imaginis* here; and although his quotation of Liv. 3.72.4 to support *imago* = *splendor, decus* is inadmissible (cf. Ogilvie ad loc.), his other quotation of Vell. 27.5 (where he originally proposed the emendation *magnitudinis*!) seems far nearer the mark: 'hodieque tanta patris imagine non obscuratur eius memoria'. And in fact two other passages of Livy seem to contain *imago* in this sense: 3.58.2 'uirum honoratissimae imaginis futurum', 36.40.9. In view of this evidence, tenuous though it may be, I have retained the paradosis.

The basic sense of the clause is: Licinius failed to achieve a fame that was exalted up to the highest point or to the point reached by his father. *euectae ...imaginis* would be either genit. of definition or objective genit., depending upon whether *consummatio* = 'highest achievement' or simply 'process of achieving' (cf. *OLD* s.v. 4, 3: neither sense occurs before V., unless Sen. *Contr.* is earlier); but 'one sometimes wonders whether a grammatical distinction almost impossible to make is really meaningful' (Goodyear on Tac. *A.* 1.18.3). For *euectae in (ad) fastigium* (the noun is a favourite of V.), cf. 30.3, 56.3, Val. Max. 1.6.1, Curt. 4.14.20.

116.5 neque enim iustus sine mendacio candor apud bonos crimini est Syme has objected strongly to the present chapter (*RR* 488 'Vell. delights in the language of laudation, or, as he calls it, "iustus sine mendacio candor"'), and indeed it was a topos of historiography that it was dangerous to praise people in historical writing (Sall. *C.* 3.2, derived from Thuc. 2.35.2, cf. 45.1; also Lucian, *Hist. Conscr.* 7, 9, 59; Avenarius 13ff., 157ff.; Walbank on Plb. 10.21.8). The danger was increased in the case of contemporary personalities (cf. Cic. *Fam.* 1.9.23 to Lentulus on the *De Temporibus Meis*: 'uerebar, non eos qui se laesos arbitrarentur (etenim id feci parce et molliter), sed eos quos erat infinitum bene de me meritos omnes nominare', Plin. *Ep.* 5.8.13, Tac. *A.* 4.33.4): contemporary persons were awkward for an historian because of his readers' *inuidia* (cf. 92.5, another topos). One solution was of course to omit judgement on contemporaries, as V. himself does at 36.3 ('nam uiuorum ut magna admiratio, ita censura difficilis est', cf. Ov. *Tr.* 2.467 'praestantia *candor* | nomina uiuorum dissimulare iubet'); but this means that an ancient historian would be failing in one of his primary tasks, viz. encouraging others to excellence (cf. Tac. *A.* 3.55.5). Here therefore V. quite rightly admits praise of some of his contemporaries, while claiming for himself the virtue of *candor* which Seneca attributed in a similar connection to Livy (*Suas.* 6.22 'est natura candidissimus omnium magnorum ingeniorum aestimator T. Liuius'). In view of this evidence, Michels (10f.) is clearly wrong to suggest that V., in writing this apologia, felt himself to be breaking new ground.

Cornelissen (1877) wished to delete *sine mendacio*, but the pleonasm with *iustus candor* is typically Velleian (97.2n., cf. also Löfstedt, *Synt.* 2.184ff.); for *mendacium* applied to historiography cf. e.g. Cic. *Rep.* 2.28, Liv. 8.40.4, 26.49.3, 40.29.8, Amm. 31.16.9, Oros. 5.3.4. For *apud bonos* cf. Tac. *H.* 1.29.2; for *quaerere* in the sense of irrelevant searching cf. Liv. 9.17.1.

117–120 THE *VARIANA CLADES* AND ITS AFTERMATH (A.D. 9–10)

The disaster which befell Varus and his legions in the Teutoburg Forest in A.D. 9 ranked with Carrhae as one of the worst in Roman history (cf. 119.1). V. has divided the episode into two main sections, the *causa* and *summa* of the disaster (117–18 and 119–20 respectively),[1] each of which is subdivided in its turn in the interests of dramatic writing. In 117–18 a character sketch of Varus introduces an account of his *segnitia*, after which V. has a contrasting sketch of his opponent Arminius, highlighting his alertness and treachery (see above, p. 42). The two parts of this section are clearly separated by a dramatic *tum* (118.2), and V. concludes with a long *sententia* on fate (118.4). The second main section opens with a brief recapitulation of the three themes of the preceding section (119.2 'marcore ducis, perfidia hostis, iniquitate fortunae') and with a summary account of the *clades* itself which 'clearly owes much to the stories of survivors encountered by V. in camp' (Sumner 274 n. 105). Then, as in the previous section, there follows a *peripeteia*, which this time consists of the dramatic intervention of Tiberius (120.1): he proceeds to deal with the rebellious areas in a campaign whose speed V. captures by a series of quick-fire phrases (120.1–2). The episode as a whole concludes with a tribute to the bravery of some of Varus' soldiers and a final reminder of the unsuitability of Varus himself (120.3–6).

At first sight it is perhaps surprising that V., himself a former soldier in Germany and now writing a work whose guiding principle is brevity, should choose this notorious defeat for the longest example of literary *exaedificatio* in his history. But the preceding analysis, not to mention V.'s introduction to the episode (117.1 'in hoc saltem tantummodo indulgente nobis fortuna, ne occupato duce...'), shows that his primary intention is praise of Tiberius. 'Per questa via si pongono maggiormente in rilievo le virtù belliche di Tiberio, che, afferrando saldamente in pugno la situazione confusa e pericolosa dopo la disfatta, prontamente ristabilisce la sicurezza' (Lana 110).

---

[1] In my earlier analysis of the episode I was perhaps wrong to term the second of these sections the *ordo* of the disaster, although that is, in effect, what it is (Woodman, *EA* 7–8).

117–118 THE 'CAUSA'

117.1 Tantum quod ultimam imposuerat...Caesar manum 'Scarcely had Caesar put the finishing touch upon...' (Shipley). For *tantum quod* cf. K–S 2.272; for *ultimam imposuerat manum* cf. 33.1, 87.1, 88.1, Virg. *Aen.* 7.572f., Ov. *Her.* 16.117, Donat. on Ter. *Andr.* 412. The disaster took place in the latter half of September, A.D. 9 (cf. John 955–8).

funestae...epistulae For this apt and forceful expression cf. Liv. 4.20.9 'annales uelut funesti', 45.24.11 'hanc funestam legationem'; F. adds Cic. *Pis.* 92 'funesta indicia'. The news of the disaster went first of all to Rome (John 956): it was only afterwards that Tiberius, who of course was still in Illyricum at the time, was informed, whereupon he naturally returned to Rome (120.1 below). For *consummati...operis* above cf. Colum. 4.8.3, Sen. *Ep.* 65.14, Amm. 16.11.11 (*consummare bellum* is of course common: *TLL* 4.600.80ff.).

***** uelut in hoc saltem tantummodo indulgente nobis fortuna, ne...** *epistulae* above lacks a main verb: Burman suggested *uenerunt*, an anonymous scholar suggested *redditae sunt*, and Kreyssig *attulere nuntium* – each placing their supplement before *uelut*. Halm, however, who agreed with Kreyssig's suggestion, placed the supplement after *epistulae*. I think Halm is wrong: as Kritz observes, *uelut* and its phrase occur with undue abruptness immediately after *cohortium*, and it is likely that not only a main verb but also some other material has been omitted. But since it is impossible to know precisely what has fallen out, I have preferred simply to mark a lacuna in what I consider to be the right place.

Scholars have naturally objected to the pleonasm of *saltem tantummodo*, but it is in V.'s manner: cf. 49.4 'tantummodo contentus', 78.2 'interim Caesar per haec tempora' (Freitag 10ff.). For the rest of V.'s phrase cf. Flor. 1.30.5 'hoc quoque illi in malis suis indulgente fortuna ut...', Cels. 3.6.2 'magis aegris in potione quam in cibo indulgere'; *indulgens fortuna* is a cliché (Liv. Manil. Phaedr. Sen. Curt. etc.).

ne occupato duce * et causa ⟨et⟩ persona moram exigit** Here there seems little doubt that the lacuna should be marked before *et*. Of the many earlier supplements listed by Kritz, none is at all convincing. Halm proposed *duce ⟨tanta clades inferretur sed⟩ et*; but I think we need more than simply *sed* to introduce the clause *et causa...exigit* (cf. 1.16.1, 41.1, 108.2). Again, however, it is impossible to guess exactly what the omission should be. Ruhnken wisely contented himself with remarking, 'totus hic locus variis lacunis misere foedatus est'.

For the apologetic manner in which V. introduces the more elaborate sections of his narrative, as here, cf. 108.2n. I have suggested elsewhere that *mora*, a natural word to use in the context of a 'speedy' narrative such as V.'s, may perhaps be a technical term = 'digression' *uel sim.* (Woodman (1975), 284 n. 1). The apparent correlation between *causa* and *persona* (words which are contrasted in a different context at 30.3) is further evidence that V., like other Latin historians, saw history in terms of the characters who took part in the action (see above, pp. 30–44). For *causa exigit* cf. Quint. 12.9.8.

117.2 Varus Quintilius P. Quin(c)tilius Varus, *RE* 24.907–84 = Quinctilius 20 (John); *PIR*² 3.118ff., no. 27; also Timpe, *Arminius* 120ff. But V.'s treatment of the man is by no means as harsh as Timpe or indeed Lana 116ff. would have us believe (cf. esp. 120.5; John 958ff.); and what criticism there is can be justified (Wells 238f.).

inlustri magis quam nobili ortus familia V. thus introduces an extended portrait of Varus which comprises the conventional elements of his *genus, ingenium, mores* etc. (see above, p. 41); note also the use of *is* at 3 below (cf. 109.5n.; Leo 309). The contrast between *inlustri* and *nobili* is noteworthy because these words are often coupled, as in Cic. *Verr.* 2.3.93, 2.5.40, 2.5.166 (F.). For *ingenio mitis* below cf. Liv. 34.5.6, Tac. *A.* 6.15.1 (*mite ingenium* at Juv. 4.82f., 13.184f.).

ut corpore et animo immobilior Thus the paradosis, which is retained by Orelli and Schoepfer; Bucretius proposed *et...et*, Acidalius *ut...ita*. Halm, Ellis, Bolaffi and Stegmann print one or other of these emendations, but H. Paessens argued that here *ut...et* = *ut...ita et*, and his contention is upheld by L–H–S 633. Paessens' evidence is that this construction appears twice elsewhere in the text of V. (25.3 'nam ut consulem, ut praediximus, exarmatum...et multos alios...dimisit incolumes', 125.1 'tulit protinus ut uoti et consilii sui pretium res publica'), and also twice in Seneca (*Ep.* 78.17 'si longus est (morbus)...multum temporis donat, necesse est, ut exsurgit et desinat', 95.37 'ceterum ut illos in bonum pronos citius educit ad summa, et hos imbecilliores adiuuabit malisque opinionibus extrahet').[1] Though the point is admittedly uncertain, I think this evidence justifies our retaining the paradosis. For *animo immobilior* cf. Plin. *NH* 7.52 'immobiles animi' (Ruhnken); for *otio...castrorum* below cf. Varro in Gell. 1.25.1 'pax castrensis'.

---

[1] The first of the Senecan exs. is uncertain: *exsurgit* is Haase's emendation of the paradosis *exsurgat* and L. D. Reynolds accords it a 'fort. recte' in his app. crit. (OCT, 1965); Madvig wrote *et* for *ut*. But the second ex. has not been questioned: on the contrary, it is supported by Winterbottom 88, who adduces two further exs. of the construction in Quintilian.

quam non contemptor...declarauit The adjectival use of *contemptor* is possibly in imitation of Sall. *J.* 64.1 (Woodman (1968), 799 n. 1), but the usage is also found before V. in Virg. *Aen.* 9.205, Liv. 44.22.7. For *declarare quam* cf. Cic. *Red. Sen.* 22, *Phil.* 14.29 (F.). For Varus' governorship of Syria cf. John 911ff.

quam pauper diuitem ingressus diues pauperem reliquit The effect of V.'s word play, involving chiastic polyptoton and two parallel series of nom. / acc. / verb, may be appreciated by a comparison with the same idea, but prosaically expressed, in Jos. *AJ* 17.307 (quoted by John 961). The technical name for this device is *commutatio*, 'cum contrariae sententiae relatione uerba quoque conuertantur' (*Rhet. Herenn.* 4.39). For some other exs. cf. Val. Max. 3.2.14 'dignitas sine uita quam uita sine dignitate', 4.4.9, 6.2.5, 6.9.11, 7.5.6 (Lundberg 90–1); Quint. 1.6.41 'ut nouorum optima erunt maxime uetera, ita ueterum maxime noua', 10.3.10, 12.6.4 (X. Gabler, *De Eloc. Quint.* (1910), 102).

117.3 qui nihil praeter uocem membraque haberent hominum Cf. Liv. 29.17.11 'nec hominis quicquam est...praeter figuram et speciem ...pestis ac belua immanis' (Ruhnken), 34.24.4 'linguam tantum Graecorum habent sicut speciem hominum...immanes beluae uiuunt' (John 960), Curt. 5.5.7 'non homines uidebantur, nec quicquam in illis praeter uocem poterat agnosci' (Verhaak 109). V.'s expression, which like the others quoted is derived from typical Roman invective (cf. I. Opelt, *Die lat. Schimpfwörter* (1965), 143, 183, 187), leads naturally into the description of German *feritas* at 118.1. The hyperbaton of *nihil...hominum* is emphatic.

Since the present clause represents V.'s, not Varus', thought, *haberent* should strictly be indic. like the following *poterant*; Cornelissen (1877) emended to *habebant*. But this 'illogical' use of the subjunctive is not unknown elsewhere (cf. Handford, *Lat. subjunctive*, p. 154 top).

quique gladiis domari non poterant, posse iure mulceri 'Difficilius est prouincias obtinere quam facere: uiribus parantur, iure retinentur. igitur breue id gaudium. quippe Germani uicti magis quam domiti erant' (Flor. 2.30.29). With the benefit of hindsight, both V. and Florus are able to recognise the shortcomings of Augustus' policy (for which cf. e.g. Wells 239, Seager 44).

117.4 agendoque pro tribunali ordine trahebat aestiua He 'dragged out the campaigning season with regular judicial activities'. Some scholars have questioned *ordine*, preferring a further allusion to Varus' *segnitia* (e.g. *socordius*, Ellis). But such an allusion is already present in *trahebat*: *ordine*, which is adverbial (so Krause, Boot), adds an ironical touch, contrasting Varus' naivety with the Germans' cunning. For *agere pro tribunali* cf. Cic.

Fam. 3.8.2; for *pacis gaudentes dulcedine* above cf. Liv. 31.15.10 'gaudentes utcumque composita cum Philippo pace'.

118.1 quod nisi expertus uix credat 'It is impossible for a man with no experience of war to write well about what happens in war' (Plb. 12.25g.1). We are once again reminded that V. took part in many of the events which he describes (cf. 101.3n., 104.3n.), and that he fully satisfies Polybius' demands for the ideal historian (cf. F. W. Walbank, *Polybius* (1972), 42, 71–2). For the phraseology cf. Plin. *Ep.* 5.8.1 'id enim temere credas nisi expertus' (Heinsius).

in summa feritate uersutissimi natumque mendacio genus 'highly cunning despite their extreme wildness, a race of liars from birth.' The description smacks of the conventional. Foreign peoples in general and Germans in particular were often accredited with *feritas* (106.2n.): V. stresses it again below and at 119.5. Similarly Roman enemies were traditionally treacherous (cf. Otto 291, Opelt (as above, 117.3n.) 182ff.): for Germans cf. Caes. *BG* 4.13.4. Yet this latter aspect of the German character is explicitly denied by Tac. *G.* 22.3 'gens non astuta nec callida'; but Tacitus, with his ambivalent attitude towards Roman imperialism, tended to idealise the heroes of less civilised societies (see B. Walker, *The 'Annals' of Tac.* (1952), 225ff.). V., on the other hand, who had experienced several years' hard campaigning on the northern frontier and who took part in Tiberius' mopping-up operations after the *clades*, had no such illusions and was in a position to know better (cf. *expertus* above). As so often in V., truth lies behind the literary convention (see also below, 2n.; and above, 106.3n.).

feritasque sua...mitesceret 'Nolite existimare beluas tantum recens captas feritatem illam siluestrem primo seruare, dein, cum diu manibus humanis alantur, mitescere, in hominum feritate mulcenda non eandem naturam esse' (Liv. 38.17.15: compare the whole passage). The irony of V.'s account brings out only too vividly the tragedy of the situation. For the antithesis *ferus* (*uel sim.*)/*mitescere* cf. Acc. *Trag.* 683–4 Ribbeck, Hor. *Epist.* 1.1.39, Liv. 33.45.7, Lact. *Mort. Pers.* 3.5. For *iustitia finiret* above cf. Liv. 34.6.10 'ut (ista lex) finiret libidinem muliebrem'; the pleonasm of *nouitate incognitae* below, which worried older edd., is in V.'s manner (cf. *simulantes fictas* above, also 117.1n., 97.2n.).

solita armis discerni iure terminarentur Cf. Liv. 28.21.5 'quidam quas disceptando controuersias finire nequierant aut noluerant...ferro decreuerunt' (Kritz).[1] *socordiam* below, a preeminently Sallustian word (cf.

[1] But the quotation should not be used to support Gronovius' emendation *decerni*: for *discerni* in the sense that V. uses it here cf. e.g. Caes. *BC* 1.35.3, Liv. 22.61.10.

Syme, *Sall.* 268) found nowhere else in V., aptly sums up Varus' character before we proceed to hear about Arminius.

praetorem urbanum So too Flor. 2.30.31 'quasi uiolentiam barbarum lictoris uirgis et praeconis uoce posset inhibere'.

118.2 Tum iuuenis...sensu celer The second part of the *causa cladis* is introduced by a dramatic *tum* and a contrasting sketch of Arminius (σύγκρισις, see above, p. 42). Whereas Varus was epitomised by *socordia*, Arminius is a *iuuenis* (b. 19 B.C. when Varus was almost 30), he is *celer* and *promptus*, a second Sextus Pompeius (cf. 73.1 'hic adulescens erat studiis rudis, sermone barbarus, impetu strenuus, manu promptus, cogitatu celer', a sketch itself based on Cethegus in Sall. *C.* 43.3). V.'s graphic portrait (on which see also Verhaak 119–22) is culpably ignored by Tacitus in his obituary notice of Arminius (*A.* 2.88 'Romanis haud perinde celebris, dum uetera extollimus, recentium incuriosi'), but acknowledged by E. Norden: 'Wir Deutsche dürfen ihm noch besonders Dank wissen, dass wir uns von den grossen Gestalten unserer ältesten Geschichte, Arminius und Marbod, nur aus ihm ein greifbares Bild machen können' (*Die röm. Literatur*[6] (1961), 91). For *sensu celer* cf. also Auson. 195.1 'ingenio celer'.

ultra barbarum promptus ingenio Cf. Tac. *H.* 4.13.2 'Ciuilis ultra quam barbaris solitum ingenio sollers'; for *promptus ingenio* cf. Liv. 5.3.1. In view of these and other parallels which I quote elsewhere in this section, E. Bickel perhaps went too far when he wrote as follows (*Arminius-biographie und Sagensigfrid* (1949), 73): 'Was...Vell. sagt, ist frei von ethnographischen Gemeinplätzen...Reines Erlebnis ist die Arminius-charakteristik des Vell.' V.'s account, as in 1 above, is doubtless an amalgam of rhetoric and reality.

Arminius *RE* 2.1.1190–200 = Arminius 1 (v. Rohden); *PIR*[2] 1.207–8, no. 1063; Timpe, *Arminius* (with earlier bibliog.).

Sigimeri *RE* 2A.1.1073 = Segimerus 1 (Stein).

ardorem animi uultu oculisque praeferens Verhaak (121) is reminded of the dying Catiline (Sall. *C.* 61.4 'ferociam...animi...in uoltu retinens') and of Hannibal (Liv. 21.4.2 'eundem uigorem in uoltu uimque in oculis...intueri'); cf. also Liv. 6.13.2 'uultum hostis ardore animi micantem', Curt. 8.6.16 'uultuque et oculis motum praeferens animi'. For other exs. of *uultu praeferre* cf. 94.2n., Curt. 6.9.1 'uultu praeferens dolorem animi'.

adsiduus militiae nostrae prioris comes, iure etiam ciuitatis Rom⟨an⟩ae ius equestris consequens gradus The historical problems raised by both these phrases have caused a vast amount of argument: the latest contribution is that of Timpe, *Arminius* 21ff., who fully reports and discusses the views of earlier scholars. The problems are particularly acute because the interpretation of *iure...gradus* has been thought to depend upon that of *adsiduus...comes*; nevertheless I prefer to start by discussing *iure... gradus* because it involves questions of a textual nature which scholars have not always appreciated.

With the exception of E. Hohl, all scholars have accepted Burer's (not Burman's, as Timpe 27 says) *Rom⟨an⟩ae* for the paradosis *Romae*: it is true that the normal phrase is simply *ius ciuitatis* (*TLL* 7.2.687.3ff.), but Arminius' German background supports the addition of the adjective here. Next, Hohl agreed with Mommsen that the interpretation of *iure...gradus* depends upon A's reading *eius equestris consequens gradus*: although I do not myself accept this assumption, we may briefly pursue its implications, the first of which is that *equestris...gradus* must be acc. plural. To what, then, would *eius* refer? Hohl ('Um Arminius, Biographie oder Legende?', *SDAW* (1951), 1.24 Anm. 35) believed that it referred to *ciuitatis* just mentioned, 'equestrian grades of *ciuitas*'; but Timpe 28 rightly follows those who had already pointed out that there are no such grades. Mommsen, on the other hand, believed that *eius* should refer to *militiae* in the preceding phrase, 'equestrian grades of *militia*'. Such a meaning, if taken out of context, would make sense: *militiae gradus* is a common phrase, used by V. of his own military tribunate at 101.3 (n.), and for *equestris militia* cf. 111.3, again with reference to V. himself. But Mommsen's interpretation means that *eius* = *militiae* in the sense of 'military service', whereas its natural sense in the preceding phrase is 'campaign': the change of meaning is intolerable. Finally, there is a single argument which ought to dispose of the interpretations of both Hohl and Mommsen: *eius*, given the position which it occupies in the phrase and the context in which it is found, is devoid of any meaning whatsoever.

And in fact *eius* has no genuine authority at all but is a typical error by Amerbach. P reads *ius*, which, since Burer raises no objection but rather confirms it (see app. crit.), was presumably the reading of (M) and not, as Timpe 28–9 apparently believes, a conjecture of Rhenanus. Of course the appearance of the word in (M) need not mean that it is what V. wrote: I can find no exact parallel for the expression *ius equestris gradus* (Burman's *decus* has been accepted by many edd., but there seems no parallel for this expression either). But the lack of a precise parallel need not on this occasion imply that the paradosis *ius* is wrong. Bolaffi reasonably suggested that the polyptoton *iure...ius* is intentional: it would certainly be in V.'s manner, and Krause acutely noted that V. uses *ius* in exactly the same way at 43.4 'reuocati ad ius dignitatis proscriptorum liberi' (cf. 28.4 'onera ordinis sustinerent et iura perderent'). Finally, there is no difficulty over *equester gradus*

= *equester ordo* or over *consequens* (which both Gelenius and Heinsius emended to *consecutus*) in a past sense: for *equester gradus* cf. Liv. 2.1.10, Plin. *Ep.* 2.13.4, 3.2.4, 8.22.2, Suet. *Galba* 14.2; and for the present part. in a past sense cf. K–S 1.757 (so, rightly, Timpe 28 n. 49). The sense of the phrase is that given by Kritz. 'Eo, quod iure civitatis Romanae *vel* civitate Romana donatus est, etiam id consecutus, ut ius equestris gradus, *i.e.* equitis Romani locum ac dignitatem obtineret.' This interpretation seems to me unexceptionable.

What, then, of the phrase *adsiduus...comes*? In the same work as mentioned above, Hohl (pp. 60f.) returned to his earlier interpretation: 'ständiger Begleiter meiner früheren Dienstzeit'. That is: he takes *militia* not as 'Feldzug' but as 'Militärdienst', *nostrae* not as 'our' (in the sense of 'Roman') but as 'my', and *prioris* as meaning the equestrian in contrast to the senatorial part of V.'s own military service (cf. 111.3). Since the equestrian part of V.'s service ended when the Pannonian revolt began (loc. cit.), Hohl's interpretation would mean that Arminius was present during Tiberius' German campaigns of A.D. 4 onwards but not during the war in Illyricum (cf. E. Bickel, *RhM* 98 (1955), 233); it would also mean some small support for Mommsen's interpretation of *eius* (see above), although Hohl himself, as we have seen, adopted a completely different hypothesis for that word. But I do not believe that Hohl is right in his view of *adsiduus... comes*. As Timpe argues (*Arminius* 21–7), his is hardly the natural interpretation of V.'s phrase; and when V. uses the expression *militiae comes* elsewhere (59.3 'quem C. Caesar...Hispaniensis militiae adsecutum se postea comitem habuit'), *militia* = 'campaign' as clearly as it does at Val. Max. 9.11.4 'Pompeianae militiae comes'.

I therefore conclude that V.'s two phrases mean what Timpe says they mean (*Arminius* 30). 'Arminius hatte in dem vergangenen Krieg auf unserer Seite gekämpft, selbst das römische Bürgerrecht erhalten, ja, er war sogar darüber hinaus zum Ritterrang gelangt.'[1] This meaning is admittedly vague, but I can see no justification in V.'s text for assuming that anything more precise was intended. And such an interpretation in no way precludes the more detailed suggestions which Timpe proceeds to make about Arminius' career: that he was an equestrian prefect in command of auxiliary units and served in both Germany and Illyricum.

For the combination of *adsiduus* and *comes* cf. 1.9.6, Sen. *Phaedr.* 1077, *Dial.* 6.4.3, Mart. 11.39.2.

---

1 Timpe's actual words are 'zu ritterlichen Positionen (oder: zum Ritterrang) gelangt': his indecision arises from his failure to dispense firmly with *eius*, which I hope I have succeeded in doing. Given that Arminius was a soldier (*militiae comes*) and had reached the equestrian rank (*ius equestris consequens gradus*), his position(s) in the army would naturally be of equestrian status.

segnitia ducis A stock charge in Latin historiography (cf. Heubner on Tac. *H.* 2.40; also Ogilvie on Liv. 2.58.6), but our sources are agreed on this aspect of Varus' incompetence: Tac. *A.* 1.58.2 'segnitia ducis', Suet. *Tib.* 18.1 'temeritate et neglegentia ducis', Sen. *Contr.* 1.3.10 'neglegentia'. It is difficult to see why V. should be criticised for pointing this out (Timpe, *Arminius* 120ff.). For *in occasionem sceleris* below cf. Tac. *H.* 1.80.2, Just. 12.1.6.

haud imprudenter speculatus *** No editor, so far as I know, has been troubled by *speculari* + acc. and infin., yet the construction is unparalleled elsewhere in Latin and the normal usage of the verb makes it unlikely that the construction is possible (indirect questions are quite different). I therefore suggest a lacuna, which would contain not only some such word as *fortunam* (cf. 1.9.2) or *opportunitatem* (120.4), but also a verb of saying or thinking to introduce the acc. and infin. clause.

neminem celerius opprimi quam qui nihil timeret The maxim, which is naturally applicable to the present disaster (cf. Flor. 2.30.34 'itaque improuidum et nihil tale metuentem ex improuiso adorti...'), is a topos of Latin historiography: Liv. 37.4.9 'eo ipso quod nihil tale timerent, opprimi incautos posse' (Ruhnken), 6.6.10, 21.43.11, 29.3.8, Curt. 5.4.27, 6.3.11. Some of these exs. are taken from Lipsius, *Opera omnia* (1675), 4.159, to whom Boeclerus refers. See too next n.

frequentissimum initium esse calamitatis securitatem Again a topos (Cato, *Or.* fr. 122 Malc., Liv. 21.61.2, 23.27.3; Häussler, *Nachträge* 123, 248), but appropriate to the *clades* (Flor. 2.30.34 'cum ille – o securitas! – ad tribunal citaret, undique inuadunt'). The gnomic character of sections 2 and 4 of this chapter is noteworthy: the moral is drawn at 120.5 below (see p. 42).

118.3 decretis facta iungit Cf. 110.5n.

118.4 Segesten *RE* 2A.1.1070–1 (Stein).

postulabat etiam * fata consiliis** Lipsius thought that *postulabat etiam* was a corruption of *obstabant sed iam,* but since Segestes actually did make demands of Varus (Tac. *A.* 1.58.2 'ut me et Arminium et conscios uinciret flagitaui', cf. 55.2), *postulabat* may well be right. Yet Lipsius' notion is too attractive to be dismissed completely. If V. had written (e.g.) *postulabat etiam a Varo ut uincirentur conscii, sed obstabant iam fata consiliis,* a scribe's eye might have jumped straight from *postulabat etiam* to *fata* on account of homoeoteleuton (*obstabant iam*). *fata obstant* is in origin a Virgilian phrase

(*Aen.* 4.440), and we should note that in the only comparable passage to this, 57.3, V. also uses Virgilian phraseology. The phrase recurs in Ov. Val. Fl. Stat.; *obstare consiliis* is at Stat. *Theb.* 7.423 (Ruhnken).

omnemque animi eius aciem praestrinxerant V.'s regular fondness for Ciceronian phrases confirms Gelenius' emendation *praestrinxerant*: cf. *Phil.* 12.3, *Fin.* 4.37 'aciem animorum nostrorum uirtutis splendore praestringitis', *Rab. Post.* 43, *Diu.* 1.61, *Diu. Caec.* 46. The metaphor is that of blunting the sharpness of vision or eyesight. Just as a vivid light will diminish the sharpness of one's vision (Liv. 40.58.4 'fulguribus praestringentibus aciem oculorum', cf. Luc. 1.154, Sil. 1.358), so the sharpness of one's metaphorical vision or of one's mind can be diminished (Cic. *Vatin.* 25 'Domitii dignitas et splendor praestringebat oculos Vatinii', *Senec.* 42 'mentis ut ita dicam praestringit oculos'). We should remember that 'non...solum ipsa fortuna caeca est, sed eos etiam plerumque efficit caecos quos complexa est' (Cic. *Amic.* 54; cf. Otto 142).

cuius fortunam mutaturus ⟨est⟩ deus, consilia corrumpat It is impossible to know precisely how V. expressed this well known aphorism here. The paradosis offers *qui*, which Vossius emended to *cui*: whether or not Vossius intended as much, Kritz assumed that *cui* was not the relative pronoun (in which case *est* would have to be understood with *mutaturus*) but the indefinite pronoun (thus *mutaturus* has an almost conditional force): 'si cui fortunam mutaturus est, consilia (sc. eius) corrumpat'. Yet this seems unduly oblique, and does not square with V.'s expression of the same idea at 57.3 'fatorum uis, cuiuscum⟨que⟩ fortunam mutare constituit, consilia corrumpit', where a relative pronoun is used. Whether we should retain Vossius' *cui* as a relative, or follow the Bipontine ed. in preferring *cuius*, is uncertain; but in the light of 57.3 I have opted for the latter (the series of corruption *cuius* > *cui* > *qui* is not implausible; for *cuius* corrupted to *cui* cf. e.g. Hor. *C.* 2.4.23). It is again uncertain whether we should understand *est* with *mutaturus*, or supply it: despite V.'s fondness for ellipse, I have again followed the Bipontine ed. in supplying *est* (ellipse with the future participle seems much less common, except in or. obl., than the type noted at 111.4n.). In this note I have not made use of examples of the same *sententia* in other authors: the version 'quem Iuppiter uult perdere, dementat prius' is extremely late (cf. Jebb's edn of Soph. *Ant.*, pp. 255–6), and the relative pronoun is not invariable (cf. Otto 145, where however note Publil. Syr. 612 'stultum facit fortuna, quem uult perdere'). For *consilia corrumpat* cf. Sall. *H.* 1.77.6, Gell. 1.13.4 (F.).

quod accidit, ei etiam merito accidisse uideatur Kritz aptly emended *et* (BA) to *ei*,[1] but his quotation of Sall. *C.* 51.26 indicates that we should

[1] There is a similar corruption at 104.2 (see app. crit.).

punctuate before, not after, *ei* ('illis merito accidet quicquid euenerit'); cf. also Cic. *Verr.* 2.1.70 'idque ita illi merito accidisse existimatum', *Fam.* 5.17.5 'tibi nihil merito accidisse'; Klebs quoted Sulp. *Chron.* 2.22.6 'merito sibi illa accidisse' (291–2). For *quod miserrimum est* above cf. 130.4, Sall. *J.* 14.4, Cic. *Quinct.* 49, *Rab. Perd.* 6, Liv. 6.24.9, 37.53.16.

casus in culpam transeat The antithesis between *casus* or *fortuna* and *culpa*, which probably derives from legal terminology (cf. *Rhet. Herenn.* 2.24, and similar phrases in late legal works), is conventional: Cic. *Verr.* 5.131, *Leg. Man.* 10, *Pis.* 43, *Rab. Post.* 29, *Att.* 11.9.1, *Fam.* 6.2.3, 7.28.3, 9.13.3, 15.15.2, Sen. *HF* 1201, *Clem.* 1.2.1, Tac. *A.* 4.64.1. For the opposite cf. Tac. *A.* 1.28.3 'quae casus obtulerat, in sapientiam uertenda ratus', *G.* 36.1.

spe⟨cie⟩mque in se beneuolentiae ex merito aestimare While it makes sense to say *beneuolentiam aestimare* or *spem beneuolentiae habere*, it does not make sense to say *spem beneuolentiae aestimare.* Burman rightly wrote *speciem*, observing that the two words are often confused. For *ex merito* cf. Sall. *J.* 85.37, Liv. 26.31.9, Ov. *Ex P.* 4.7.16, *H.* 2.62 *al.*, Tac. *H.* 4.50.3; Hand, *Turs.* 2.655.

119–120 THE 'SUMMA'

119.1 Ordinem...iustis uoluminibus ut alii ita nos conabimur exponere As John 934–5 rightly observes, we cannot tell whether *alii* alludes to writers who have already treated the *clades* or to those who will do so in the future. If the former (as assumed without question by Timpe, *Arminius* 119), there is no way of knowing whom V. means. For V.'s references to his own future work cf. 96.3n. Note that V. here refers to himself in the plural, *nos*: 'the plural of authorship is not pompous, but (if anything) more urbane than *ego*' (Nisbet–Hubbard on Hor. *C.* 1.6.5 with further reff., to which add M. P. Pieri, *SIFC* 39 (1967), 220–1, on Cicero's letters; S. Lilja, *Eranos* 69 (1971), 89–103, on Pliny's: the former remarks that when Cic. alludes to his own future works, he tends to use the singular, i.e. the opposite of V. here). For *ordinem...exponere* cf. Liv. 40.55.5 'ordinemque omnem facinoris...exposuit', Sen. *Contr.* 7.8.5.

119.2 marcore ducis, perfidia hostis, iniquitate fortunae circumuentus This tricolon summarises the three main themes or topoi of the first section of V.'s account (see above, p. 188). Note that both Augustus (Dio 56.24.2) and Tacitus (*A.* 1.55.3) also saw the workings of fate behind the catastrophe, and that the latter, despite his admiration for Arminius, admits to the man's *perfidia* at *A.* 1.55.1. For *iniquitas fortunae* cf. Sen. *Contr.* 10.4.2 (*iniquitas fatorum* at 97.3, Sen. *Dial.* 12.11.1, Apul. *Met.* 9.38.4). *circumuentus* is not literally 'surrounded' (which follows later with *inclusus*):

the word is rather metaphorical, 'ensnared', 'victimised'. *marcor*, a rare word, seems not to be found before V. and Celsus. For *manu*. . .*princeps* above cf. Manil. 4.688–9 'Sparta manu. . . | princeps'.

cum ne pugnandi quidem egredien⟨di⟩ue occasio iis, in quantum uoluerant, data esset †immunis, castigatis etiam quibusdam graui poena quia Romanis et armis et animis usi fuissent A desperate passage, which may be discussed in three parts.

(1) It seems clear from B that (M) read *egrediē*; (R) copied the word in such a way that A did not know whether to write *egredie* or *egregie*, while P opted for the latter (not unnaturally, since *pugnare egregie* is a set phrase: Liv. 3.29.7, 43.5, 10.30.2 etc.). Vossius acutely suggested that V. wrote *egrediendi*: he was supported strongly by Kritz, who showed that the verb is almost a technical military term 'quo significatur eos, qui aliquo impedimento clausi vel circumventi tenentur. . .vel erumpere vel exire conari' (cf. *TLL* 5.2.279. 24ff.). It is perhaps less certain whether we should also follow Vossius in emending *aut* to *-ue*, or follow Haase in transposing *egrediendi* and *aut*. On balance, I think the preceding negative makes the former more likely.

(2) From *data esset* in the paradosis it appears that the two gerunds *pugnandi* and *egrediendi* depend upon a feminine singular noun in the nominative; but no such noun is there given. One possibility is to supply a noun, e.g.: . . .*egrediendiue aut occasionis*. . .*data esset ⟨potestas⟩ immunis* (after Rhenanus); but this would mean that *occasio* = 'surprise attack', a sense which, despite L&S, the supposed parallels do not support. The same objection applies to those who would emend the difficult word *immunis* as did Friebel: *occasionis* . . .*immunitas* (Rosenheyn realised this when he proposed *occisionis*. . . *impunitas*). Most scholars have believed, I think rightly, that V. wrote *occasio*: this gives perfect sense in itself, and the only problem is to decide how the corruption may have occurred. Of the various suggestions which have been made, I am attracted to only three: *occasio iis* (Vossius), *occasiones*. . . *datae essent* (Fröhlich), *occasio nis⟨i iniqua nec⟩ in quantum*. . . (Ellis). Despite the brilliance of Ellis' proposal, Vossius' emendation involves only the smallest change and the corruption is entirely credible (e.g. *iis* > *hiis* > *his* > *-nis*).

(3) As constituted so far, the text means: 'since no *occasio immunis* even of fighting or of sallying forth had been given to them to the extent they had wished'. This seems to be one of those places where *immunis* takes its precise significance from its context (so *TLL* 7.1.507.5ff.): we must therefore understand V. to mean an *occasio* which was *immunis* from the *graui poena* mentioned in the following phrase. But what exactly is the *graui poena*, and by whom was the *occasio* not given (*ne*. . .*quidem*. . .*data esset*)? Timpe adopts an interpretation which is at least as old as Burman and which was also accepted by, among others, Kritz and Ellis. He believes (*Arminius* 110) that V. is

referring to the 'Kampfverbot des Varus': the soldiers naturally expected to fight, but Varus prevented them from so doing on pain of punishment (*ne pugnandi quidem...occasio iis, in quantum uoluerant,...immunis*); moreover he chastised very severely those who actually *did* fight (*castigatis etiam quibusdam graui poena quia Romanis et armis et animis usi fuissent*). The main argument in favour of this interpretation is that it explains the troublesome word *immunis*. Yet it has serious disadvantages.

(*a*) There is no hint of such behaviour on the part of Varus anywhere in Dio's relatively detailed account[1] or in Tacitus. Indeed such behaviour is almost unthinkable for a Roman general, however *socors*, and has no parallel (so far as I am aware) elsewhere in Roman military history.[2] Besides, such behaviour is, it seems to me, psychologically and militarily improbable: Varus could not hope to gain anything by it. (*b*) To say that Varus did not guarantee his men immunity *in quantum uoluerant* is to imply that on other occasions a Roman general would guarantee such immunity; but this is nonsense, since the primary duty of soldiers is to fight. Gruter and Vossius did indeed delete the words *in quantum uoluerant*, but their reappearance at 120.3 below confirms, rather than refutes, their genuineness here (cf. 100.5n.). (*c*) The subjunctive *usi fuissent* suggests that this is not V.'s own comment but a reported reason (*haberent* at 117.3 is not parallel, since there the verb has been attracted into the subjunctive on account of the or. obl.): the words are hardly applicable to Varus, but could very naturally be seen as coming from a barbarian enemy. (*d*) The passage *cum ne pugnandi quidem... usi fuissent* far more naturally refers to the difficulties in which the Romans found themselves as a result of the enemy's surprise attack (*inclusus siluis* etc., below) and to the treatment which the captured soldiers received at the hands of the enemy, a point to which V. returns at the end of his account (120.6, cf. Tac. *A.* 1.61.3–4). For this almost metaphorical use of *poena* cf. 121.1.

These four points suggest that the interpretation of Burman and Timpe is incorrect; and the last two points indicate that V. means that no *occasio*

---

1 Timpe however implies the opposite, noting that at 56.20.4–5 Dio refers to the Romans' lack of resistance. But Dio explicitly (γάρ) gives other reasons for this failure: the irregular marching order, the Romans' inferior numbers, and their inability συστραφῆναί πῃ ῥᾳδίως. Besides, Dio later (56.21.2) states that the Romans did resist.

2 John (941) regards the incidents described at Liv. 22.25.8–10 and Plut. *Mar.* 16.1 as comparable. But, as Mr J. F. Lazenby points out to me, the former is a tendentious representation of Fabius' over-all strategy by a prejudiced *tribunus plebis* (the whole passage is in or. obl.); and the latter is part of a deliberate tactical policy on the part of Marius. In neither case is the military situation in any way comparable to the plight in which Varus suddenly and unexpectedly found himself.

immunis had been given to Varus' troops by the enemy. But under what conditions could a Roman army possibly expect an *immunis occasio* from the enemy? If the Romans were in a vastly superior position and all the advantages lay with them, then they might expect an *occasio immunis* either to fight or, possibly, to sally forth. Thus in Dio's account of this same encounter we are told that the Germans τὴν ἐξουσίαν καὶ τῆς ἐφόδου καὶ τῆς ἀναχωρήσεως ἀδεᾶ ἔχουσιν (56.21.4). But of course the passage of Dio merely goes to prove that the Romans were in no such position on this occasion: the last thing they were entitled to expect was an *occasio pugnandi egrediendiue* which was *immunis*. Yet Wopkens noted that a hostile army would sometimes offer a *libera occasio* to an encircled enemy in order to entice them out and destroy them (Front. *Strat.* 3.11.2): 'paulum regressus tamquam ad alios actus liberam recedendi occasionem iis dedit; non multo post milite reducto destitutos Phocenses superauit'. And it is indeed true that a similar move was suggested by Arminius himself in Germany later (Tac. *A.* 1.68.1 'Arminio sinerent *egredi egressosque* rursum per umida et impedita circumuenirent suadente'). Yet it is extremely unlikely that Varus' soldiers were hoping for the enemy to adopt this tactic so that, when it came, they could use it to launch a last, desperate counter-attack. The Germans already had the Romans exactly where they wanted them, viz. in the *umida et impedita* (cf. *inclusus siluis, paludibus* below): the Romans were in no position to anticipate this move from the enemy, and, even if they had been, it is almost impossible to deduce as much from what V. says. In any case, the context of the operation described by Frontinus (above) is quite different.

Thus, either *cum ne pugnandi quidem...usi fuissent* refers to Varus' *Kampfverbot*, in which case *immunis* makes sense, or it refers to the desperate position in which the Romans found themselves as a result of the Germans' attack, in which case *immunis* does not make sense. It will be evident from the preceding discussion that I favour the latter interpretation and that I therefore regard *immunis* as an error. Indeed even Burman, who of course preferred the former interpretation, believed that *immunis* was wrong: he conjectured *comminus*, which has the advantage of agreeing with Dio 56.20.5 (quoted above, p. 200 n. 1) but which is inappropriate with *egrediendi*; Burman was compelled to emend this word to *congrediendi*, but adverb and verb are still intolerably far apart. Mommsen proposed *immo* (for *immo...etiam* cf. Sen. *Contr.* 2.1.7, Plin. *NH praef.* 13, Petron. 110.2), but it is hard to see how the corruption might have occurred. In fact no conjecture carries complete conviction, and I have reluctantly obelised *immunis*.

For *in quantum* cf. 114.5n.; for *armis et animis* cf. 115.1n.; for *animis usi* cf. Cic. *Att.* 15.4.2 'animis...usi sumus uirilibus' (F.).

inclusus siluis... The exact site of the disaster is still unknown: 'the only indication of locality is the vague statement of a writer who had no occasion to be precise' (Syme, *CAH* 10.375, with ref. to Tac. *A.* 1.60.3 'ad ultimos Bructeros, quantumque Amisiam et Lupiam amnes inter uastatum, haud procul Teutoburgiensi saltu, in quo reliquiae Vari legionumque insepultae dicebantur'). For discussion and refs. to earlier literature cf. John 951ff.

more pecudum trucidauerat 'Slaughtering like animals' originates in Latin with Sall. *C.* 58.21 'sicuti pecora trucidemini', *H.* 4.67; it rapidly became a commonplace, esp. of historical writing: cf. [Sall.] *Ep. Caes.* 1.4.1, Liv. 5.44.7, 25.16.19, 28.16.6, 38.17.6, Tac. *A.* 4.25.3, Amm. 14.2.7. 'Dying like animals' is at Thuc. 2.51.4 (expanded in Lucr. 6.1237); other animal comparisons at Sall. *H.* 3.48.6, Liv. 5.48.3, Flor. 1.5.13, Plut. *Pericl.* 34. See too E. Skard, *Sallust u. s. Vorgänger* (1956), 21 n. 1, adding Suet. *Aug.* 15.

uitam aut mortem eius nunc ira nunc uenia temperaret 'dont la vie et la mort dépendaient de leur colère ou de leur pitié' (H–W).

119.3 ad moriendum...animi fuit *animus ad* is Livian, cf. 8.1.5, 10.36.3, 29.17.11 (F.). For the death of Varus' father after Philippi cf. 71.3.

119.4 L. Eggius *RE* 5.2.1986 = Eggius 1 (Stein); *PIR*[2] 3.68, no. 4. For *exemplum...prodere* cf. Liv. 5.27.13, Sen. *Ep.* 78.21, Apul. *Met.* 10.6.

Ceionius *RE* 6.1828 = Ceionius 1 (v. Rohden); *PIR*[2] 2.134, no. 597. For *longe*+superl. below cf. K–S 2.403 Anm. 2; Landgraf on Cic. *Rosc. Am.* 33.

supplicio quam proelio mori maluit Cf. 35.5 'quem spiritum supplicio debuerat, ⟨proelio⟩ reddidit' (Acidalius), Val. Max. 6.3.3 'effecitque ut quem spiritum profundere in acie noluerat, turpiter in catenis consumeret' (Verhaak 110). *auctor deditionis* above is technical (Cic. *Off.* 3.109, Liv. 6.10.5, 28.20.11, Curt. 9.7.13).

Vala Numonius C. Numonius Vala, *RE* 17.2.1461–2 = Numonius 2 (v. Petrikovits).

cetera quietus ac probus Ancient historians regularly draw attention to two contrasting aspects of a man's character by such words as (ἐς) τἄλλα, *alioqui* or *cetera* (cf. e.g. 2.2.2, 2.7.3, 33.1, 33.4, 46.2, Thuc. 6.72.2, Sall. *H.* 4.70, Liv. 1.35.6, Tac. *Agr.* 16.2; K–S 1.286 Anm. 1). The trait presumably derives from their recognition that *nemo sine uitio est* (Sen. *Contr.* 2.4.4), a topos for which cf. also Catull. 22.20 (and Kroll's n.), Cic. *Inu.* 2.165, Sen. *Ep.* 114.12, Plin. *Pan.* 4.5. See also Vell. 91.2.

119.5 gentilicii tamen tumuli sepultura honoratum est 'Varus, quamquam tantae calamitatis auctor, *tamen* gentilicii tumuli sepultura honoratus est' (Kritz). For *gentilicii...tumuli* cf. *CIL* 8.23126; for *sepultura honoratum* cf. 62.4, Stat. *Silu.* 2.1.69f., Lact. *Mort. Pers.* 4.3.

120.1 His auditis reuolat ad patrem Caesar V. clearly states that Tiberius, on hearing of the disaster, returned to Rome. We do not know when he arrived, but it was presumably quite some time after the disaster had happened (cf. 117.1n.). The triumph, which he had been voted for his conquests in Illyricum, was deferred (Suet. *Tib.* 17.2); and having dedicated the temple of Concordia early in A.D. 10 (EJ p. 45), he set off for Germany (Suet. *Tib.* 18.1 'proximo anno repetita Germania'). Dupraz 178–9 uses this last statement of Suetonius ('*re*petita') to argue that Tiberius had already gone to Germany late in A.D. 9 after the disaster had taken place and that, having returned to Rome in the winter of A.D. 9/10, went *back* to Germany early in A.D. 10. This view, taken by some other scholars also, would mean that V.'s statement *reuolat ad patrem* is incorrect. But by *repetita* Suetonius of course means nothing more than does V. when he says 'perpetuus patronus...*adsuetam* sibi causam suscipit' just below: *repetita* is a natural word to use of someone going to Germany for at least the seventh time, as was Tiberius (the other certain occasions were in 9, 8, 7 B.C., and A.D. 4, 5, 6). Tiberius even remarked himself upon the regularity of his trips to Germany (Tac. *A.* 2.26.3). Dupraz has misunderstood Suetonius' statement, which therefore in no way contradicts what V. says here. For *reuolat*, a characteristically Tiberian action, cf. 123.1n.

The section which begins *His auditis* and ends with *in hiberna reuertitur* (2, below) was transposed to the end of this chapter by Haase. This bold suggestion, accepted by Kritz, merits serious consideration, mainly because the style and contents of 120.3–6 strongly resemble those of 119.4–5: these two sections arguably form a single unit, which 120.1–2 apparently interrupts. Despite the obvious attraction of Haase's transposition, however, I do not think it is right.

(1) V.'s narrative of the *Variana clades*, as of the revolt in Illyricum, is broadly annalistic. The *clades* was reported within days of the victory in Dalmatia in A.D. 9, as V. explicitly states (117.1). V. then sketches in the background to the disaster (117.2–118.4), focusing on the *aestiua* of A.D. 9 (117.4). The disaster is related (119), after which we are told that Tiberius rushed back to Augustus' side (120.1): no date is given, but it was presumably late in A.D. 9. We are then given an account of Tiberius' return to Germany in A.D. 10 and of his actions of that year, up to his return to winter quarters (120.1–2). Again no dates are given, but the phrase *in hiberna reuertitur* (120.2) implies that the preceding section has described only the events of the year immediately following the disaster, viz. A.D. 10.[1] In V.'s

[1] Dupraz 177ff. is hopelessly wrong in his interpretation of 120.1–2: he believes that V. is referring to the events of A.D. 9–11.

eyes the aftermath of the *clades* is now over; and in 121.1ff. he passes quickly on to the years A.D. 11–12 (see below, pp. 209–15). What is more natural than a series of *testimonia* in 120.3–6 to separate the events of A.D. 9–10 from those of A.D. 11–12? V.'s practice here is directly comparable to that in the revolt in Illyricum: 120.3–6 here fulfils exactly the same function as did ch. 116 there (see above, p. 183). This seems to me the strongest argument that Haase's transposition is mistaken. But there are others.

(2) The intervention of Tiberius follows more dramatically after the disgraceful *exempla* described in 119.4–5 than after the accounts of bravery in 120.3–6. (3) The final judgement on Varus (120.5 *ex quo apparet Varum...*) forms a natural conclusion to the episode and is more suitably placed as in the paradosis than anywhere else (see above, p. 42). (4) Haase's transposition would be particularly damaging to the climactic incident described at 120.6 (see n.).

perpetuus patronus Romani imperii adsuetam sibi causam suscipit An excellent example of V.'s use of language. During the later republic a *patronus* was someone who agreed to protect another person, a *cliens*; the *patronus* could protect him by legal assistance, while the *cliens* would support his *patronus* by electoral backing. The relationship between the two stands at the very heart of Roman politics; and as individual politicians became increasingly more powerful, so the word *patronus* (or its Greek equivalent προστάτης) came to be used widely, and almost metaphorically, of highly influential persons. Under the empire, the emperor's relationship with his subjects was a natural extension of the *patronus/cliens* relationship: thus Tiberius in his funeral speech for Aug. calls him προστάτην αὐτὸν καὶ πατέρα δημόσιον (Dio 56.41.9), and the same title is used of Claudius (Jos. *BJ* 2.208). Moreover, the emperor's role as *patronus* was fostered and reaffirmed by his complementary roles as *custos* (104.2n.) and *pater patriae* (123.1n.; *patronus* is of course etymologically derived from *pater*, hence Tiberius' words as given in Dio above), in both of which he was expected to concern himself with the *tutela* and *cura imperii* (105.3n., 106.3n.). *patronus* thus takes its place in the vast complex of imperial propaganda.[1]

V. here says that Tiberius, as *patronus*, 'takes up the cause of the Roman empire'. He thus keeps alive the original function of a *patronus*, for *causam suscipere* is a metaphor derived from legal terminology (Cic. *Verr.* 1.51, 2.1 'suscepi causam rei publicae', *Sest.* 87, Ov. *Ex P.* 2.2.45 etc.). For V. Tiberius is also '*perpetuus* patronus' (for the phrase cf. *IG* 14.277; cf. also Dio 44.2.5 on Caesar: προστάτην διατελῆ τῆς πόλεως καὶ τῆς ἀρχῆς ἁπάσης), recalling

---

[1] Cf. how Livy makes Manlius Capitolinus sound like Augustus, 'ego me patronum profiteor plebis' (6.18.14; cf. Vict. *Vir. Ill.* 24.3.5, also Liv. 2.31.9).

the notion of *perpetuitas* which featured so prominently during the empire, and never more so than during Tiberius' own reign (103.4n.). V. reinforces the notion with *adsuetam*, which is conceivably an echo of Sall. *C.* 35.3 'publicam miserorum causam pro mea consuetudine suscepi' (a passage which Livy too was able to recall, cf. 3.15.9).

On *patronus* etc. cf. Premerstein *passim* (index under 'Klientel' and προστασία/προστάτης: for V. see p. 128); also L. R. Taylor, *Party politics in the age of Caesar* (1964 edn), 41ff.; Hellegouarc'h, *VL* 350ff. and elsewhere; Gelzer 62ff.

se magnitudine sua non fiducia hostium metiens Thus P, with *qui...minabantur* below; A reads *et se* and *qui...minabatur*. Burer notes as follows: 'sic legendum uidetur, quamquam ex uet. cod. nihil certi conijci queat. praesidia munit, & se magnitudine sua, non fiducia metiens' (i.e. with *et* but without *hostium*); then below, 'ex. uet. habet, minabatur'. Kritz explained this diversity of testimony as follows. Since Burer was concerned only to reinstate *et*, which P had omitted, his omission of *hostium* does not imply that that word was missing in (M): Burer omitted the word either through conjecture or through a desire to be brief. A, concludes Kritz, confirms the presence in (M) of both *et* and *hostium*; and P's *minabantur* below is Rhenanus' necessary correction of an earlier error which also was present in (M).

Kritz's view was attacked by Haupt (1.265–7), writing after Fechter's demonstration that both P and A depend upon (R). Haupt argued that Burer would not omit *hostium* for reasons of brevity (why write the phrase *non fiducia metiens* at all?), nor could its omission be a conjecture ('sinnlos'). Haupt considered a third possibility, viz. that Burer or Froben's printers omitted *hostium* in error, only to dismiss it: since Burer's 'vorsichtiges *quamquam ex uet. cod. nihil certi conijci queat* bezieht sich gewiss nicht auf das wörtlein *et*, dessen tilgung oder ausfall ihm schwerlich wichtig erschien', it follows that Burer was referring to the omission of *hostium*. Haupt therefore assumed that *hostium* was, on Burer's testimony, not present in (M) and that it had been added to (R) either by the apograph's copyist or by Rhenanus himself: hence it found its way into both P and A, and Rhenanus was forced to make the subsequent change to *minabantur*. But since the text makes no sense without some such word as *hostium*, and since we know from BA that (M) read *minabatur*, Haupt conjectured that what V. wrote was *non fiducia hostis metiens*.

Haupt's argument was accepted by Halm, but it cannot be right, since it is based upon the false premiss that Burer's formula *sic legendum uidetur* introduces a reading of (M). As I have explained above (pp. 8–10), Burer's readings of (M), as in the case of *minabatur* here, are introduced by the phrase *exemplar uetustum habet*, while his own conjectures are introduced by such phrases as *sic legendum uidetur*. I therefore conclude that Burer's note *sic legendum...metiens* does not report that (M) offered *et* and omitted *hostium*; on the contrary the note represents a conjecture by Burer.

What exactly was Burer's conjecture? Did he wish both to supply *et* and to omit *hostium*? Or did he wish only to supply *et*? Like Haupt, I find it unlikely that Burer would have conjectured the omission of *hostium* (although it would be no worse than several of his other proposals): he doubtless omitted the word for reasons of brevity (so Kritz; Haupt is wrong to think that Burer does not do similar things elsewhere), or through error (so Haupt).[1] In my opinion Burer was concerned only to supply *et*; and the appearance of the same word in A is due (so I believe) either to a similar conjecture by Amerbach or to error.

We must now try to decide whether *et* is right. I argue below, on quite different grounds, that there is no sentence break after *transgreditur* but that, contrary to what edd. have believed, *ultro...contenti erant* forms one complete sentence. If this sentence is the conclusion to the list of actions which have gone before, *et* should be retained. But if the sentence is the beginning of a new set of actions, *et* should be omitted. Everything which precedes *ultro* concerns stabilisation (*confirmat, praesidia munit*), whereas everything which follows *contenti erant* concerns aggression (*penetrat, aperit, gloria*). And since the sentence *ultro...contenti erant* itself concerns aggression, I conclude that *ultro* marks a new stage of Tiberius' strategy and that a new sentence begins at this point. Thus the preceding sentence ends *Italiae minabantur* (– ∪ – – –, as often in V.), and *se...metiens* is a participial phrase which naturally cannot be joined to *praesidia munit* by *et*.

For *se...metiens* cf. Curt. 9.6.18, Plin. *Pan.* 88.3 'ut se non tua fortuna sed sua metiantur'; F. adds Luc. 8.346, Sen. *NQ* 4 *praef.* 15, *Ep.* 124.24. V.'s expression is not unlike the proverb in Otto 221.

ultro Rhenum cum exercitu transgreditur ⟨et⟩ arma infert quae arcuisse...contenti erant Both *ultro* (the reading of A but brilliantly conjectured by Freinsheim before A was discovered) and *infert* (Lipsius' conjecture) are guaranteed by Livian parallels: 3.8.3 'non solum arcere bellum sed ultro etiam inferre', 10.28.2 'Romani...arcebant magis quam inferebant pugnam', 21.21.10 'partiens curas simul in inferendum atque arcendum bellum', 44.4 'inferentis uim quam arcentis'. The phrase *ultro arma* (or *bellum*) *inferre* is so standard (Liv. 3.42.7, 7.28.4, 23.38.6, 25.37.19, 31.18.3, 38.38.16, Curt. 7.7.11, Tac. *H.* 3.2.2 etc.) that it is clear that *ultro* should qualify *infert* as well as *transgreditur*; but since the asyndeton is harsh, I have supplied *et*. The sense is: 'crossing the Rhine with his army, Tiberius carried ⟨to the enemy⟩ the war which Augustus had been content merely to

[1] Burer similarly omits *ferme* at 1.14.6 and *gladiorum* at 22.2.

prevent'. Kritz plausibly explains how *infert* became corrupted into the paradosis *interfecti*.

Massauer agrees with the numerous scholars who have believed that Tiberius did not cross the Rhine until A.D. 11. But since Tiberius returned to Germany in A.D. 10 (see above), and since 120.1–2 of V.'s account naturally refers to the events of only one year (cf. *in hiberna reuertitur* below), I agree with Seager 45 that Tiberius did cross the Rhine in A.D. 10. The conflicting testimony of Dio 56.24.6, a passage which is attributed to A.D. 10 and which states that Tiberius did not cross the Rhine, must therefore be discounted (it derives from Zonaras). Seager also follows Timpe (*Germanicus* 31f.) in saying that Tiberius' expedition was no mere 'Demonstrationszug' (Massauer), but a symptom of the imperialist ambitions still cherished by Augustus; if so, V. has misunderstood Augustus' intentions (*arcuisse... contenti*).

120.2 aperit limites 'opened up roads' (on the analogy of *aperire uias*, cf. 2.1.1). It is however possible that V. means 'broke through the frontier lines (fortifications)'; cf. Liv. 24.34.9 'murum...aperuit', and for *limes* in this sense cf. Tac. *A.* 2.7.3, *G.* 29.3, *Agr.* 41.2. The expression, being ambiguous, is thus of little help in explaining the controversial statement made by Tac. at *A.* 1.50.1 (see Goodyear's n.). Timpe's comment on this part of V.'s account is as follows: 'Es fehlt nur ein Punkt: die Deportation der Gefangenen und Überläufer, an der es nicht gemangelt haben wird' (*Germanicus* 31 n. 19, referring to Tac. *A.* 1.58.5, 71.1).

120.3 L. Asprenati L. Nonius Asprenas, *RE* 17.1.867–72 = Nonius 16 (Groag). I find it hard to agree with Lana 118ff. that V. in his general treatment of Asprenas 'lancia la sua frecciata maligna, con quel procedimento che sarà poi tipico di Tacito'. For *incolumi...numero* above cf. Cic. *Verr.* 2.3.125, Apul. *Met.* 4.8.6 (F.); for *immunem...calamitate* below cf. 115.2 (n.).

uacillantium etiam cis Rhenum sitarum gentium animos *situs* of persons is not common (*gens sita* is also at Plin. *NH* 7.28, Flor. 2.3.2; cf. also Tac. *A.* 12.10.1, *Agr.* 30.2); V. may be imitating Sall. *H.* 4.69.17 (so Milkau 99). We might have expected *uacillantes animos*, as at Sen. *Ep.* 114.2, but V. has transferred the adj. as at 83.2 and elsewhere.

excisi exercitus So P; A reads *occisi*, and B is silent. In believing that A has simply substituted one synonymous word for another, as often, Halm (1875), 547, does the apograph's reading less than justice by implying that *occisi exercitus* is impossible. On the contrary, the expression is possible (cf. Liv. 5.28.12), and A's is the *lectio difficilior*. Nevertheless B's silence implies that *excisi* was the reading of (M), and it is this which we must retain.

hereditatem adire is technical legal phraseology = 'come into an inheritance' (cf. *TLL* 1.627.84, 628.1ff.); but its application here to *excisi exercitus* is an effective twist from its more regular use, as Professor Goodyear points out. For *in quantum* cf. 114.5n.

120.4 L. ...Caedicii *RE* 3.1245 = Caedicius 4 (Stein); *PIR*[2] 2.23, no. 113.

difficultatibus superatis quas...faciebat insuperabiles 'Having surmounted all the difficulties which the lack of provisions was making intolerable and the enemy strength was making insurmountable': the word play of *superatis...insuperabiles* is typically Velleian (cf. e.g. 115.4 'pugnandi scientia...inexpugnabiles'; Verhaak 77–8). Although *intolerabiles* is almost certainly acc. plur. (P reads *-abileis*, A *-abilis*), V may be recalling Sall. *H.* 2.45 'annonae intolerabilis saeuitia': for this type of 'associated reminiscence' cf. A. B. Cook, *CR* 15 (1901), 338–45. For *difficultates superare* cf. Plin. *Ep.* 9.39.6, Amm. 14.2.9.

nec temerario consilio nec segni prouidentia uicti Not only is E. Thomas' *uicti* closer to B's *uiti* than other conjectures, but *uinci consilio* is also at Liv. 6.23.8, Tac. *H.* 2.40, Just. 2.13.7. Thomas noted that *uit-* and *uict-* are confused by A at 97.1. *temerarium consilium* is a cliché (Cic. Liv. Curt. etc.); for *segni prouidentia* cf. perhaps Tac. *A.* 2.2.3 'segni cura'.

120.5 destitutum Herel unjustifiably deleted this word: the *abundantia* with *defectum* is typically Velleian (97.2n.), and for the two words combined cf. e.g. Manil. 2.732–5. For *defectum consilio* above cf. Cic. *Clu.* 184, Val. Max. 3.1 *ext.* 1 (F.).

John, drawing attention to what V. says of Varus here (*grauem et bonae uoluntatis uirum*), observes that 'vollends bezeigt er dem Varus eine fast respektvolle persönliche Achtung' (959). But Timpe, noting V.'s numerous references to Varus' *segnitia*, concludes that 'das alles wiegt die beschränkte Anerkennung 120.5 nicht auf' (*Arminius* 125 n. 25). Yet since Varus' *segnitia* is attested in other sources including Tacitus (above, 118.2n.), V.'s decision to add this extra comment here surely supports John's contention. The fact that Varus' family was under attack in the late twenties (Timpe, *Arminius* 123–4, following Lana; cf. Tac. *A.* 4.66) shows that V.'s judgement was independent of such intrigues rather than, as Lana and Timpe believe, influenced by them.

120.6 ad uetustatem familiae suae dignissimus Ruhnken wrote *ad⟨ulescens⟩*, but for *dignus + ad* cf. Plaut. *Mil.* 968 'ad tuam formam... dignast', Manil. 5.134 'dignas ad fulmina uires', Sil. 15.564 'dignas tanta ad conamina dextras'; also Cic. *Rep.* 1.30, Sil. 10.109. For Coelius Caldus cf. *RE* 4.195 = Coelius 11 (Stein); *PIR*² 2.297, no. 1242.

protinus pariter sanguinis cerebrique effluuio exspiraret Such deaths offered a combination of moral rectitude (contrast the *turpe exemplum* at 119.4 and n.) and almost 'epic' goriness (cf. e.g. Ov. *Met.* 12.238–9 'sanguinis ille globos pariter cerebrumque merumque | uulnere et ore uomens') that was hard to resist, and they become a topos of ancient writing: cf. 2.7.2 'quem cum haruspex Tuscus amicus flentem in uincula duci uidisset, "quin tu hoc potius", inquit, "facis?", protinusque inliso capite in postem lapideum ianuae carceris effusoque cerebro exspirauit', Val. Max. 9.12.6, Sen. *Ep.* 77.14 'exempla nunc magnorum uirorum me tibi iudicas relaturum?...ut primum iussus est (Lacon ille) seruili fungi...ministerio, illisum parieti caput rupit', Plin. *Ep.* 3.16.12, Tac. *A.* 4.45.2 'eo nisu proripuit se custodibus saxoque caput adflixit ut statim exanimaretur', Plut. *Cat. Min.* 68, *Mor.* 234C.

The paradosis here reads *in fluuio,* which cannot be right. I have preferred Lipsius' *effluuio* to the other conjectures on account of 2.7.2 (quoted above): if this is right, it provides an *aabb* alliterative pattern which is typical of V. (129.3n.) and brings the whole of the Varian episode to an effective conclusion.

121–122 THE POWER, TRIUMPH AND MODERATION OF TIBERIUS (A.D. 11–12)

It is clear, particularly from the phrase *subsequenti tempore* at 121.1 (n.) and from the contents of 121.3–122, that V. has for the moment abandoned the annalistic method of writing which he has been using since 104.2; instead, he returns to a more 'topical' method of arrangement (on which see above, p. 96). From our point of view this is perhaps unfortunate, because the chronology of the events of A.D. 11–13 has given considerable trouble to modern scholars.

Tiberius emerges from this section as Augustus' acknowledged equal in political power, as a triumphant general, and as a man of *moderatio* – a virtue which was to characterise much of his reign (122.1n.). 'Tiberius was now more secure than he had ever been, his position as Augustus' successor clear' (Seager 47). But the confidence implied in V.'s account of these years is dramatically upset by the crises which come to be described in chh. 123–5.

121.1 et uirtus et fortuna For this combination cf. 97.4n. A omits the first *et*, but cf. 97.4.

subsequenti tempore Whereas in his narrative of the revolt in Illyricum V. was usually careful to introduce a new year by some such phrase as *insequenti aestate* (114.4, cf. p. 154), his use of *tempore* here is vague by comparison. The reason must be that he has now stopped annalistic writing; *tempore* embraces the events of more than one year: the problem is to know how many years are intended (see below).

accensaque plebe Viennensium dissensiones...mollisset B tells us that (M) read *accensaque plebis*, which, since it is nonsense, P emended to *accensasque plebis*. Ellis (188) finds this reading attractive in view of Sall. *H.* 1.77.14 'omnes discordiae accensae' ('qui locus mirum quantum ad hunc Vellei accedit'). But *Viennensium* in apposition to *plebis* is highly unusual (we should expect *Viennensis*). A, whether through error or emendation (see above, p. 17 n. 4), wrote *accensaque plebe*, the correctness of which is proved by Sall. *J.* 73.6 'plebes sic accensa'.

No other historical source mentions the trouble in what is now modern Vienne, but a poem by Crinagoras (*Anth. Pal.* 9.283) alludes to a Roman victory which was witnessed by the Pyrenees and the Alps. Hitherto no one has been able to determine what event is being alluded to, despite numerous widely divergent conjectures (cf. A. S. F. Gow and D. L. Page, *The Garland of Philip* (1968), 2.234ff.); but the uprising in Vienne fits the geography of the poem exactly, since the town lies between these two mountain ranges. Can the uprising be dated? V. attributes the victory to Tiberius, while Crinagoras' victory is attributed to Germanicus; but the two are not inconsistent if we assume that Tiberius was commander-in-chief. According to Dio (56.25.2) Germanicus was with Tiberius on campaign in A.D. 11, although we are told that they stayed in the Rhine area and accomplished nothing of note; we also know that Germanicus was consul in A.D. 12, and Suetonius states that he remained in Rome throughout that year (*Cal.* 8.3). Thus the evidence implies that, if Germanicus' victory is the same as that referred to here by V., it took place probably in A.D. 11.

For *dissensiones...mollisset* cf. perhaps Prop. 4.4.62 'molliet arma', Ov. *Tr.* 3.5.53–4 'molliat... | poenam'. For the combination of *coercitio* and *poena* cf. Tac. *A.* 3.26.1.

ut aequum ei ius in omnibus prouinciis exercitibusque esset... decreto complexus est Two questions are prompted by this statement: was Tiberius' new power different from that which he possessed already, and when did he receive it? Both V. and Suetonius (*Tib.* 21.1 'lege per consules lata ut prouincias cum Augusto communiter administraret') clearly imply that Tiberius received greater power than he already had. But since Tiberius, in all probability, had been given *imperium proconsulare* in A.D. 4, we conclude that this earlier grant had possibly been limited to his area of operations in Germany. The new power had no such geographical limitation. See Goodyear, *Comm. Tac.* 1.112 with n. 2; P. A. Brunt, *ZPE* 13 (1974), 171–3.

The date at which Tiberius received this power has been much discussed (see Dupraz 174). Suetonius' account is as follows (*Tib.* 20–21.1): 'a Germania in urbem post biennium regressus triumphum...egit...ac non multo post lege per consules lata, ut prouincias...administraret...in Illyricum profectus est.' That is: Germany, triumph, *imperium*. In V.'s account the order of events is: Germany, *imperium*, triumph (121.1–2). The discrepancy may be resolved as follows. V. nowhere states when Tiberius actually received the *imperium*; he merely implies that the voting of *imperium* preceded the celebration of the triumph (*senatus...decreto complexus est*: see below). Since the triumph was almost certainly celebrated in October A.D. 12 (below, 2n.), it follows that the senate's decree preceded that date. Suetonius does not contradict this, provided we assume that his phrase *ac non multo post* refers not to *lege per consules lata* but to *in Illyricum profectus est*: 'and not long after his triumph, a law having ⟨earlier⟩ been passed that he should govern the provinces jointly with Augustus, he set off for Illyricum'. The evidence of Suetonius and V., thus interpreted, is admittedly of no help in solving the vexed problem of when exactly Tiberius received his *imperium*; but the arrangement of V.'s narrative implies that the *imperium* was decreed before October A.D. 12, presumably before Tiberius returned to Rome from campaign (cf. *in urbem reuersus* at 2 below). Finally, note that the speculations of Dupraz should be discounted (183–5), because he wrongly bases his chronology of events on the assumption that Tiberius' triumph was celebrated in January of A.D. 12.

quam erat ipsi Orelli proposed *atque* for *quam*, but *quam* after the adverb *aeque* in non-negative sentences is found elsewhere: e.g. Liv. 31.1.3, Ov. *Met.* 10.185–6, Sen. *Contr.* 2.1.5, Val. Max. 9.2 *ext.* 2, Colum. 8.10.2, Plin. *NH* 2.196, Quint. 9.4.85; cf. Draeger, *Hist. Synt.* 2.635, L–H–S 593, *TLL* 1.1044.24ff. (but Ter. *Ad.* 702 is not a certain ex.). It seems that V. has extended the usage to the adjective (so Kritz, Georges 26–7).

decreto complexus est Some alteration of the paradosis is required if this sentence is to make sense, and I prefer Ellis' *est* for *esset* here rather than Rhenanus' *mollisset* ⟨*et*⟩ above. *est* produces a far better sentence structure, and could easily have been corrupted to *esset* following *ut*.

V.'s expression is technical, = 'effected by decree that', but is wrongly classified in most lexica: it is analogous to such exs. as Plin. *Ep.* 10.22.1 (Trajan writing) 'ut (numerus) daretur illi mandatis meis complexus sum', Gai. *Inst.* 4.166*a* 'quod praetor interdicto complexus est', Ulp. *Dig.* 40.5.30.7 (see too Liv. 32.34.11 'decreta...omnes honores complexa'). It is thus clear that V.'s *ut*-clause depends equally upon *decreto complexus* and *postulante* above.

121.2 ad opem ferendam primus In V.'s opinion Tiberius should not be 'oneratus magis quam honoratus' (Liv. 22.30.4, cf. Otto 167). Note the chiasmus of the whole sentence as well as of its first colon, the antitheses of *sub/ab*, of the gerundival phrases, and *primus ad/parem ad* (for the former cf. Ter. *Phorm.* 533 'prior ad', Tac. *A.* 1.28.5; for the latter cf. Cic. *Verr.* 3.23, Liv. 1.5.7, 2.11.10 *al.*); also the polyptoton of *uindicabantur/uindicandum.*

dilatum...egit triumphum 'The day is certain, the year disputed' (Seager 45 n. 6). The day was 23 October (cf. EJ p. 54); the year was almost certainly A.D. 12 (cf. Sumner 274 n. 107; also E. Hohl, 'Die Siegesfeiern des Tib.', *SDAW* (1952), 1.8ff.). For *debitum triumphum* cf. Liv. 39.4.6, Suet. *Vesp.* 12; for *dilatum triumphum* cf. Suet. *Tib.* 17.2, 20 (of this same occasion). Tiberius' triumph had been deferred from A.D. 9/10 (120.1n.).

121.3 quippe...hostium duces non occisos fama narrauit sed uinctos triumphus ostendit Despite *fortunae indulgentia* above, V. is delighted by the survival of these princes not for any humanitarian reason but because they provided visible evidence of Tiberius' military success. As Burman in a lengthy note observes, the notion 'homines amplius oculis quam auribus credunt' was proverbial (Sen. *Ep.* 6.5, cf. Otto 251); but it was particularly applicable to historiography (cf. Plb. 12.27.1 and Walbank's n.) and to panegyric (Plin. *Pan.* 59.3 'aequum est...oculis nostris, non famae semper et rumoribus credere', *Pan. Lat.* 2.24.4, 4.32.4). For descriptions of triumphs as a topos of panegyric cf. Plin. *Pan.* 17 and Durry 35 (to his refs. add Cic. *Verr.* 5.77, and Nisbet–Hubbard on Hor. *C.* 1.37.20). For *fortunae indulgentia* cf. Heubner on Tac. *H.* 2.84.2; for *fama narrauit* cf. 93.2, 102.1; for *triumphum...comitari* below cf. Suet. *Dom.* 2.1.

122.1 singularis moderatio Ti. Caesaris Moderation was by no means a new concept for leaders to adopt. Brasidas, for ex., claimed it in the fifth century B.C. (Thuc. 4.108.2), it was attributed to Romulus in the first century B.C. (Weinstock 181), and then Ovid (*Tr.* 2.41–2) and Suetonius (*Aug.* 21.3) ascribed it to Augustus. But scholars are generally agreed that it was Tiberius who appropriated *moderatio* as his own 'peculiar and distinctive virtue' (Rogers 88). The emperor publicised it himself, both on the coinage (*RIC* 1.108) and in official correspondence (EJ 102), and authors follow suit: Suet. *Tib.* 32.2 'parem moderationem minoribus quoque et personis et rebus exhibuit', and elsewhere in V. at 2 below, *modum... temperauit*, and at 130.1 *magnificum animi temperamentum.* The witness of two other authors is interesting but paradoxical. Val. Max., a contemporary, wrote a chapter *De moderatione* (4.1), but surprisingly did not mention Tiberius: as Professor Goodyear remarks to me, this silence perhaps attests Tiberius' *moderatio* better than any mention might have done. Conversely Tacitus, who might have been expected to disparage this quality of the emperor, seems to acknowledge it (see Goodyear on Tac. *A.* 1.8.5). Even a sceptical modern scholar, speaking of the imperial virtues in general, admits that 'not all stand the test, but some come off without reproach, such as the MODERATIO of Tiberius Caesar' (Syme, *Tac.* 754). See further Rogers 60–88; Sutherland 97ff. and in *JRS* 28 (1938), 129ff.; Grant, *RAI* 49 (with later dating of the coinage); Levick (1975), with further refs.

For *elucet atque eminet* below cf. Plin. *Ep.* 1.10.5 'multa in Euphrate sic eminent atque elucent'.

septem triumphos meruerit, tribus contentus fuit Weber (4* n. 15) notes that V.'s present definition of Tiberius' *moderatio* resembles Ovid's of Caesar's (*Met.* 15.757 'et multos meruisse, aliquos egisse triumphos') and Augustus' of his own (*RG* 4.1 'decernente plures triumphos mihi senatu, quibus omnibus supersedi'). 'Also [he concludes] keine rhetorische Formel des Vell., sondern Topos, der zum Bild des moderatus gehört.' Cf. also *Eleg. Maec.* 1.31 'maius erat potuisse tamen nec uelle triumphos'. Levick (1975), 123, is thus mistaken to say that V. singles out Tiberius' *moderatio* 'in a trivial connection'.

As Massauer, following Hohl (above, 121.2n.), points out, Tiberius' triumph in 9 B.C. was strictly no more than an *ouatio*; but V. had earlier described it as if it were a triumph (96.3 and n.). Here at 122.1 V. similarly suggests that Tiberius deserved four more triumphs, whereas his actual phrase *ouans triumphare* below makes it clear that one of these would also be no more than an *ouatio*. Tiberius' other curule triumph was in 7 B.C. for exploits in Germany (97.4).

I have adopted Haase's *fuit* for the paradosis *fuerit*. Either construction is possible, but V.'s preference is for the indicative (cf. 1.5.3, 1.16.2, 115.5, 122.2) and the corruption is entirely credible after *meruerit*. Novák (1907), 147, observes that *fuit* preserves the superior clausula – – – ∪ –. *sine ulla dubitatione* above has a Ciceronian flavour (*Cat.* 4.5, *Font.* 21, *Har. Resp.* 56 etc.) and is found in other subsequent authors besides V.

ex Armenia recepta et ex rege ⟨ei⟩ praeposito 20 B.C. (cf. 94.4 and n.). The paradosis reads *praepositi*, an error which is best explained by Rhenanus' ⟨*ei*⟩ *praeposito* (viz. homoeoteleuton). Heinsius' *praeposito* ⟨*ei*⟩ is less satisfactory because *cuius* follows. Note word play of *praeposito*/*imposuerat*.

Vindelicorum...uictor 15 B.C. (cf. 95.2, 39.3). The phraseology *uictor* *curru urbem ingredi* is conventional, cf. 30.2, Liv. 45.39.8, Ov. *Met.* 13.251ff. etc. The *continua triennii militia* in Germany below is a ref. to A.D. 4–6 (cf. 104.2–109).

122.2 totius * prosperrimo rerum euentu** We know from BA that (M) read *totius*; although this is nonsense by itself, order is restored if we posit a lacuna (I suggest *totius* ⟨*militiae eius*⟩, the error having occurred through parablepsy). The phrase *summi ducis* later in the sentence then has point: after 'the most successful outcome of his military career', Tiberius is now the *summus dux*. The twin dependent genitives *totius*... and *rerum* are not an objection to my suggestion: *rerum euentus* is a set phrase in which the genitive is hardly felt (cf. *TLL*), and V. anyway does similar things elsewhere (e.g. 121.1 above, 'res Galliarum maximae molis', 58.4; cf. Kritz on 50.4).

Rhenanus' conjecture *ocius* is unlikely. Since Suetonius tells us that this campaign was deliberately slow (*Tib.* 17f.), there would be little point in saying *either* 'Germany was destroyed quicker this time (sc. than immediately after Tiberius' adoption)' *or* 'Germany was destroyed quickly' (i.e. taking *ocius* in a non-comparative sense as does Stegmann, referring to Wölfflin 175).

excisa Germania This phrase, which contrasts strongly with the claim made by Aug. himself (*RG* 3.2 'externas gentes, quibus tuto ignosci potuit, conseruare quam excidere malui'), is evidence of V.'s apparent indifference to the fate of foreigners (cf. Hellegouarc'h (1974), 82).

triumphus summi ducis adornari *adornare* = 'make ready' is used of such events as weddings (Plaut. *Aul.* 157, *Cas.* 419), funerals (Apul. *Apol.* 18), mock battles (Tac. *A.* 12.56.1), and perhaps even real battles (Liv. 10.38.2). Despite the lack of an exact parallel, I think *triumphus* too can qualify.

For the military and political connotations of the title *dux* cf. Béranger 47ff.

nescias utrum magis mireris It was a recognised trick of the panegyrical style to express one's inability at describing the attributes of the *laudatus*: such expressions may be classified according to various formulae (cf. e.g. 104.4n.), the present instance being the formula of the 'unresolved alternative', as it has been called (W. S. Maguinness, *Hermath.* 48 (1933), 124f.). Exs. are found either in direct form (e.g. Plin. *Pan.* 14.4 'initium laboris mirer an finem?') or indirect form (e.g. *Pan. Lat.* 10.4.3 'nescio utrum magis fortitudine repressum sit an clementia mitigatum'), the latter being V.'s favourite, cf. 40.1 'incertum est', 97.2 'in incerto est', 125.5 'nescias'.

For *modum...temperauit* below cf. Cic. *ND* 2.49, *Orat.* 60, Plin. *NH* 17.249; also Non. p. 837.19–20L.

123–125 THE DEATH OF AUGUSTUS AND SUCCESSION OF TIBERIUS

The last five months of A.D. 14 are conceived by V. in dramatic terms. He sees three areas of activity: 123 the death of Augustus, 124 the succession of Tiberius (home affairs), 125 the revolts in Germany and Illyricum (foreign affairs). Each of these three begins on a note of crisis (123.1 'plurimum metus', 124.1 'senatus trepidatio, populi confusio, orbis metus', 125.1 'rabie quadam et profunda confundendi omnia cupiditate') followed by a περιπέτεια calculated to bring out the excellence of the new emperor (123.1–2 'ille...exspectato reuolauit maturius. *tum* securum se Augustus praedicans'; 124.1 'cuius orbis ruinam timueramus, eum *ne* commotum *quidem* sensimus, *tanta*que unius uiri maiestas fuit *ut*...'; 125.3 '*sed* haec omnia ueteris imperatoris [sc. Tiberii] maturitas...sopiit ac sustulit').

Dramatically the most effective of these chapters is 123,[1] which is not unnatural since there was a tradition of emotional death-scenes in Latin historiography (cf. esp. Tac. *A.* 4.33.3), and V. here combines some of the conventional ideas of consolatory literature with a telling selection of specific events.[2] The most problematic chapters, however, are 124 and 125: detailed discussion appears below, but one point may be dealt with here. V.'s description of popular feeling at Rome in ch. 124 is castigated by Syme as 'exaggeration...palpable and shameless' (*RR* 437). It is of course true that by now Tiberius was co-regent with Augustus and thus inevitably destined to succeed him (cf. 121.1); but I doubt whether this constitutional consideration weighed very heavily in the mind of the average Roman, senator or not. It had been Augustus who had ended the civil wars and kept the state unified for forty-five years: some kind of apprehension was only natural, and is indicated also by Tacitus (*A.* 1.4.2 'aderatque finis et spes

---

1 What amounts to a commentary on this ch. is provided by Weber 3–6 and 5*–9*. A comparison of V.'s account with those of Suetonius, Tacitus and Dio is given by Steffen 29–34.

2 In referring to *consolationes*, I do not wish to imply that V. had this genre in mind. As a rhetorical historian he is simply describing an *exitus illustris uiri* in emotive terms, and many of the relevant techniques are naturally appropriate also to the writer of *consolationes*.

nouae, pauci bona libertatis in cassum disserere, plures bellum pauescere, alii cupere', cf. 1.46.1 'trepida ciuitas').[1] The evidence of V. as a contemporary witness cannot be dismissed.

123 THE DEATH OF AUGUSTUS

123.1 quippe Caesar Augustus cum Germanicum...reliqua belli patraturum misisset 'Wie alle anderen Personen, war auch der Kaiser seit 2.94 eindeutig hinter dem eigentlichen Helden der Darstellung zurückgetreten', remarks Steffen 29; but now V. contrives 'Augustus noch einmal in den Mittelpunkt der Geschehnisse zu rücken'.

Germanicus was not sent to Germany until A.D. 13 (Suet. *Cal.* 8.3 'exacto consulatu', i.e. after A.D. 12). If we are right in assuming that chh. 121–2 recount only the events of A.D. 11–12 (cf. 121.1n.), it follows that the present allusion to Germanicus is V.'s only reference to A.D. 13. Yet nothing much happened in that year that was worth recording, unless Dio 56.28.1 is right in placing Tiberius' renewal of *trib. pot.* then (the statement is controversial, cf. Goodyear on Tac. *A.* 1.3.3). However that may be, V.'s narrative now returns to a chronological arrangement, in contrast to the vaguer structure of 121–2 (see p. 209).

For the phraseology Weber (5* n. 21) compares Nicol. Dam. *FGrH* 2A.127.14 τὰ λειπόμενα τοῦ ἐκεῖ μεταστάντος πολέμου καθέλοι (47 B.C.), Tac. *H.* 4.51.2 'ad reliqua Iudaici belli perpetranda'; for *reliqua belli* cf. also Liv. 28.2.14, Curt. 9.1.1 (and above, 114.4n., where also *bellum patrare*). For the future participle of purpose, frequent from Livy onwards, cf. e.g. 74.1; E. Laughton, *The participle in Cicero* (1964), 118ff.

ad firmanda pace quae bello subegerat Burer's *firmanda*, for the paradosis *formanda*, is strongly supported by Liv. 1.15.6 '(urbis) non bello ac pace firmandae' (cf. also Vell. 1.8.5 'firmare urbem nouam'), and I think Kritz and others are right to print his emendation. For a comparable case, where however Burer's suggestion is rejected, see 110.6n.

certamini ludicro Cellarius' *certamini*, which also avoids the juxtaposition of two genitives, restores the standard phraseology *certamen ludicrum* (1.8.1, Liv. 40.6.6, 7.3, 42.63.2, Mela 2.5, Sen. *Ag.* 935, Tac. *H.* 3.83.1). For *athletarum certamini* cf. Liv. 39.22.2, Val. Max. 2.4.7. For *honori* as dative of purpose, below, cf. Suet. *Aug.* 98.5, Plin. *NH* 16.9, Plin. *Ep.* 10.75.2 (F.).

iam Dramatically effective: Aug. had often been ill before, and 'uota pro ualetudine mea suscipi per consules et sacerdotes quinto quoque anno

---

[1] Steffen 54–5 also notes that V.'s account is confirmed by Tacitus.

senatus decreuit...uniuersi ciues pro ualetudine mea supplicauerunt' (*RG* 9.1–2; but on the text cf. Weinstock 317). This was the final attack.

motus imbecillitatis Cornelissen (1883) preferred *notas*, but *motus* is a technical medical term, for which cf. Cic. *ND* 3.2 'febrium...motu', Cels. 3.9.1 'initium quoddam noui motus', Sen. *NQ* 6.14.2.

inclinataeque in deterius principia ualetudinis senserat The language is again technical, cf. Cels. 3.6.12 'ubi inclinata iam in melius ualetudo est', 2.14.5 'ualetudo longa et iam a primo impetu inclinata', 1 *pr.* 56, 2.15.1, 3.2.2 'inclinatis morbis'. For *principia* of illness cf. Cels. 3.9.4, 22.8 'fereque id posse inter principia corpus pati debet'; for *sentire* of illness cf. Scrib. Larg. 84 (p. 35.21 Helmr.), Cels. 1 *pr.* 70, 6.7.1, Curt. 8.10.29. For the absol. use of *obnitens* below cf. 89.5, Tac. *A.* 13.12.6; for *ui animi* below cf. 35.3.

ipse Nolam petiit Augustus left Beneventum on 9 Aug. and was in Nola on 11 Aug. (Massauer).

ingrauescente in dies ualetudine Quoting Tac. *A.* 1.5.1 'grauescere ualetudo' (also of Aug.; cf. 6.46.5), C. Brakman (*Mnem.* 47 (1919), 412) saw this as one of Tacitus' 'rare allusions' to V.; but *ingrauescere* is the proper verb with such nouns as *ualetudo, dolor, morbus* (cf. *SHA Hadr.* 23.16; Plin. *Ep.* 1.12.5; Cic. *Diu.* 2.16, *Cat.* 1.31, Liv. 4.21.5, 41.16.3; Suet. *Cal.* 23.3).

uolenti omnia post se salua remanere An echo of one of Augustus' own edicts: 'ita mihi saluam ac sospitem rem publicam sistere in sua sede liceat... ut optimi status auctor dicar et moriens ut feram mecum spem, mansura in uestigio suo fundamenta rei publicae quae iecero' (Suet. *Aug.* 28.2). For the Grecism *uolenti* cf. K–S 1.322*b*.

reuocauit filium: ille ad patrem patriae...reuolauit Steffen, pointing out that the word *filium* occurs three times in this section, remarks: 'Auf diese Weise wird die enge Verbundenheit zwischen Vater und Sohn immer stärker betont' (36). In view of this it could be argued that Acidalius was right to delete *patriae*: the official title, which occurs nowhere else in V., could have been added by a scribe insensitive to the pathos of V.'s account. Yet it can also be argued that *patriae* is an effective παρὰ προσδοκίαν, reminding us not only of Augustus' relationship to Tiberius but also of his hitherto sole responsibility towards the state. After some hesitation, I have retained it. For public service as a theme of consolatory literature cf. Esteve-Forriol 134–5. On the title *pater patriae* in general cf. Béranger 276f., Weinstock 200–5.

exspectato reuolauit maturius Weber (6* n. 31) compares Constantine's dash to the death-bed of his father Constantius in A.D. 306 (Euseb. *Vit. Const.* 1.21, Lact. *Mort. Pers.* 24.8 'ille incredibili celeritate usus peruenit ad patrem iam deficientem...atque ita in lecto suo requiem uitae, sicut optabat, accepit'), which became an appropriate motif for panegyric (*Pan. Lat.* 6.7.5). Weber also points out (n. 33) that speed of travel was characteristic of Tiberius (cf. 120.1 'reuolat ad patrem Caesar', 107.3), notably on the comparable occasion of his brother's death in 9 B.C. when he dashed from Ticinum to be with Drusus in Germany (Liv. *per.* 142, Plin. *NH* 7.84), a journey which Val. Max. (5.5.3) takes as an example of *beneuolentia fraterna*.

For *exspectato* cf. *ante exspectatum* at Virg. *G.* 3.348, Ov. *Met.* 4.790, 8.5, Sen. *Ep.* 114.17, Sil. 2.31.

123.2 securum Augustus is now *sine cura*, first because Tiberius' arrival has ensured his equanimity (it was reckoned good fortune to die with one's relatives nearby, cf. [Plut.] *Cons. Apoll.* 117B, Tac. *Agr.* 45.4), and second because he has now handed over *cura imperii* (106.3n.) to Tiberius (cf. Suet. *Aug.* 98.5 'neque post ulli maiori negotio animum accommodauit').

praedicans...amplexibus...commendans 'Ein rhetorisches Schaustück ohne Wahrheit ist das letzte Wiedersehen des Augustus und Tiberius' (Sauppe 62). But Sauppe bases his comment on Dio 56.31.1, where it is stated that Augustus was dead before Tiberius reached him. Yet Dio himself admits that the matter is uncertain (so too Tac. *A.* 1.5.3), while Suetonius' far more detailed account essentially agrees with V. (cf. *Aug.* 98.5, *Tib.* 21.1). Most modern scholars accept the validity of Suetonius' and V.'s accounts (Seager 48; Goodyear on Tac., loc. cit). Suet. however says that Augustus' last conversation was a *secretus sermo* (locc. citt.), whereas V. gives us its supposed content; Steffen (38–9) defends V. by arguing that an 'official version' of the scene was made known, possibly in the speech which Drusus read to the senate shortly afterwards (Suet. *Tib.* 23) and which V. doubtless heard for himself. However that may be, *nouissima uerba* (and more particularly a dying man's last wishes or commands) were conventionally effective: cf. Tac. *Agr.* 45.4 'adsidere ualetudini, fouere deficientem, satiari uultu complexuque...excepissemus certe mandata uocesque quas penitus animo figeremus'; Esteve-Forriol 141–3 (also embraces).

opera For this sense of political works or achievements cf. 124.3, 126.1, Val. Max. 5.1.10. For *recuso* with acc. and *de*+abl., below, cf. Cic. *Planc.* 3 'nihil de poena recusabo'; for *finis* = *mors* below Ruhnken refers to Val. Max. 3.3 *ext.* 4, Georges to Boetticher, *Lex. Tac.* s.v.; cf. also Sen. *NQ* 6.32.8 'ego recusem mei finem?'; Krebs–Schmalz 1.594.

si fata poscerent Comparing similar phraseology at Virg. *Aen.* 7.272 and Sen. *Tro.* 352, where *fata* = 'Schicksalssprüche' (add esp. *Aen.* 6.45 with Norden's n.), Weber (6*–7* n. 35) sees here a reference to the oracular responses which in the previous May had predicted Augustus' death within a hundred days (Suet. *Aug.* 97.2). Even if we do not accept this interpretation, the refs. to *fata* here and just below cannot fail to add to the drama of V.'s account. For the expression cf. also Virg. *Aen.* 8.477, Petron. 111.11. *subrefectus* below is ἅπαξ λεγόμενον.

carissimi sibi spiritus In wishing to delete *spiritus*, Cludius did not realise that the word can refer to a person (cf. Val. Max. 1.1.14 'religiosissimi spiritus tam crudeliter uexati', 4.4.11 'in hac ille pecunia futurus senatus princeps nutritus est spiritus', Front. p. 253 Naber = p. 43 Van den Hout), in the same way as *anima* (e.g. Cic. *Fam.* 14.14.2, Hor. *S.* 1.5.41f.).

in sua resolutus initia 'resolved into his own elements'. *sua* may have the same implications as *caelestem* below (see n.), but is more probably just the natural expression, cf. Cic. *Acad.* 1.27 'omnia...etiam interire, non in nihilum sed in suas partes' (it is clear from 1.26 that Cic. is using *partes, elementa* and *initia* as synonyms). V. is clearly referring to the Four Element Theory which had so pervasive an influence on many branches of ancient philosophy including Epicurean and Stoic (Von Arnim, *SVF* 2.405, 412ff., 616; Cic. *Diu.* 2.11, *ND* 2.82 with Pease's n., cf. Sen. *NQ* 3.12.3). The elemental theory was so widespread that for V. it affords merely a way of describing death in the language of popular philosophy; nevertheless there is a strong Stoic flavour in his subsequent remarks about Augustus' *anima* (see below). In fact what V. says here may ultimately derive from the funeral speech which Tiberius delivered and which V. may well have heard for himself (cf. Dio 56.41.9 τὸ μὲν σῶμα αὐτοῦ τῇ φύσει ἤδη ἀποδοῦναι, τὴν δὲ ψυχὴν ὡς καὶ θεοῦ ἀεὶ ἀγάλλειν). See too Ov. *Ex P.* 4.13.25–6; Weber 8* n. 37.

Pompeio Apuleioque consulibus Sex. Pompeius, *RE* 21.2265–7 = Pompeius 62 (Hanslik); Sex. Apuleius, *RE* 2.259 = Appuleius 18 (v. Rohden); *PIR*[2] 1.187, no. 962. Augustus died on 19 Aug. (EJ p. 50).

animam caelestem caelo reddidit A's *deo* is clearly wrong (cf. 124.3 'post redditum caelo patrem'); Amerbach has been 'Christiana religione deceptus' (Orelli), as at 114.1 (see p. 14 n. 2).

V.'s expression here is not simply characteristic word-play but rests upon a tenet of Stoic philosophy. Though the Stoics had various views on the afterlife (sometimes denying its existence completely, e.g. Cic. *Tusc.* 1.79, Sen. *Ep.* 54.4, *Cons. Marc.* 19.5, sometimes even claiming immortality, e.g.

Sen. *Ep.* 57.9), nevertheless they generally believed that the soul must survive in some form because of its physical affinity with its destination (cf. Cic. *Tusc.* 1.42 'is autem animus, qui si est horum quattuor generum ex quibus omnia constare dicuntur, ex inflammata anima constat...superiora capessat *necesse est*; nihil enim habent haec duo genera proni, et supera semper petunt...hoc etiam magis *necesse est ferantur ad caelum*', Sen. *Ep.* 79.12 'animus noster...*caelo* redditus *suo* fuerit, cum receperit locum quem occupauit sorte nascendi. sursum illum uocant *initia sua*'). A refinement of the Stoic view was that only the *boni* or men of wisdom attained true happiness in afterlife, the physical state of their souls being a precise reflection of their moral worth (Von Arnim, *SVF* 2.811, 813 = Lact. *Diu. Inst.* 7.20 'animas (iustorum)...ad sedem caelestem, unde illis origo sit, remeare'). Such a viewpoint naturally suited the writer of *consolationes* (cf. H. Johann, *Trauer und Trost* (1968), 120ff.), but was even more suited to the panegyrical attitude which writers adopted towards great men in general (e.g. Scipio Africanus at Sen. *Ep.* 86.1 'animum quidem eius in caelum, ex quo erat, redisse') and emperors in particular (e.g. Hor. *C.* 1.2.45 with Nisbet-Hubbard's n., Manil. 4.57 'Augustus caelo genitus caeloque receptus', German. *Arat.* 560). Emperors were of course conventionally *optimi* (126.5n.).

V. has presumably come to these notions through the medium of popular philosophy, but note that Tiberius brought Augustus' immortality to the attention of the citizens of Rome in the concrete form of coins issued with Augustus' radiate head and a star over it (*RIC* 1.140–1). It had long been believed, by Pythagoreans as well as by Stoics, that the stars were divine, and they came to be recognised as gods (Cic. *ND* 2.39, 42–3, with Pease's nn.), a belief upon which the Stoics and others capitalised by affirming that 'uirorum animas...in modum siderum uagari in aere et esse sic immortales' (*SVF* 2.817). V. has no mention of stars here, but the idea was popular under the empire (e.g. Hor. *C.* 3.3.10–12 (33–6), Ov. *Ex P.* 4.8.63, 4.9.125–34, Luc. 1.46, Stat. *Theb.* 1.31). Perhaps the best parallel comes from the roughly contemporary Manilius (1.758ff.): 'an fortes animae dignataque nomina caelo | corporibus *resoluta* suis terraeque remissa | huc migrant ex orbe *suum*que habitantia *caelum* | aetherios uiuunt annos... [799–80] descendit caelo caelumque replebit, | quod reget, Augustus'. See further Ruhnken on this passage of V.; Weber 8* n. 37, 24* n. 124, 87* n. 404; L. R. Taylor, *The divinity of the Roman emperor* (1931), 228–38; Richter on Virg. *G.* 4.219ff.; Weinstock 370–84; also below, 131.2n.

124 THE SUCCESSION OF TIBERIUS

124.1 confusio 'anxiety', for which sense cf. *TLL* 4.269.8–12.

salutis exitiique confinio The 'margin between safety and disaster'; for the metaphor cf. Tac. *A.* 4.58.3 'patuit breue confinium artis et falsi'; *TLL*

4.217.27ff. *salus* and *exitium* are commonly collocated, esp. in Cic. (e.g. *Mil.* 100).

mihi tam festinanti The speed of V.'s narrative (for which cf. 108.2n.; Woodman (1975), 277–87) prevents him from going into details: the *recusatio* is more likely to confirm the items of which V. speaks rather than, as Syme seems to believe (*Tac.* 367), invalidate them. Professor C. O. Brink has suggested to me that we are perhaps also intended to think of the goal to which V. is hurrying, viz. Tiberius' actual reign: such a suggestion is supported by *Pan. Lat.* 3.2.6 'tamen illa...nunc ex parte maxima praetermittam ut quanto ocius ad ea quae propria sunt perueniat oratio' (cf. also Nep. *praef.* 8, Liv. *praef.* 4). For *exprimere* introducing an indirect question, below, cf. Cic. *Part. Or.* 57, Plin. *Ep.* 5.14.2 (F.).

dixisse †habeo In view of the frequency of the phrase *dicere habeo* = 'I am able to say', esp. in Cicero, it is tempting to suggest that V. is here varying the standard phrase by means of the perfect infinitive. But although many auxiliary verbs in Latin can take the perf. infin. instead of the pres. (K–S 1.133–5), the present is invariable in the case of *habeo* = 'I am able' (cf. P. Thielmann, *ALL* 2 (1885), 50ff.; *TLL* 6.3.2454.12ff.). I have thus thought it safer to obelise; most edd. supply *satis* before *habeo*: cf. also 103.4n. For *uoce publica* above cf. 131.1n.

orbis ruinam...eum ne commotum quidem Possibly a sustained metaphor from earthquakes, as at 1.3.1, 2.2.1 (cf. Sall. *J.* 41.10): for *ruina* of earthquakes cf. Lucr. 6.544, 572; for *commouere* of earthquakes cf. Sen. *NQ* 6.7.6, 22.2, 25.3, Sil. 5.388: see also Val. Max. 9.11 *ext.* 4 'totius orbis ruina conlaberentur', to which Professor D. A. West adds Hor. *C.* 3.3.7–8 'si fractus illabatur orbis, | impauidum ferient ruinae'.

unius uiri maiestas Steffen (55 n. 3) acutely points out that this language was used of Tiberius in the years after A.D. 4, quoting Suet. *Tib.* 21.5 (Aug. to Tib.) '*unus homo* nobis uigilando restituit rem', 15.2 'nihil ex eo tempore praetermissum est ad *maiestatem* eius augendam'. See also 99.4n. *maiestas* naturally played a part in panegyric (cf. Burdeau 22).

ut nec bonis * neque contra malos opus armis foret** I do not think that V.'s love of contrast extends to the weak tautology of the paradosis. Since none of the proposed emendations (listed by Kritz) attempts to solve this problem, I have posited a lacuna: it is quite possible that V. may have mentioned some such matter as that in Tac. *A.* 1.8.5–6 'populumque edicto monuit (Tiberius) ne, ut quondam nimiis studiis funus diui Iulii turbassent...die funeris milites uelut praesidio stetere'.

124.2 una tamen ueluti luctatio ciuitatis fuit Thus introduced, this section deals with the debate in the senate on 17 Sept. A.D. 14, in the course of which there occurred Tiberius' *recusatio imperii* (see below).

luctatio is followed by two different types of genitive, (1) subjective or possessive (*ciuitatis*), (2) definitive or explanatory (*senatus* etc. and *illius*). The double genitive is not essentially different from those instanced at K–S 1.416 Anm. 3, except that here the second genitives are elaborated by the participle *pugnantis* which at first sight appears to qualify *ciuitatis*. The arrangement may be clumsy, but there is nothing wrong with the text: there is a similar, but less awkward, expression at 101.2 'spectaculum stantis... Parthorum exercitus'.

stationi paternae succederet *statio* is originally a military term = 'post', 'station' (cf. Caes. *BG* 4.32.2 'duas in stationem cohortes succedere ...iussit'), but one which in the early empire came to be used to designate the office of the *princeps* – not unnaturally, since the *princeps* himself was often described by such military terms as *custos* (104.2n.). As with the comparable term *status* (91.2, 131.1n.), Aug. may have started the trend himself, since in a letter to his grandsons Gaius and Lucius (on the subject of the succession) he says: 'ἀνδραγαθούντων ὑμῶν καὶ διαδεχομένων stationem meam' (Gell. 15.7.3). The notion had clearly become current by A.D. 8/9, since Ovid writes (*Tr.* 2.219–20): 'scilicet imperii princeps, statione relicta'; later *statio* is thus found in such authors as Tac. *D.* 17.3, Plin. *Pan.* 7.3, 86.3, Suet. *Claud.* 38.3, Front. p. 168 Naber = p. 160 Van den Hout. The word has agreeable connotations of 'permanency', counteracting the idea of *ruina* above. Cf. in general E. Koestermann, 'statio principis', *Philologus* 87 (1932), 358–68; Béranger 184–6, also in *REL* 21–2 (1943–4), 144–54 and *Mus. Helv.* 5 (1948), 194 n. 109; C. Mohrmann, *Vigiliae Christianae* 7 (1953), 235–8; H. J. Mette, *Gymn.* 68 (1961), 272. Also below, 131.2n.

ut potius aequalem ciuem quam eminentem liceret agere principem Again and again our sources stress Tiberius' reluctance at assuming the full responsibility of running the empire: e.g. Ov. *Ex P.* 4.13.27f., Suet. *Tib.* 24.1 (with verbal similarities to V.'s next sentence, but different sense), 24.2, 25.2, Dio 57.2.3, Vict. *Epit.* 2.6; and we know from Tac. that Tiberius' reluctance expressed itself in the senatorial debate of 17 Sept. which V. presumably attended (*A.* 1.11.1, 12.1). Such *recusationes imperii* become a common feature of later imperial life and are frequently used as a panegyrical topos (e.g. Plin. *Pan.* 5.5, 6.3–5, 7.1, 9.2–4, *Pan. Lat.* 2.11.1, 6.8.3–6, 10.3.1). The subsequent regularity of this charade, together with the hostile scepticism of Suetonius (24.1 'impudentissimo mimo') and Tacitus (1.11.2), has led many scholars to conclude that Tiberius' reluctance was insincere. But since there had never before been a succession of one *princeps* after the death of another, it is hard to see how Tiberius could have been conforming to 'attitudes and language preordained' (Syme, *Tac.* 410), especially since there are many features of Tiberius' character and career which seem to confirm his reluctance for public life in general (most notably his retirements to Rhodes in 6 B.C. (cf. 99.1n.), to Campania in A.D. 21–2, and to Capri in 26, and his statement at Suet. 24.2 that he would not remain *princeps* indefinitely).

The fact that Tiberius had earlier been made co-regent with Augustus, possessing powers which were equal to those of the emperor (121.1n.) and which he did not refrain from using after Augustus had died (Tac. *A.* 1.13.4), does not cast doubt on his reluctance. Included in the senatorial debate of 17 Sept. was a *relatio* of the consuls (Tac. loc. cit.), the content of which is unknown but which may have been intended to confirm Tiberius' sole tenure of the provinces which he had hitherto been jointly administering with Augustus (cf. P. A. Brunt, *ZPE* 13 (1974), 180). It is clear from the ancient evidence that Tiberius responded to this *relatio*, whatever its content, by stressing that the empire was a burden which involved too much responsibility for one man alone (Tac. *A.* 1.11.1 'solam diui Aug. mentem tantae molis capacem: se...didicisse quam arduum, quam subiectum fortunae[1] regendi cuncta onus. proinde in ciuitate tot inlustribus uiris subnixa non ad unum omnia deferrent: plures facilius munia r.p. sociatis laboribus executuros', 12.1 'se ut non toti r.p. parem', Suet. *Tib.* 24.2 'querens miseram et onerosam iniungi sibi seruitutem', 25.2 'uniuersae (r.p.) sufficere solus nemo posset nisi cum altero uel etiam pluribus', Dio 56.33.4). From Tiberius' encouraging attitude towards the senate in subsequent years (126.2n.) there can be little doubt that Tiberius' response to the consular *relatio* was to suggest a diminution in the size of the *prouincia* which he already held and a corresponding increase in the administrative role of the senate itself.

As it was, of course, the senate fought against Tiberius' proposal and, as V. says and as every other senator must have known (next n.), Tiberius himself realised that in the end he could not refuse to continue in the role in which he had been placed by Augustus' death. Even if the senate had found Tiberius' suggestions acceptable, that would hardly have made him the *aequalis ciuis* which, according to V., he wished to be. Yet it is clear from Suetonius that V.'s statement is not without foundation (*Tib.* 26.1 '*ciuilem* admodum inter initia ac paulo minus quam priuatum *egit*'), and such a wish is by no means inconsistent with what we know of Tiberius' character. In time, naturally, this too became a panegyrical topos (Plin. *Pan.* 2.3–4 'non enim de tyranno sed de ciue...loquimur...').

---

[1] *subiectum* combines with *arduum* to produce a striking cliff-metaphor which commentators seem to have missed. The empire is an uphill task, exposed to fortune's whim.

For a comparison of V.'s account of this and other matters in ch. 124 with those of other authors see Steffen 40–53. For *recusatio imperii* as a motif cf. Béranger 137ff., also in *Mus. Helv.* 5 (1948), 178–96, esp. 183; for that of Tiberius in particular cf. Grenade 394–443; Seager 50–7; Goodyear, *Comm. Tac.* 1.171ff. with further bibliography, adding Weber 25* n. 126. For *onus imperii* cf. 127.3n.

cum quicquid tuendum non suscepisset, periturum uideret In his account of the senatorial debate of 17 Sept., Tacitus represents Asinius Gallus as taking it for granted that this was Tiberius' own belief: 'idcirco interrogatum ait...ut sua [i.e. Tiberius'] confessione argueretur unum esse r.p. corpus atque unius animo regendum' (*A.* 1.12.3). We may reasonably assume that Gallus was not alone in his opinion. For other exs. of the inevitability of autocracy cf. *A.* 1.6.3, 9.4, 4.33.2, *H.* 1.1.1, Flor. 2.14.6.

V. has here used typically conventional language. Tiberius' assumption of office is described by the verb *suscipere*, almost a technical term (Béranger 175 n. 30, adding Plin. *Ep.* 10.1.1), and an oblique reference to the principate as an *onus*; the character of the office is described by the gerundive *tuendum*, recalling the notion of the principate as *tutela* (105.3n.). Cf. esp. Tac. *A.* 1.12.1 'dixit forte Tiberius se...quaecumque pars sibi mandaretur, eius *tutelam suscepturum*'.

paene diutius recusare principatum quam, ut occuparent eum, alii armis pugnauerant Grenade 403 has suggested that V. means the ten years from A.D. 4 to 14, i.e. from Tiberius' first refusal of *trib. pot.* (103.3): these ten years 'correspondent exactement à la durée de la marche de César vers le principat de 59 à 49'. K. Wellesley, on the other hand, has suggested that V. refers to Sulla's march on Rome from Nola, which would have taken barely a week; but Wellesley believes that Tiberius accepted the principate between 1 and 3 Sept. and that his hesitation extended over 'four, five or six days in a number of senatorial sessions' (*JRS* 57 (1967), 29 and n. 20). Neither of these suggestions seems to me convincing, and Wellesley's view of Tiberius' *dies imperii* has not found widespread acceptance (see Goodyear on Tac. *A.* 1.11–13). It may of course be that V. is simply indulging in rhetorical exaggeration, yet the specific nature of his expression seems to indicate that he has some definite incident in mind. A possibility might be Marius' march on Rome in Aug./Sept. 87 B.C., which might correspond in time to the month which elapsed between Augustus' death and the senatorial debate in Aug./Sept. A.D. 14. But unfortunately none of our authorities for Marius' action reveals the exact period of time involved, and I do not regard my suggestion as much more convincing than those given above. For a slightly different contrast but in a similar context cf. Tac. *H.* 1.15.1 'principatum de quo maiores nostri armis certabant, bello adeptus quiescenti offeram'.

124.3 corpus eius humanis honoribus, nomen diuinis honoratum V. refers respectively to Augustus' funeral (Tac. *A.* 1.8.6, Suet. *Aug.* 100.3–4, Dio 56.34–42; L. R. Taylor, *The divinity of the Roman emperor* (1931), 228–9) and his deification (Taylor 229ff., also below, 126.1n.). V. distinguishes between them since the former was discussed at an earlier meeting of the senate (Tac. *A.* 1.8.1), the latter at the meeting of 17 Sept. Krause tentatively suggested that we should read *numen*, but *nomen* seems a most appropriate way of referring to Augustus' new title of 'diuus Augustus'; Kritz's argument that the antithesis *corpus/nomen* is inept is refuted by 54.2 'nusquam erat Pompeius corpore, adhuc ubique uiuebat nomine'. For *honoribus... honoratum* cf. Sall. *C.* 35.3 'honore honestatos', *Pan. Lat.* 3.25.5 (Ruhnken; the phrase is also at Plaut. *Capt.* 247, 356, cf. Syme, *Sall.* 72n.); for *nomen... honoratum* cf. Just. 38.6.7.

primum principalium eius operum fuit Contrast 'primum facinus noui principatus' (Tac. *A.* 1.6.1, with Goodyear's n.). V. seems to be the first to use *principalis* in the sense of 'imperial' (e.g. 56.3, 93.2, 127.3): thereafter it is common (Tac. Plin. Suet. etc.).

ordinatio comitiorum quam manu sua scriptam diuus Augustus reliquerat Since we know from Tacitus that a change was effected in the role of the *comitia* at elections and that this change came early in the reign (*A.* 1.15.1), it would be exceptionally perverse to hold that Tiberius' *primum opus*, to which V. here refers, is not this change in the role of the *comitia.* We must therefore translate *ordinatio comitiorum* as something like 'the rationalisation of the electoral assemblies', giving the phrase a different meaning from that which it has at Plin. *Pan.* 72.1. What this rationalisation was, and whether it mattered, are topics which have caused an immense amount of discussion, centring principally on the statements of Tacitus at *A.* 1.14.4–15.1 and the notorious tabula Hebana (EJ 94*a*). Bibliographies of this discussion are provided by Goodyear, *Comm. Tac.* 1.191–2 and by Seager 124 nn. 2–3: add J. Béranger, 'La démocratie sous l'Empire romain', *Mus. Helv.* 14 (1957), 216–40; M. Pani, *Comitia e senato: sulla trasformazione della procedura elettorale a Roma nell'età di Tiberio* (1974) (I regret that this latter work came to my attention too late to be of use: I know of it only through a review in *JRS* 65 (1975), 201). In what follows I shall discuss the whole matter only in so far as it affects what V. says here and at 126.2.

In accordance with his plan to give autocracy an appearance of republicanism, Augustus restored to the electoral assemblies (*comitia*) their former authority, retaining of course the right to recommend certain candidates himself (Dio 53.21.6–7, Suet. *Aug.* 40.2). This meant that, e.g. in 27 B.C., the *comitia centuriata* and the *comitia tributa* met to vote on the greater (consuls and praetors) and lesser magistracies respectively (cf. Dio 53.21.6 ὅ τε δῆμος

[= *com. centuriata*] ἐς τὰς ἀρχαιρεσίας καὶ τὸ πλῆθος [=*com. tributa*] αὖ συνελέγετο). There were subsequent modifications to this procedure. First, the disturbances which accompanied Roman elections became so serious on occasion that Aug. was compelled to elect all the magistrates himself (e.g. in A.D. 7, cf. Dio 55.34.2). Second, we know from the tabula Hebana that by the lex Valeria Cornelia of A.D. 5 ten '*destinatio* centuries' were formed to 'pre-elect' candidates before the voting of the assemblies. How much importance is to be attached to this move, and what Augustus' purpose was, are matters about which there is little scholarly agreement; but note that neither Tacitus nor V. mentions this recent innovation: both authors refer to the changes of A.D. 14 as affecting the *comitia* alone. It would be tempting to suppose that the provisions of the lex Valeria Cornelia lapsed, were it not for the fact that the tabula Hebana implies the opposite (cf. J. H. Oliver, *AJPh* 75 (1954), 239; G. W. Clarke, *Historia* 13 (1964), 383–4). We must assume that since the ultimate authority still rested with the *comitia*, there was no need for Tacitus or V. to mention the lex.

However that may be, we know for certain that with the accession of Tiberius a change in election procedure took place. Tacitus says (*A.* 1.15.1): 'tum primum e campo comitia ad patres translata sunt: nam ad eam diem, etsi potissima arbitrio principis, quaedam tamen studiis tribuum fiebant'. In view of the double contrast between *campo* and *tribuum* and between *potissima* and *quaedam*, it looks at first sight as if Tacitus is referring to the elections of both greater and lesser magistracies, i.e. those of the *comitia centuriata* (which met on the *campus*) and of the *comitia tributa* respectively (so L. Canesi in his comm. (1955), ad loc.; also W. K. Lacey, 'Nominatio and the elections under Tiberius', *Historia* 12 (1963), 171–2). But since the rest of Tacitus' paragraph, both before and after this crucial sentence, concerns the praetorship exclusively, it would be difficult to assume that in this sentence he is talking about anything other than the praetorship elections, i.e. those in the *comitia centuriata* (so D. C. A. Shotter, 'Elections under Tiberius', *CQ* 16 (1966), 323 and n. 3). Tacitus is therefore no evidence for the election procedure of lesser magistrates in A.D. 14, only for the praetors. V. however at 126.2 says: 'summota e foro seditio, ambitio campo'. By the figure metonymy he is referring to the *comitia tributa* and *comitia centuriata* respectively, and his statement there clearly implies a change in the roles of *both* electoral assemblies (see n.). This is confirmed by Dio's account of the election procedure in A.D. 32 (58.20.3–4): τῶν δὲ δὴ τὰς ἄλλας ἀρχὰς αἰτούντων [i.e. other than the consulship] ἐξελέγετο ὅσους ἤθελε, καί σφας ἐς τὸ συνέδριον ἐσέπεμπε...καὶ μετὰ τοῦτο ἔς τε τὸν δῆμον καὶ ἐς τὸ πλῆθος οἱ προσήκοντες ἑκατέρῳ...ἐσιόντες ἀπεδείκνυντο. The combined testimony of V. at 126.2 and Dio at 58.20.3–4 is the only evidence we have for the transference of the elections of the lesser magistrates to the senate in A.D. 14, a point which seems to have escaped the modern historians (e.g. Lacey, as above). And this evidence, taken with that of Tacitus at *A.* 1.15.1, gives us a picture of all election changes in A.D. 14 with the exception of the consulship. Here at 124.3 V. does not specify which *comitia* were affected; but since he is, as we have seen, aware of changes to *both* electoral assemblies, we may assume (*pace* J. Béranger, *Mus. Helv.* 14 (1957), 231–2) that he is here referring to both.

Although the changes in the roles of the *comitia* were made after Tiberius had succeeded Augustus, it is not an open question whether Aug. himself had left instructions for the changes (despite Frei-Stolba 145–6 and n. 71). V. expressly states that the *ordinatio comitiorum* had been left by Aug. and in his own handwriting: the *ordinatio* presumably therefore formed part of the fourth book which Aug. left on his death (Dio 56.34.3), or, if Dio is not to be believed, possibly an addition to the third book, the *breuiarium totius imperii* mentioned by Suet. *Aug.* 101.4. Again, there is little agreement on what Augustus' purpose might have been in this change; but the transference certainly suited Tiberius' encouraging policy towards the senate. For the senate thus acquired additional prestige and 'largitionibus ac precibus sordidis exsolutus libens tenuit' (Tac. *A.* 1.15.1). As a senator himself, V. appreciated the change, and returns to it in his panegyric of the reign at 126.2 'summota...discordia curia' (see n.).

124.4 mihi fratrique meo See Frei-Stolba 266 and 271–2. For V.'s brother cf. also 115.1n., 121.3.

candidatis Caesaris...destinari praetoribus...commendaret A person who was 'commended' by the *princeps* became a *candidatus Caesaris* and was therefore 'destined' for inevitable election. All three terms are technical and have caused much discussion, for which cf. the bibliography referred to above (3n.). Tacitus tells us that there were four such *candidati* (*A.* 1.15.1); and since V. and his brother had also been commended by Augustus, it is reasonable to suppose that the other two (unfortunately anonymous) had been too.

proxime a nobilissimis ac sacerdot⟨al⟩ibus uiris Scholars are divided on the question of whether *a* indicates the agent ('by most noble...') or is to be taken closely with *proxime* ('next after most noble...'): see Frei-Stolba 143–4 and n. 63 for a survey of such opinions. There are three main reasons why the latter interpretation is correct: (1) *proxime* by itself makes nonsense after *quo tempore*; (2) Velleian usage elsewhere favours *proxime a*, cf. 76.4, 127.1; (3) 'what interests V. is...the social prestige of the other candidates' (Syme, *Tac.* 759). Frei-Stolba gets it right and well compares Tac. *A.* 11.21.2 on Curtius Rufus, 'et mox nobiles inter candidatos praeturam principis suffragio adsequitur' (where Koestermann quotes V.).

125 MUTINIES IN GERMANY AND ILLYRICUM

125.1 Tulit protinus ut uoti et consilii sui pretium res publica 'The state soon reaped the benefit of its wish and resolve' (*uoti* and *consilii* are references to the *luctatio ciuitatis* etc. at 124.2). For *tulit pretium* cf. 45.2, Naev. *Trag.* 9 Ribbeck, Sen. *Phoen.* 590, Juv. 13.105, Suet. *Tib.* 16.2; for *uoti et consilii* cf. Suet. *Nero* 23.1. For *ut...et* = *ut...ita et* cf. 117.2n.

neque diu latuit...quid impetrando profecissemus For the (panegyrical) idea cf. *SHA Max. Balb.* 17.4 'quae, quanta et cuiusmodi sit (felicitas), iam in ipso exordio principatus uestri cognoscere potuimus' (on this ch. of the *SHA* see below, p. 234).

praesentisque Germanici imperio regebatur 'Zu Anfang des Cap. der Name des Germanicus als des Inhabers der höchsten Befehlsgewalt am Rhein fiel und deshalb mit Recht ein ausführlicher Bericht über das Verhalten des obersten Kommandeurs erwartet werden durfte' (Steffen 73): see further below, 4n. For the common combination *imperio regere*, the most famous instance of which is Virg. *Aen.* 6.851, cf. Munro on Lucr. 5.1130.

profunda confundendi omnia cupiditate An echo of Sall. *H.* 4.69.5 'cupido profunda imperi et diuitiarum' (Ruhnken). Unlike Sall., however, who prefers *cupido* to *cupiditas* (20:3), V. prefers to write *cupiditas*, as here (6:1): in this he resembles Cicero, Caesar and the elder Seneca, none of whom uses *cupido* at all. Tacitus, on the other hand, shows an increasing fondness for *cupido* as his writing develops (Goodyear on *A.* 1.3.6). For *confundere omnia* cf. Liv. 42.13.9; for *rabies* of mutinies, above, cf. Liv. 28.34.4, Tac. *A.* 1.31.1 (the latter with ref. to A.D. 14).

nouum ducem, nouum statum, nouam quaerebant rem publicam The political nature of the German mutiny is not in doubt (Tac. *A.* 1.31.1, 35.3, Suet. *Tib.* 25.2), but V. sees also the Illyrian mutiny in similar terms (*quaerebant* refers to both armies, although modern historians fail to note the point). There is some evidence for this. Tacitus describes the Illyrian mutineers as threatening civil war and possibly a march on Rome (*A.* 1.16.1, 17.1), while Dio explicitly states that the Illyrian army threatened to march on Rome and even to oust Tiberius in favour of someone else if their demands were not met (57.4.2–3). Mr Paterson however points out to me that V. does not take the notion of revolution quite as seriously as the above grandiloquent tricolon suggests. *quin etiam* below indicates that the climax is still to come: what disturbs V. is the fact that the soldiers of both armies were prepared to take the law into their own hands in defiance of senate and *princeps* (cf. *ausi sunt, sibi ipsi*). His reaction is what we should expect from a senatorial supporter of Tiberius, for the emperor's characteristic policy was to involve the senate as much as possible in discussing the soldiers' grievances (Tac. *A.* 1.25.3 'acturum apud patres de postulatis eorum...cetera senatui seruanda'). For *nouum statum* cf. Suet. *Aug.* 28.2: the phrase quite clearly means 'a new political system' (Steffen 67–8).

125.2 minari daturos senatui, daturos... Orelli's ⟨*se*⟩ *senatui* is attractive because it is the more 'normal' construction and because V. rarely omits *se* in or. obl. (according to J. N. Adams, *CQ* 22 (1972), 370 and n. 5). But (1) omission of *se* in or. obl. is very common, esp. in historians (cf. K–S 1.700–1; Kühnast, *Liv. Synt.* 106ff.; Draeger, *Hist. Synt.* 2.440–1): for an ex. with *minari* cf. Cic. *Fin.* 5.31 and Madvig's judicious n.; (2) *daturos se* is slightly ambiguous; (3) the omission of *se* here produces a speedy and effective anaphora (*daturos senatui, daturos principi*).

modum stipendii, finem militiae Not elegant variation but a precise summary of the soldiers' demands (Tac. *A.* 1.17.5 'sextus decimus stipendii annus finem adferret, ne ultra sub uexillis tenerentur'). For *processum etiam*... below cf. Ascon. *Scaur.* p. 25.11 Clark 'ad ferrum et ad arma processit'.

paene in ultimam ⟨cladem⟩ gladiorum erupit impunitas It is clear from BA that (M) read *ultimam*, which P emended to *ultimum*. The emendation is not possible: since *gladiorum impunitas* is a Ciceronian phrase which V. uses elsewhere (2.3.3, cf. Cic. *Phil.* 1.27, *Fam.* 10.2.1), it follows that *ultimum* here has no dependent genitive; but *ultimum* (sing.) can never = τὰ ἔσχατα unless there is a dependent genit. (as Liv. 2.45.10 'rem ad ultimum seditionis erupturam'; at id. 1.29.3 *ultimum* is followed by *illud*). Vossius suggested *ultima*; but it is equally possible that in this lacunose chapter a noun has fallen out, as Cornelissen (1887) also believed, proposing *ultimam* ⟨*uim*⟩. I suggest tentatively *in ultimam* ⟨*cladem*⟩, for which phrase cf. Liv. 5.22.8; for *clades* omitted before *gladium* cf. the plausible supplement of Madvig (2.425f.) at Sen. *Clem.* 1.9.1 'in communi quidem rei publicae ⟨clade⟩ gladium mouit'. For *erumpo* (a favourite verb of V.) in contexts of sedition etc. cf. *TLL* 5.2.839.78ff., 841.40ff.

defuitque qui contra rem publicam duceret, non qui sequerentur Since it was Germanicus whom the troops wished to overturn Tiberius (Suet. *Tib.* 25.2, Tac. *A.* 1.31.1 etc.), V.'s statement must be a tribute to his refusal of their demands. Ruhnken notes that the phrase is Sallustian (*H.* 1.77.8 'quin praeter idoneum ducem nihil abest ad subuortundum imperium'), but the notion of 'lacking a leader' is also at 61.1, Liv. 7.39.8, Tac. *A.* 1.55.2. For *contra rem publicam duceret* cf. Cic. *Phil.* 13.14; for the 'heroic clausula' cf. 95.2n.

125.3 sed haec omnia ueteris imperatoris maturitas... Since this and the two previous chh. are aimed at demonstrating the excellence of Tiberius (above, p. 215), it seems likely that the *uetus imperator* is Tiberius himself, the veteran campaigner (so too Steffen 70–1). The general policy adopted by Tiberius, identical to that which he used when in the field himself (114.3 and n.), is described in the present sentence; the instruments of his policy, Germanicus and Drusus, are described in the following sentence (*quidem* at 4 below almost = *enim*). That this is V.'s sequence of thought is confirmed by Tac. *A.* 1.46–7. The emperor was criticised for not visiting the troubled areas himself (46.2 'ire ipsum et opponere maiestatem imperatoriam debuisse cessuris ubi principem *longa experientia*...uidissent'), but Tiberius was ready with his reply (47.2 'at *per filios* pariter adiri maiestate salua, cui maior a longinquo reuerentia'). Tiberius' policy, which was undoubtedly correct (Marsh 57, Seager 70), was thus not to intervene personally until it was absolutely necessary: this is exactly reflected in V.'s account, and Steffen's objection to it (72 'Von persönlichen Massnahmen des Tiberius...ist nichts bekannt') is misguided.

For this sense of *maturitas* cf. Cic. *Sen.* 33, Tac. *H.* 1.87.2, Amm. 16.10.21 'Seuero, bellorum usu et maturitate firmato'. In supportof J. F. Gronovius' correction *noxiorum* below cf. e.g. Tac. *A.* 1.44.1 'orabant puniret noxios'.

sopiit ac sustulit For V.'s fondness for alliteration with verbs cf. e.g. 75.3 *peruenit...peruecta*, 89.2 *concipi...consummari*; Milkau 19f. The pleonasm of the two verbs is equally typical (cf. 97.2n.). For *sopiit* cf. 89.3; for *mitis...castigatio* above cf. Liv. 1.28.11 'mitiores poenas', Quint. 6.4.16; for *castigatio* with a transitive verb cf. Sen. *Ep.* 94.36.

125.4 ut pleraque ignouit Germanicus Steffen, having already suggested that V. pointedly mentions Germanicus' presence at the German mutiny (above, 1n.), remarks that V. here dismisses Germanicus' countermeasures in the present 'einziges Satzglied' whereas he deals with those of Drusus at some length (see below). Steffen concludes (73–7) that V. disapproved of Germanicus, and he traces the reason for this disapproval to Tiberius himself, who after the mutinies addressed the senate in terms which, while their proportions were ironically the opposite of V.'s here, nevertheless betrayed his hostility (Tac. *A.* 1.52.2–3): 'rettulit tamen ad senatum de rebus gestis multaque de uirtute eius [sc. Germanici] memorauit, magis in speciem uerbis adornata quam ut penitus sentire crederetur. paucioribus Drusum...laudauit, sed intentior et fida oratione.' While I agree that V.'s manner of treating Germanicus and Drusus is significant, as Timpe also believes (*Germanicus* 17), Kritz aptly reminds us that V. refers to Germanicus in honorific terms at 116.1, 129.2 and 130.3. The fact is that relations between Germanicus and Tiberius were necessarily complicated and ambiguous (Seager 110f.), and these qualities are reflected in Tacitus' account of Germanicus in *A.* 1.31–52 (Goodyear, *Comm. Tac.* 1.239–41): it is hardly surprising that V.'s attitude to the man should be equally ambiguous. See too above, 2n.

Steffen also discusses the text of this phrase (72 n. 2). The paradosis reads not *ignouit* but *ignaue*: the former is the emendation of the Bipontine ed.; Boeclerus suggested *gnaue*, an emendation which (according to Ellis) was also proposed independently by Bentley.[1] Ruhnken improved on this latter proposal by reading *egit naue*, the verb balancing that in the *ita*-clause below. Steffen argues that *ignouit* is impossible because it would make 'allzu stark den Kontrast zwischen dem Verhalten des Germanicus und dem entschlossenen Durchgreifen des Drusus'; he therefore prefers ⟨*haud*⟩ *ignaue*, an emendation not essentially different from those of Boeclerus and Ruhnken. But Steffen's assumption that *ignouit* is a culpable action is refuted by V.'s own description of Tiberius at 114.3 'non sequentibus disciplinam... ignouit'; and ⟨*haud*⟩ *ignaue* (*uel sim.*) destroys the balance of the sentence: the action of the *ut*-clause is extremely vague, whereas that of the *ita*-clause is most specific. I believe that *ignouit* is exactly what is wanted. We know that Germanicus' policy was one of leniency (e.g. Tac. *A.* 1.52.3 'cunctaque quae Germanicus indulserat'), and *ignouit* follows entirely naturally after *mitis... castigatio* in the previous sentence: Germanicus shows the leniency there mentioned, and Drusus the severity. For *ut...ita* of two contrasting actions cf. K–S 2.451.2; L–H–S 633; for *ignosco* + acc. rei cf. *TLL* 7.1.318.27ff.

Drusus Tiberius' own son, Drusus Iulius Caesar: *RE* 10.1.431–4 = Iulius 136 (Gardthausen); *PIR*[2] 4.173–6, no. 219; also Rogers 91ff.

igne emicans incendium militaris tumultus *incendium* is often used metaphorically of sedition etc., e.g. *CIL* 6.526.2 'incendio tumultus ciuilis'; cf. *TLL* 7.1.864.82ff. B. Rehm (*TLL* 5.2.483.57–60) proposed *micans* for *emicans* here, saying that the latter is found nowhere else with a simple abl., that *micans igne* is the usual phrase, and that *emicare* is not used 'sensu durativo'. While his suggestion is obviously possible, it is hard to believe that *igne emicare* is wrong: *ignis emicat* is a perfectly normal expression (ib. 488.62ff.), and there is no need to assume that V. has an extended period of time in mind. For *emicans incendium* cf. Apul. *Mund.* 34.

prisca antiquaque seueritate usus The two adjj. are combined also at 89.4, Sen. *Phaedr.* 916; the pleonasm is of course Velleian (97.2n.). The phrase *prisca seueritas* (also at 92.2, 127.4) is an example of V.'s habit of

[1] Ellis also states that *gnaue* was proposed by Salmasius, presumably before Boeclerus. I have however been unable to verify this.

comparing with the past those more recent or contemporary actions of which he approves: cf. 78.3 'grauissimum comparandumque antiquis exemplum', 80.3 'non ab Scipionibus aliisque ueteribus Romanorum ducum quicquam ausum patratumque fortius', 92.5 'factum cuilibet ueterum consulum gloriae comparandum'.

ancipitia sibi ⟨sus⟩tinere ⟨maluit⟩ quam exemplo perniciosa The paradosis offers no main verb; and BA read *timere*, while P reads *tam re*. Many emendations have been proposed (see Kritz), almost all of which fail because they accept P's reading, as if the contrast were between *re* and *exemplo*. That this cannot be so is seen from the analogous case of Germanicus in Germany. When the German troops mutinied, Germanicus was confronted with two alternatives: he could take a firm line, thereby putting himself at risk, or he could give in completely, thereby acting shamefully (Tac. *A*. 1.36.2 'periculosa seueritas, flagitiosa largitio'). Drusus was doubtless confronted with a similar choice in the Illyrian mutiny (cf. esp. Tac. *A*. 1.29.1–3): the (chiastic) contrast is between *ancipitia sibi* and *exemplo perniciosa*. It seems clear from the following clause ('*et*...obsidentes coercuit') that a finite verb has been omitted from the present clause: most scholars now accept Madvig's supplement *maluit*. *timere* however is still awkward, and none of the proposed emendations (cf. Stegmann 176) is quite satisfactory. I suggest tentatively *sustinere* ('he preferred to face personal danger rather than things which would prove a harmful precedent'): *sus-* might have dropped out after *sibi*, which explains why I place *maluit* before *quam*. No exact parallels, but cf. Liv. 2.20.11 'partem periculi sustinentes'.

For *anceps* + dat. cf. Val. Max. 9.15 *praef*., Tac. *H*. 1.5.2. *exemplo* is of course abl., as at 114.3 (see n.): cf. also Hor. *C*. 3.5.15f. 'exemplo trahentis | perniciem'.

obsessus...obsidentes A familiar contrast, cf. 51.2, Liv. 5.26.9, 6.33.9, 23.37.5, 25.11.11, Val. Max. 1.6.3, Tac. *H*. 3.73.1. For *ipsis* almost = *isdem*, above, cf. Loefstedt on *Per. Aeth*. 2.3.

125.5 Iunio Blaeso Q. Iunius Blaesus, the *auunculus* of Sejanus mentioned at 127.3: cf. *RE* 10.1.967 = Iunius 41 (Riba); *PIR*² 4.330–1, no. 738. For *nescias* below cf. 122.2n.; for the combination *castris*...*toga* below cf. Sil. 6.617.

†Ad Hispanias exercitumque† A desperate passage. (1) The sudden reference to Spain seems quite extraordinary: every other event mentioned takes place either in Germany or Illyricum, and the chapter ends with the words *in maritima parte Illyrici*. If V. were here giving details of Blaesus' earlier career (as each ed. before Haase believed), a desirable link with the rest of the ch. would be provided. In that case, however, the elaborate *praediximus*-clause which follows would refer back no further than the previous sentence, which is intolerably inept. (2) If, then, V. is not discussing Blaesus, he must be discussing someone whose name is lost to us through a lacuna but whose valour in Illyricum V. has 'previously mentioned' (*praediximus*). Conjecture thus seems restricted to M. Valerius Messalinus (112.1–2), M. Aemilius Lepidus (114.5–115.3) and L. Aelius Lamia (116.3), each of whom has been suggested by one scholar or another. The presence of Messalla in Rome during September A.D. 14 (Tac. *A.* 1.8.4) would seem to rule him out, and the choice must lie between Lepidus and Lamia. Here I think one must draw the line: neither of these individuals is elsewhere attested in any source as having ever been to Spain (the same is also true of Blaesus and Messalla), and it is quite irresponsible of historians to use Madvig's conjecture to 'prove' the presence of Lepidus in Spain (Syme, *RR* 438; *Tac.* 382 n. 9; *TST* 35; *PIR*² 1.61; G. Alföldy, *Fasti Hispanienses* (1969), 12–13; L. Hayne, 'The last of the Aem. Lepidi', *Ant. Class.* 42 (1973), 500). Only if we had concrete evidence of whom V. is discussing would we be able to determine why he, alone of our sources, appears to make any reference to Spain here at all. The most that can be said is that the paradosis is nonsense and that something has been omitted.

cum imperio obtineret In view of the uncertainties discussed above (last n.), we cannot be sure whether *cum* is the conjunction or preposition. The latter is perhaps more likely since, as Kritz notes, *cum imperio* is a standard expression (e.g. Cic. *Fam.* 1.9.13 'cum tu Hispaniam citeriorem cum imperio obtineres'). On the subconscious repetition *obtinendi* below cf. 100.5n. For *in pace...continuit* below cf. Hirt. *BG* 8.49.3; for *pace* ⟨*et*⟩ *quiete* below cf. Tac. *G.* 40.3, *H.* 4.1.3.[1]

pietas rectissima sentiendi et auctoritas quae sentiebat obtinendi A character judgement not unlike that which Pericles passes on himself at Thuc. 2.60 (see Gomme's n.): οὐδενὸς ἥσσων οἴομαι εἶναι γνῶναί τε τὰ δέοντα καὶ ἑρμηνεῦσαι ταῦτα. I can find no parallel for this use of *pietas*: Cornelissen (1883) would emend to *peritia*, Mr DuQuesnay to *potestas*, *uel sim.* *curam ac fidem* below is a favourite combination of Livy: to the exs. in *TLL* add Liv. 35.25.8.

Dolabella P. Cornelius Dolabella, *RE* 7.1.1308–10 = Cornelius 143 (Groag); *PIR*² 2.318–19, no. 1348. For *simplicitatis generosissimae* below cf. *nobilissima simplicitas* at 2.10.2, 72.3. *ora* for *parte* below was conjectured by Bolaffi, but cf. Caes. *BG* 5.12.2, Cic. *Fam.* 3.5.3 (F.). For *per omnia* below cf. 100.3n.

[1] As at 100.3, I have avoided printing two paired words in asyndeton: whether I am right must perhaps remain doubtful (see Winterbottom 70).

126–130 THE REIGN OF TIBERIUS

It is clear from the phraseology at 129.1 that V. has divided his treatment of Tiberius' reign into two complementary sections (126 the reign as a whole, 129–30 the details of the reign), and that the latter section is intended mainly to illustrate or confirm many of the general statements made in the former (so too Steffen 80; see further below, p. 263). This neat arrangement appears however to be disturbed by the anomalous discussion of Tiberius' treatment of Sejanus in chh. 127–8; but since V. has subdivided 129–30 into (*a*) the achievements of the reign (129–130.2) and (*b*) its disappointments (130.3–5), it might be argued that 126–8 is also subdivided, its latter section being devoted to the discussion of Sejanus. But even if we accept this structural correspondence, chh. 127–8 remain extremely awkward: V. clearly experienced some difficulty in dealing with its uncongenial subject matter (see below, pp. 246–8).

126 A GENERAL SURVEY OF TIBERIUS' REIGN

The reign of Tiberius forms the climax of V.'s summary of all Roman history. He describes it as a period of restoration (*reuocata, redditae*), in the same way as he had already described the aftermath of Actium (89.3ff. *reuocata, restituta, redactum, reuocata*) and the adoption of Tiberius by Augustus (103.1ff. *reddiderat, reuersus, repleuerat, refulsit*). 'Per Velleio la storia contemporanea è dunque scandita da questi tre momenti, evidentemente paralleli, per lui, e nel significato e negli effetti che producono' (Lana 178).

The emphasis upon restoration is not to be taken as implying criticisms of Augustus' reign: on the contrary, it is one of several hints that V. has in this ch. resorted to the techniques of panegyric (below, 2n.). Scholars such as Peter (*GL* 1.388) and Leo (241f.) had of course commented on the panegyrical tone of V.'s final pages (see above, pp. 28ff.), but it was not until J. Mesk in 1911 that anything like its full extent was realised.[1] If we compare ch. 126 with an actual panegyric (an excellent parallel, in view of its similar length, is the epistolary panegyric at *SHA Max. Balb.* 17),[2] we see that the correspondences are remarkable: it is almost as if V. has written a panegyric proper (see nn. below).[3]

---

[1] 'Zur Quellenanalyse des Plinianischen Panegyricus', *WS* 33 (1911), 85–7.

[2] The probable fictitiousness of the letter in no way detracts from its value as an example of a literary form.

[3] Although most of the supporting evidence is later than V., I have suggested elsewhere that he would be familiar with panegyrical motifs through their appearance in Cicero and Horace, and in the *gratiarum actiones* which newly elected consuls customarily delivered on their assumption of office (Woodman (1975), 292–3). Dr B. M. Levick has, however, kindly pointed

Yet we should beware of thinking that this panegyric bears no relation to historical fact. Almost every statement which V. makes can be corroborated in other ancient authorities, an especially instructive parallel being the comparable survey of the years A.D. 14–23 given by Tacitus at *A.* 4.6.[1] V. has written a manifesto based on the government's record, a type of 'factual panegyric' which his own history did much to develop. 'Velleius avait eu le mérite d'inaugurer sur le mode des rhéteurs des thèmes d'actualité propres au régime alors récent, des thèmes romains et impériaux' (Durry 31).

126.1 Horum XVI annorum V. intended that his work should be published in A.D. 30 (100.2n.): if we count backwards from that year, as he also intends (cf. 100.2, 103.3 *abhinc*), we reach the sixteenth year in A.D. 14, the first year of Tiberius' reign. To reckon from A.D. 14 to 29 inclusively is another way of saying the same thing, and these are the sixteen years to which V. refers. Sumner 285–6 believes that A.D. 30 is also included, but this seems to me impossible (Woodman (1975), 275–6).

cum inhaereant oculis animisque omnium *insera*, the reading of BA, was emended by Rhenanus to *inserta sint.* Though credible (cf. Val. Max. 8.9 *ext.* 3 'imagine audientium pectoribus inserta', 6.3.1*a* 'aeternae memoriae nota inserta est'), the emendation does not square with similar expressions at 1.14.1 'cum facilius cuiusque rei in unum contracta species quam diuisa temporibus oculis animisque inhaereant', 36.3 'paene stulta est inhaerentium oculis ingeniorum enumeratio'. Orelli's *inhaereant* thus seems to me more likely. For other conjectures see Kritz.

(quis)...[in] partibus eloquatur? V. here implies that he is unable to set down in detail the achievements of Tiberius' reign. The ostensible reason for his inability is the proximity of these events to his readers (*cum inhaereant oculis animisque omnium*, cf. 36.3 quoted in last n.), but he does in fact proceed to a detailed account in chh. 129–30 (cf. 129.1 '*singula* recenseamus'). Why this contradiction? It was a convention of the panegyrical style to confess one's inability to deal properly with the subject under discussion (104.4n.).

---

out to me that Durry's discussion of these *gratiarum actiones* (3–5) does not prove that as early as A.D. 8 there existed a *senatus consultum* stipulating such speeches of gratitude (as I there stated). Nor do I wish to imply that V. derived his panegyrical technique only from the three sources just mentioned. There doubtless existed a well worn literary tradition which the advent of autocracy only served to confirm.

1 For a detailed comparison of ch. 126 with other authorities see Steffen, esp. 90–109. His discussion corroborates the accuracy of V.'s statements, although he notes that V.'s main fault is one of omission: there is in ch. 126 no reference to the treason trials.

One of the methods of expressing this topos is to declare that a person's achievements are so many as to defy even enumeration (cf. Cic. *Red. Sen.* 1, *Marc.* 4 'nullius dicendi aut scribendi tanta uis, tanta copia, quae non dicam exornare, sed enarrare, C. Caesar, res tuas gestas possit', *Pan. Lat.* 8.1.3, *SHA Max. Balb.* 17.3 'nulla oratio tam felix, nullum ingenium tam fecundum umquam fuerit quod possit publicam felicitatem digne exprimere... [5] haec enumerare difficile est, nedum prosequi consentanea dicendi dignitate'; Gutzwiller 93, quoting Menand. rhet.). In view of the word *partibus* it seems to me that V. is alluding to this topos, being more concerned to place Tiberius' achievements in a eulogistic light by means of a recognisable panegyrical motif than to worry about the subsequent illogicality of 129.1.

Vossius rightly deleted *in*, as the similar phraseology at 38.1 (despite corruption elsewhere in the sentence) shows: *quae partibus notauimus*. The corruption may well be due to the final *m* of *omnium*.

sacrauit parentem suum Caesar non imperio sed religione 'So bringen diese Worte zum Ausdruck, dass die im folgenden aufgezählten Taten des Tiberius im Geiste und Sinne des Vaters, als Fortsetzung der augusteischen Politik, vollbracht wurden' (Steffen 81). Note also that the deification of one's predecessor was to become one of the possible introductory topoi of panegyric (Plin. *Pan.* 11; Durry 31); and though V. has already mentioned the subject at 124.3, he now returns to it.

The sense of V.'s phrase appears to be: 'he deified his father not by ukase but by his own instinctive reverence'. *non imperio* is illustrated by Sen. *Clem.* 1.10.3 'deum esse non tamquam iussi credimus: bonum fuisse principem Augustum...fatemur'; *religione* by Plin. *Pan.* 11.2 'tu sideribus patrem intulisti...quia deum credis'. That *sacrauit* = 'deified' does not destroy the force of *fecit deum* below has been pointed out to me by Professor West, quoting Ov. *Ex P.* 4.8.55 '*di* quoque carminibus (si fas est dicere) *fiunt*... [63–4] et modo, Caesar, *auum*, quem uirtus addidit astris, | *sacrarunt* aliqua carmina parte *tuum*.'

non appellauit eum sed fecit deum For *facere deum* cf. Ov. *Ex P.* 4.9.108, Manil. 4.934, *Octau.* 528f., Sen. *Apoc.* 9.3. Pliny perhaps echoes V. at *Pan.* 11.3 'deum et facis et probas'.

126.2 reuocata in forum fides When we read Tacitus' account of the financial crisis of A.D. 33 (*A.* 6.17: the ch. concludes *sic refecta fides*), we realise why V. here lays so much stress on *fides*, 'credit'. Heinsius illustrated V.'s point by quoting Cicero: *Off.* 2.84 'nec enim ulla res uehementius rem p. continet quam fides', *Leg. Agr.* 1.23 'fidem de foro...sustulistis' (compare the whole passage), 2.8 'sublata erat de foro fides non ictu aliquo nouae calamitatis sed suspicione ac perturbatione iudiciorum'. And indeed V. seems to be echoing Cicero's panegyrical *Pro Marcello* 23 'reuocanda fides' (again compare the whole passage, and cf. Fraenkel 451). For economic security as a panegyrical motif cf. Claud. *IV Honor.* 498 (and perhaps 501f.), Prisc. *Laud. Anast.* 203 (text in *PLM* 5.264ff.).

In the carefully arranged antitheses which follow, and about which Steffen 83–4 has some interesting remarks, Kaiser saw evidence of Sallustian influence (38f., quoting Caesar's speech at *C.* 52.21f.); Bolaffi also compared Sall. *H.* 1.55.11–51, a less cogent parallel (*Sallustio* 194).

summota e foro seditio, ambitio campo, discordia curia The forum was the traditional meeting place of the *comitia tributa*, responsible for the election of lesser magistrates; the Campus Martius was the traditional meeting place of the *comitia centuriata*, responsible for the election of consuls and praetors; the curia was of course where the senate met. By the figure metonymy V. here describes each of these meetings by its locale, as Liv. 9.46.11 'forum et campum corrupit' (for discussion of the figure cf. Cic. *De Or.* 3.167 'appellare...campum pro comitiis').

Elections at Rome were traditionally opportunities for *ambitio* and *seditio* (rioting), instances during Augustus' reign being 19 B.C. (Dio 54.10.1–3) and A.D. 7 (id. 55.34.2), since at that time all magistrates were still elected by the people. As was seen at 124.3n., however, Augustus had been planning to transfer the elections from the people to the senate: he died before he could carry out the plan, which was put into operation by Tiberius in A.D. 14. As a result there was no longer any opportunity for popular rioting, which is what V. means when he says that *ambitio* and *seditio* were abolished from the *comitia tributa* (*foro*) and *comitia centuriata* (*campo*). The senate for its part naturally welcomed the change as bringing increased dignity to its members (Tac. *A.* 1.15.1 'senatus largitionibus ac precibus sordidis exsolutus libens tenuit'), of whom V. of course was one (hence *summota... discordia curia*). Thus, although V.'s language may appear merely vague or eulogistic (and *forum*, *campus* and *curia* are a standard trio: Cic. *Cat.* 2.1, Sen. *Dial.* 2.12.2, Quint. 11.1.47 etc.), his statement is in fact an accurate representation of what happened to election practice during Tiberius' reign. The same is true of much of this chapter as a whole.

The verb *summouere* can take either *a*+abl., *ex*+abl., or simple abl. (K–S 1.366): here V. uses the two latter constructions – to the concern of some older edd., although such *uariatio* is quite common: cf. 56.2 'apparatus ex citro...ex acantho...testudine...ebore...argento...constitit', Cic. *De Or.* 3.177 'ex alio genere...alio...sumuntur', Lucr. 1.841, 6.279f., Liv. 36.28.5, Cels. 7.7.10, Sen. *Ep.* 59.2, Quint. 8.6.19, Apul. *Apol.* 65. See further *TLL* 5.2.1127.83ff., 1129.72ff.; K–S 1.580f., 2.636; G. Sörbom, *Variatio sermonis Taciti* (1935), 49 and n. 1; E. Loefstedt, *Per. Aeth.* 275f., *Arnobiana*

89. For a possible verbal echo of V. cf. Plin. *Pan.* 29.1 'pulsus ambitus campo' (Trajan's relations with the *comitia* form a major section of this work: 69–75).

sepultaeque ac situ obsitae iustitia, aequitas, industria In this vivid image V. sees justice etc. as first being buried and then covered over with the decay which attacks objects, either physically (Tib. 1.10.50 'occupat arma situs') or metaphorically (Hor. *Epist.* 2.2.11–13 'speciosa uocabula rerum | ...nunc situs informis premit et deserta uetustas'). The nearest parallel to V.'s metaphor is Gell. 20.1.10 'passus enim est leges...situ atque senio emori', but cf. also Plin. *Pan.* 45.2 'bonos autem otio ac situ abstrusos et quasi sepultos'. The sparkle of V.'s language is well seen when compared with the prosaic *SHA Max. Balb.* 17.4 'leges Romanas aequitatemque abolitam et clementiam...reduxistis'.

The paradosis *oppositae* was rightly emended by Gelenius to *obsitae*, the correct word for being covered with filth etc.: Liv. 29.16.6 'legati...obsiti squalore', Tac. *A.* 4.28.1 'inluuieque ac squalore obsitus', 6.43.2; for the metaphorical use cf. Val. Max. 2.9.5 'istud horridae uetustatis rubigine obsitum imperium' (F.). Ruhnken notes a similar confusion of words at Liv. 24.39.1. The paronomasia '*sit*u ob*sit*ae' is typically Velleian (cf. 1.17.6 *accendit/ascendit*, 2.4.6 *uelato/elatum*, 2.5.1 *aditis/audita*, 2.15.2 *fastigium/fastidire*, 19.1 *urbe exturbauit* etc.).

The three qualities mentioned here by V. are described as being *ciuitati redditae*, in the same way as, just above, *fides* was described as *reuocata*. This language implies that these qualities were absent from at least the last years of Augustus' reign, an absence which is apparently confirmed by the strong expression *sepultae ac situ obsitae*. Now we know from other sources that the last decade of Augustus' reign was fraught with disappointment and disaster (see above, p. 46 n. 4), and it has been argued that V. is here admitting as much (so Schäfer 24). Yet, as Steffen 90–1 has observed, it is hardly likely that V. would intend overtly to criticise the man upon whom Tiberius modelled himself and of whom he said: 'omnia facta dictaque eius uice legis obseruem' (Tac. *A.* 4.37.3; cf. Grant, *Aspects* 39f.; Seager 174–7). Another explanation seems required.

It was conventional for panegyrical writers to praise a present ruler by comparing him with his predecessor(s). Such comparison could take two forms. The present ruler is compared with his predecessors 'great though they were' (cf. Menand. rhet. 376.31ff. ἥξεις δὲ ἐπὶ τὴν τελειοτάτην σύγκρισιν, ἀντεξετάζων τὴν αὐτοῦ βασιλείαν πρὸς τὰς πρὸ αὐτοῦ βασιλείας, οὐ καθαιρῶν ἐκείνας (ἄτεχνον γάρ) ἀλλὰ θαυμάζων μὲν ἐκείνας, τὸ δὲ τέλειον ἀποδιδοὺς τῇ παρούσῃ, Maguinness (1932), 46–8, with further exs.); alternatively, the present ruler is compared with his predecessors because his achievements or virtues are so different from their deficiencies (Plin. *Pan.* 53.1 'nihil non parum grate sine comparatione laudatur. praeterea hoc primum erga optimum imperatorem piorum ciuium officium est, insequi dissimiles... [6] sic maxime laudari incolumem imperatorem, si priores secus meriti reprehendantur'; Maguinness (1932), 45–6, with further exs.). A further convention, which is clearly related to the latter type of comparison, was to state that the present ruler has 'brought back' or 'restored' the good things of life (e.g. Hor. *C.* 4.15.4–5 'tua, Caesar, aetas | fruges et agris rettulit...', 6 'restituit', 12 'ueteres reuocauit artes', *CS* 57–9 'Fides et Pax et Honos Pudorque | priscus et neglecta redire Virtus | audet', Tac. *Agr.* 3.1 'nunc demum redit animus'; above, 103.1n.; and esp. Fraenkel 450–1).

Now there can be little doubt that V. here, as at 89.3ff. and 103.1ff., is resorting to this last topos; equally there can be little doubt that if he really intended to develop the contrast between Tiberius and Augustus, he would have chosen the first method of comparison mentioned above. As it is, however, he has employed a technique which is more closely connected with the second method, thereby implying criticism of Augustus which I find it hard to believe that he intended but which he has unfortunately underlined by the expression *sepultae...obsitae.* This conclusion may seem unsatisfactory, but the illogicality which it imputes to V. here is in no way different from that which we have already noted in a similar connection at 1 above (see n.).

The three qualities themselves are the natural slogans of propaganda and panegyric. *iustitia* appeared on the coinage of Tiberius (*RIC* 1.160, A.D. 22) and was one of the distinctive virtues of his reign (see the excellent remarks of Sutherland 97f.; also Weinstock 247). *aequitas* appears at Plin. *Pan.* 77.3 and on the coins of Vespasian, Nerva and Hadrian (*BMC Emp.* 1.381, 2.112, 3.478f., 548; *RIC* 2.79–81, 223ff., etc.; cf. *CIL* 8.26487, 14.2860). *industria* was a quality much admired under the republic (cf. Earl 12, 100 etc.), but it needed to be seen in a different context under the empire: contrast *Rhet. Herenn.* 4.27 'industria uirtutem comparauit' with Tac. *A.* 16.18.1 'utque alios industria, ita hunc ignauia ad famam protulerat' or with *Agr.* 6.3 'inertia pro sapientia fuit'. V. certainly welcomes *industria* here, but we should not forget his admiration for men whose lives displayed anything but *industria* (Piso at 98.3 and Saturninus at 105.2). For *iustitia* and *industria* combined cf. Tac. *A.* 16.23.1 (F.).

accessit magistratibus auctoritas The paradosis *militibus* seems quite out of place in this context. Bernays (in Haase xii) anticipated H. Dahlmann (*Hermes* 68 (1933), 126f.) in suggesting *comitiis*, but V. has already dealt with this topic (last n. but one). K. Scott (*CPh* 26 (1931), 205f.) suggested ⟨*praepositis*⟩ *militibus* or ⟨*praefectis*⟩ *militibus* ('the authority of those placed in command of the troops was increased'); but this seems unnecessarily awkward. The traditional reading is Gelenius' *magistratibus*, which, although it is hard to see how the corruption might have arisen, is much more appropriate to the context (next n.).

senatui maiestas The central phrase in a tricolon which, taken as a whole, is V.'s testimony to the part which Tiberius encouraged the senate to play in the everyday administration of the government: for this cf. Tac. *A.* 4.6.3 (and Koestermann's n.), Suet. *Tib.* 30, Dio 57.7.2ff., 11.3; Seager 123ff.; Syme, *Tac.* 427. The re-establishing of the senate's authority eventually became a topos: cf. Plin. *Pan.* 66.2–3 (esp. 'omnes ante te eadem ista dixerunt, nemini tamen ante te creditum est'), *SHA Max. Balb.* 17.2 'senatui...reddidistis pristinam dignitatem' to which identical wording is found in *Pan. Lat.* 12.20.1.

iudiciis grauitas This Ciceronian phrase (F. quotes *Diu. Caec.* 8, 27 'grauitatem iudiciorum', 37) testifies to Tiberius' excellence in judicial matters, something which even Tacitus, as Mr Paterson points out to me, is forced to admit: 'iudiciis adsidebat...multaque eo coram aduersus ambitum et potentium preces constituta' (*A.* 1.75.1). See in general A. H. M. Jones, 'Imperial and senatorial jurisdiction in the early principate', *Historia* 3 (1955), 464ff. (= *Studies in Roman government and law* (1960), 67ff.); Seager 123ff. As Steffen however remarks, 'das Bild, das Tacitus von den Majestätsprozessen entwirft, scheint in schroffem Widerspruch zu den Angaben des V. zu stehen' (90).

compressa theatralis seditio Theatrical disturbances were a legacy from Augustus' reign which Tiberius, at the expense of some popularity, attempted to eliminate: cf. Dio 57.14, Tac. *A.* 1.77, Suet. *Tib.* 37.2 (and Rietra's n.); Steffen 100; Yavetz 11, 21.

recte faciendi omnibus aut incussa uoluntas aut imposita necessitas The older edd. remark that *incutere* is commonly used with such words as *terror* or *metus*, but there is nothing sinister about V.'s phrase: cf. *incutere* used with *amor* at Lucr. 1.19, 924, *admiratio* at Liv. 29.22.4 (cf. 45.37.14), and *misericordia* at Sen. *Dial.* 4.17.1. V.'s point is this: 'doing right' involves adhering to the spirit of the law (*uoluntas*) as well as its letter (*necessitas*), based on a system of rewards and punishments (*honorantur recta, praua puniuntur*, below). The best example of 'doing right' was Tiberius himself (5n.), and it rubbed off on to his loyal subjects (129.1n.).

126.3 suspicit potentem humilis 'looks up to'. A negative expression of the same sentiment is at Tac. *D.* 40.4 'nulla fuit in foro pax, nulla in senatu concordia, nulla in iudiciis moderatio, nulla superiorum reuerentia, nullus magistratus modus' (cf. too Plin. *Ep.* 8.14.7). It is interesting to ask whether Tac. is here looking back to V.: Gudeman ad loc. makes no ref. to V. at all, which is perhaps hardly surprising in view of his claim elsewhere (edn of *Agr.* and *Germ.* (1928), 351) that Tacitus does not show 'the faintest trace of indebtedness' to V. anywhere in his works.

For *humilis* used as subst. cf. Pompon. *Praetext.* 1 Ribbeck, Cic. *Off.* 2.70, Liv. 3.56.13, 9.46.11, Sen. *Contr.* 1.5.6; for *potens* as subst. cf. Cic. *Fam.* 9.16.5, Liv. 2.3.4, 9.1.8, Phaedr. 1.5.1 etc.; for the somewhat proverbial contrast between *humilis* and *potens* cf. Hor. *C.* 3.30.12, Phaedr. 1.30.1, Cassiod. *Var.* 1.10.1.

quando annona moderatior? The adj. shows that *annona* here = 'price of corn', as 77.1. The *annona* had been one of Tiberius' first concerns in public life (94.3), and during his reign he did his best to alleviate what could prove a difficult problem: cf. Tac. *A.* 2.87 'saeuitiam annonae incusante plebe statuit frumento pretium', 4.6.4 'plebes acri quidem annona fatigabatur, sed nulla in eo culpa ex principe: quin infecunditati terrarum aut asperis maris obuiam iit, quantum impendio diligentiaque poterat'. 'So ergibt sich, dass die Angaben des V. in diesem Punkt durchaus der Wahrheit entsprechen' (Steffen 101). Durry 31 remarks that these three words of V. 's'allongent en un chapitre entier' of Plin. *Pan.* (viz. 29): this presupposes that Pliny was directly influenced by V., which is not unreasonable in view of the seemingly close verbal parallels given above (2n.) and below (4n., 5n.).

quando pax laetior? The adj. *laetior*, coming after *annona* above, perhaps indicates the notion of fertility (cf. esp. Plin. *Pan.* 32). For the expression cf. Liv. 1.13.6 'laeta repente pax'. See too next n.

diffusa in orientis occidentisque tractus...pax augusta Foreign affairs and the *pax augusta* are topics to which V. returns in more detail at 129.1–4, corroborating his general statements here.

It was conventional for panegyrical writers to stress the extent of the ruler's dominion, to say that his *imperium* stretched from east to west, or that it was co-extensive with the boundaries of the universe. For the former motif cf. *Pan. Lat.* 2.23.1; for the latter cf. ib. 10.10.1 (an echo of Cic. *Cat.* 3.26). For exs. concerning Tiberius himself and his exploits during Augustus' reign cf. Hor. *C.* 4.14.45ff., *Anth. Pal.* 16.61; other exs. in general at Cic. *Arch.* 23, Tib. 2.5.57ff. (with Smith's n.), Hor. *C.* 3.3.53ff., 4.15.14ff., Curt. 7.8.12 (and Wilhelm 41); esp. Fraenkel 451 n. 4. It was also conventional to claim that the ruler has brought widespread peace: cf. 89.3 'reuocata pax', Hor. *C.* 4.5, Tac. *D.* 38, Menand. rhet. 372.26ff., 375.5ff., esp. 12. V. has here combined the two ideas, describing the imperial *peace* in terms which are usually reserved for the imperial *power*. The conceit thus neatly anticipates what V. says in the following clause (next n.).

V.'s language here is solemn and traditional (*quicquid...finitur*: *finire* is the proper word for both geographical limits (e.g. Liv. 28.39.14) and the limits of an empire (ib. 37.35.5)); and to the conventional 'east and west' he has added the less usual 'north and south' (*meridiano aut septentrione*): this is not simply rhetorical elaboration but, like most of his other statements in this ch., a direct reflection of Tiberian policy (e.g. in Germany and Africa, cf. *CAH* 10.643ff.). Compare Flor. 2.34.61 'omnibus ad occasum et meridiem pacatis gentibus ad septentrionem quoque...[64] sic ubique certa atque continua totius generis humani aut pax fuit aut pactio.'

For *diffusa...pax* cf. 32.5 'bellum tam late diffusum', Hor. *Epist.* 1.3.8 'bella quis et paces longum diffundit in aeuum?' (different sense), Sen. *Contr.* 9.2.11 'maiestas p. R. per omnes nationes, per omnes diffusa prouincias', Sen. *Ep.* 91.2 'diffusa securitas'.

per omnes terrarum orbis angulos * a latrociniorum metu seruat immunes Similar phraseology elsewhere (120.3 'exercitum immunem tanta calamitate seruauit', 86.2 'at Sosium...seruauit incolumem') shows that *immunes* is here predicative and that a direct object is therefore required for *seruat*. Haase's deletion of *per* is accepted by most edd., yet the word is in place after *diffusa* (cf. Sen. *Contr.* 9.2.11, quoted above). Cornelissen (1887) suggested ⟨*homines*⟩ *immunes*, which, while otherwise attractive, destroys the clausula, one of V.'s favourites (cf. Woodman, *EA* 24 n. 64). Heinsius' supplement of *nos* after *angulos* introduces a personal note which is absent from the remainder of V.'s panegyric (note all the passive verbs); but I think Heinsius was right to place the supplement here: in my opinion something has been omitted after *angulos*, although we cannot know what it was. *ciues* is perhaps a possibility, looking forward to *ciuium* in the next sentence. For *a metu...immunes* cf. Sen. *Clem.* 1.19.5 (F.).

The meaning of *latrociniorum* is illustrated by 90.4, a similarly eulogistic context: 'has igitur prouincias...tam feras ad eam pacem...perduxit Caes. Aug. ut...postea etiam latrociniis uacarent' (i.e. freedom even from 'terrorist activities'). V. may well be thinking of the suppression of Julius Florus and Tacfarinas (cf. 129.3–4). The reference to *latrocinia* and to Rome's ability to suppress them shows that V. is seeing the *pax augusta* (last n.) in terms of the military power which made *pax* possible. This attitude, fostered by Augustus himself (*RG* 26.2), is typical of the Augustan age: cf. Virg. *Aen.* 1.286ff., esp. Val. Max. 2.7 *init.* 'praecipuum decus et stabilimentum Romani imperii, salutari perseuerantia ad hoc tempus sincerum et incolume seruatum, militaris disciplinae tenacissimum uinculum, in cuius sinu ac tutela serenus tranquillusque beatae pacis status adquiescit'; S. Weinstock, *JRS* 50 (1960), 45f., 49f.

126.4 fortuita non ciuium tantummodo sed urbium damna principis munificentia uindicat *munificentia*, having been a virtue of Caesar

(41.3) and of Augustus (81.3), was a prominent feature of Tiberius' reign: Tac. *A.* 1.46.2 'principem...munificentiae summum', 2.26.1 'addidit munificentiam Caesar', 4.64.2 'ignotos etiam et ultro accitos munificentia iuuerat', 6.45.1. V. himself is quite specific, stating that Tiberius aided individuals and cities alike (cf. Dio 57.10.3 πολλὰ δὲ καὶ πόλεσι καὶ ἰδιώταις ἐπαρκῶν): the former statement he illustrates at 129.3 and 130.2 (for ample additional evidence see Rogers 3ff.), the latter directly below (*urbes Asiae*) and at 130.1 (further corroborative material in Rogers 14ff., Lana 183ff.).

As a concept *munificentia* found its way into the panegyrist's repertoire, cf. Plin. *Pan.* 25.5, 50.4 'magnum hoc tuum non erga homines modo sed erga tecta ipsa meritum, sistere ruinas, solitudinem pellere, ingentia opera eodem quo exstructa sunt animo ab interitu uindicare' (an apparently close imitation of V.'s sentence), *Pan. Lat.* 5.2.2. It first appears on the coinage of Antoninus Pius, in connection with public spectacles (*RIC* 3.134 etc.).

For *damna uindicat* (presumably = 'restores') cf. Apul. *Met.* 8.18, Gai. *Inst.* 3.217. For the subconscious repetition *uindicat/uindicatae* (below) cf. 100.5n.; for *non...tantummodo...sed* (*etiam*) cf. 110.5; Krebs–Schmalz 2.644f.

restitutae urbes Asiae An earthquake in A.D. 17 had destroyed several cities in Asia Minor, and Tiberius assisted in the relief by financial contributions and tax remissions, cf. Tac. *A.* 2.47, 2.48.1 'magnificam in publicum largitionem', Dio 57.17.7 etc.; also Orth 97. Coins with the legend *ciuitatibus Asiae restitutis* were issued in commemoration (*RIC* 1.105: cf. Lana 185f.; but the issue is dated later by Grant, *RAI* 65f.). Provincial gratitude, on this as on other occasions, was spontaneous (Rogers 15ff., Orth 116–17, also Koestermann on Tac. *A.* 2.47.2). Steffen however notes (105) that Suetonius puts Tiberius' generosity in a different perspective (*Tib.* 48.2): 'ne prouincias quidem liberalitate ulla subleuauit, excepta Asia, disiectis terrae motu ciuitatibus'. For rebuilt cities in panegyric cf. Prisc. *Laud. Anast.* 184 'prostratas recreasti funditus urbes'.

uindicatae ab iniuriis magistratuum prouinciae We learn from what follows that Tiberius' provincial policy, like his domestic policy above, was based on a system of rewards and punishments. He described his principle in a famous maxim, 'boni pastoris esse tondere pecus non deglubere' (Suet. *Tib.* 32.2), and Tacitus' evidence bears this out: 'et ne prouinciae nouis oneribus turbarentur utque uetera sine auaritia aut crudelitate magistratuum tolerarent, prouidebat' (*A.* 4.6.4: on the suggestive *prouidebat* see next n.); see Steffen 107–9. It must be noted however that Tiberius' provincial policy has been attacked by P. A. Brunt, *Historia* 10 (1961), 189–227; G. Alföldy, *Latomus* 24 (1965), 824–44 (who also attacks V.'s remarks on the subject in this chapter); Orth, *passim*. For provincial policy as a panegyrical topos cf. *SHA Max. Balb.* 17.2, *Pan. Lat.* 11.5.3; for taxation cf. Menand. rhet. 375–6. For *iniuriae magistratuum* cf. Cic. *Verr.* 2.2.8, Liv. 3.56.13, Tac. *A.* 2.54.1.

honor dignis paratissimus The immediate context suggests a reference to Tiberius' well known policy of prolonging the provincial tenure of successful procurators, which Tacitus treats with characteristic *insinuatio* at *A.* 1.80 (cf. also 4.6.3), but which Jos. *AJ* 18.172 describes as προμήθεια, the Greek equivalent of *prouidentia*, one of the distinctive virtues of Tiberius' reign (115.5n.). Yet V.'s phrase need not exclude other *honores* (cf. 129.2n.).

poena in malos sera sed aliqua It was proverbial throughout Greek and Latin literature that *divine* vengeance works slowly but surely (see Dodds on Eur. *Bacch.* 882–7, Nisbet–Hubbard on Hor. *C.* 1.15.19, Orelli on ib. 3.2.31f., Ogilvie on Liv. 3.56.7, Smith on Tibull. 1.9.4, Mayor on Juv. 13.100, Otto 111). Now Tiberius' attitude to his own divinity was one of well attested contempt (cf. e.g. Seager 144ff.); V. thus only hints at it by describing Tiberius' leniency in terms usually reserved for a god. V.'s subtlety is clear when compared with the unambiguous articulation of Horace at e.g. *C.* 3.5.1–4 or 1.2.25ff. (see Nisbet–Hubbard's nn. on this poem). For the panegyrical technique of alluding to someone in divine terms see also Cairns 218.

It should be clear from the preceding paragraph that V.'s phrase cannot be interpreted as criticism of Tiberius' leniency towards provincial governors as Orth claims (69–70); on the contrary, V. is praising Tiberius' *clementia*, one of the characteristic virtues of the reign: cf. Rogers 35ff.; Wirszubski 150–3; Grant, *RAI* 47–51; Béranger 271; Levick (1975), all with further refs.

For this use of *aliqui* cf. *OLD* s.v. 4*a*; for the contrast between *ambitio* and *uirtus* below cf. Titin. *Com.* 11 Ribbeck, Sall. *C.* 52.22, *SHA Pesc.* 4.3.

126.5 nam facere recte...faciendo docet V. here elaborates the point which he made at 2 above: it now transpires that Tiberius is the cause of the citizens' *recte faciendi uoluntas*. The expression is reminiscent of *rex erit qui recte faciet* (*FPR* 56.4, cf. Hor. *Epist.* 1.1.59f. and Porph. ad loc.), a proverbial sentiment whose implication is that he who is (morally) best deserves to lead the rest: for this convenient defence of autocracy cf. Plato, *Theaet.* 146A, Rut. Nam. *Red.* 1.91 'quod regnas minus est quam quod regnare mereris', *Pan. Lat.* 7.5.3 'uirtutibus tuis debitum...meruisses', *SHA Tac.* 2.3, 4.2–3, *El.* 34.5. And V. proceeds to place Tiberius' excellence beyond question with the word *optimus* (next n.). Grenade 120 has some good remarks on this point.

For *faciendo docet* cf. Sen. *Ep.* 81.19 'iniurias quas posse fieri faciendo docuerunt' (F.).

princeps optimus This title is applied elsewhere to Tiberius (Val. Max. 2 *praef.*, *CIL* 6.902, 904, cf. 6.93), who is the first emperor of whom it is used: it was also applied to Claudius (cf. Plin. *Ep.* 8.6.13), Nerva (Front. *Aqu.* 2.64.1) and of course Trajan (*RIC* 2.534ff. etc.). V. as usual reflects the current political language of the day, and the description of Tiberius as *optimus* accords well with allusions to Tiberius' right to rule (last n.) and to his being an example to the citizens (next n.). See in general Wirszubski 153–4; Frei-Stolba (1969), 21ff., esp. 23.

It should be clear from this note that the emendation *optime*, made by Mommsen before Pluygers, cannot be right.

cumque sit imperio maximus, exemplo maior est 'and though he is greatest in authority, he is still greater in the example which he sets' (Shipley): for the contrast cf. Plin. *Pan.* 45.6 'nec tam imperio nobis opus est quam exemplo', Tac. *G.* 7.1 'duces exemplo potius quam imperio... praesunt'. The 'leader being an example to the rest' is a motif which has its origins in Greek thought, e.g. Solon fr. 5, Democr. B39, 79, but above all Plato, *Laws* 711, Xen. *Cyr.* 8.1.12, 21ff., 6.13, 8.5, *Ages.* 7.2, Isocr. *Areop.* 21–2, *Nicocl.* 31, 37.[1] It is taken over into Latin literature (e.g. Cic. *Leg.* 3.31, *Rep.* 1.47, 2.69, *Fam.* 1.9.12), often proverbially (Cic. *Att.* 5.11.5, Petron. 58; Otto 119, 300). It is significantly a regular topos in panegyric, or in other writings about the *princeps*: Augustus implied it himself (*RG* 8.5), and Ovid acknowledged it (*Met.* 15.834 'exemploque suo mores reget'); Pliny devotes two whole chh. to Trajan as a model for his citizens (*Pan.* 45–6), and for other exs. cf. Sen. *Clem.* 1.1.6, 2.2.1, *Pan. Lat.* 2.14.4, 4.29.3, Claud. *IV Honor.* 269–74, 299–302, *Stil.* 1.168, Paul. Petr. *Vit. Mart.* 2 (61.1018D Migne). See also Weber 168*–174* n. 611; Häussler, *Tac.* 355ff.

127–128 TIBERIUS' TREATMENT OF SEJANUS

The ancient authorities are agreed that in A.D. 14 Tiberius came to the throne reluctantly (124.2n.), ventilating the suggestion that the empire should not be governed by himself alone (127.3n.). Most modern historians, like many of their ancient counterparts, are inclined to dismiss this evidence as mere posturing by the emperor; but Tiberius' diffidence, if we accept it, goes a long way towards explaining the otherwise astonishingly rapid career of the distinguished *eques* L. Aelius Seianus. There is no need to go over his

[1] I owe some of these references to Dr T. J. Saunders.

career here,[1] except to observe that a symptom of his success was Tiberius' custom of referring to him as *adiutor imperii* and *socius laborum* (127.3n.). Such nomenclature must have had an incalculable effect upon the senatorial order at Rome, and we may safely assume that for as many influential senators who followed Sejanus' lead, there would be at least a similar number committed to opposing him.[2] Such opposition will have been intensified by Sejanus' equestrian status. He was an upstart, a *nouus homo*, who had been catapulted to a position of almost unprecedented authority over the heads of many experienced, distinguished and aristocratic senators. Even Drusus, Tiberius' own son and hitherto the most illustrious person in the state (cos. 15, 21; *trib. pot.* 22), felt cheated and insecure (Tac. *A.* 4.3.2, 7.1).

We must remember that such opposition to Sejanus had started at least as early as A.D. 20, and was not confined to the senatorial order but extended to the people also. In that year Sejanus' daughter was betrothed to Claudius' son Drusus, and Tacitus notes the hostility with which this news was generally received (*A.* 3.29.4). The same hostility was present in 29, when Tiberius had written to the senate with accusations against Agrippina and Nero (*A.* 5.4.2–3). It is easy to imagine opposition of this kind existing throughout the twenties. Sejanus' unique position and his equestrian status were two sides of the same coin: these were the two issues which combined to alienate loyalist support at Rome. No clearer evidence of this could be found than in the interchange of letters which, according to Tacitus, took place between Tiberius and Sejanus in A.D. 25.[3] Sejanus had written to Tiberius requesting the hand of the princess Julia Livilla in marriage (Tac. *A.* 4.39). In his reply Tiberius isolated exactly the two causes of discontent which people levelled against Sejanus, his equestrian status and great power (*A.* 4.40.5): 'illi magistratus et primores, qui te inuito perrumpunt omnibusque de rebus consulunt, excessisse iam pridem equestre fastigium longeque antisse patris mei amicitias non occulti ferunt'. Moreover, Tiberius goes on to say that opposition towards Sejanus means criticism of himself: 'perque inuidiam tui me quoque incusant'. For it is essential to remember that Sejanus' elevation was, and was seen to be, the personal responsibility of Tiberius. Sejanus could not have risen to such heights, or maintained his supremacy, without the emperor's continual blessing.[4] And it is undoubtedly this criticism of the emperor himself which prompted V. to devote the present section to a defence of Tiberius' treatment of Sejanus.

In chh. 127 and 128 respectively V. defends the two causes of complaint

---

1 For which see Seager 178–223.

2 Senatorial opposition is rightly emphasised by Steffen 186–7.

3 On the sources of the correspondence see Koestermann on *A.* 4.39.1.

4 This aspect is well brought out in a speech in Tac. *A.* 6.8.3–4: Tac. adds that the speech voiced everyone's thoughts, and we have no reason to assume otherwise (cf. also *A.* 5.6). Marsh 189f. rightly stresses this point.

attaching to Sejanus, that he is the emperor's *adiutor* and a *nouus homo*. Each of these chh. is subdivided in its turn: 127.1–2 precedents, 3–4 character sketch of Sejanus; 128.1–3 precedents, 4 conclusion. The first and third of these subdivisions correspond to each other not only in function (they are carefully calculated introductions to the second and fourth subdivisions respectively), but also in method: using the techniques of contemporary rhetoric, V. moves with dexterity from initial *sententiae*, to illustrations from past history (*exempla*), and finally back to subtle re-statements of his original propositions (see below). The precision of his material is often impressive (e.g. 128.2n.), but the language throughout is prosaic and ordinary (esp. 127.1), and instead of the elegant reminiscences of Cicero to which we have been accustomed and which are seen in profusion in the following chh., we are given officialese and propaganda (127.3–4nn., 128.4nn.). V. has sacrificed embellishment of style for clarity of argument in a way which is entirely uncharacteristic. The tone and structure are those of a political pamphlet, not a work of history. There is a further untypical feature. On other occasions when V. expands his rapid narrative to deal with a single large topic, as here, he invariably begins with some suitable introductory formula; but at 127.1 (see n.) the opening *sententia* follows abruptly and illogically after 126.5. Similarly at 129.1, when the discussion is over, V. begins: 'sed proposita quasi uniuersa principatus Ti. Caesaris ⟨imagine⟩, singula recenseamus', where *proposita imagine* refers not to the discussion of Sejanus, immediately preceding, but to ch. 126, three chh. previously. The present discussion is thus isolated from the surrounding narrative in a way which is unique in V.'s work. The section has clearly been inserted to meet an immediate need, to counter contemporary criticism of Tiberius.[1] But both style and structure have suffered.

Although many scholars have deduced from this section that V. was himself an adherent of Sejanus,[2] this view is completely without foundation. We know from Tac. *A.* 1.24.1–2 and Dio 57.19.6 that when the army in Illyricum revolted in A.D. 14, Tiberius sent out Drusus and Sejanus to deal with the revolt. V.'s account of the revolt was given in ch. 125: if he were the enthusiastic supporter of Sejanus which, on the basis of chh. 127–8, he is usually claimed to be, he would surely have referred to Sejanus' presence in Illyricum. As it is, we are indeed told of Drusus' mission (125.4), but there is no mention of Sejanus.[3] Again, we know from Tac. *A.* 3.72.2–3 and Sen. *Marc.* 22.4 that when Pompey's theatre caught fire in A.D. 22 it was Sejanus who played a major part in controlling the blaze, as a result of which the

---

[1] Steffen, who notes the inconsistency of 129.1, suggests (193–5) that chh. 127–8 are a *later* addition to the main narrative; but see below, 128.4n.

[2] Notable exceptions are Abraham 13f.; Dihle 640; Steffen 181ff.; Sumner 288–97.

[3] Steffen 194f. also makes this point.

senate voted for the erection of his statue on the site. The fire was clearly a famous incident, and it is naturally mentioned by V. in his detailed survey of Tiberius' reign (130.1); yet he makes no reference either to Sejanus' sterling work or his subsequent honour.

Now these are both occasions on which it would have been more than natural for V. to introduce the name of Sejanus into his narrative, yet each time he declines the opportunity.[1] Instead we are given the present awkwardly inserted discussion, where neither style nor method nor tone rings true. Such evidence hardly adds up to enthusiasm for Tiberius' minister:[2] it would seem, with far more probability, that V. belonged with those senators who were antagonised by Sejanus (above, p. 246). If this is true, we must conclude that chh. 127–8 are aimed, not at defending Sejanus himself, but at justifying Tiberius' treatment of him.[3]

127.1–2 *Adiutor imperii*: precedents

We have seen that the primary cause for complaint against Sejanus was his position as Tiberius' *adiutor*. V. begins his defence of Tiberius with the generalisation that powerful men have often had recourse to powerful assistants, a point which he then illustrates by four examples grouped in two sets of two, the second of which shows that being a *nouus homo* is no obstacle to political success. This in turn leads to a confirmation of the original statement in slightly different form (but the verbal repetition of *magnis adiutoribus* at 2 indicates the circular movement of the argument), together with the additional qualification that essential state service should bring its own kind of distinction. The accent is all on public expediency and political necessity (see the accumulation of such words as *usu, utilitatem*), but by introducing,

---

[1] There may have been a similar opportunity at 101–2, from which we know that V. was on the staff of Gaius Caesar in the east. It is usually assumed that Sejanus was there too (cf. Tac. *A.* 4.1.2), and it is also assumed (e.g. by Syme (1956), 265) that V.'s acquaintance with Sejanus must date from this period. Yet V. makes no mention of it at any point during his elaborate account of Gaius' oriental activities, even though this is the kind of personal detail he usually includes. But since the Tacitus passage is not in fact decisive for Sejanus' presence in the east (cf. Sumner 292 n. 197), the reason for V.'s silence may simply be that Sejanus was not there at the time.

[2] Contrast Syme, *Tac.* 571, 'When Vell. has to concoct an encomium [for Sejanus]...the thing can be done without discomfort.'

[3] This conclusion was also reached by Kritz xvii sqq. and Sumner 292, although they both call V.'s treatment of Sejanus a 'eulogy'. That chh. 127–8 are not a eulogy I have already argued elsewhere (Woodman (1975), 296–303), and much of what I said there is inevitably repeated here. There are also some brief but sensible remarks in Paladini 474.

with apparent casualness, the names of two famous *noui homines* from recent history V. at the same time prepares us for what will prove to be the main debating point in 128.1–3.

127.1 Raro eminentes uiri non magnis adiutoribus...usi sunt On other occasions when V. digresses on a single large topic, he either begins with some temporal or logical connective (e.g. 2.9.1 *eodem tractu temporum*, 90.2 *in quas prouincias*) or with an apologetic formula (e.g. 1.14.1, 1.16.1, 36.2, 66.3). Only here is no such introduction used, this opening *sententia* being completely divorced from anything in ch. 126 (see above, p. 247).

The *sententia* itself is an attempt to see Sejanus' appointment in terms of past precedents (cf. too Grenade 467f., 478f.), and V.'s four *exempla* (see below) are all instances of political *amicitia*, a concept with a long history which stretches back, perhaps conveniently, into the days of the republic. It would seem, however, that the concept assumed a heightened significance in Tiberius' reign: having come to the throne reluctantly (124.2n.), he went out of his way to associate others in the management of the empire (see also below, 3n.). Thus Strabo, writing about A.D. 18, states that Tiberius' sons Drusus and Germanicus are ὑπουργοῦντες τῷ πατρί in the government (6.4.2, p. 396 Meineke). Germanicus died in 19, Drusus in 23; but within a few years we find V. in the present passage alluding to Sejanus in a similar manner as the emperor's *adiutor*. In fact by A.D. 28 the senate had voted for the erection of an *ara amicitiae*, to be flanked by statues of Tiberius and Sejanus (Tac. *A.* 4.74.2, cf. Grant, *Aspects* 54); and when Val. Max. comes to refer to Sejanus' fall, he twice describes it as a violation of *amicitia* (9.11 *ext.* 4).

Tiberius' concern at associating others in the running of the empire has provided useful material for two modern scholars. Kornemann (5f.) attempted to show that Augustus and most subsequent emperors occupied the highest position in the state along with another person (or other persons), forming a kind of 'double principate': in 18–13 B.C., e.g., Augustus and Agrippa formed a *Doppelprinzipat* (12ff.). Then Grenade (444ff.) wrote a ch. on 'les charges du pouvoir et la théorie des "adiutores imperii"', based on the reigns of Augustus and Tiberius. I have considerable sympathy with each of these scholars, and Grenade in particular makes some interesting and valuable remarks to which (it will be clear) I am indebted. But in my opinion Grenade fails to appreciate the distinctive character of Tiberius' reign as compared with Augustus', while Kornemann fails to see the full extent to which the years A.D. 23–31 were a *Doppelprinzipat* of Tiberius and Sejanus (44–6).

ut duo Scipiones duobus Laeliis These are (1) P. Cornelius Scipio Africanus (*RE* 4.1.1462–70 = Cornelius 336 (Henze)) and C. Laelius Maior (*RE* 12.400–4 = Laelius 2 (Münzer)). Laelius, described as a *nouus* *homo* (*Rhet. Herenn.* 4.19), had an *artissima familiaritas* with Scipio (Val. Max. 5.5.1); and in a ch. on *amicitia* Val. Max. (4.7.7) compares the *amicitia* of the two men with that of Agrippa and Augustus in much the same way as V. does here, attributing to both Laelius and Agrippa many of the standard virtues to be expected from those whose lives are devoted to the welfare of the state (cf. Grenade 467f.). Laelius was thus an apposite forerunner of Sejanus; on Agrippa see below. (2) P. Cornelius Scipio Africanus Aemilianus (*RE* 4.1.1439–62 = Cornelius 335 (Münzer)) and C. Laelius the orator (*RE* 12.1.404–10 = Laelius 3 (Münzer)), men also characterised by *amicitia* (Val. Max. 8.8.1).

M. Agrippa On Agrippa, 'quem...*amicitia principis* euexerat' (90.1), see 96.1nn. He was *par excellence* the appropriate precedent for Sejanus: his stoico-military characteristics, described at 79.1 (and cf. Val. Max. as above), happily found their parallel in the image of himself which Sejanus projected to the world and which V. faithfully reproduces at 3 below (see nn.). The astuteness of the parallel has been recognised by modern scholars, e.g. L. Levy, *Quomodo Tiberius se gesserit* (1901), 78; Syme, *Tac.* 402f.; Grenade 168f., 466ff.

Statilio Tauro T. Statilius Taurus (*RE* 3A.2.2199–203 = Statilius 34 (Nagl)) was an *amicus* of Augustus (J. Crook, *Consilium principis* (1955), 184, no. 310) and a *nouus homo* (Wiseman 263, no. 413).

Scheffer's correction *proxime* for the paradosis *maxime* above is clearly right: for the corruption cf. 110.4n.; for *proximus* (*-e*) *ab* cf. 76.4, 124.4. For *multiplices consulatus triumphosque* below cf. Liv. 10.6.11 'multiplices consulatus censurasque et triumphos'.

eueherentur Vascosanus' emendation of the paradosis *enumerentur* is preferable to Gelenius' *eniterentur* or Heinsius' *emererentur* (deleting *ad* above) for two reasons: (1) it is the natural verb for elevating to honours (e.g. Tac. *D.* 13.1 *ad consulatus*) and is used regularly by V., esp. in this sense (e.g. 53.3, 90.1); (2) V. is defending Tiberius' treatment of Sejanus, not what Sejanus has achieved for himself.

127.2 etenim magna negotia magnis adiutoribus egent For the polyptoton and somewhat similar sentiment cf. Heliodor. 9.24.3 τὰ μεγάλα τῶν πραγμάτων μεγάλων δεῖται κατασκευῶν (F.), Charit. 2.10.3 τὰ μεγάλα τῶν πραγμάτων...μεγάλαις ἐπινοίαις κατορθοῦται.[1]

†neque in parua paucitas ministeria defecit† From the long lists of emendations provided by Kritz and Bolaffi it is clear that most scholars have

---

[1] I owe the latter reference to Dr D. M. Bain.

attempted to produce Latin which has the following meaning: 'in small affairs, as in great ones, there is need of proper assistance' (Rockwood). But such a sentiment is utterly irrelevant to V.'s otherwise compact and carefully elaborated argument, as was realised by both Vossius and Madvig (2.312f.). Vossius deleted the words as a gloss ('sane si tota haec periodus tolleretur, sensus optime procederet') and was followed by Boeclerus; Madvig emended to *atque impar capacitas ministeria deficit*. Each of these suggestions has its merits, but I am not sufficiently convinced by either to deviate from Ellis' judicious policy of obelising the whole phrase.

interestque rei publicae... V.'s argument seems to be this. If the services of a certain man are required for the good of the state (*quod usu necessarium est*), that man should be given the political status appropriate to his actual (as opposed to his hereditary) importance (*dignitate eminere*); otherwise he will not be seen to possess the proper influence (*auctoritate muniri*), and his activities on behalf of the state will run the risk of being disregarded. This analysis shows that each word of the argument counts, and that *dignitate* and *auctoritate* are not synonymous, as usually thought.

dignitas here = political status, something not always associated with the equestrian order (Hellegouarc'h, *VL* 457f., but note the reservations of C. Nicolet, *L'ordre équestre* (1966), 1.237ff.) and therefore relevant to V.'s argument. But that need by no means imply a reference to the consulship: see 128.4n.

For *auctoritate muniri* cf. Sall. *J.* 28.4 (F.); for *usu necessarium* cf. Curt. 5.1.8; Cicero toys with the concepts of *utilitas, auctoritas* and *honestas* somewhat similarly to V. at *Off.* 3.109f.

127.3–4 *Adiutor imperii*: Sejanus' character

It is clear from the opening phraseology of this subsection (*sub his exemplis*) that the preceding argument in 1–2 has been a calculated introduction to the character sketch which now follows. To say that the sketch follows 'by the irony of fate', as does H. Stuart Jones (*CAH* 10.177), is simply perverse. The information that we are about to be given about Sejanus (that he is Tiberius' *adiutor* and a *nouus homo*) is a direct sequel to the points made in 1–2. But there is more than this to the sketch: we are also given a list of Sejanus' *uirtutes* which opens the way for a wider discussion on the relationship of morality to politics (128.1–3), a topic of eternal concern to *noui homines* (128.1n.).

127.3 sub his exemplis An unusual expression which became a mannerism of the younger Pliny: cf. *Ep.* 1.18.5, 2.6.6 (Ruhnken), 3.18.2, 6.5.2; F. adds *Pan.* 53.5, 76.1, Val. Max. 8.9 *init.*, Tac. *A.* 3.68.1, 4.11.3.

Ti. Caesar Although chh. 127–8 are concerned with Sejanus, he is in fact referred to only twice, here and at 128.4, and on each occasion he is seen as the recipient of honours from Tiberius or from Tiberius acting with the senate and people. It was the contemporary view (see above, p. 246) that Sejanus owed his supremacy to the emperor, a view which V. reflects here quite clearly. This vital point is rightly appreciated by Hellegouarc'h (1964), 679, and also (but wrongly interpreted) by Grenade 478f.

Seianum Aelium *RE* 1.529–31 = Aelius 133 (v. Rohden); *PIR*[2] 1.41–3, no. 255. Also D. Hennig, *L. Aelius Seianus* (1975), which I regret I have been unable to see.

principe equestris ordinis patre viz. L. Seius Strabo, *RE* 2A.1.1125–6 = Seius 15 (Stein). On the title *princeps equestris ordinis* cf. Hellegouarc'h, *VL* 456f.

materno uero genere clarissimas ueteresque et insignes honoribus complexum familias Cf. Tac. *A.* 15.48.1 'multas insignesque familias paterna nobilitate complexus' (Fletcher): the echo of V.'s words, though doubtless subconscious, suggests that Tacitus had read V.'s description of Sejanus for himself (see further below).

On Sejanus' maternal pedigree Syme has said, 'the "potentia" of Aelius Seianus is entwined about the very roots of the dynasty' (*Tac.* 384); but I am not sure whether V. is really 'justifying the promotion of the new man ... on the ground that his newness is not absolute and unqualified' (Sumner 292).

consulares fratres, consobrinos On who these might be see esp. G. V. Sumner, 'The family connections of L. Aelius Seianus', *Phoenix* 19 (1965), 137ff.; also F. Adams, *AJPh* 76 (1955), 70ff., and below, 128.3n. His *auunculus* was Q. Iunius Blaesus (125.5n.).

ipsum uero laboris ac fidei capacissimum, sufficiente etiam uigori animi compage corporis We are told that Tiberius, after the blaze at Pompey's theatre, 'simul laudibus Seianum extulit, tamquam *labore uigilantiaque* eius tanta uis unum intra damnum stetisset' (Tac. *A.* 3.72.3); and later Tacitus reports an exchange of letters between Sejanus and Tiberius (see above, p. 246) in which Sejanus is said to have claimed '*excubias ac labores*, ut unum e militibus, pro incolumitate imperatoris malle' (4.39.2); to this Tiberius replied by first praising his loyalty (4.40.1 'laudata pietate'). From these remarkably close correspondences between V. and Tac. it is possible to conclude (with Steffen 186, 194; Koestermann on *A.* 4.39.2) that during the twenties Sejanus cultivated an 'official image' of himself, modelled perhaps on Agrippa, the archetypal man of *labor* (cf. 79.1). It was the image of an indispensable state servant, just the kind of assistant that the diffident Tiberius would appreciate: 'l'habile homme sait parler à son maître le langage qui lui va droit au cœur' (Grenade 467). On *uigilantia* see further below.

Much of V.'s description also recalls Tacitus' famous portrait of Sejanus at *A.* 4.1.3 ('*corpus* illi *laborum* tolerans, *animus* audax'); but whereas V. appreciates what appear to be the true qualities of Sejanus (*uigor animi*, for ex., was a special quality of Julius Caesar at 41.1), Tacitus depreciates them (*animus audax* echoes Sallust's description of Catiline at *C.* 5.4). Koestermann has conveniently and (I believe) correctly summarised what our conclusions from this evidence should be (p. 24 of his comm. on Tac. *A.* 4–6): 'Die Möglichkeit kann nicht völlig von der Hand gewiesen werden, Tacitus habe bei der Wahl seiner eigenen Formulierungen den Geschichtsabriss vor Augen gehabt [see above, last n. but one], um alsdann in seiner Weise die Ausführungen seines Vorgängers in ihr Gegenteil umzubiegen.'

Sumner 293–4 properly acknowledges the parallelism between Tac. and V., but also states that 'the obvious literary parallels' for V.'s sketch are Livy's portrait of Hannibal (21.4) and Sallust's of Catiline (*C.* 5.1ff.): from this and other points he concludes that V.'s sketch of Sejanus is less congenial than usually thought. While I would of course agree that V. was in no way attracted to Sejanus, I think his sketch merely reflects current thinking and that the portraits of Hannibal and Catiline belong to a quite different tradition (cf. B.-R. Voss, *Der Pointierte Stil des Tac.* (1963), 76).

For *compage corporis* cf. Cic. *Senec.* 77.

singularem principalium onerum adiutorem in omnia habuit atque habet This statement must be considered in conjunction with four others, all equally important: Tac. *A.* 4.2.3 'facili Tiberio atque ita prono ut *socium laborum* non modo in sermonibus sed apud patres et populum celebraret'; 4.7.1 'set crebro querens (Drusus) incolumi filio *adiutorem imperii* alium uocari'; Dio 57.19.7 καὶ σύμβουλον καὶ ὑπηρέτην πρὸς πάντα ἐποιεῖτο, 58.4.3 καὶ ὕπατόν τε αὐτὸν ἀπέδειξε καὶ κοινωνὸν τῶν φροντίδων ὠνόμαζε. From the remarkably similar phraseology used by each historian it is reasonable to conclude that Sejanus was known as Tiberius' *adiutor*. Whether this was ever an official appointment, as has been suggested (Abraham 8; Rogers 139; Steffen 188; Koestermann on Tac. 4.2.3), is perhaps doubtful; but Tac. 4.2.3 and a further most important passage of Dio (58.8.4 τῇ τε γερουσίᾳ...γράφων Σεϊανὸν ἁπλῶς αὐτὸν ὠνόμαζε, μηδὲν ὧνπερ εἴθιστο προσθείς) leave us in no doubt that Tiberius' references to Sejanus were frequent, were made in front of both the senate and the people, and used the same formula. V. was of course himself a senator, and will often have been subjected to hearing the title *adiutor* used of Sejanus. It is in no way surprising that on this matter he so closely resembles our other sources (see further below, 128.1n., 4n.). I have argued elsewhere that Tiberius began referring to Sejanus as his *adiutor* in the early months of A.D. 23 (Woodman (1975), 301–2).

When Tiberius adopted Sejanus as his *adiutor*, he seems to have done so on the grounds that he himself had excessive responsibility (cf. *onerum* in V., *laborum* in Tac., φροντίδων in Dio). It of course became a commonplace from the early empire onwards for writers to stress the effort, toil or responsibility required of the *princeps* if he was to rule with the appropriate *cura*. As usual a few key words presented themselves to express this notion: *moles* (131.1n.), for ex., and *onus*: cf. Ov. *Met.* 15.819f. 'qui nominis heres | impositum feret unus onus', Sen. *Dial.* 6.2.3 'in quem onus imperii reclinare', *Clem.* 1.1.6 'ingens tibi onus imposuisti', Vict. *Epit.* 12.3. A main difficulty, esp. at this early period of the empire, is to try and decide on which occasions these topoi reflect the genuine attitude of an emperor. In the case of Tiberius there is strong evidence that he came to the throne reluctantly, considering his task one of almost impossible magnitude (Tac. *A.* 3.69.4 'satis *onerum* principibus'), and from the very start expressing a belief that ruling the empire was too much for one man alone (124.2n.). Certainly the first sixteen years of his reign show Tiberius going out of his way to associate others in the administration of the government (above, 1n.; also Kornemann 35ff.). In general on this topic see refs. at 1n. and 124.2n.; and esp. Béranger 175–8 (who concludes, as do I, that Tiberius' reluctance is probably sincere).

127.4 uirum priscae seueritatis, laetissimae hilaritatis V. depicts Sejanus as a man of mixed disposition, combining the gravity and gaiety which Pliny recommended (*Ep.* 8.21.1). The only question is to decide in which order the words should be printed. Should we read the paradosis *seueritatis laetissimae, hilaritatis priscae* (with the vast majority of edd.), or *priscae seueritatis, laetissimae hilaritatis* (with Bothe)? The paradosis is suspect not because of the oxymoron *seueritas laetissima* (its supporters have long been quoting Sil. 8.611 'laeta uiro grauitas' and Cic. *Mur.* 66 in its favour) but because Velleian and other usage tells against it. On two other occasions V. uses the phrase *prisca seueritas* to describe people – once as recently as 125.4 of Drusus, and again at 92.2 of Sentius Saturninus (a man who is at the same time *hilaris*: 105.2).[1] In addition (as pointed out by W. D. Lebek, *Verba prisca* (1970), 144), *prisca seueritas* is a standard phrase, cf. Cic. *Har. Resp.* 27, Liv. 22.60.5, Tac. *A.* 6.13.8, 11.25.13.[2] A further consideration is that *prisca*

[1] Drusus and Saturninus are men of whom V. strongly approves, whereas of course I believe that he did not approve of Sejanus; but I do not think this affects my argument here since the sketch of Sejanus is *prima facie* congenial.

[2] Lebek himself quotes the paradosis of our passage and is thus compelled to say that V. has varied the standard phraseology.

makes little or no sense combined with *hilaritas* whereas it makes excellent sense with *seueritas.* I therefore accept Bothe's emendation. Both Ellis and Bolaffi, not mentioning Bothe, attribute to Cornelissen (1877) the suggestion *seueritatis priscae, laetissimae hilaritatis*, which is not what that scholar proposed: his conjecture was identical to Bothe's but forty years late.

hilaritas was later to become an official virtue of Hadrian (*RIC* 2.321, 355, 360, 483n.; cf. Syme, *Tac.* 756), having already been applied unofficially to Trajan by Pliny (*Ep.* 10.1.2).

actu otiosis simillimum I have noted elsewhere (98.3n.) that V. attributes *otium* to persons of whom he approves since it is something which betokens their loyalty to the emperor. It therefore seems to me significant that V. refrains from attributing it to Sejanus, allowing him only a semblance of *otium.* Subsequent events were to prove V. right.

actus in the sense of *agendi ratio* is modelled on Sall. *H.* 5.4; cf. also Manil. 2.635. For *actus/otium* cf. Sen. *Dial.* 8.6.2.

nihil sibi uindicantem eoque adsequentem omnia In the exchange of letters between Tiberius and Sejanus, already mentioned, the latter claimed 'neque fulgorem honorum umquam precatum', with which Tiberius agreed, 'uis tu quidem istum intra locum sistere' (Tac. *A.* 4.39.2, 40.5). But Tiberius added, as does V. here, that Sejanus' actual power was nevertheless considerable (see above, p. 246). Once more V. clearly reflects the attitude of the times.

V.'s phraseology is Sallustian: cf. *C.* 54.6 'quo minus petebat gloriam, eo magis illum adsequebatur' (Ruhnken), also *J.* 6.1 'plurumum facere et minumum ipse de se loqui'. For *adsequi omnia* cf. also Cic. *Fam.* 15.4.11, *Att.* 10.8.5 (F.).

uultu uitaque tranquillum Cf. Tac. *A.* 4.1.3 'palam compositus pudor', another of the close correspondences between the sketches of V. and Tac.

animo exsomnem A quality which Sejanus shares with Maecenas (88.2 'uir ubi res uigiliam exigeret, sane exsomnis') and which occurs in Sejanus' description of himself in his letter to Tiberius (above, 3n.). The virtues in question are *industria* and *uigilantia*, often claimed by *noui homines* (Gelzer 28 and n. 207), and appearing also in Tacitus' sketch of Sejanus, where they are typically twisted: 'haud minus noxiae quotiens parando regno finguntur'.

128.1–3 *Nouus homo*: precedents

Rockwood described this subsection as an 'excursus on eminent Romans of humble origin', and it is certainly true that, as has often been pointed out (e.g. by Mayor on Juv. 8 intro.), V.'s theme is not unlike the familiar rhetorical topos 'de his qui humili loco nati clari euaserunt' (Val. Max. 3.4, cf. e.g. 3.5, 4.4.11, Sen. *Ben.* 4.30, *Ep.* 44 etc.). Yet V. is not simply indulging in an exclusively rhetorical excursus: the section is closely and explicitly connected to the preceding character sketch of Sejanus (see first n. below), and its argumentation is similar in both relevance and method to that in 127.1–2.

We have seen that Sejanus' supremacy was made more irksome by his equestrian origins, and it is to this which V. now turns. He begins with the generalisation that what is most meritorious is also the most noble, a familiar theme in the political literature of the late republic and one from which readers would recognise that, as in 127.1–2, V. is still discussing the public service of *noui homines*. But whereas in 127.1–2 the accent was upon public expediency and political necessity, the emphasis is now on the relationship of morality to politics (*uirtutum*, *optimum*, *uirtus*), a topic for which V. has prepared the way by listing Sejanus' moral qualifications in 127.3–4. The opening generalisation is then illustrated by seven examples arranged in five unequal groups which eventually lead, as at 127.2, to a confirmation of the original proposition, suitably modified in the light of the preceding *exempla*.

128.1 In huius uirtutum aestimatione...iudicia ciuitatis cum iudiciis principis certant The repetition of *aestimatio* from 127.4 is not a 'subconscious repetition' of the type discussed at 100.5n. but is essential to V.'s logic. It expresses a strong contrast while establishing the close connection of this ch. to the preceding subsection: 'Sejanus always reckoned himself below the estimation of others [127.4], but there was no doubt about the estimation which others made of his true worth [128.1].' For a somewhat similar use of repetition cf. Brink on Hor. *AP* 42.

V.'s sentiment, perhaps reminiscent of Sall. *C.* 9.2, is not baseless: public eulogies of Sejanus were recited, listing his virtues (Dio 57.21.3), and in the letters between Sejanus and Tiberius, already mentioned, Tiberius is reported to have said: 'id tantum aperiam, nihil esse tam excelsum quod non *uirtutes istae* tuusque in me animus mereantur, datoque tempore *uel in senatu uel in contione non reticebo*' (Tac. *A.* 4.40.7). V.'s phraseology has an authoritative ring (cf. e.g. Cic. *Brut.* 281 'cum honos sit praemium uirtutis iudicio studioque ciuium delatum ad aliquem', *Fam.* 1.9.14). For *uirtutum aestimatione* cf. Val. Max. 5.3.2*e*, Sen. *Ben.* 4.21.3.

quod optimum sit, esse nobilissimum This brief *sententia*, essential to V.'s argument, cannot be understood without an excursion into the somewhat confusing terminology of republican politics.

During the republic a family was called *nobilis* if at least one of its members had attained the consulship. *nobilitas* thus depended upon achieving the highest honour in the state: it was a term of political significance. In practice, however, the consuls were traditionally supplied by a relatively small group of aristocratic families, and since this group was almost self-perpetuating, it was exceedingly hard for any non-*nobilis* (*nouus homo*) to reach the consulship and so ennoble his own family. Moreover the *nobiles* regarded themselves as not only socially but also morally superior to the rest: they were the *boni*, the *optimi*, or (in the later language of party politics) the *optimates*. The *nobiles* regarded *uirtus* as their inalienable right and as something inseparable from their *nobilitas* (cf. Cic. *Phil.* 4.13 'uirtus...quam uobis tamquam hereditatem maiores uestri reliquerunt'); and it is clear from Cicero, who on several occasions describes the *nobilissimi* as being also *optimi* (*Rosc. Am.* 142, *Cael.* 72, *Phil.* 13.26 etc.), that the equation of heredity and moral rectitude continued till the end of the republic. To be *nobilis* was to be *optimus*.

Yet experience, esp. in the post-Gracchan era, showed that if a *nouus homo* had the right combination of ambition and both practical and moral qualities, he was able to rise to the consulship on his own merit, becoming automatically *nobilis*. Men like Cato, Marius and Cicero proved that *nobilitas* depended, not on family, but on what they described as *uirtus*. This view was quite contrary to the conventional assumptions of the aristocracy, wherefore *noui homines* emphasised it all the more, esp. since it could be expressed (like so many thoroughly Roman concepts) in the pseudo-intellectual language of Greek philosophy (evidence in E. Skard, *SO* 21 (1941), 98–102, but with mistaken conclusions). Hence Sallust records Marius as claiming that 'fortissumum quemque generosissimum' (*J.* 85.15: *generosus* = *nobilis*, as often; cf. Gelzer 38), and 'ex uirtute nobilitas coepit' (85.17). Cicero too, whatever he may have said on other occasions, wrote to Hirtius that 'nobilitas nihil aliud sit quam cognita uirtus' (*Ep. Hirt.* fr. 3 Watt). The *noui homines* staunchly contended that merit was the measure of *nobilitas*. To be *optimus* was to be truly *nobilis*.

There thus arose a contrast between the traditional *nobilitas* of the *nobiles*, dependent upon *genus*, and the *nobilitas* of the *noui homines*, attainable through *uirtus*. This contrast is to be seen in many passages of late republican literature (e.g. Cic. *Sest.* 136 'uosque adulescentes, et qui nobiles estis, ad maiorum uestrorum imitationem excitabo, et qui ingenio ac uirtute nobilitatem potestis consequi, ad eam rationem, in qua multi homines noui et honore et gloria floruerunt, cohortabor'), and the terminology impressed itself upon later writers. Thus Livy, writing about the earliest periods of Roman history for which such language was almost meaningless, represents Tanaquil as saying 'in nouo populo ubi omnia repentina atque ex uirtute nobilitas sit' (1.34.6), and Canuleius as arguing 'dum nullum fastiditur genus in quo eniteret uirtus, creuit imperium Romanum' (4.3.13).

In the present passage of V. we are given the familiar contentions of

Marius and Cicero. No one, on reading V.'s statement that what is most meritorious (*optimum*) is also the most noble (*nobilissimum*), could have failed to recall this background: each reader would instantly have been aware that this was preeminently the language of the *noui homines*. The connection with the argument in 127.1–2 could hardly have been made more explicit.

There is one conclusion which in my opinion should not be drawn from this discussion. We should not think that V. is here defending Tiberius' general policy of granting more responsibility to *equites* and *noui homines*. This thesis, which has been argued by Lana and others, was rightly refuted by Hellegouarc'h (1964), 679, who said that V. wrote the present section 'uniquement parce que Séjan est lui-même un homme nouveau, et non pas en vertu d'une position de principe qui le conduirait à soutenir l'action des *homines noui*'.

The bibliography on the terms discussed above is vast. A selection is as follows: H. Strasburger on *nobiles* (*RE* 17.785–91), *noui homines* (*RE* 17.1223–8) and *optimates* (*RE* 18.773–98); Syme, *RR*; Wirszubski; Earl; Hellegouarc'h, *VL*; Gelzer; Wiseman, esp. 107ff. on 'the ideology of *nouitas*'.

illi antiqui ⟨qui⟩ ante primum bellum Punicum Following an earlier suggestion of Fröhlich, Halm rightly supplied *qui* (for such haplography cf. Kritz cvii–cix). The proposals of Ellis (*illi qui ante bellum*) and even of Bolaffi (*illi qui primi ante bellum*) are wrongly influenced by an excessive adherence to the nonsense in A.

Ti. Coruncanium *RE* 4.1663–4 = Coruncanius 3 (Münzer). He was cos. 280, dict. 246, and pont. max. *c.* 254, the first plebeian to attain the honour (next n.). He is quite a common *exemplum*, usually of old fashioned virtue, but sometimes (e.g. Cic. *Sull.* 23) of the 'humble birth' topos: cf. Litchfield 50 and n. 2, Wiseman 108 and n. 1.

ad principale extulere fastigium On the significance and unique importance of the office of pont. max. see Wiseman 169f. For similar expressions cf. 1.11.6, 30.3, 40.4.

128.2 et ⟨qui⟩ equestri loco natum P reads *et equestri*, A *et eque aequestri*. Fröhlich rightly believed that V. wrote *et qui equestri*, but he wrongly saw the traces of this reading in A, which, in common with other scholars, he thought to be a more trustworthy guide than P. In fact A's reading is no more than yet another instance of Amerbach's habit of transcribing part of a word, stopping, then transcribing the whole word: sometimes he stops because he had begun to transcribe wrongly, sometimes for no apparent reason at all; sometimes he crosses out the partially transcribed word, sometimes (as here) not. For examples of this habit see above, pp. 89–92. Thus, while I have printed Fröhlich's *qui*, I have indicated that the word is a supplement. Rhenanus failed to supply *qui* because he had already failed to supply *qui* at 1 above, where the word was clearly missing either in (M) or (R) or of course both.

Sp. Caruilium *RE* 3.1630 = Carvilius 9 (Münzer). He was cos. in 293, again in 272, and cens. in (?) 289. Unlike Coruncanius, Sp. Carvilius is apparently obscure, not mentioned by Cicero or Val. Max. Why is he mentioned here? The answer has been ingeniously supplied by Syme (1956), esp. 262–5. Carvilius had built a shrine to Fors Fortuna (Liv. 10.46.14), the 'most patently plebeian of the Roman deities'. This goddess assumed particular significance in Tiberius' reign: not only did the senate vote for the erection of a temple to her in A.D. 16 (Tac. *A.* 2.41.1), but Sejanus had in his house a famous statue of her which had earlier been in the temple of Fortuna in the Forum Boarium (Dio 58.7.2–3). This latter fact may illustrate Sejanus' anxiety to gain popular support, something in which he resembled Tiberius himself, although neither was very successful in the event (Yavetz 109–13). V.'s mention of Carvilius here is a subtly oblique reminder of the *nouus homo* who had in an important manner contributed to the cult of a plebeian deity whose appeal in the reign of Tiberius had undoubted significance.

M. Catonem M. Porcius Cato, *RE* 22.108–65 = Porcius 9 (Helm). He was a familiar example of the topos under discussion: cf. e.g. Val. Max. 3.4.6; Litchfield 33; Wiseman 108ff.

nouum etiam Tusculo, urbis inquilinum 'also a new man from Tusculum, not a native of the city of Rome'. Suitably for his theme, V. is being archaistic. *nouus* (subst.) = *nouus homo* is rare but was a mannerism of Sallust (*J.* 8.1, 63.7, 65.5): *Tusculo* is an abl. of origin, a fairly regular usage in early Latin (e.g. Plaut. *Asin.* 499 'Periphanes Rhodo', cf. Bennet, *Synt.* 2.290; Löfstedt, *Synt.* 1.297) but rare later (cf. Meusel on Caes. *BC* 1.24.4; also K–S 1.476 (but the ex. at Cic. *Clu.* 36 is invalid), L–H–S 105). The second part of the phrase recalls Catiline's famous 'inquilinus urbis Romae', applied to Cicero (Sall. *C.* 31.7, cf. App. *BC* 2.2.5).

Mummiumque Achaicum For L. Mummius cf. *RE* 16.1195–206 = Mummius 7*a* (Münzer). At 1.13.2 V. says of him: 'nec quisquam ex nouis hominibus prior Mummio cognomen uirtute partum uindicauit'. His father may in fact have been a praetor (see Wiseman 3 and n. 2, saying that V. has 'extended the concept of *nouitas* to include men of notable *uirtus*'), but he could be used as an *exemplum* of the 'humble birth' theme, cf. Litchfield 33. *prouexere* below is a technical word for elevation to honours (Liv. 39.40.5 Val. Max. 8.5.1, Sen. *Ben.* 3.30.3, Plin. *Ep.* 10.13 etc.).

128.3 C. Marium *RE* Suppl. 6.1363–425 = Marius 14 (Weynand). He was a familiar example of the present topos, cf. Sen. *Contr.* 1.6.4; Litchfield 51 and n. 4; Wiseman 108, 113, 240, no. 248. Note also T. F. Carney, 'Cicero's picture of Marius', *Wien. Stud.* 73 (1960), 83–122. For *ignotus* used of ignoble persons or families, below, cf. Cic. *Rep.* 1 'M. Catoni, homini ignoto et nouo', Liv. 2.5.6, Val. Max. 9.7.2. The description which V. applies to Marius below, *Romani nominis...principem*, had already been used of Pompey at 53.2.

Tullio PA read *Fuluio*; 'palmari coniectura ac nemini dubia Lipsius restituit *Tullio*' (Kritz).

paene adsentatione sua 'almost on his personal commendation alone'. The noun is usually pejorative ('adulation', as at 82.4, 102.3), but not here or at Petr. 17.1; cf. *TLL* 2.853.52–6.

quibus uellet principatus conciliaret The first five *maiores* listed by V. were noteworthy for emerging from humble origins to the heights of constitutional power (cos., pont. max., etc.); with the introduction of Cicero, however, V. changes ground to mention those who, even within the framework of the republic, achieved power which lay outside the constitution. In Cicero's case this meant, according to V., the authority to secure positions of prominence (*principatus*) for whomsoever he pleased. Cicero is thus an apposite precedent for Sejanus who, according to Tacitus, 'neque senatorio ambitu abstinebat clientes suos honoribus aut prouinciis ornandi' (*A.* 4.2.3). Sejanus' success at this doubtless caused much contemporary ill will, but it was an aspect of his career which could still be seen as 'official' or 'Tiberian' policy: 'ut quisque Seiano intimus, ita ad Caesaris amicitiam ualidus' (Tac. *A.* 6.8.4). The most prominent example is Blaesus, his uncle, made governor of Africa (*A.* 3.35). See H. Bird, 'L. Aelius Sejanus and his political significance', *Latomus* 28 (1969), 61ff.

For V.'s expression cf. Caes. *BG* 1.3.7 '(se) illis regna conciliaturum confirmat'.

quique nihil Asinio Pollioni negauerunt quod nobilissimis...consequendum foret Whereas the *nobiles* had to strive (*consequendum*) with the maximum of effort (*summo cum sudore*) for everything they achieved, the implication is that identical honours fell into Pollio's lap (*nihil...negauerunt*) on account of his personal merit. Thus Pollio is seen as an excellent precedent for Sejanus who, despite his humble beginnings, was granted unprecedented honours by Tiberius. In addition, Pollio had been an outstanding example of loyalty (63.3) and discretion (86.3).

For Pollio cf. *RE* 2.2.1589–602 = Asinius 25 (Groebe); Wiseman 215, no. 50. The expression *summo cum sudore* appears to be a variant on *plurimo sudore et sanguine*, 'the stock phrase for lauding a great achievement' (Ogilvie on Liv. 2.48.2; cf. Otto 334). For *profecto* below, summing up the previous string of relative clauses and at the same time emphasising the subsequent *sententia*, cf. Sall. *J.* 4.4, *Pan. Lat.* 3.10.1, 13.3.

ei plurimum esse tribuendum *plurimum* means what it says: if a man is possessed of *uirtus*, he should be admitted to the top in any capacity. In the light of the two final *exempla* V. has moved away from the careful language of 1 above.

128.4 *Nouus homo*: conclusion

It is clear from the phraseology with which this subsection begins (*haec naturalis exempli imitatio*) that the preceding argument in 1–3 has been a calculated preparation for the conclusion which we are now given. This is a pattern already observed in the previous ch. (see above). Yet the present section has an extra function in bringing together, at the close of the whole discussion, the strands of the two main arguments which have been advanced. In 127.1–2 V. discussed political expediency, in 128.1–3 the relationship of morality to politics: he now concludes by saying 'ut quod *usu optimum* intellegit, id...', where *usu* refers back to the argument of the first section (cf. 127.2 'quod *usu* necessarium est') and *optimum* to the argument of the penultimate section (128.1 'quod *optimum* sit'). Thus just as 127.1–2 and 128.1–3 were themselves miniature examples of circular composition, so the entire treatment of Sejanus has come round in a circular movement, assisted by the repetition of two key words. The ring composition unifies the whole discussion and emphasises still further its total detachment from the surrounding narrative (see too above, p. 247).

128.4 ad iuuanda uero onera principis...senatumque et populum Romanum eo perduxit The wording is not unlike Tac. *A.* 4.2.3 'ut *socium laborum* non modo in sermonibus sed *apud patres et populum* celebraret'. For *onera* cf. 127.3n.; for *exempli imitatio* above cf. Cic. *Flacc.* 24 (F.).

propulit The required sense is 'impel', a meaning which the paradosis *protulit* can never have (despite L&S s.v. IIF, whose instances are invalid: at Cic. *Sull.* 64 read *propulisset*; and Plin. *Pan.* 48.3 is different, cf. *Ep.* 1.13.1). For the confusion of *p* and *t* cf. 94.1.

eo perduxit ut... BA have *produxit*, but *eo perducere ut* is the usual construction, cf. 96.1 (*in hoc*), Nep. *Dion.* 5.6, Planc. in Cic. *Fam.* 10.7.2, to which F. adds Sen. *Clem.* 1.13.2 (see too K–S 2.219*e*). *per-* and *pro-* are of course often confused (e.g. 96.2). At *Rhet. Herenn.* 1.4 *producere* is used differently, of progress made in a discussion.

in tutelam securitatis suae V. concludes with a characteristically propagandist expression: for *tutela* cf. 105.3n., for *securitas* cf. 103.4n. R. A. Bauman (*Impietas in Principem* (1974), 123–4) rightly says that we cannot tell whether V.'s phrase here is technical; but his observation that V. 'is expressing his admiration for Sejanus' systematic exploitation of the *lex maiestatis* in somewhat exaggerated terms' seems to me utterly without foundation.

Sumner 286 has recently argued that V.'s statement here, taken in context, 'undoubtedly refers to the promotion of the Praetorian Prefect to the consulship, which he was to come from Capri to assume at Rome on 1 January A.D. 31'. Sumner supports his theory by observing that each of the precedents mentioned in 1–3 were consuls.[1] Yet I cannot believe that V. is here defending a different moment in Sejanus' career from that which is defended at 127.1–4 (*contra* Steffen 191). The whole discussion appears to centre on one issue (though treated from the different viewpoints of Sejanus' actual power and his equestrian status in chh. 127 and 128 respectively), and the language is the same in both places: 127.3 'principalium onerum adiutorem', 128.4 'ad iuuanda onera principis'. And since we know from the independent evidence of Tacitus and Dio that Tiberius regularly referred to Sejanus as his *adiutor* (127.3n.), and since *adiutor* is the term upon which V. insists throughout ch. 127 (3 times), it is reasonable to assume that it is this honour which V. is defending at 128.4. I therefore believe that the present discussion was not composed in the light of Sejanus' impending consulship; it would have been appropriate at any moment from A.D. 23 onwards, that being the date at which Tiberius began referring to Sejanus as his *adiutor* (Woodman (1975), 301–2). Steffen 191ff. has argued that chh. 127–8, taken in conjunction with 131.2, belong to A.D. 29/30 and anticipate the nomination of Sejanus as Tiberius' successor.[2] But Sumner has shown that such an interpretation of 131.2 is mistaken (see n.).

---

[1] 'It could be held that V. manages to hint at more than the consulship for Seianus, but it will not be denied that he alludes to the consulship specifically' (Sumner 286 n. 157). While in fact I firmly deny the latter part of this statement, it will be clear from 128.3nn. that I readily accept the former part. Sejanus' position as *adiutor* carried more *auctoritas* than any of the conventional offices traditionally arrogated by the *nobiles*.

[2] Steffen 193–5 tries to support this thesis by suggesting, in the light of the inconsistency of 129.1, that chh. 127–8 are a later addition by V. to his narrative, intended to defend the imminent elevation of Sejanus to this unprecedented position (see above, p. 247).

aduocet The word has suitable connotations of 'helping', cf. *TLL* 1.894.70ff.

129–130.2 THE ACHIEVEMENTS OF TIBERIUS' REIGN

V. now proceeds to justify, by individual examples (129.1 *singula*), some of the claims which he made in ch. 126. The most important of these concern foreign policy, which, having been mentioned at 126.3–4, now takes up almost the whole of ch. 129.[1] The nature of Tiberius' foreign policy was well known, 'destinata retinens, consiliis et astu res externas moliri, arma procul habere' (Tac. *A.* 6.32.1). Tacitus selects two episodes in particular to illustrate it, Tiberius' relations with Maroboduus and with the king of Thrace (2.64.1–2 'laetiore Tiberio quia pacem sapientia firmauerat quam si bellum per acies confecisset. igitur Rhescuporim quoque, Thraeciae regem, astu adgreditur'), but his judgement on Tiberius' policy as a whole is one of disappointment: there were no great wars to challenge the historian's art or stimulate the imagination of the citizens (*A.* 4.32.2). Like Tacitus, V. chooses as examples of Tiberius' policy his treatment of the king of Thrace and of Maroboduus; but unlike Tacitus (*A.* 2.65.1), he uses these episodes to defend the emperor's position. Indeed, in his allusion to Maroboduus, V. appears to echo the speech which Tacitus reports Tiberius as having delivered in the senate (129.3n.): this is something which happens on two other discernible occasions in ch. 129 (there could well be others), from which we must conclude that V., in writing these last chh. of his history, was referring back to senatorial debates which he had attended himself.

There was of course a certain amount of campaigning during the reign, for instance on the northern frontier and in Africa. In mentioning these incidents V. naturally admits the attractions of military achievement (e.g. 129.2 'respondente cultu triumphi rerum magnitudini'), but firmly points out the speed with which the campaigns were conducted (129.3 *mira celeritate*, 4 *breui*). It was only by these methods – by diplomacy or (failing that) by swift action – that the citizens of the empire could properly enjoy the benefits of the *pax augusta* already described at 126.3–4.

129.1 proposita quasi uniuersa principatus Ti. Caesaris ⟨imagine⟩ Without supplement this abl. absolute is incomplete. Rhenanus, followed by Burer, supplied *forma* after *Caesaris*, arguing that the word had been wrongly transposed from here to the following sentence, which ends, nonsensically, *formam euocauit*. This argument has attracted many edd., but it cannot be right since *formam* in the following sentence needs to be retained, albeit

[1] Steffen discusses Tiberius' foreign policy at some length under both ch. 126 (102ff.) and ch. 129 (114ff.).

slightly altered (see below).[1] We thus still require a noun to complete the abl. abs.: *forma* is perhaps a possibility on its own merits (cf. Tac. *A.* 13.4.2 'formam futuri principatus'), but many other supplements have been proposed (cf. the list given by L. Alfonsi, *Aevum* 29 (1955), 580). Although we cannot know what the truth should be, the expression at 89.6 *uniuersam imaginem principatus eius* (i.e. of Augustus, cf. Flor. *praef.* 3 'totam eius imaginem') led Friebel to emend *quasi* to *imagine,* and T. Sinko (*Eos* 20 (1914–15), 113) to retain *quasi* but supply *imagine* after *Caesaris.* On the whole I prefer Sinko's suggestion. The *proposita imago* is ch. 126 (see above, pp. 234 and 247).

singula recenseamus 'let us recount details' (for this sense of the verb cf. Ov. *Her.* 9.105, Apul. *Apol.* 51.13, *Met.* 9.26.1; also Curt. 3.3.6). V. has in fact already expressed an inability to recount details (126.1): but the *recusatio* was doubtless inserted for its immediate panegyrical effect (see n.), since V. elsewhere likes to give both a general survey and a detailed account (38.1 '...ut quae partibus notauimus, facilius simul uniuersa conspici possint', cf. 1.14.1). This method of approaching one's subject matter from two different angles is closely paralleled in Suet. *Aug.* 9 'proposita uitae eius uelut summa, partes singillatim neque per tempora sed per species exsequar, quo distinctius demonstrari cognoscique possint', where Casaubon quotes V. At first sight this parallel might be thought to support those who have described V. as a 'biographer' of Tiberius (see above, pp. 28f.). But Leo 241 has rightly pointed out the differences between Suetonius and V.: 'bei Sueton das *singillatim* den Sinn eines genauen Eingehens auf alles Einzelne hat, während Vell. nur das Einzelne herzählt.' And besides, such an approach is by no means the exclusive province of the biographer: cf. e.g. Tac. *A.* 4.4.3 '*percensuitque* (Tiberius) cursim numerum legionum et quas prouincias tutarentur. quod *mihi quoque* exsequendum reor...[6.1] congruens crediderim *recensere* ceteras quoque r.p. partes...'.

qua ille prudentia Rhascupolim, interemptorem... 'L'entusiastica enumerazione delle buone opere di Tiberio...è suscettibile di critica per il tono eccessivamente panegiristico che assume, ma esaminata punto per punto risulta veritiera nelle sue linee essenziali' (Paladini 476); cf. also the apposite remarks of M. L. W. Laistner, *The greater Roman historians* (1963 edn), 110. For a comparison of V.'s brief reference with Tacitus' account of the episode (*A.* 2.64ff.) see Steffen 114–16, concluding that 'das Schwer-

[1] Stegmann wrongly states that Burer found the *formam* of the second sentence in the margin of (M); but Burer is in fact discussing *Rhenanus*' marginal note on *formam euocauit,* which, as he remarks, contradicts Rhenanus' previous note on ⟨*Caesaris*⟩ *forma.*

gewicht liegt in seinem Bericht auf der "prudentia" des Kaisers, und das Lob, das dieser prudentia zuteil wird, besteht zweifellos zu Recht'. For Tiberius' *prudentia* cf. also 115.5n.

Since a similar spelling of Rhascupolis is found in some MSS of Suetonius (*Tib.* 37.4, see Ihm's edn), and since the name is spelled inconsistently on coins and inscriptions (see Walther on Tac. *A.* 2.64.2, Rietra on Suet. loc. cit.), I have retained the form found in the paradosis. Rhascupolis was the brother of Rhoemetalces (cf. 112.4): for him cf. *RE* 6A.447–9 (Lenk); for his nephew Cotys cf. *RE* 11.2.1554 = Kotys 8 (Kahrstedt); *PIR*² 2.381, no. 1554. *interemptor* is not a common word and occurs in Latin first here and at Val. Max. 6.1.2 (Ungewitter 10); for *consortisque*...*imperii* below cf. Tac. *H.* 3.75.2, Suet. *Otho* 8.1.

Romam euocauit The paradosis *formam euocauit* makes no sense (see above): Ursinus therefore made the easy change to *Romam*. This suggestion, accepted by Ellis and Bolaffi, is surely right since it was to Rome that Rhascupolis was actually summoned in A.D. 19 (cf. Tac. *A.* 2.67, Suet. loc. cit.). For the expression cf. Cic. *Verr.* 2.1.85 'Pericles Ephesius...Romam euocatus est' (*euocare* is almost a technical term for summoning someone from a distance and/or to justice: *TLL* 5.2.1055–7).

Flacci Pomponii consularis, uiri nati ad omnia... L. Pomponius Flaccus, *RE* Suppl. 14.439–40 = Pomponius 46*a* (Eck). I have ventured to punctuate after *consularis* in the light of V.'s great fondness for *uir* used in apposition: cf. e.g. 69.1 'C. Trebonium consularem...uirum aduersus merita Caesaris ingratissimum' (where *consularis* is used absolutely, as here and at 112.4 and perhaps 2.2.3), 114.5, 116.2, 3, 125.5 'singulari adiutore in eo negotio usus Iunio Blaeso, uiro nescias utiliore in castris an meliore in toga'; and also Cic. *Sest.* 50 'uirum...natum ad salutem huius imperii', Aufid. Bass. fr. 2 'uir natus ad r.p. salutem'. Compare also 102.1 'uirum... genitum'. Yet V. apparently writes *consularem uirum* as a phrase at 24.1 and *praetoriis uiris* at 69.2; and cf. 116.1.

omnia quae recte facienda sunt Pomponius is thus a living example of the effectiveness of Tiberius' reign as given at 126.3 'recte faciendi omnibus aut incussa uoluntas aut imposita necessitas'. Like L. Piso (98.3n., cf. Sen. *Ep.* 83.14) he was one of Tiberius' drinking companions (Suet. *Tib.* 42.1). For *simplici uirtute* below cf. Sen. *Ep.* 95.13.

merentis semper quam captantis gloriam 'always deserving rather than seeking *gloria*'. Misled by the appearance of *semper* and the omission of *magis*, Orelli proposed *merentis semper, numquam captantis*. Yet for *semper* cf. 116.3 'uir...priscam grauitatem semper humanitate temperans'; and

Ruhnken rightly observed that *magis* is often omitted in comparisons, e.g. Val. Max. 1.1 *ext.* 2 'factum Masinissae animo quam Punico sanguini conueniens' (for such ellipse cf. K–S 2.463, L–H–S 593f.). I can therefore see no fault in the paradosis. For *gloriam mereri* cf. Liv. 2.1.3, Val. Max. 5.1 *ext.* 1, Plin. *Ep.* 3.11.4; for *gloriam captare* cf. Ov. *Tr.* 5.1.75, Sen. *Ben.* 4.11.1.

129.2 non ut princeps * et causas pressius audit** Two main lines of approach have been used to elucidate this sentence. (1) Some edd. have believed *pressius* to be wrong and have emended the word: *praesens* (Lipsius), *Drusi Libonis* (Madvig 2.313). Madvig's suggestion is unlikely to be right since Libo Drusus is mentioned below at 130.3. Lipsius' suggestion has the support of Tac. *A.* 1.75.1 (quoted above, 126.2n.), but I do not believe that *pressius* is wrong; on the contrary, it is an uncommon word (and thus unlikely to have been a scribal invention) but one which exactly suits a legal context such as this (cf. Cic. *Fin.* 4.24, *Tusc.* 4.14, Sen. *Dial.* 9.1.14, Reid on Cic. *Acad.* 2.29). (2) If *pressius* is right, we must agree with those other edd. who have placed a lacuna after *princeps* or *et*: e.g. *et* ⟨*Caesar*⟩ (ed. Bipont.). Yet another question at once presents itself. Is *pressius* an example of comparative for positive (cf. Wölfflin 174ff.), or is it a genuine comparative? The latter is perhaps more likely in view of the following *quam celeriter* in the paradosis. The whole sentence might originally have read thus: 'cum quanta grauitate ut senator et iudex, non ut princeps ⟨et dux quaestionibus praeest⟩, et causas pressius audit quam ⟨seuerius! quam⟩ celeriter...' ('with what gravity, as senator and judge not as emperor and ruler, does he preside over trials and hear cases more with scrupulousness than with severity': for the comparative *seuerius* after *quam* cf. K–S 2.474*b*). But the whole matter is extremely uncertain, and I have simply marked lacunae in what (in my opinion) are the two most likely places.

quam celeriter ingratum * et noua molientem oppressit Unless we accept Madvig's emendation of *pressius* (last n.), it is clear from the acc. forms that a person's name has been omitted somewhere in the sentence. The most popular suggestion has been Libo Drusus, but this is unlikely in view of what was said about Madvig's emendation above. Vossius suggested *Clementem* before *ingratum* (for him see Tac. *A.* 2.39f., Suet. *Tib.* 25), although such a supplement should perhaps rather be placed after *molientem* (parablepsy). Better is Krause's supplement *Archelaum*, although the possibility of parablepsy suggests that the name should be supplied after, rather than before, *ingratum*. Archelaus was as good an ex. of Tiberius' foreign policy as Rhascupolis and Maroboduus (cf. Suet. *Tib.* 37.4), he was supposed to have had treasonable designs (Dio 57.17.4 ὡς καὶ νεωτερίζοντά τι), and he more than qualifies for the epithet *ingratus* since he once owed his acquittal in a court case to the young Tiberius (Suet. *Tib.* 8). Krause's suggestion is a serious possibility; my only doubt is whether *oppressit* describes with sufficient accuracy the treatment Archelaus received from Tiberius and the senate: cf. Tac. *A.* 2.42.3, Dio loc. cit. On account of this slight doubt I have, perhaps too timorously, simply marked a lacuna.

For such words as *ingratus* used in a political context cf. Hellegouarc'h, *VL* 202ff.; for *noua molientem* cf. Tac. *A.* 12.32.1, Sil. 2.149 (also Cic. *Rep.* 1.31).

praeceptis instructum Germanicum As Steffen remarks, V. sees Germanicus solely as an extension of Tiberius' own *Kriegskunst* (122–3; so too Timpe, *Germanicus* 16f.); yet there is no doubting the honorific manner in which Germanicus himself is described in this section. Steffen also suggests that V.'s reference to Germanicus' *honores* (below) is an illustration of the point which V. made at 126.3 'honorantur recta...[4] honor dignis paratissimus': this is of course in the nature of the present ch. (see above pp. 234 and 263). The events to which V. alludes here and below are Germanicus' recall to Rome in A.D. 17, his subsequent triumph, and mission to the eastern provinces with *maius imperium* (cf. *quanto cum honore* at 3 below). See in general Seager 87–9 and 96ff., with further refs.

For *praeceptis instructum* cf. Sen. *Ep.* 13.1, Petron. 140.2; for *instructum... imbutumque* below cf. Tac. *D.* 19.5 (F.); for the metaphor of 'heaping up' in *exaggerauit* below cf. Cic. *Parad. Sto.* 41 'animo excelso et alto et uirtutibus exaggerato' (and compare Tac. *A.* 1.4.4 'congestos iuueni...triumphos', 14.53.2 'tantum honorum...in me cumulasti').

129.3 cum id senatu auctore facere potuit V. must be referring to incidents such as that described at Tac. *A.* 1.75.3–4 when, after Propertius Celer had been given financial support by Tiberius, the emperor 'temptantis eadem alios probare causas senatui iussit' (a passage which invalidates the conclusion to which Steffen 126 comes in his discussion of this matter). Cf. also e.g. Tac. *A.* 2.37.1, Dio 57.10.3. This is an example of Tiberius' policy of restoring to the senate its *maiestas* (126.2). Tiberius' generosity towards the senate here and towards the people above (*quotiens...congiariis*, cf. Tac. *A.* 2.42.1, 3.29.3, Suet. *Tib.* 54.1, but note the scepticism of Yavetz 107) is to be seen in terms of his *liberalitas*, for which cf. Kloft 86–7 (who in n. 7 remarks that much of what V. says in 129.3–130.2 may be paralleled in Menand. rhet.'s prescriptions for panegyric).

ut...neque honestam paupertatem pateretur dignitate destitui V.'s wording is almost exactly echoed in Tacitus' account of an instance of Tiberius' *liberalitas* (*A.* 2.48.1–3): 'magnificam in publicum largitionem auxit Caesar haud minus grata liberalitate, quod bona Aem. Musae...

Aem. Lepido...et Pantulei...hereditatem...tradidit M. Seruilio... nobilitatem utriusque pecunia iuuandam praefatus...ceterum ut *honestam* innocentium *paupertatem* leuauit...'. The italicised phrase is not found elsewhere before V. and Tac. (later in Amm. 24.3.5), and it seems to me highly likely that both authors are alluding to an actual remark which Tiberius made in the senate: V. presumably reproduces it because he heard it himself, Tacitus because he found it in the *acta senatus*. See below on two other such echoes.

The *aabb* alliteration of *paupertatem pateretur dignitate destitui* is typically Velleian, cf. 1.4.2, 1.9.4, 25.4 'tabula testatur aerea intra aedem', 120.6. For the use of *inuitare* above cf. e.g. *OLD* s.v. 7.

pace maiestatis eius dixerim Freitag notes that V. has similar parentheses at 1.7.4 and 1.17.3; for V.'s opinion of Maroboduus cf. 108.2 and nn. The king's capitulation seems to have been in A.D. 18 (Seager 94–5). For *ministro et adiutore* above cf. 41.2, Plin. *Ep*. 6.9.2.

uelut serpentem This simile has been prepared for by *inhaerentem* above, the *mot juste* for clinging creatures (Cic. *ND* 2.100 'beluarum partim ad saxa natiuis testis inhaerentium', Apul. *Met*. 1.4 'baculo...serpentem... inhaerere'), and is rounded off by *medicamentis* below (for *medicamenta* used in overcoming reptiles cf. Cels. 5.27.3 'stupente ea (colubra) quod per quaedam medicamenta circulatores faciunt'; Ruhnken quotes Solin. 30.17 (p. 133 Mommsen) '(draconibus) obiiciunt gramina medicata'). For *serpens* used in metaphor or simile cf. e.g. Cic. *Har. Resp*. 55, *Vatin*. 4; for the metaphorical use of *inhaereo* cf. Flor. 1.22.41, 57 'inhaerentem atque incubantem Italiae' (F.).

abstrusam terra The paradosis reads *terrae*. Though there is no clear ex. elsewhere in Latin of *abstrusus* + dat., that does not mean the construction is impossible (cf. Virg. *Aen*. 2.553 'lateri capulo tenus abdidit ensem'). A case can be made for a 'final-locative' dative, *terrae* being perhaps one of the commonest words used in this way (cf. Landgraf, *ALL* 8 (1893), 72); but I am not sufficiently convinced by the evidence to reject Cludius' very easy change to *terra* here. See also Goodyear on *Aetna* 138. P. Thomas (1921), 21, suggested *abstrusam terrae ⟨latebris⟩ salubribus*..., which is supported by Tac. *A*. 2.45.3 'Hercyniae latebris defensum' (of Maroboduus).

salubribus consiliorum suorum medicamentis Ellis follows Ruhnken in deleting *consiliorum suorum* as being dittography from *qua ui consiliorum suorum* above. Yet the phrase is explicable either as one of V.'s many subconscious repetitions (100.5n.) or as evidence of V.'s desire to stress Tiberius' diplomacy (for such repetitions cf. Löfstedt, *Synt*. 2.174 n. 2). For *salubribus* ...*medicamentis* cf. Liv. 8.18.8.

ut honorate ita secure continet The paradosis reads *ut*...*nec*, which was defended by Baehrens 311 and Paessens on the grounds that *secure* can mean 'negligently' (cf. Plin. *Ep.* 1.4.3) and that *nec* here = 'auch nicht'. Yet they fail to take proper account of the fact that, according to Tac. *A.* 2.63.2, Tiberius wrote to Maroboduus saying that '*tutam* ei *honoratamque* sedem in Italia fore, si maneret'. It may be inferred from the following section ot Tacitus' account (3 'apud senatum disseruit') that Tiberius related the contents of his letter to the senate; and the close similarity of Tacitus' phraseology to that of V. suggests that both authors are recalling an official utterance of Tiberius, as also above (*honestam paupertatem*) and below (*ante*... *nuntius*).[1] If so, it is highly unlikely that V. would use *secure* in a sense which is opposite to that of *tutam*: it is far more reasonable to assume that *secure* here has its normal meaning of 'securely', in which case *nec* cannot be right.

The obvious emendation of *nec* is *sic* (Burman), but Novák (1906), 291–2, pointed out that V. never uses *ut*...*sic*: he much prefers *ut*...*ita* (23 times, according to Paessens). Novák thus argued that *nec secure* arose from a scribal correction of an earlier error *sec secure* (dittography), and that *ita* had dropped out. Whether or not this was in fact the genesis of the error, I nevertheless agree with Novák that *ita* is more likely to be correct than any of the other suggestions which have been made.

The adverb *honorate* occurs first here in V.; comparative adv. at Val. Max. 5.1.11, superlative adv. at id. 2.10.2, 5.1 *ext.* 4 (Ungewitter 10, Lundberg 44).

Sacrouiro Floroque Iulio For Julius Sacrovir cf. *RE* 10.1.796–8 = Iulius 452 (Stein); *PIR*² 4.267f., no. 529; for Julius Florus cf. *RE* 10.1.589 = Iulius 238 (Stein); *PIR*² 4.214, no. 315. Their rebellion was in A.D. 21 (Tac. *A.* 3.40–6). For *quantae molis bellum* above cf. 95.1n.; for *bellum ciente* above cf. 54.2, 75.1, Liv. 5.37.2, Tac. *H.* 3.41.3 and Heubner ad loc.; for *uirtute compressit* below cf. *SHA Tac.* 13.2.

ante p. R. uicisse se quam bellare cognosceret nuntiosque periculi uictoriae praecederet nuntius Each of these conceits may be paralleled in writers whose aim is to emphasise the *celeritas bellandi* of the person(s) with whom they are dealing: cf. e.g. Liv. 2.64.6 'dum se putant uincere uicere', 3.18.9 'prius uicit quam pugnare sine duce sentiret', 44.32.5 'hoc unum bellum prius perpetratum quam coeptum Romae auditum est', Curt. 3.5.6, 7.4.14, Sen. *Dial.* 3.11.2, *Ben.* 6.31.9, Flor. 1.18.6, 1.29.2 'denique hoc

1 Baehrens in fact never mentions the Tacitus passage, while Paessens denies that both V. and Tac. derive 'irgendwie aus gemeinsamer Quelle'; but he was naturally unaware of the other occasions when the two authors apparently echo Tiberian phraseology.

bellum ante finitum est quam geri Romae nuntiaretur', 2.13.63, Just. 11.2.10, *Pan. Lat.* 10.5.4; C. v. Morawski, *Eos* 5 (1898–9), 5; Wilhelm 7 Anm. 2; D. Korzeniewski, *Die Zeit des Q. Curt. Rufus* (1959), 61f. For *celeritas* (which V. couples with *uirtus*, cf. also Cic. *Phil.* 10.11, *Flacc.* 29) as a topic of panegyric cf. W. S. Maguinness, *Hermathena* 47 (1932), 55: for some exs. cf. Cic. *Leg. Man.* 34f., 40f., *Marc.* 5, *Pan. Lat.* 8.6.1, 12.5.5, 12.15.3.

Yet despite the conventional nature of the wording, I agree with Ruhnken that V. here 'expressisse uidetur literas Tiberii, de hoc ipso bello ad senatum scriptas': Tacitus describes Tiberius' report of the war as if it contained phraseology not unlike that which V. uses (*A.* 3.47.1 'Tiberius *ortum patratumque* bellum senatu scripsit'), and I think we have here another example of both historians' echoing the emperor's own words (*contra* Stein, *RE* 10.1.797).

129.4 bellum Africum...breui sepultum est The war in fact lasted 8 years (A.D. 17–24, cf. Tac. *A.* 2.52, 4.23ff.). Steffen points out (138–40) that Tiberius believed the war to be over in A.D. 22 (Tac. *A.* 3.74.4); but that hardly explains V.'s *breui*. For *bellum...sepultum* cf. 75.1, 89.3, 90.1, Cic. *Leg. Man.* 30, *Aetna* 204, *Octau.* 524, Amm. 26.9.9.

130.1 Quanta suo suorumque nomine exstruxit opera It came to be expected of emperors that they should demonstrate their *liberalitas* and *munificentia* by the erection of public buildings (Kloft 115ff.). Tiberius, however, notoriously failed in this respect (Tac. *A.* 6.45.1, Suet. *Tib.* 47), and both Seager (140) and Kloft (115) criticise V. for allegedly implying here that Tiberius erected numerous public buildings. But V. writes *quanta*, not *quot*: he is referring to splendour, not number.

Seager and Kloft also imagine that the *opera* to which V. refers are those which he mentions in the next two sentences, the temple to Augustus and Pompey's theatre, the two important building projects of the reign. But since neither edifice was dedicated before Tiberius' death (Tac. loc. cit.), and since we are expressly told that he did not place his own name upon the restored theatre of Pompey (Dio 57.10.2), it is hardly likely that *suo nomine opera* can be a reference to these two buildings. V. must here be alluding to other buildings, which in my opinion are the temple to Castor and Pollux and the temple of Concord. The former was dedicated in A.D. 6, the latter in A.D. 10, and both of them were dedicated in Tiberius' own name and that of his brother Drusus (cf. Suet. *Tib.* 20 'dedicauit et Concordiae aedem, item Pollucis et Castoris, *suo fratrisque nomine*', Dio 55.27.4 τὸ Διοσκόρειον ὁ Τιβέριος καθιερώσας οὐ τὸ ἑαυτοῦ μόνον ὄνομα αὐτῷ...ἀλλὰ καὶ τὸ ἐκείνου ἐπέγραψε, 56.25.1 τὸ Ὁμονοεῖον ὑπὸ τοῦ Τιβερίου καθιερώθη, καὶ αὐτῷ τό τε ἐκείνου ὄνομα καὶ τὸ τοῦ Δρούσου τοῦ ἀδελφοῦ αὐτοῦ καὶ τεθνηκότος ἐπεγράφη). It is of course true that neither building belongs actually to

Tiberius' reign, and to this extent V. is being misleading; but it is clear from Suetonius and Dio that both buildings were regarded as Tiberius' own responsibility.

In this note I have assumed that we should read, not the paradosis *sua*, but Acidalius' *suo*, which seems amply confirmed by the parallels in Suetonius and Dio. *suorum* is a rhetorical plural, frequent when allusion is being made to one's relatives (K–S 1.87, L–H–S 16).

quam pia munificentia superque humanam euecta fidem *munificentia* is another of Tiberius' virtues which V. has already mentioned in ch. 126 (4); *pia* is of course a natural adj. to use of Tiberius' relationship with Augustus (e.g. 105.3n.). For such expressions as *super humanam euecta fidem* cf. 41.1 'super humanam et naturam et fidem euectus', 51.3, 56.1 'quod humanam excedat fidem', Liv. 8.24.15, Val. Max. 3.2 *ext.* 24, 5.7 *ext.* 2, Plin. *NH* 34.38, Sen. *Ep.* 97.3, 114.1, Curt. 3.13.11, 5.6.8, Suet. *Diu. Iul.* 57 *Claud.* 29.3.

quam magnifico animi temperamento...munera absumpta igni restituit The fire was in A.D. 22 (Tac. *A.* 3.72.2). *temperamento* is an allusion to Tiberius' characteristic *moderatio* (122.1n.) and perhaps also to his *clementia*, a virtue which, as Steffen remarks (143 n. 1), Augustus too had shown in the case of Pompey's theatre (cf. *RG* 20.1 'Pompeium theatrum... refeci sine ulla inscriptione nominis mei').[1]

qui quicquid umquam...ueluti cognatum censet tuendum The paradosis *qui quidem quam* is clearly wrong, and Rhenanus' emendation highly credible: the postulated haplography is easy, and *u* and *e* are often confused (cf. e.g. 105.1; Kritz lxxxviii, xci); cf. perhaps 124.2 'cum quicquid tuendum non suscepisset, periturum uideret', where the sentiment and wording have something in common with this passage. I can find no precise parallel for the bold expression *ueluti cognatum*.

130.2 incenso monte Caelio A.D. 27 (Tac. *A.* 4.64, Suet. *Tib.* 48.1): see too Kloft 119. For *iacturae...succurrit* below cf. Claud. *Rufin.* 2.201 'succurrere damnis' (F.).

sine trepidatione dilectus 'without the fear one normally associates with a levy'. On this sentence cf. P. A. Brunt, *Italian manpower* (1971), 414, 637; on the precise meaning of *dilectus* and *supplementum*, ib. 635–8.

---

1 Kloft 87 notes that Tiberius' *liberalitas* to men 'omnis ordinis' at 2 below also has an Augustan precedent (Suet. *Aug.* 41.1 'liberalitatem omnibus ordinibus...exhibuit').

130.3–5 THE DISAPPOINTMENTS OF TIBERIUS' REIGN

After surveying in detail the achievements of the reign, V. now concludes the narrative part of his work by enumerating some of its disappointments, both political and social. The subject matter is delicate, and V.'s uneasiness apparent: his account is perhaps more revealing in what it omits (e.g. Tiberius' departure to Capri in A.D. 26) than in what it includes. Even so, this brief section, with its tale of treason and thwarted hopes, is the last thing that might have been expected from a historian as devoted to Tiberius as V. It is a striking deviation from the traditional pattern (see above, pp. 53–4) and more than sufficiently depressing to warrant the *uotum* with which the book concludes (below, pp. 275ff.).

130.3 Si aut natura patitur aut mediocritas recipit hominum The expression (cf. also 97.2) is indebted to Cic. *Rep.* 3.18 'nec uirtus recipit nec ...natura patitur'. V. professes to talk generally of men (*hominum*), but he is really referring only to himself (*audeo*, below): *mediocritas* is thus one of those formulae of self-depreciation which, while common in imperial times for addresses to the emperor (104.3n.), were also appropriate in other contexts (cf. *Inscr. Christ.* 615 'incomparabilissimae feminae, queius de uitae documenta non sufficit *mediocritas hominum* at cumulum laudis peruenire', where Diehl quotes V.), particularly in approaches to divinities (*cum deis queri*, below).

audeo cum deis queri Heinsius' emendation[1] is superior to the others listed by Kritz because of its Ciceronian heritage (*Rabir.* 24 'queri est ausus', *Acad.* 2.81 'quererer cum deo'), thus completing the Ciceronian flavour of the whole sentence (last n.). On *queri cum* cf. also Ov. *Met.* 10.724; Hand, *Turs.* 2.148; Nägelsbach 531. The allusion to the gods in this context provides a significant introduction to the *uotum* in 131: see below, p. 276.

scelerata Drusus Libo iniret consilia On him see *RE* 2A.1.885–7 = Scribonius 23 (Fluss); on his name cf. Sumner 275 n. 113; on his conspiracy cf. also EJ p. 52 'nefaria consilia quae de salute Ti. Caes. ... inita ab M. Libone erant' (A.D. 16). For *scelerata consilia* cf. Cic. *Ep. Brut.* 18.3, Liv. 28.28.8.

Steffen 146 notes that the effect of 130.3–5 is cumulative: starting with Libo and the behaviour of other *nobiles*, V. proceeds to mention the setbacks which Tiberius experienced within his own family, concluding (*auxit*) with the death of Livia herself. The narrative could hardly end on a more gloomy note.

---

[1] Stegmann wrongly attributes it to Halm.

Silium Pisonemque The former is C. Silius A. Caecina Largus (*RE* 3A.1.74–7 = Silius 12 (Nagl)), who in A.D. 24 was charged with treason and anticipated the verdict by committing suicide (Tac. *A.* 4.18ff.). The latter is Cn. Calpurnius Piso (*RE* 5.1380–2 = Calpurnius 70 (Groag); *PIR*² 2.58–61, no. 287),[1] who was brought to trial in A.D. 20 on various charges and also anticipated the verdict by suicide (Tac. *A.* 3.8ff.). Of the former it could perhaps be said that Tiberius *dignitatem constituit*, since he was granted the *ornamenta triumphalia* in A.D. 15 (Tac. *A.* 1.72.1); of the latter it could certainly be said that Tiberius *dignitatem auxit*, since he held his consulship in 7 B.C. with Tiberius as his partner (EJ p. 38) and was made *legatus Syriae* in A.D. 17 at the instigation of Tiberius (Tac. *A.* 2.43.2, Suet. *Tib.* 52.3, *Cal.* 2).

ut ad maiora transcendam Reminiscent of such Ciceronian phraseology as *Phil.* 2.78 'ad maiora ueniamus', 5.38 'magna haec, sed ad maiora properat oratio', cf. *Sest.* 5 'non adgrediar ad illa maxima', 52. For *transcendere* in this sense cf. Tac. *A.* 4.56.1, Quint. 7.1.21.

iuuenes amitteret filios Germanicus (116.1n.), adopted son of Tib., d. A.D. 19 (EJ p. 53); Drusus (125.4n.), Tiberius' own son, d. A.D. 23 (EJ p. 52).

nepotem ex Druso suo Ti. Germanicus Iulius Caesar (*PIR*² 4.189, no. 224), b. A.D. 19, d. A.D. 23 (Tac. *A.* 4.15.1). For this use of *ex*+abl. noun expressing relationship cf. 2.2.1 'ex filia nepos'; *TLL* 5.2.1095.76ff.

130.4 dolenda adhuc rettulimus; ueniendum ad erubescenda est V. refers to the items of 130.3 as *dolenda*, even though it is not until 130.4 that *dolor* and its derivatives are mentioned: this indicates not so much careless writing as failure to come to terms with subject matter which is extremely distressing. For the combination of *dolere* and *erubescere* cf. Sen. *Dial.* 12.9.6, Drac. *Med.* 10.290. *erubescenda* is only here as subst. in classical Latin; for *dolenda* cf. Ov. *Tr.* 5.1.26, *RA* 226 (F.).

hoc triennium A.D. 27–9, on the system of reckoning mentioned at 126.1n. Since all the events which V. records in 130.4–5 are attributable to A.D. 29, it is hardly likely that *triennium* includes A.D. 30.

abstruso...incendio *abstruso* goes with *incendio* (cf. Virg. *G.* 1.135 'abstrusum...ignem'; also *Aen.* 6.6f.), and not, as E. Wölfflin says (*ALL* 6

[1] As Lana (140 n. 523) points out, Shipley, Bolaffi and Stegmann wrongly identify Piso with L. Calpurnius Piso (cos. 1 B.C.), Gnaeus' elder brother; but it could not be said of him that Tiberius *dignitatem auxit* (below). Krause got it right.

(1889), 549), with *dolore* (which has to be understood). For *quod miserrimum est* cf. 118.4n.

quod ex nuru, quod ex nepote The former is Agrippina, wife of Germanicus; the latter is their son, Nero Julius Caesar (*RE* 10.1.473–7 = Iulius 146 (Gardthausen); *PIR*² 4.187–9, no. 22). For Tiberius' attack on them in A.D. 29 cf. Tac. *A.* 5.3ff.; below, p. 276 n. 2.

quod is either the conjunction or the relative pronoun, the latter perhaps being more likely: for *dolere, indignari* and *erubescere*+acc. cf. K–S 1.261f., L–H–S 358 (on *erubescere* esp. cf. Austin on Cic. *Cael.* 8, R. G. M. Nisbet, *JRS* 51 (1961), 267).

130.5 temporis aegritudinem V. sums up the current state of affairs with a bold illness metaphor which seems to have no exact parallel, although the adj. *aeger* was often used similarly (e.g. Liv. 5.3.6, Sen. *Ep.* 114.11 'aegrae ciuitatis indicia') and other illness metaphors are common, e.g. in Sallust (E. Skard, 'Die Bildersprache des Sall.', *Serta Eitremiana* (1942), 145f.). The metaphor has been prepared for by *doloribus* and *lacerauit* in 4 above (cf. Cic. *Acad.* 2.23 'dolore lacerari', *Tusc.* 3.27 'aegritudo lacerat...animum'), and for *aegritudo* coupled with *dolor* elsewhere cf. Cic. *Tusc.* 4.18, Gell. 9.2.9, Front. p. 86.1 Naber = p. 80.19f. Van den Hout (a passage full of illness words), Arnob. *Nat.* 1.18.

amissa mater, eminentissima et per omnia deis quam hominibus similior femina Livia, who opened the Tiberian narrative at 94.1, now closes it with her death (A.D. 29, cf. Tac. *A.* 5.1). Steffen rightly remarks (178) that whenever the name of Livia occurs in V.'s history, 'spricht der Autor von der Kaiserin im Tone der grössten Hochachtung und Verehrung'; and R. A. Bauman (*Impietas in Principem* (1974), 103 and n. 193) says that this section implies that V. took badly to Tiberius' refusal to deify Livia. I have considerable sympathy with these views. The panegyrical force of *deis...similior* is clear from such other exs. of the phrase as 35.2 (of Cato Uticensis), Cic. *Marc.* 8 (of Caesar), Liv. 26.50.13 (of Scipio), Plin. *Pan.* 1.3 (of Trajan), 7.5 (of Nerva); Livia was in fact worshipped as a deity (e.g. *ILS* 119 'Liuiae Augustae, deae', 120); and she had the admiration of the people everywhere (see the excellent remarks of Charlesworth, *CAH* 10.633f.). V.'s fondness for her is clear from the moment she enters his history as 'genere, probitate, forma Romanarum eminentissima' (75.3).

cuius potentiam nemo sensit nisi... V. describes the dead Livia in terms which may be paralleled in consolatory writing: Sen. *Cons. Pol.* 3.2 'nemo potentiam eius iniuria sensit', *Eleg. Maec.* 1.15f., *Cons. Liu.* 47 'nec nocuisse ulli et fortunam habuisse nocendi' (Ruhnken): for the consolatory theory cf. Cic. *De Or.* 2.342, Theon rhet. 111.18; Esteve-Forriol 136. For some other exs. of the same idea cf. Sen. *Cons. Pol.* 13.1, *PLM* 4.15.3 (p. 60 Baehrens), Ov. *Her.* 12.75. See further next n.

aut leuatione periculi aut accessione dignitatis V.'s topos (above) is not without foundation in historical reality. Livia had, e.g., saved C. Cornelius Cinna Magnus from Augustus' wrath (Sen. *Clem.* 1.9, Dio 55.14ff.), and had used her influence to gain senatorial rank for M. Salvius Otho, grandfather of the emperor (Suet. *Otho* 1.1). V.'s phraseology is again Ciceronian: *leuatio* (not found in Caes. Liv. Curt. Phaedr. Plin. Tac.) is in Cicero's letters and philosophical works, though not in his speeches or *rhetorica*; and for the second phrase cf. *Fam.* 2.1.2 'accessiones...dignitatis'.

131 THE *VOTVM*

Through lack of comparative evidence it is impossible to be certain whether other Roman historians ended their works with a *uotum*. We may find it credible that Livy, who had begun his work with an allusion to the gods (*praef.* 13), concluded Book 142 with a prayer; but if so, there is no trace of it in the *periocha* of that book. Florus, another historian whose general tone is not dissimilar to V.'s or Livy's, has no such ending. And it is certainly unthinkable that Sallust or Tacitus resorted to such a technique.[1] I would judge that V.'s choice of ending is a departure from tradition and requires some explanation.

Perhaps the most obvious explanation is that V. is yet again employing the techniques of the panegyrists, who found it suitable to end their works with a prayer (Plin. *Pan.* 94, *Pan. Lat.* 12.26.1–4, cf. Menand. rhet. 377.21–2 τί δὲ μεῖζον αἰτεῖν παρὰ τῶν θεῶν ἢ βασιλέα σώζεσθαι;). And it is indeed true that the content of V.'s prayer is not unlike that found in panegyric (cf. *SHA Max. Balb.* 17.8–9 'di praestent praestabuntque hanc orbi Romano felicitatem...ita ego precor ut in eo statu uobis rem publicam seruent in quo eam uos adhuc nutantem collocaritis'). Equally, however, V.'s prayer has much in common with imperial *uota*, of which there were two kinds: routine *uota* which were performed on behalf of the emperor every year at the beginning of January (cf. Weinstock 218–19), and other *uota* which were reserved for times of crisis.[2] And there can surely be no doubt that

---

1 Admittedly Tac. *Agr.* ends on a somewhat religious note, but the content of ch. 46 and the genre in which it occurs are both quite different from V. (As for Livy, I do not of course wish to imply that the silence of *per.* 142 is necessarily decisive for the absence of a prayer; on the other hand, a prayer, if there had been one, would be so unusual that it might well have been recorded in the *periocha*.)

2 Cf. Ll. W. Daly, *TAPA* 81 (1950), 165; Warde Fowler 203ff.

A.D. 29, the year in which V. apparently finished his work,[1] was a year of crisis.

In A.D. 26 Tiberius had retired to the seclusion of Capri, abdicating from *cura imperii*; from that moment the power of Sejanus inevitably increased still further, and the treason trials continued. Then in 29 Livia died, whom V. so much admired (130.5n.) and whose death, according to Tacitus, released 'praerupta iam et urgens dominatio' (*A.* 5.3.1). In the same year came the attack on Agrippina and Nero, possibly charged with conspiracy.[2] The general picture in A.D. 29 was thus scarcely optimistic, even to the most casual observer, and V. acknowledges as much by the strikingly depressing section with which he concludes his history and which forms the immediate background to the *uotum* (above, p. 272). The *uotum* is an apprehensive response to the current political situation rather than a panegyrical effusion divorced from the harsh realities of the time.[3]

131.1 Voto finiendum uolumen est Compare Plin. *Pan.* 94.1 'in fine orationis praesides custodesque imperii diuos ego...precor'. By *uolumen* V. of course means the whole of the present work, as at 1.14.1: see T. Birt, *Das antike Buchwesen* (repr. 1974), 320–1.

Technically a *uotum* was a bargain made with the gods. It was expressed in a conditional form (cf. Latte 46), and in republican times traditionally consisted of two types: there were private *uota* for the benefit of an individual (e.g. the parody at Catull. 36.4–8) and public *uota* for the benefit of the state (e.g. Liv. 22.10.2–3 '*si* r.p. pop. Rom. Quiritium...salua seruata erit hisce duellis...*tum* donum duit pop. Rom.', cf. Val. Max. 4.1.10). Under the empire, however, 'the two practices combine in public vows for the welfare of an individual, the emperor' (Ll. W. Daly, 'Vota publica pro salute alicuius', *TAPA* 81 (1950), 164). Excellent exs. of these imperial *uota* are found in the prayers of the *fratres Aruales*, e.g. Henzen 110–11 (Domitian's reign): 'Iuppiter O.M. Capitoline, *si* imp. Caesar diui Vespasiani f. Domitianus Aug....quem nos sentimus dicere, uiuet domusque eius incolumis erit...et eum diem eumque saluum seruaueris, custodierisque

---

[1] See Woodman (1975), 273–82.

[2] So *CAH* 10.635 (*contra* Syme, *Tac.* 405 n. 2).

[3] A most helpful parallel is Hor. *C.* 1.2. By way of reference to various crises, the ode builds up to the question: 'quem uocet diuum populus ruentis | imperi rebus?' (25–6). It gradually emerges that the answer to this question is Octavian, to whom Horace, at the conclusion of the ode, addresses a prayer which opens with precisely the same topos as that used by V. at 2 below for Tiberius: 'serus in caelum redeas' (45). Yet the coincidence of topos is not as important as the way in which, in both authors, a prayer is made to spring from a background of political crisis. See also how V. himself, at 130.3, has already turned to the gods at a critical stage of his narrative.

aeternitate imperi, quod suscipiendo ampliauit...ast tu ea ita faxis, *tum tibi...uouemus...*' In addition, the imperial *uota* were regularly commemorated by coin issues: thus the *uota* of 16 B.C. were recorded as follows (*BMC Emp.* 1.18 = EJ 35): 'I.O.M.... V(ota) S(uscepta) pr(o) s(alute) imp. Cae. quod per eu(m) r. p. in amp(liore) atq(ue) tran(quilliore) s(tatu) e(st)' (cf. H. B. Mattingly, *PBA* 36 (1950), 155f.).

Now V.'s *uotum* does not fulfil the most essential requirement mentioned above: it has no formula of reciprocation, no conditional clause. Yet while V.'s ch. is thus not a *uotum* in the technical sense, its content, language and tone clearly resemble quite closely the public *uota* of imperial times.[1]

est, Orelli's correction of the paradosis *sit*, is undoubtedly right (despite Baehrens 503 and Löfstedt, *Synt.* 2.132): *est* and *sit* are common confusions, esp. in gerundival forms of the verb as here (cf. W. M. Lindsay, *Introduction to textual emendation* (1896), 20). Kritz, misguidedly quoting 2.7.2. as parallel, is followed by Stegmann in retaining *sit*.

Iuppiter Capitoline 'Rome's destiny and function were impersonated in Jupiter Optimus Maximus, who had taken up residence in the Capitoline temple' (R. M. Ogilvie, *The Romans and their gods* (1969), 16). V. adds the epithet *Capitoline* because the Capitol symbolised the permanence of Rome, cf. Hor. *C.* 1.37.6–8, 3.3.42f., 30.8f., Luc. 10.63; *TLL* Suppl. 2.164.53ff. It was conventional in prayers to mention Jupiter first, cf. Otto 178f.

et auctor ac stator Romani nominis Gradiue Mars Mars is given three different titles in the paradosis, which may be discussed in turn.

(1) Mars was the father of Romulus, who in turn was the eponymous founder of Rome and the Romans. Hence Mars was actually *auctor Romani nominis* twice over: he could be said to have started the Roman race (*auctor* = *generis conditor*, as 1.6.5; *OLD* s.v. 15; *nomen* = 'race', as 1.14.1; *OLD* s.v. 19); and he was the father of the hero who gave Rome its name (*nomen* = 'name'; *Romani* = genitive of definition). The phrase thus manages to combine literary effect with the emotive associations of early Roman legend. By referring to Mars as *auctor*, V. reminds us of Rome's military heritage (cf. Liv. *praef.* 7), and also of the fact that it was Mars who was there from the beginning of Rome, spanning its history from inception to the climax of Tiberius' reign (for associated ideas cf. Pind. *Pyth.* 10.10f., Orph. fr. B6 DK ὁ μὲν δὴ θεός, ὥσπερ ὁ παλαιὸς λόγος, ἀρχήν τε καὶ τελευτὴν καὶ μέσα...ἔχων, Scythinus of Teos ap. Plut. *Orac. Pyth.* 402A, Ael. Arist. *Or.* 1.8 (p. 11 Dind.) and J. Amman ad loc., Liv. 45.39.1 'maiores uestri

---

[1] Mr Paterson also points out to me the similarity with oaths of loyalty to Tiberius, e.g. that in *JRS* 50 (1960), 75–9; cf. also EJ 315.

omnium magnarum rerum et principia exorsi ab dis sunt et finem eum statuerunt', Hor. *C.* 3.6.6 'hinc omne principium, huc refer exitum').

(2) *stator* was originally a cult title of Jupiter (cf. Wissowa, *RE* 3A.2.2226–8), and developed into a political epithet by the late republic, again always with reference to Jupiter (cf. Cic. *Cat.* 1.11 'Ioui Statori, antiquissimo custodi huius urbis', 33, Sen. *Ben.* 4.7.1 'quod stant beneficio eius omnia, stator stabilitorque est'). Mars appears to be called *stator* nowhere else in Latin, which led Puteanus to conjecture: *Iuppiter Capitoline et stator, et auctor Romani nominis...Mars.* The conjecture is admittedly attractive, but I think a case can perhaps be made for the role and title of Mars as *stator*.

As founder of the Roman race (above), Mars had a natural protective role (cf. Roscher, *Lex. Myth.* 2.2.2426); but it was in Augustus' reign that the god assumed a special significance (cf. F. Altheim, *History of Roman religion* (1938), 385f.; Syme, *RR* 470f.). When Horace asked the question to which reference has already been made (above, p. 276 n. 3), 'quem uocet diuum populus ruentis | imperi rebus?' (*C.* 1.2.25f.), he found it natural to include among his replies the *auctor* Mars (35f.). This particular devotion to Mars, like so many other features of Augustus' reign, seems to have been purposely continued in the principate of Tiberius (Grant, *Aspects* 74, 88). When the conspiracy of Libo Drusus (above, 130.3) collapsed in A.D. 16, it was to Mars (along with Jupiter and Concordia) that *dona* were decreed (Tac. *A.* 2.32.2; cf. also Henzen 121, with ref. to a conspiracy of Nero's reign). Mars, representing in Tiberius' reign an aspect of the continuity of the Augustan principate, was clearly an appropriate god to turn to at this early period of the empire.[1] A consideration of the title *stator* will confirm this.

Any consideration of Mars as *stator* must, I think, start from the third line of the *carmen aruale* of A.D. 218 and must take into account the fundamental discussion of the prayer by Norden (*AP* 149–57). The *carmen* itself is 'a ritual text originating at a very remote period which [was] handed down through successive generations of religious functionaries' (L. R. Palmer, *The Latin language* (1954), 63), and line 3 of the *carmen* is: 'satur fu fere *Mars* limen sali *sta* berber', which Norden translates 'Be sated, wild Mars, leap upon the boundary mark and *stand there.*' Norden argues that, although Mars is not in his role of war god here (*AP* 156), he is looked upon as a protective deity whose protection can be expressed in military terminology. 'Der Gott ist als *custos liminis* gedacht. Auf der Schwelle hat er seinen Standort (*statio*) als Wachposten, *uigilia*: ein militärisches Bild passend für das martialische Volk' (*AP* 154). Norden establishes a close connection between the terms involved, showing that such military words as *statio*, *uigilia* and *custodia* are almost interchangeable: when the *carmen* says 'Mars...sta', it might equally

[1] Mars is not invoked in the prayers with which Cicero sometimes concluded his speeches (e.g. *Verr.* 2.5.184, *Dom.* 144, *Sull.* 86).

well have said 'Mars custodi' or 'Mars uigila'. Indeed, as Norden proceeds to observe, when the Romans declared war, 'is qui belli susceperat curam sacrarium Martis ingressus primo ancilia commouebat, post hastam simulacri ipsius, dicens "Mars uigila"' (Serv. *Aen.* 8.3, cf. 7.603), and Norden sees in this a close analogy with the imperative *Mars sta* in the *carmen aruale.* Although the idea of Mars as a protector whose role is expressed in military language is thus extremely ancient, Norden recalls (*AP* 156f.) how important this idea was in the early empire. During this period the constitution was regularly called *status,* something which of its very nature required protection (see below): this was the duty of the emperor in his role as *custos imperii* (104.2n.), being obliged to be at his *statio* (124.2n., and below). The derivation of these key words *status* and *statio* from *stare* (cf. Sen. *Ben.* 4.7.1, quoted above) emphasises the underlying idea of conservation. Norden, commenting on this particular aspect (*AP* 288f.), quotes this passage of V. to illustrate it, 'custodite...hunc statum'; somewhat surprisingly, however, he does not comment on the word *stator.* But from the preceding remarks it should be clear how V. perhaps came to use the word. The *status* had to be protected; Mars had traditionally been invoked as a protector through the ritual expression *Mars sta*; he was currently the most appropriate god for the task, and *stator* is the obvious *nomen agentis* to describe this role. All V. needed was the imagination to apply the title, hitherto associated with Jupiter, to Mars – in the same way as the author of *ILS* 9239 applied Ultor, hitherto associated with Mars, to Jupiter.

It may be that some will still choose to emend the passage, perhaps preferring Ursinus' *et auctor ac sator* to Puteanus' conjecture mentioned above. But I think this evidence is sufficient to make one agree with Kritz's comment: 'non temere a vulgata discedendum est'.

(3) For Mars' third title *Gradiue* cf. Ogilvie on Liv. 1.20.4, and U. W. Scholz, *Studien zum altital. u. altröm. Marskult u. Marsmythos* (1970), 18ff. (who nowhere mentions Mars as *stator*).

perpetuorumque custos Vesta ignium 'Far more than any other cult, that of Vesta represents the reality and continuity of Roman religious feeling' (Warde Fowler 137). Vesta symbolised the eternity of Rome either by herself (as at Sen. *Contr.* 1.3.1), through the Vestal Virgins (as at Hor. *C.* 3.30.8f.), or through her cult fire which was never extinguished (Cic. *Leg.* 2.8 'uirgines Vestales in urbe custodiunto ignem foci publici sempiternum'). V. makes Vesta the guardian of her own fire (cf. Ov. *Fast.* 6.258 'flammae custos', also Cic. *ND* 2.67), a neat conceit from which a moral is perhaps to be drawn (2n., below). For the significance of Vesta in the early empire cf. C. Koch, *Religio* (1960), 162ff.

V.'s phraseology is here chiastic; and just as Vesta is placed in the middle of her phrase, so Jupiter is placed at the beginning of his and Mars at the end of his. The precise *uariatio* emphasises the heightened style of the prayer.

et quicquid numinum... For this standard prayer formula cf. Liv. 3.25.8 'haec sacrata quercus et quidquid deorum est audiant', 23.9.3 'iurantes per quidquid deorum est', Hor. *Epod.* 5.1 'at o deorum quidquid in caelo regit' (where Kiesseling–Heinze rightly remark that the expression 'entspricht dem sonst üblichen *di deaeque omnes*', of which exs. are found in imperial oaths of loyalty, cf. EJ 315.9; *JRS* 50 (1960), 75–6). For a comparable expression cf. Catull. 3.2 'et quantum est hominum uenustiorum'.

hanc Romani imperii molem *moles* is another of those key terms used at this period to describe the burden of ruling the empire (cf. *onus* at 127.3n.). *moles* has the additional advantage of having been used in a famous line of Virgil (*Aen.* 1.33 'tantae molis erat Romanam condere gentem', but see the reservations of Fletcher 7). For V.'s phrase cf. Liv. 1.55.3, Sen. *Oed.* 84, Stat. *Theb.* 3.387, Vict. *Epit.* 9.3; for the idea cf. e.g. Ov. *Tr.* 2.221, *Fast.* 6.645, Plin. *Pan.* 44.4, Tac. *A.* 1.4.3, 11.1; in general cf. Béranger 117–18; also above, 114.1. For *in amplissimum...fastigium extulit* below cf. Amm. 14.11.29 (also above, 30.3).

publica uoce Although V.'s *uotum* is personal, he takes it upon himself (as at 124.1) to speak on behalf of the people at large. This is what Cicero had done, of whom V. uses the same phrase, but in a bold metaphor, at 66.2 (cf. Cairns 179ff.): in a prayer for the stability of the state V. perhaps sees himself, not unnaturally, as following in the footsteps of the great conservative orator of the republic. For other exs. of the phrase, but in a different sense, cf. Ov. *Tr.* 1.8.22, Sen. *Ep.* 8.8, 21.9, 31.2, 33.2, Dio 56.35.1.

obtestor atque precor So too in the *acta* of the Arval Brethren for A.D. 101 (Henzen cxl = *ILS* 5035): 'Iuppiter O.M. te precamus, quaesumus, obtestamurque'. For similar expressions, but not this rarity here, cf. A. Szantyr, *Gymnasium* 78 (1971), 20ff. The direct imperative after *obtestor* and *precor* is uncommon, but cf. Pacuv. *Praetext.* 2, Tac. *A.* 4.8.5, Curt. 5.11.6 (F.).

hunc statum Cicero had liked to talk about *hic rei publicae status* (cf. C. Wirszubski, *JRS* 44 (1954), 4–5), but *status* came to be used by Augustus himself as a happily neutral term which aptly described the constitution which he inaugurated (cf. Suet. *Aug.* 28.2 'ut optimi status auctor dicar', Gell. 15.7.3 'statu r.p. felicissimo' (a letter of Aug.), Macrob. 2.4.8). The word appears on the coinage (*RIC* 1.75, 16 B.C.), and in such authors as V. (91.2) and Seneca (*Ben.* 2.20.2): cf. also Suet. *Aug.* 28.2, Tac. *A.* 1.2.2, *D.*

37.5. By using the word here, V. presents the system as something which requires preservation: this is the key note of the prayer, recurring in *statione* below (2n.). In general see E. Koestermann, '"status" als politischer Terminus in der Antike', *RhM* 86 (1937), 225ff. (who on p. 229 n. 9 compares the present passage with Isoc. *Nicocl.* 38 διαφυλάττετε τὴν παροῦσαν κατάστασιν καὶ μηδεμιᾶς ἐπιθυμεῖτε μεταβολῆς).

hanc pacem, ⟨hunc principem⟩ It is clear from *eique functo* below either that a masculine noun must be supplied or that *pacem* should be emended to provide one. I prefer the former solution since it produces a typically Velleian tricolon which balances two others already in the prayer (the three named deities and the three imperatives). Cf. also Tac. *A.* 3.28.2 'pace et principe'.

131.2 functo longissima statione mortali *statio*, originally a technical military term = 'post', is here used metaphorically of life. The metaphor appealed to writers of a Stoic persuasion (e.g. Sen. *Ep.* 120.18 'in hac statione morietur') and to others (e.g. Cic. *Senec.* 73 'de praesidio et statione uitae decedere'), but V. has doubtless chosen it here because of its frequent use as a description of the emperor's official position, where it again has military overtones (124.2n.). It thus reinforces the patterning of military language which pervades the prayer, and emphasises the equally prevalent notion of preservation. Just as Mars is the divine *stator* of the Roman state and Vesta the *custos* of her symbolic fire, so Tiberius is to be 'at his post' for as long as possible in his role of *custos imperii*. Cf. Luc. 1.45–6 'te, cum statione peracta | astra petes serus' (addressing Nero).

On *longissima* see next n.; for *functo statione* cf. Tert. *De Ieieun.* 10 (in Latin a dead man can be either *morte functus*, as 48.6, or *aeuo* (*uel sim.*) *functus*, as here and Hor. *C.* 2.9.13).

successores quam serissimos Independently of each other both Steffen (191ff.) and Syme (*Tac.* 367–8) suggested that V. is here anticipating the succession of Tiberius by Sejanus. Nothing could be further from the truth. The question of the succession accompanied any hint of political disturbance under the empire, and this is V.'s way of discounting, discreetly but firmly, any such possibility that might have been mooted after Tiberius' retirement to Capri. As Sumner has rightly observed (291), V. projects any possible succession far into the future (*quam serissimos*) and refuses to speculate further (cf. the repeated plural forms). Besides, it was a convention of panegyrical writers to pray or hope that the ruler's presence on earth would last as long as possible (see Nisbet–Hubbard on Hor. *C.* 1.2.45 with a host of parallels, to which add Ov. *Met.* 15.868–70, Curt. 8.5.17, Calp. Sic. 1.144–6, Plin. *Pan.* 28.6, *Pan. Lat.* 10.2.7), and one of the ways of expressing this topos was to allude to the ruler's successors – who, it is hoped, will be long delayed: cf. *Eleg. Maec.* 2.27–30 'pete sidera sero: | ...et tibi succrescant iuuenes bis Caesare digni | et tradant porro Caesaris usque genus', Plin. *Pan.* 94.5 'oro et obtestor...primum ut illum...serues, deinde ut quandoque successorem ei tribuas', Menand. rhet. 377.28–30, and the neat inversion at Plin. *Ep.* 10.1.1 'tua quidem pietas...optauerat ut quam tardissime succederes patri'). Finally, if my interpretation of V.'s opinion of Sejanus is right (above, pp. 245–8), he would hardly wish to allude to Tiberius' *adiutor* in the terms which are used in the *uotum*.

ceruices tam fortiter sustinendo The idea of the 'burden of the empire' (*molem*, above) is here continued in metaphorical terms which are derived from Cicero (*Dom.* 142 '(r.p.) quam antea uiris fortibus multis, in hac uero causa soli uestris ceruicibus sustinetis', *Sest.* 138 'qui autem praecipue suis ceruicibus tanta munia atque r.p. sustinent, hi semper habiti sunt optimatium principes auctores et conseruatores ciuitatis', *Prou. Cons.* 6). It is highly appropriate that in a prayer devoted to political stability V. should allude so unmistakably to Cicero, the arch-conservative.

For *terrarum orbis imperio* below cf. 31.1, Cic. *Mur.* 74, Vitr. 1 *praef.* 1, *Octau.* 156; for *sufficere* + dat. gerund(ive), below, cf. K–S 1.747*b*.

quam huius suffecisse sensimus The awkward circumlocution is due to the sacral language of prayers, exemplified in the *uota* of the Arval Brethren: cf. Henzen 110–11 (quoted above, 1n.), also id. cviii (= *ILS* 5033) 'si...euentumque bonum ita uti nos sentimus dicere dederis', cxv etc. See esp. Norden, *AP* 85–7; G. Appel, *De Romanorum precationibus* (1909), 146.

consiliaque omnium ciuium aut pia *** Here the text of (M) broke off, as Rhenanus on p. 70 of the *ed. pr.* remarked. Various edd. have suggested supplements (e.g. *iuuate aut impia confringite*, Halm), but Sumner, observing that V. cannot have intended to credit *all* citizens with impious designs, argued that a direct opposite of *pia consilia* (such as that proposed by Halm) is out of place (291 n. 191). I think this interpretation is over-subtle. V. surely means to say: 'Gods, with reference to the *consilia* of all the citizens, protect the *pia* and confound the non-*pia*.' It was after all conventional in oaths of loyalty to refer to the emperor's adversaries in this way (e.g. EJ 315.12ff., and line 16 of the inscription in *JRS* 50 (1960), 75), and in view of the likely background to the *uotum* (above, pp. 272–6) a suitably generalised reference to *nefaria consilia* is quite credible (cf. also *contra malos* at 124.1). *nefaria*, being the technical term (cf. EJ p. 52, quoted at 130.3n.), is perhaps preferable to Halm's *impia*; for *pium consilium* cf. Pollio in Cic. *Fam.* 10.33.2.

INDEXES

I GENERAL

INDEXES

2 LATIN WORDS

2 LATIN WORDS

3 NAMES

3 NAMES

Printed in the United Kingdom
by Lightning Source UK Ltd.
101933UKS00001B/162

9 780521 609357